BLACK PANEL
— PRESS —

presents

AL CAPONE

Story
S. MERALLI

Art
PF RADICE

By

BLACK PANEL
– PRESS –
Since 2017

Black Panel Press
Toronto, ON
Canada

www.blackpanelpress.com

First Edition
Printed in China

ISBN: 978-1-990521-16-4 (Hardcover)
ISBN: 978-1-990521-17-1 (E-book)

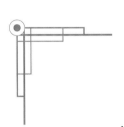

ALPHONSE GABRIEL CAPONE, AKA AL CAPONE, WAS BORN
IN BROOKLYN, NEW YORK, ON JANUARY 17TH, 1899.

IN CHICAGO, WITH HIS MENTOR JOHNNY TORRIO, HE'LL
REVOLUTIONIZE THE WORLD OF ORGANIZED CRIME.

THIS IS THE STORY OF THE GREATEST
GANGSTER OF ALL TIME.

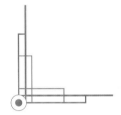

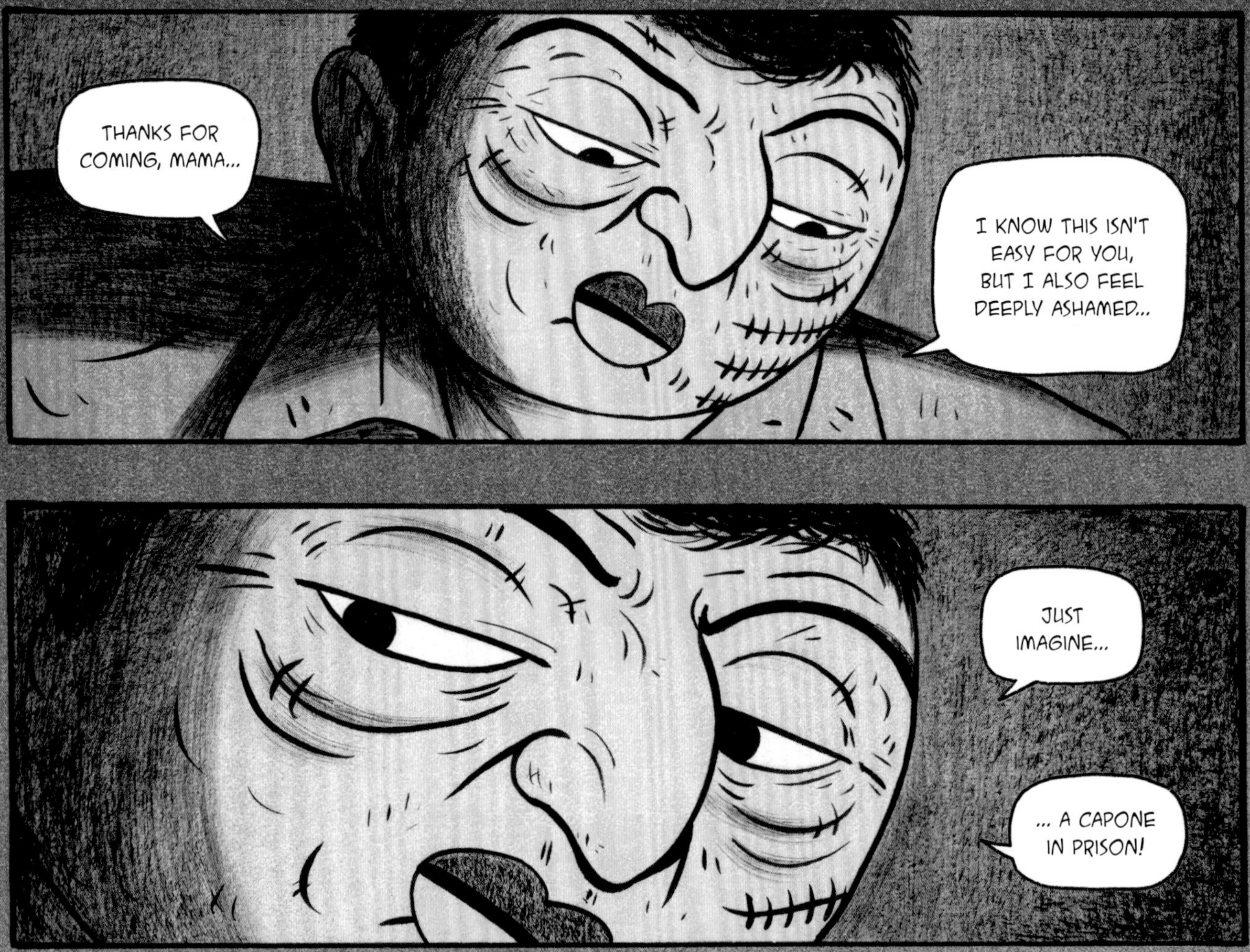
THANKS FOR COMING, MAMA...
I KNOW THIS ISN'T EASY FOR YOU, BUT I ALSO FEEL DEEPLY ASHAMED...
JUST IMAGINE...
... A CAPONE IN PRISON!
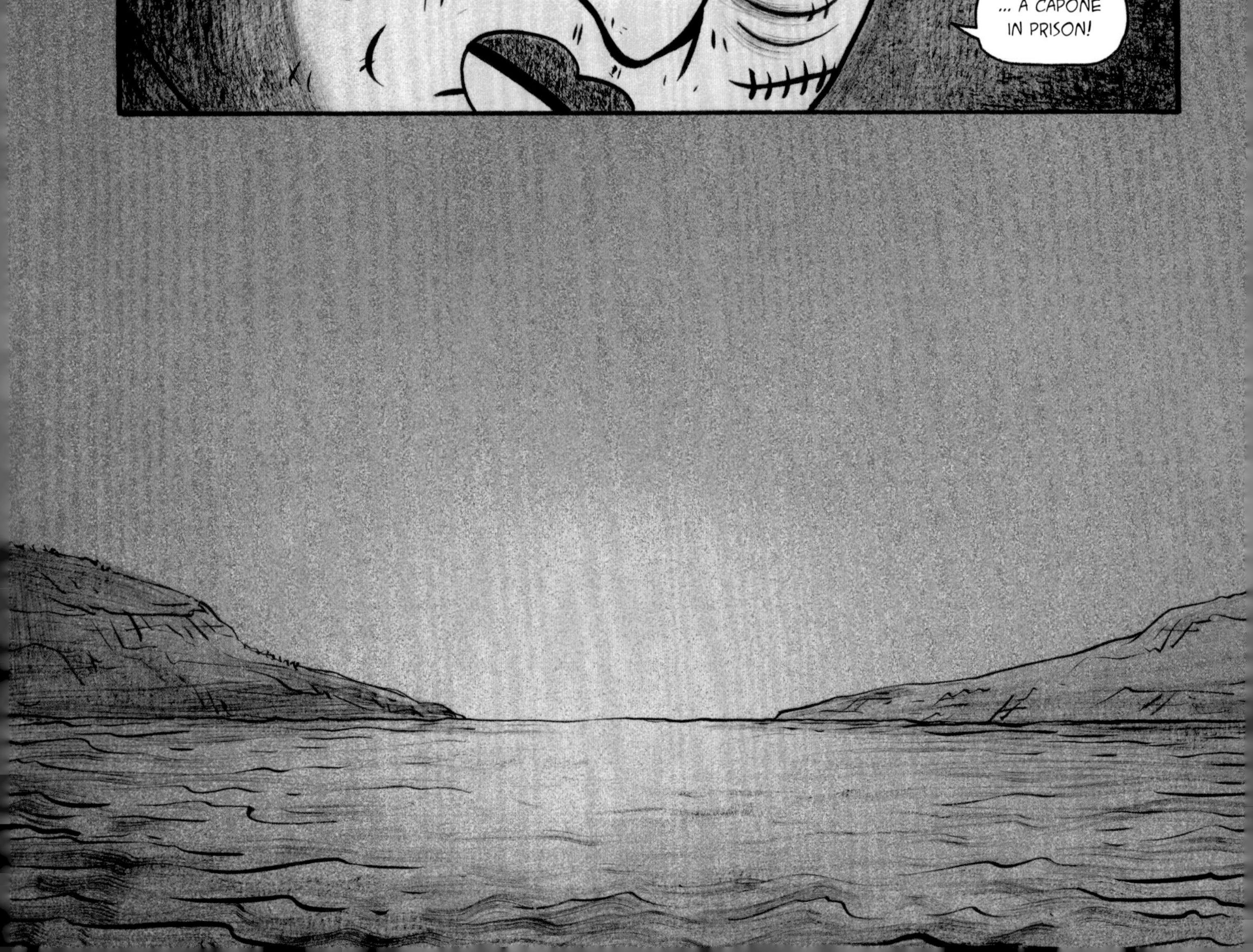

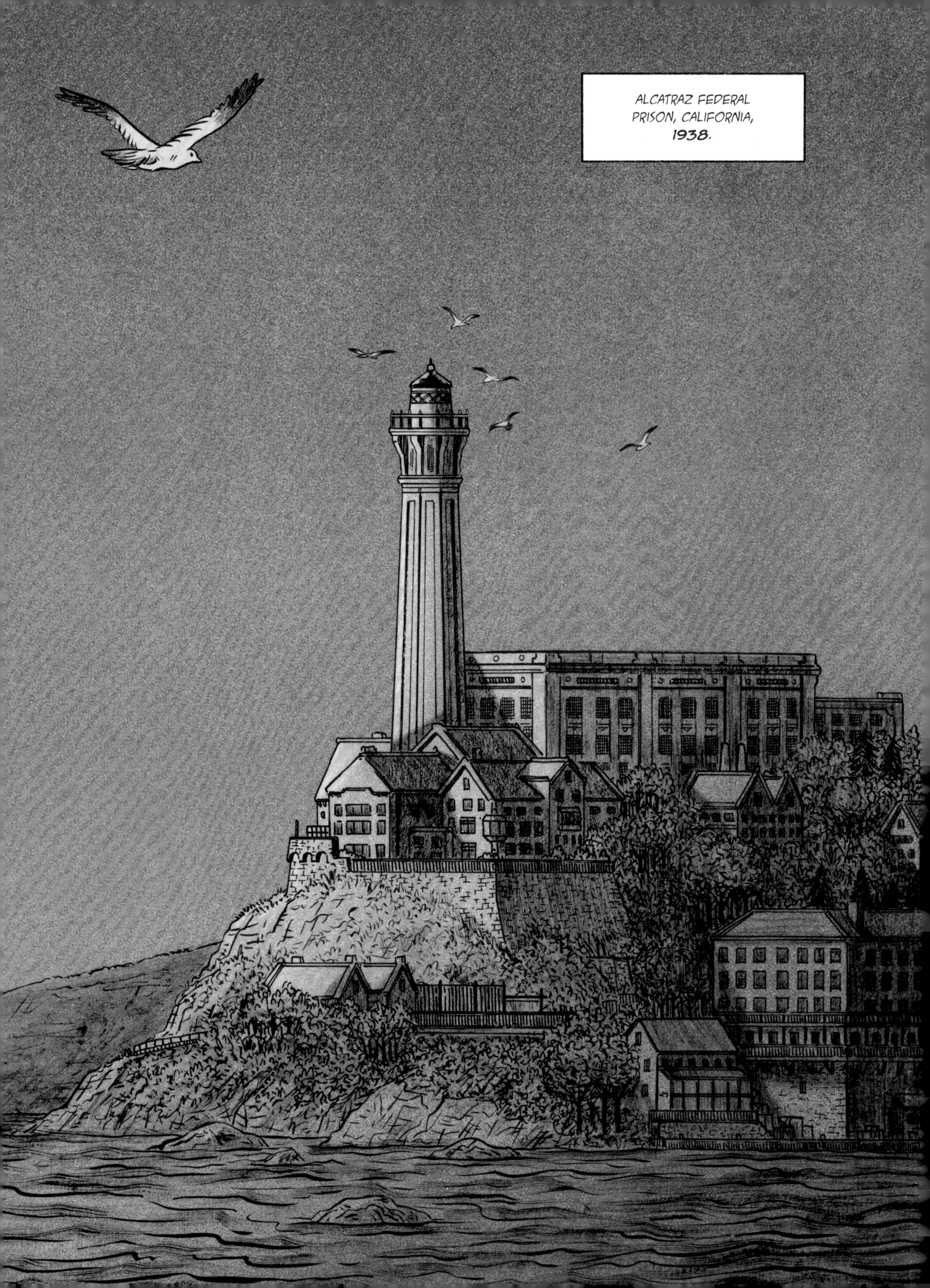
ALCATRAZ FEDERAL PRISON, CALIFORNIA, 1938.

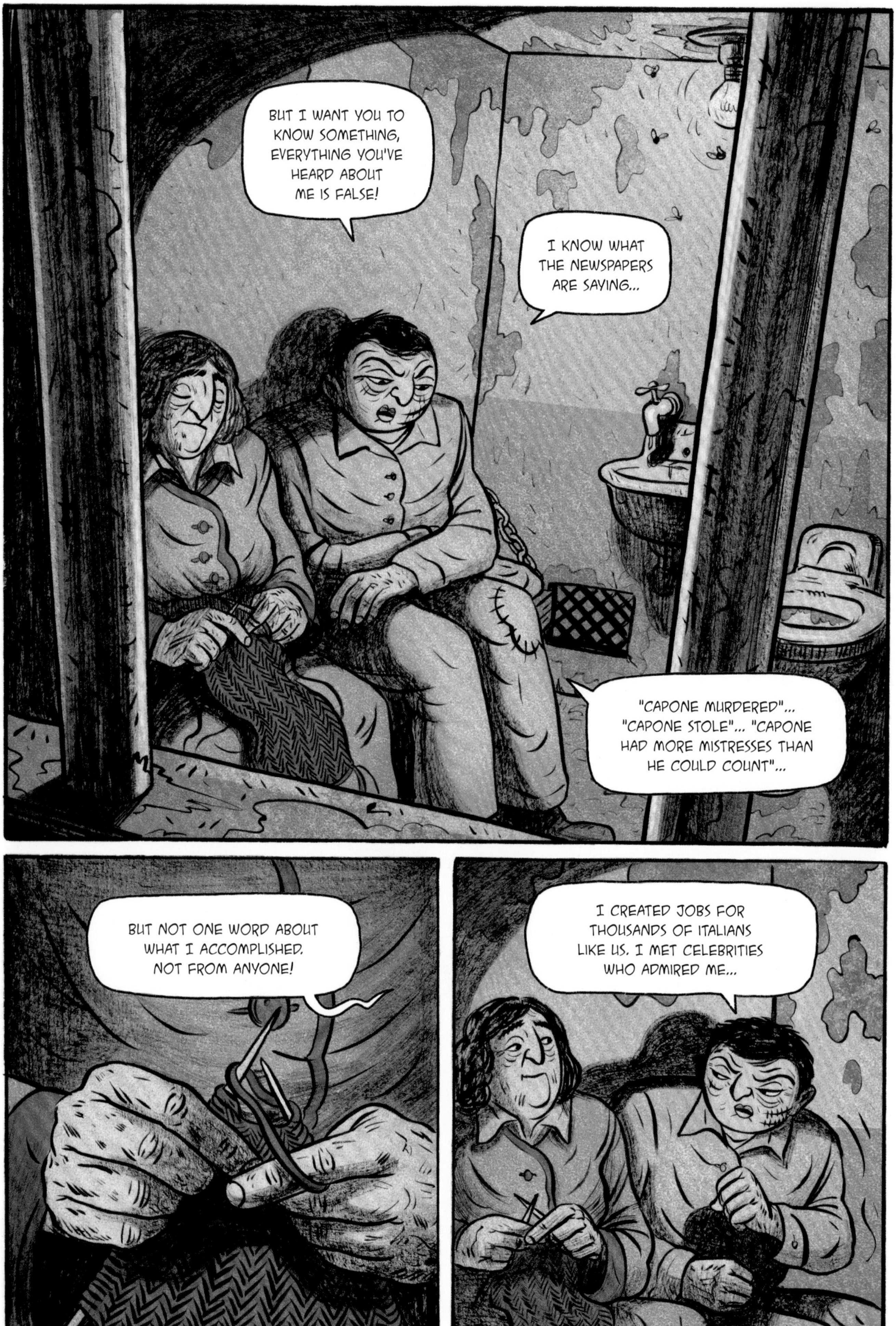
BUT I WANT YOU TO KNOW SOMETHING, EVERYTHING YOU'VE HEARD ABOUT ME IS FALSE!
I KNOW WHAT THE NEWSPAPERS ARE SAYING...
"CAPONE MURDERED"... "CAPONE STOLE"... "CAPONE HAD MORE MISTRESSES THAN HE COULD COUNT"...
BUT NOT ONE WORD ABOUT WHAT I ACCOMPLISHED. NOT FROM ANYONE!
I CREATED JOBS FOR THOUSANDS OF ITALIANS LIKE US. I MET CELEBRITIES WHO ADMIRED ME...

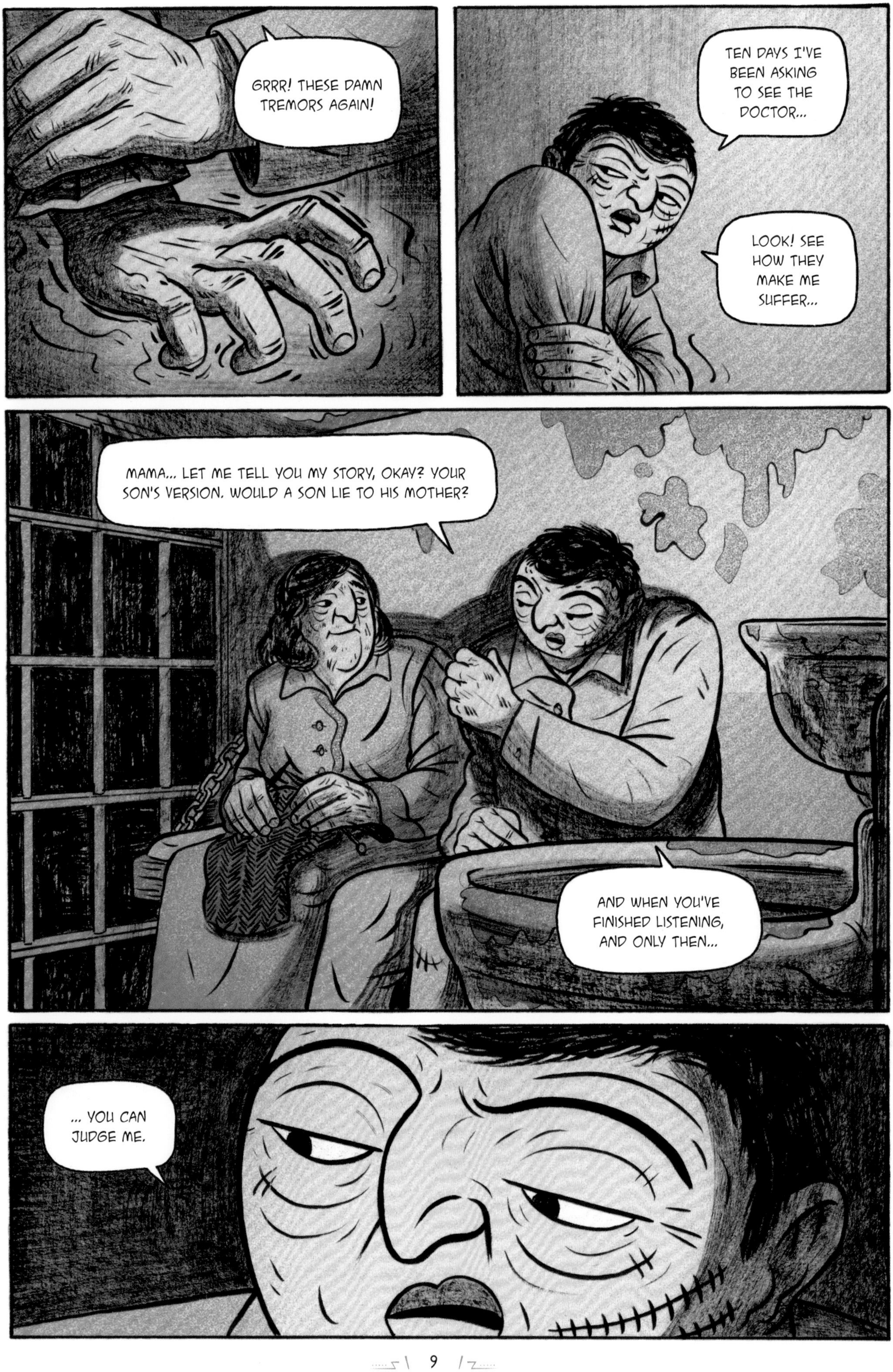
GRRR! THESE DAMN TREMORS AGAIN!
TEN DAYS I'VE BEEN ASKING TO SEE THE DOCTOR...
LOOK! SEE HOW THEY MAKE ME SUFFER...
MAMA... LET ME TELL YOU MY STORY, OKAY? YOUR SON'S VERSION. WOULD A SON LIE TO HIS MOTHER?
AND WHEN YOU'VE FINISHED LISTENING, AND ONLY THEN...
... YOU CAN JUDGE ME.

CHAPTER 1

Alphonse Gabriel
Capone

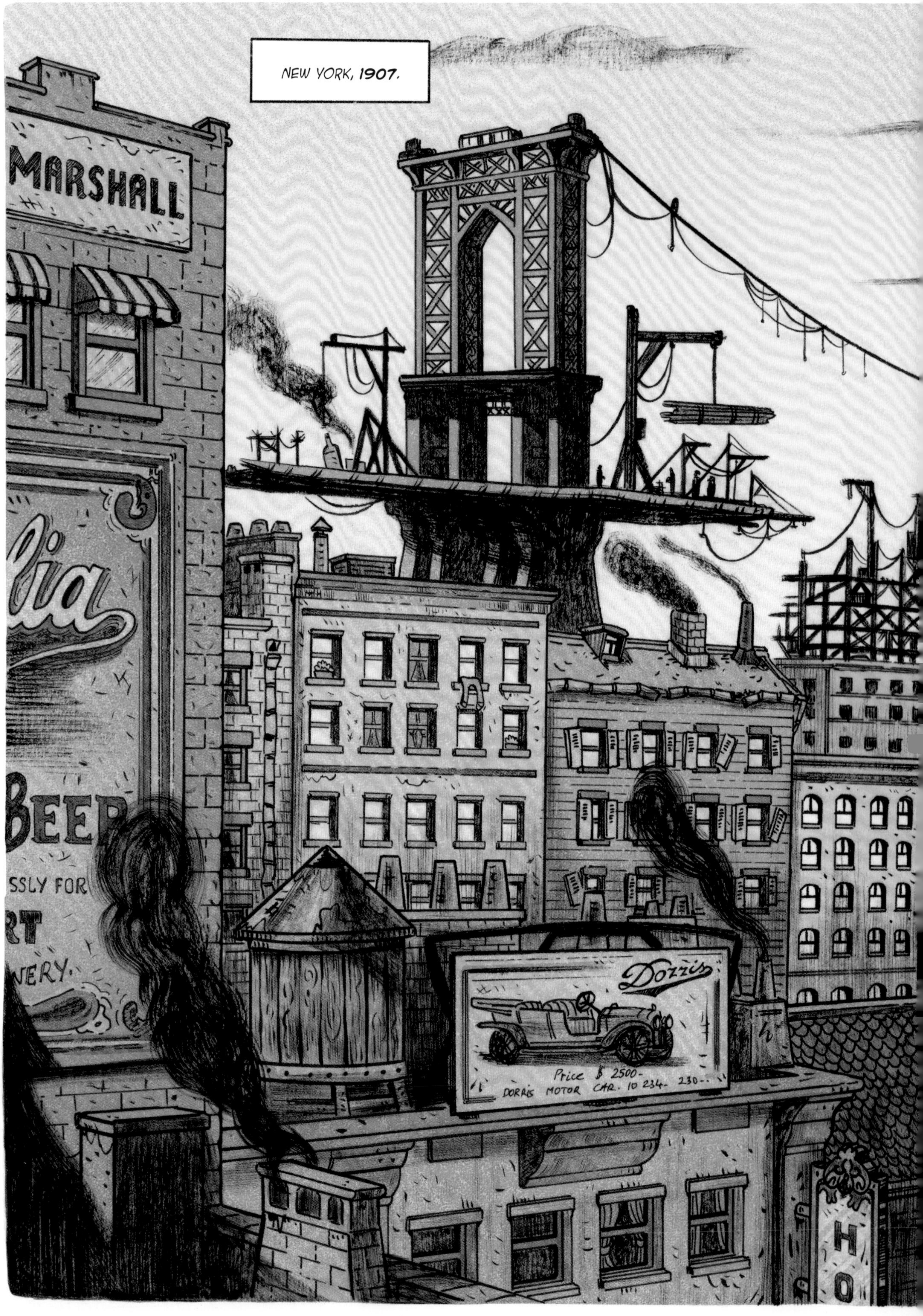
NEW YORK, 1907.
MARSHALL
BEER
SSLY FOR
RT
WERY.
Dorris
Price $ 2500-
DORRIS MOTOR CAR. 10 234- 230-
HO

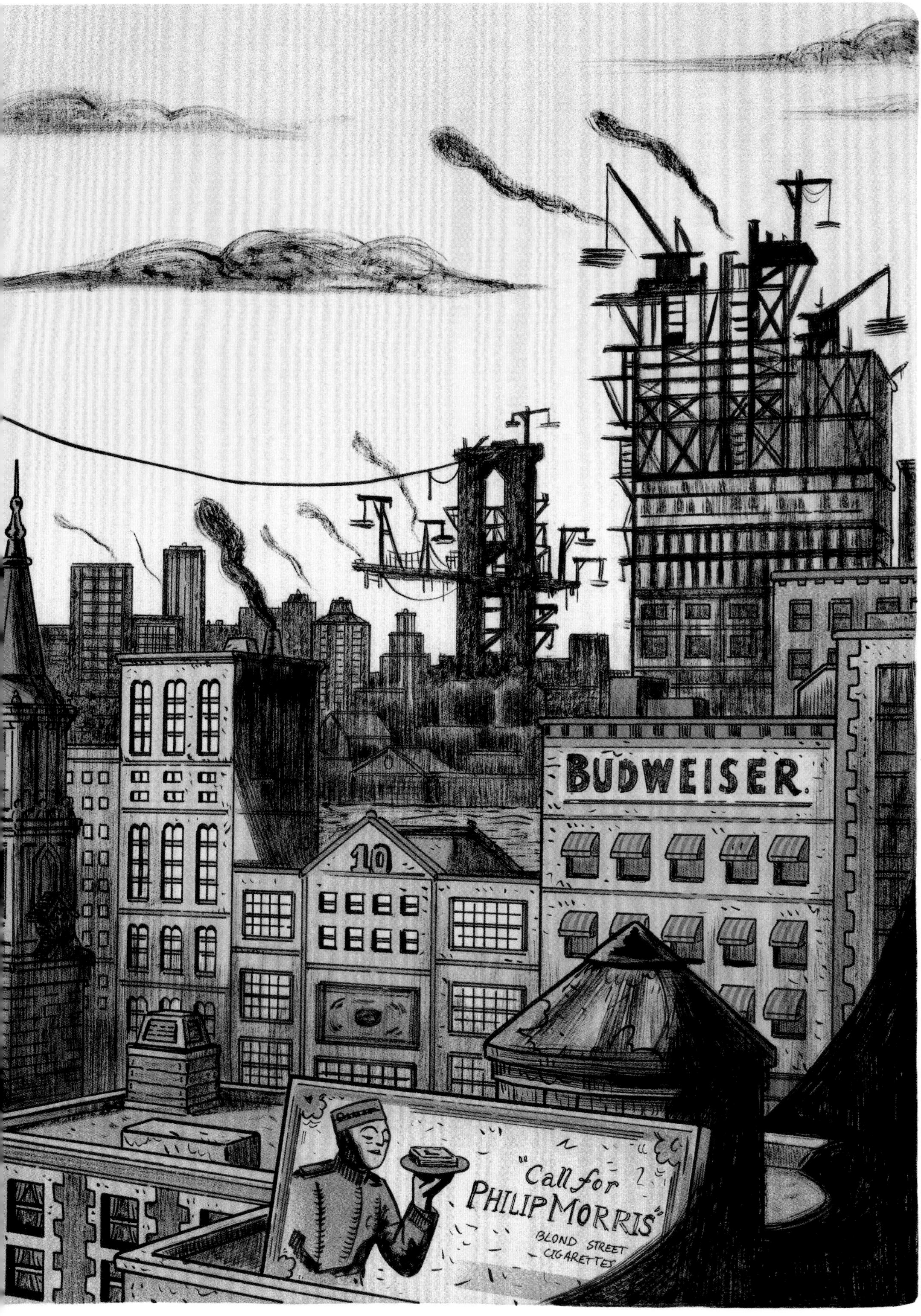
10
BUDWEISER.
"Call for
PHILIP MORRIS"
BLOND STREET
CIGARETTES

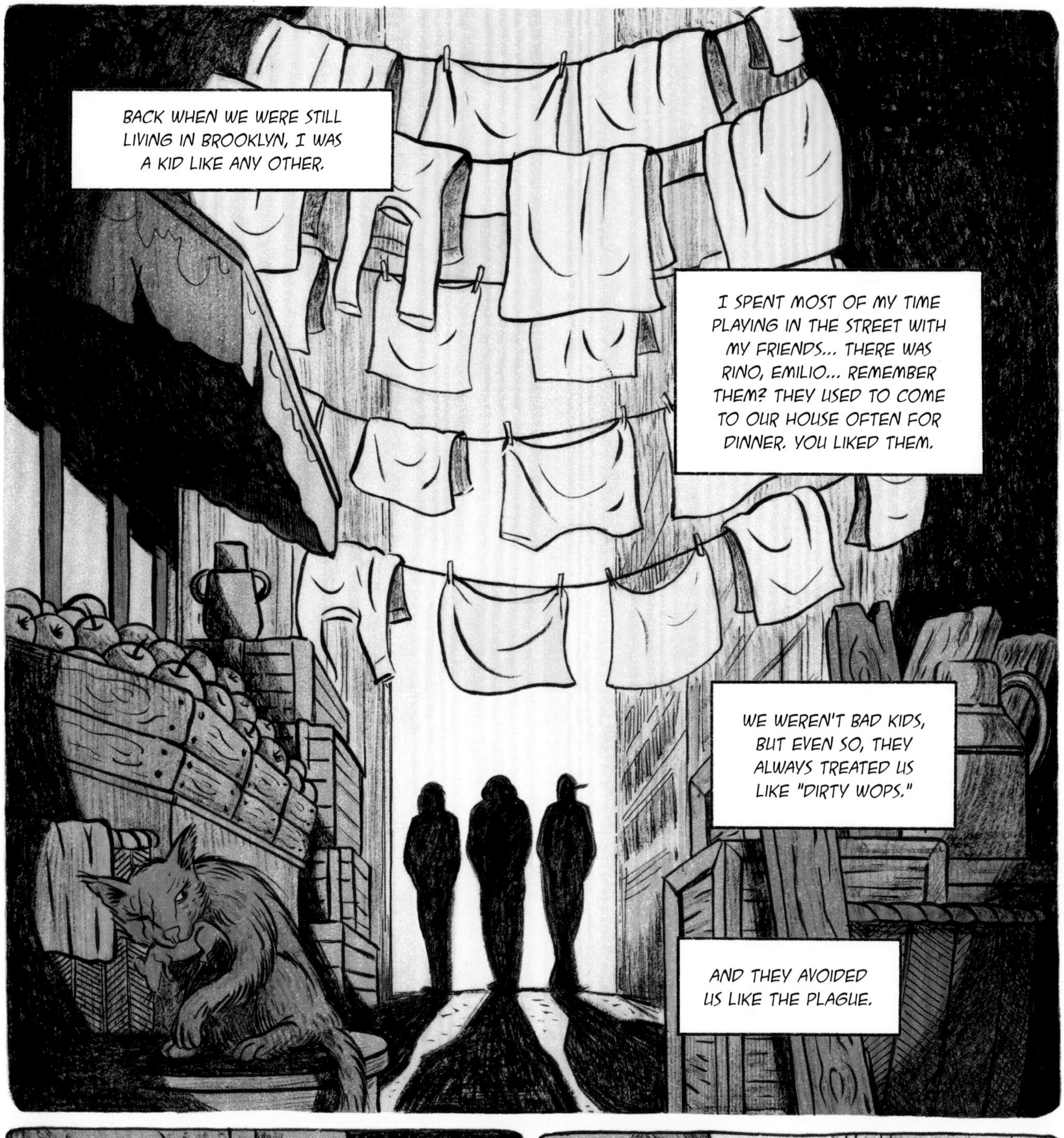
BACK WHEN WE WERE STILL LIVING IN BROOKLYN, I WAS A KID LIKE ANY OTHER.
I SPENT MOST OF MY TIME PLAYING IN THE STREET WITH MY FRIENDS... THERE WAS RINO, EMILIO... REMEMBER THEM? THEY USED TO COME TO OUR HOUSE OFTEN FOR DINNER. YOU LIKED THEM.
WE WEREN'T BAD KIDS, BUT EVEN SO, THEY ALWAYS TREATED US LIKE "DIRTY WOPS."
AND THEY AVOIDED US LIKE THE PLAGUE.

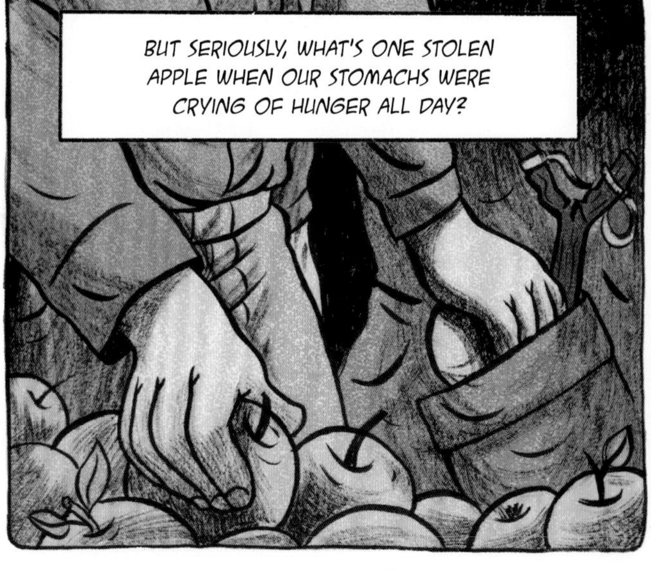
BUT SERIOUSLY, WHAT'S ONE STOLEN APPLE WHEN OUR STOMACHS WERE CRYING OF HUNGER ALL DAY?

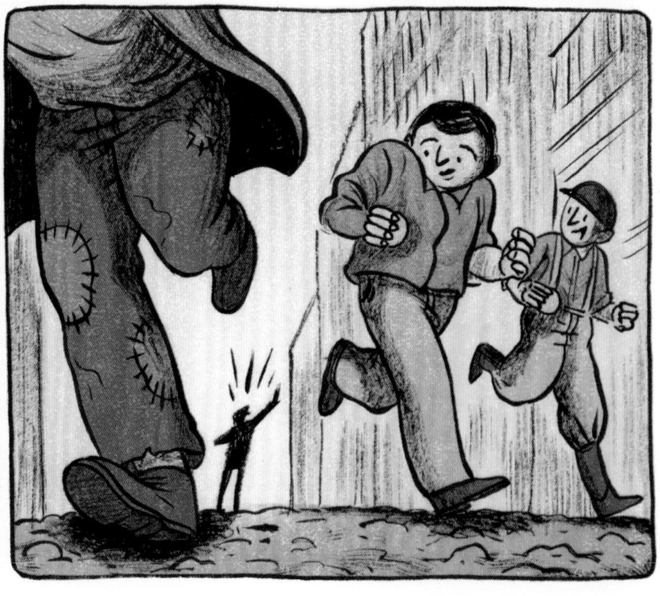

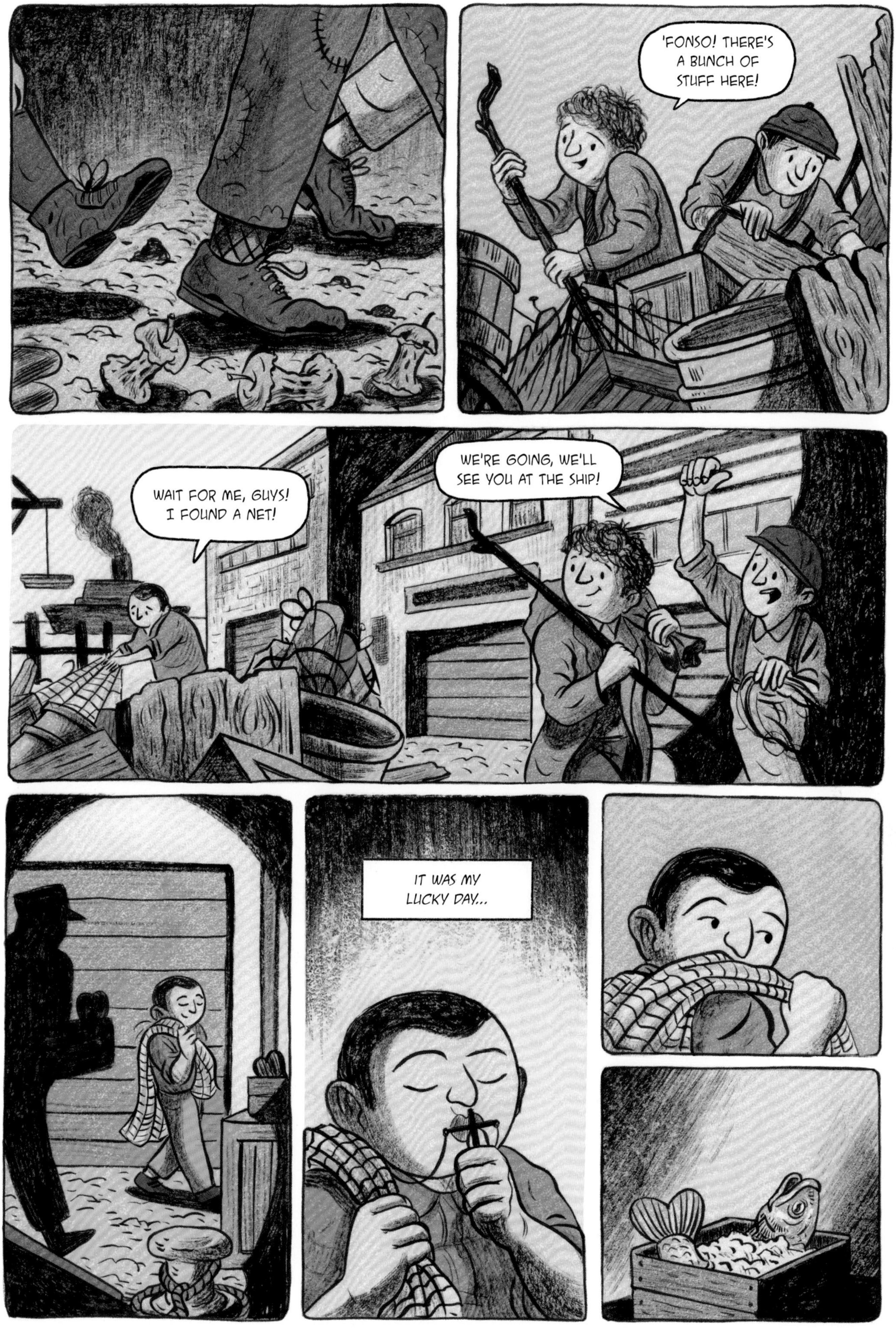
'FONSO! THERE'S A BUNCH OF STUFF HERE!
WAIT FOR ME, GUYS! I FOUND A NET!
WE'RE GOING, WE'LL SEE YOU AT THE SHIP!
IT WAS MY LUCKY DAY...

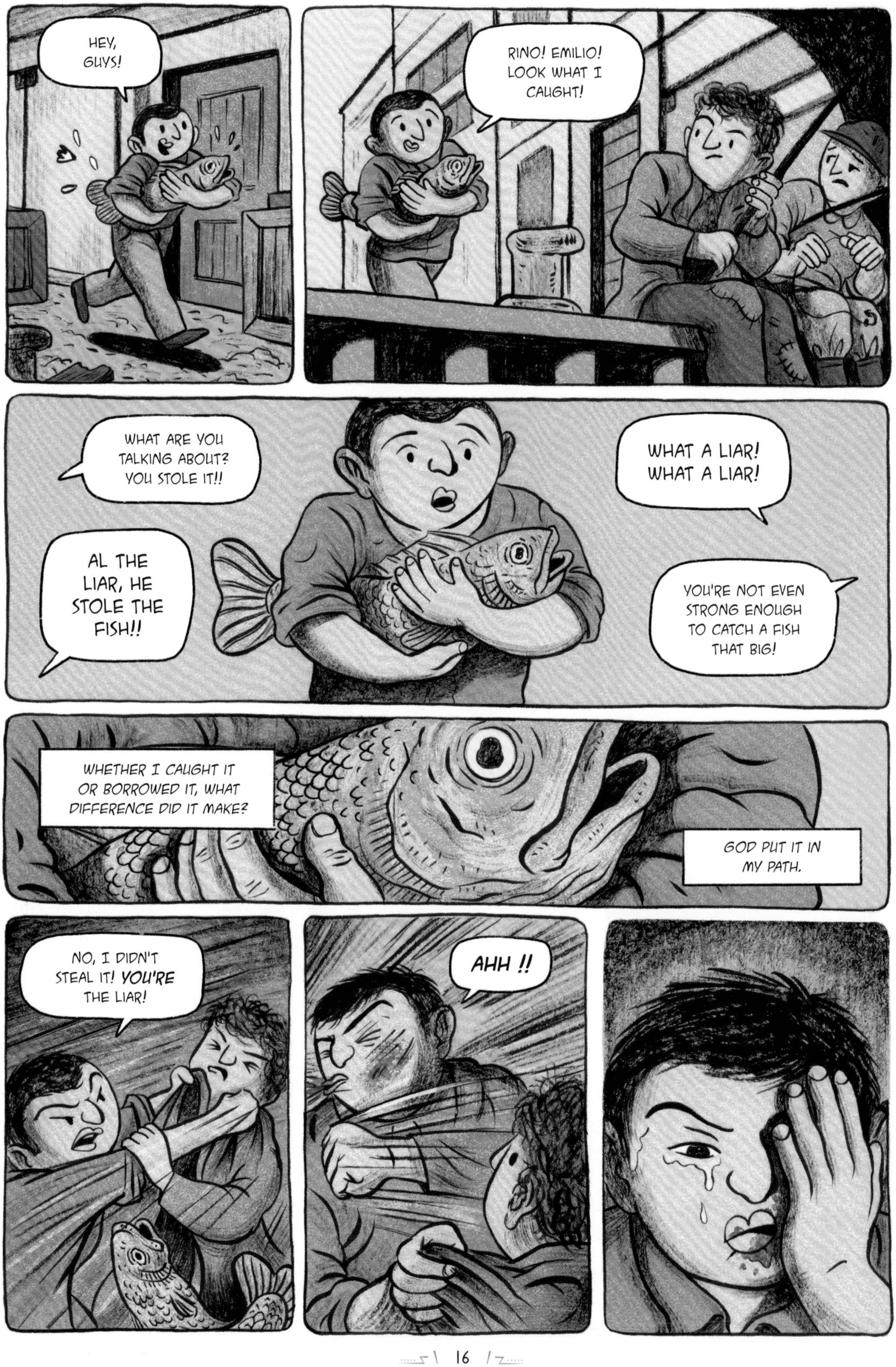
HEY, GUYS!
RINO! EMILIO! LOOK WHAT I CAUGHT!
WHAT ARE YOU TALKING ABOUT? YOU STOLE IT!!
WHAT A LIAR! WHAT A LIAR!
AL THE LIAR, HE STOLE THE FISH!!
YOU'RE NOT EVEN STRONG ENOUGH TO CATCH A FISH THAT BIG!
WHETHER I CAUGHT IT OR BORROWED IT, WHAT DIFFERENCE DID IT MAKE?
GOD PUT IT IN MY PATH.
NO, I DIDN'T STEAL IT! *YOU'RE* THE LIAR!
AHH !!

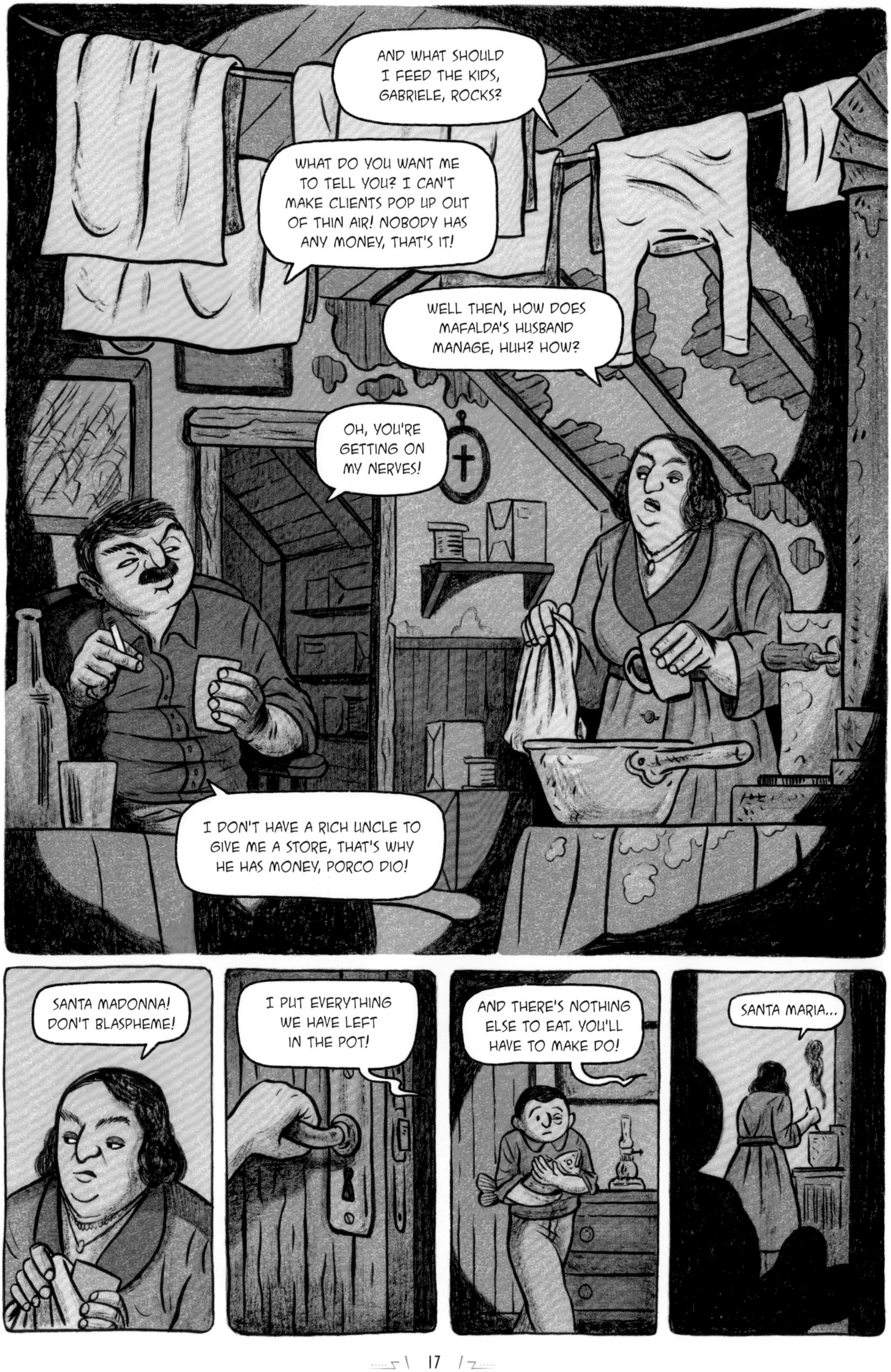
AND WHAT SHOULD I FEED THE KIDS, GABRIELE, ROCKS?
WHAT DO YOU WANT ME TO TELL YOU? I CAN'T MAKE CLIENTS POP UP OUT OF THIN AIR! NOBODY HAS ANY MONEY, THAT'S IT!
WELL THEN, HOW DOES MAFALDA'S HUSBAND MANAGE, HUH? HOW?
OH, YOU'RE GETTING ON MY NERVES!
I DON'T HAVE A RICH UNCLE TO GIVE ME A STORE, THAT'S WHY HE HAS MONEY, PORCO DIO!
SANTA MADONNA! DON'T BLASPHEME!
I PUT EVERYTHING WE HAVE LEFT IN THE POT!
AND THERE'S NOTHING ELSE TO EAT. YOU'LL HAVE TO MAKE DO!
SANTA MARIA...

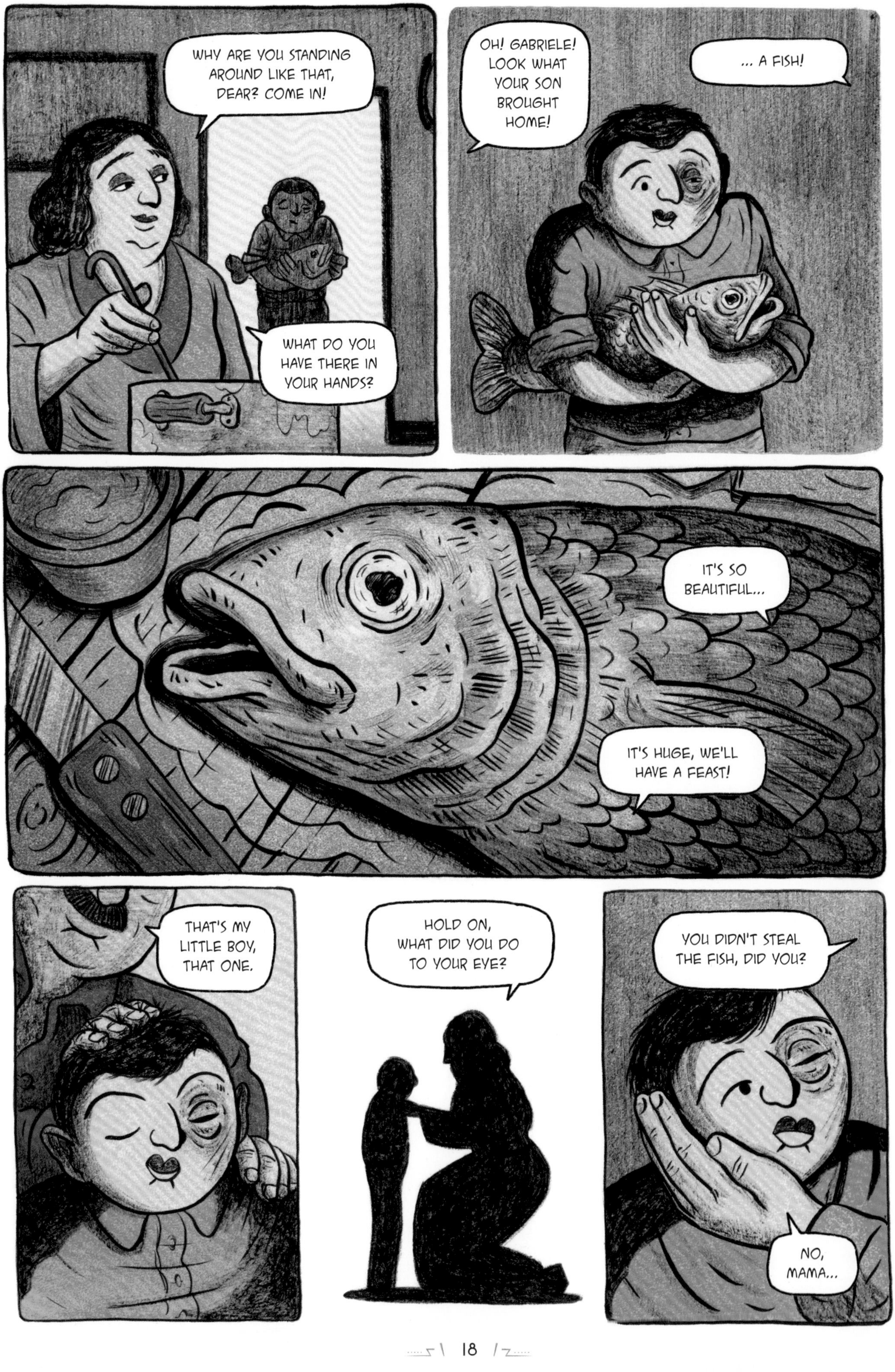
WHY ARE YOU STANDING AROUND LIKE THAT, DEAR? COME IN!
WHAT DO YOU HAVE THERE IN YOUR HANDS?
OH! GABRIELE! LOOK WHAT YOUR SON BROUGHT HOME!
... A FISH!
IT'S SO BEAUTIFUL...
IT'S HUGE, WE'LL HAVE A FEAST!
THAT'S MY LITTLE BOY, THAT ONE.
HOLD ON, WHAT DID YOU DO TO YOUR EYE?
YOU DIDN'T STEAL THE FISH, DID YOU?
NO, MAMA...

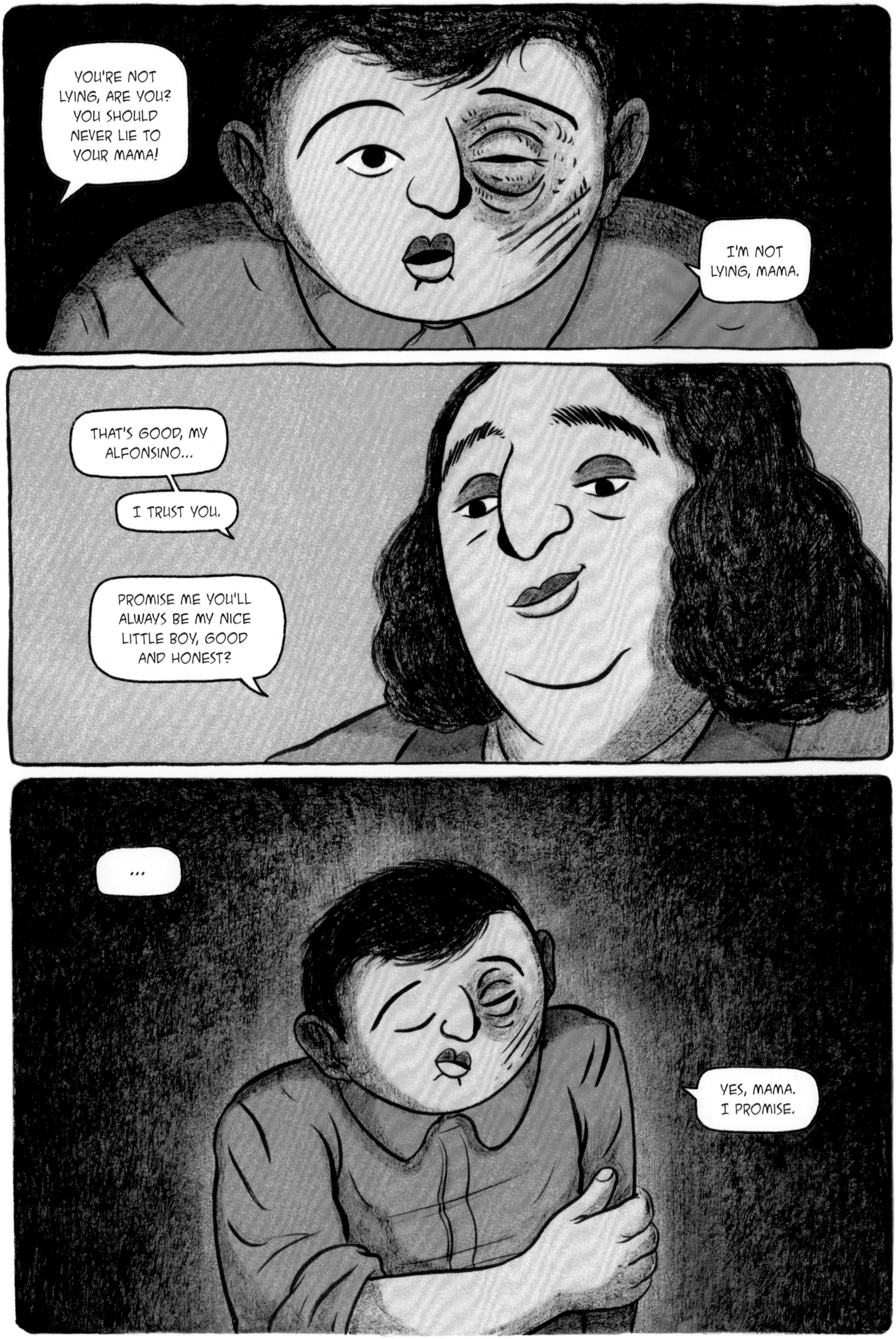
YOU'RE NOT LYING, ARE YOU? YOU SHOULD NEVER LIE TO YOUR MAMA!
I'M NOT LYING, MAMA.
THAT'S GOOD, MY ALFONSINO...
I TRUST YOU.
PROMISE ME YOU'LL ALWAYS BE MY NICE LITTLE BOY, GOOD AND HONEST?
...
YES, MAMA. I PROMISE.

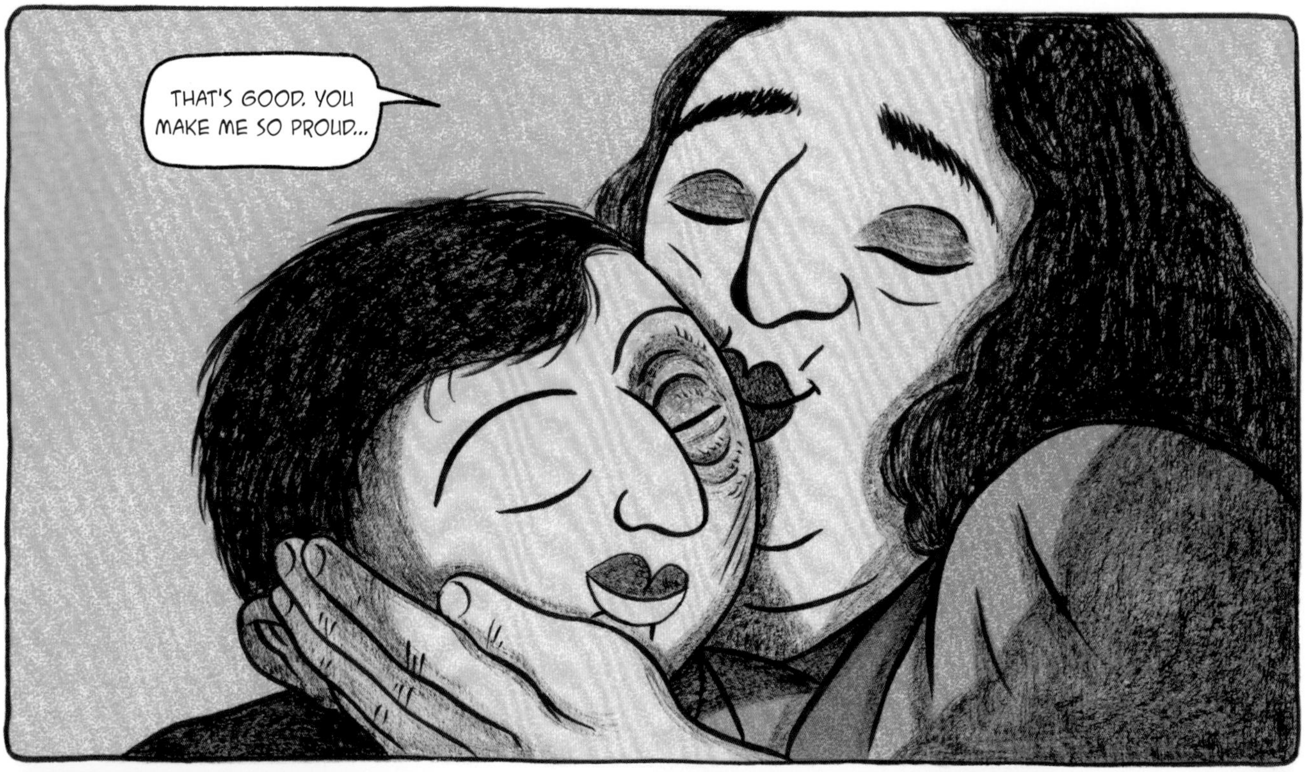
THAT'S GOOD. YOU MAKE ME SO PROUD...

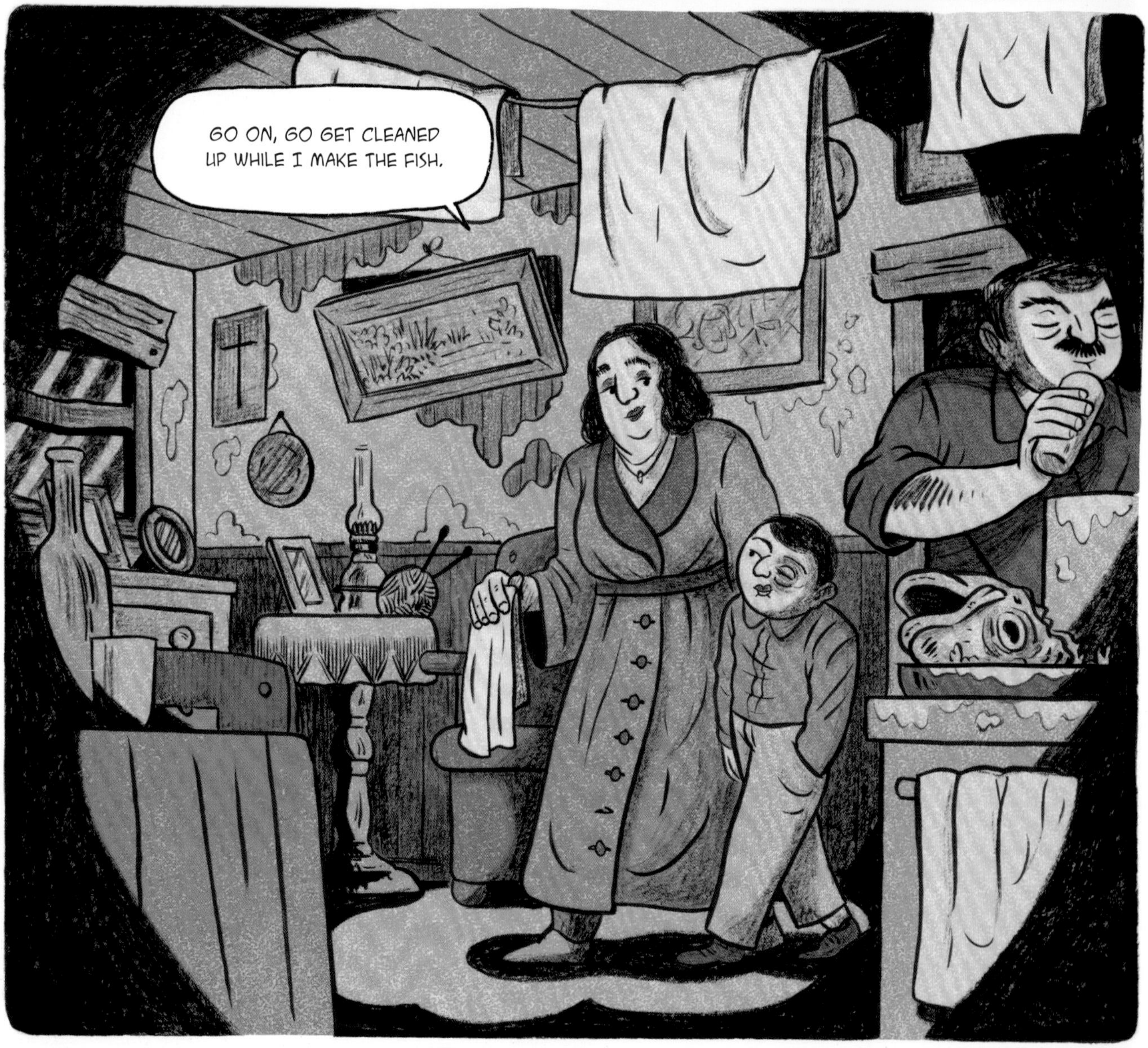
GO ON, GO GET CLEANED UP WHILE I MAKE THE FISH.

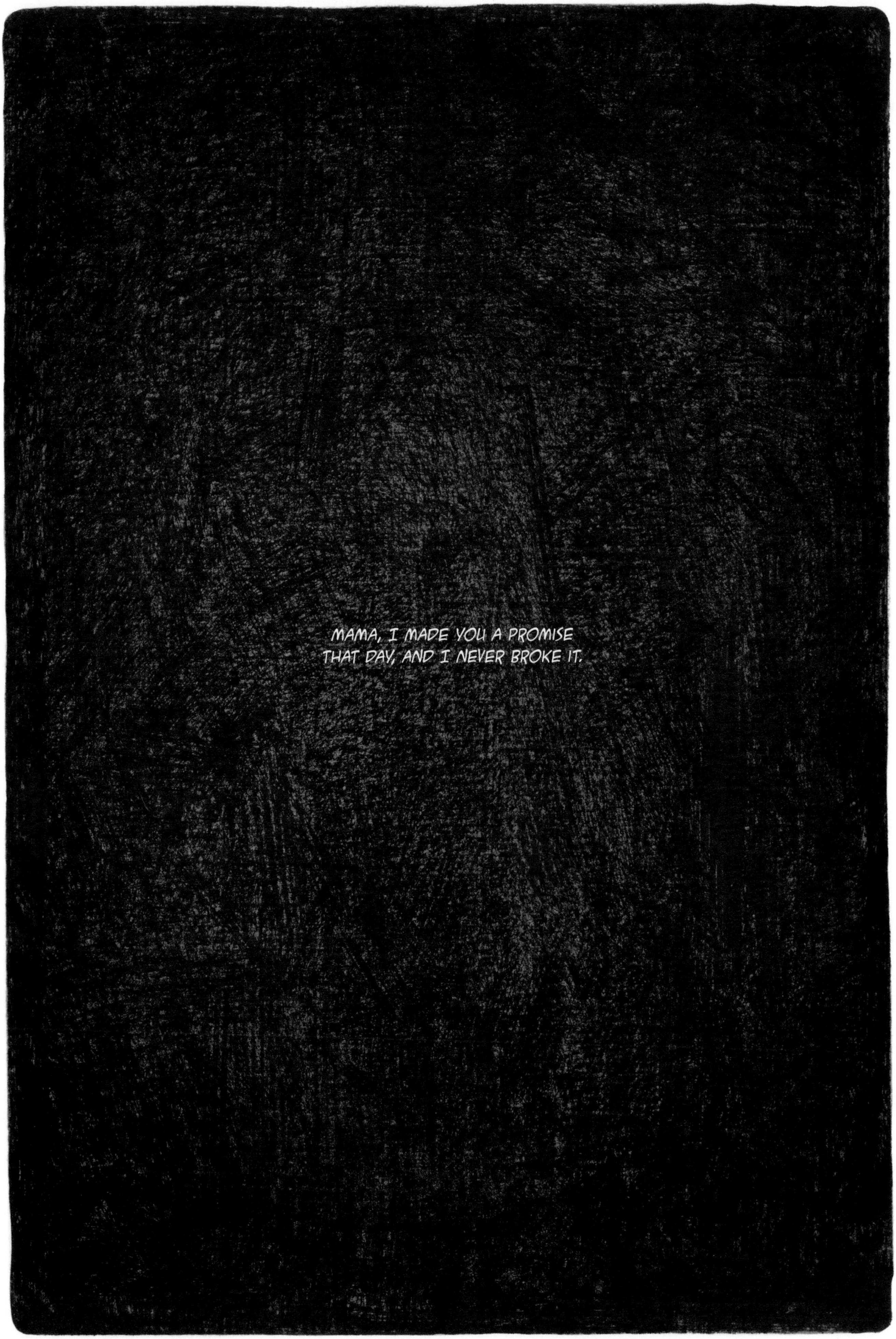
MAMA, I MADE YOU A PROMISE THAT DAY, AND I NEVER BROKE IT.

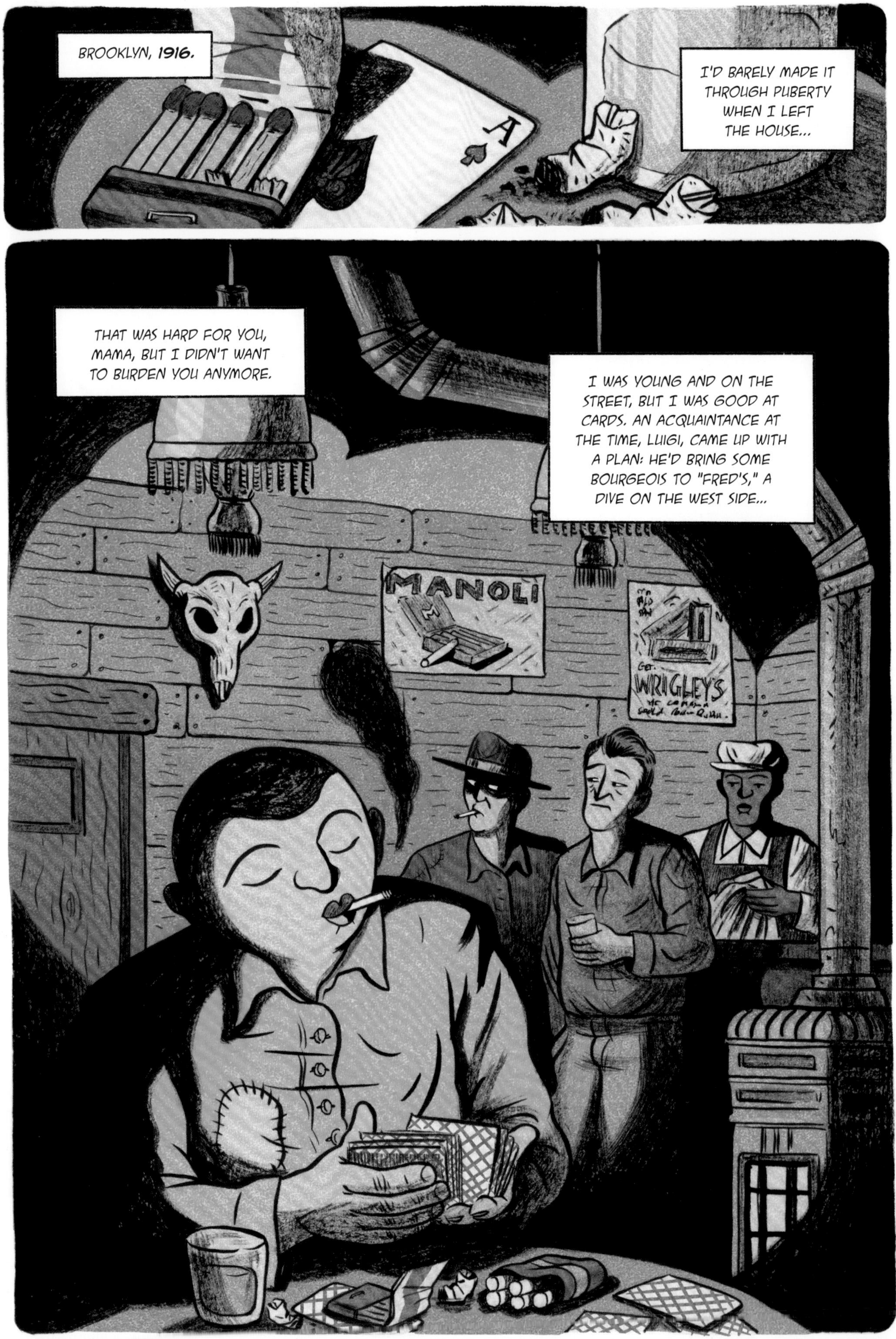
BROOKLYN, 1916.
I'D BARELY MADE IT THROUGH PUBERTY WHEN I LEFT THE HOUSE...
THAT WAS HARD FOR YOU, MAMA, BUT I DIDN'T WANT TO BURDEN YOU ANYMORE.
I WAS YOUNG AND ON THE STREET, BUT I WAS GOOD AT CARDS. AN ACQUAINTANCE AT THE TIME, LUIGI, CAME UP WITH A PLAN: HE'D BRING SOME BOURGEOIS TO "FRED'S," A DIVE ON THE WEST SIDE...
MANOLI
WRIGLEY'S

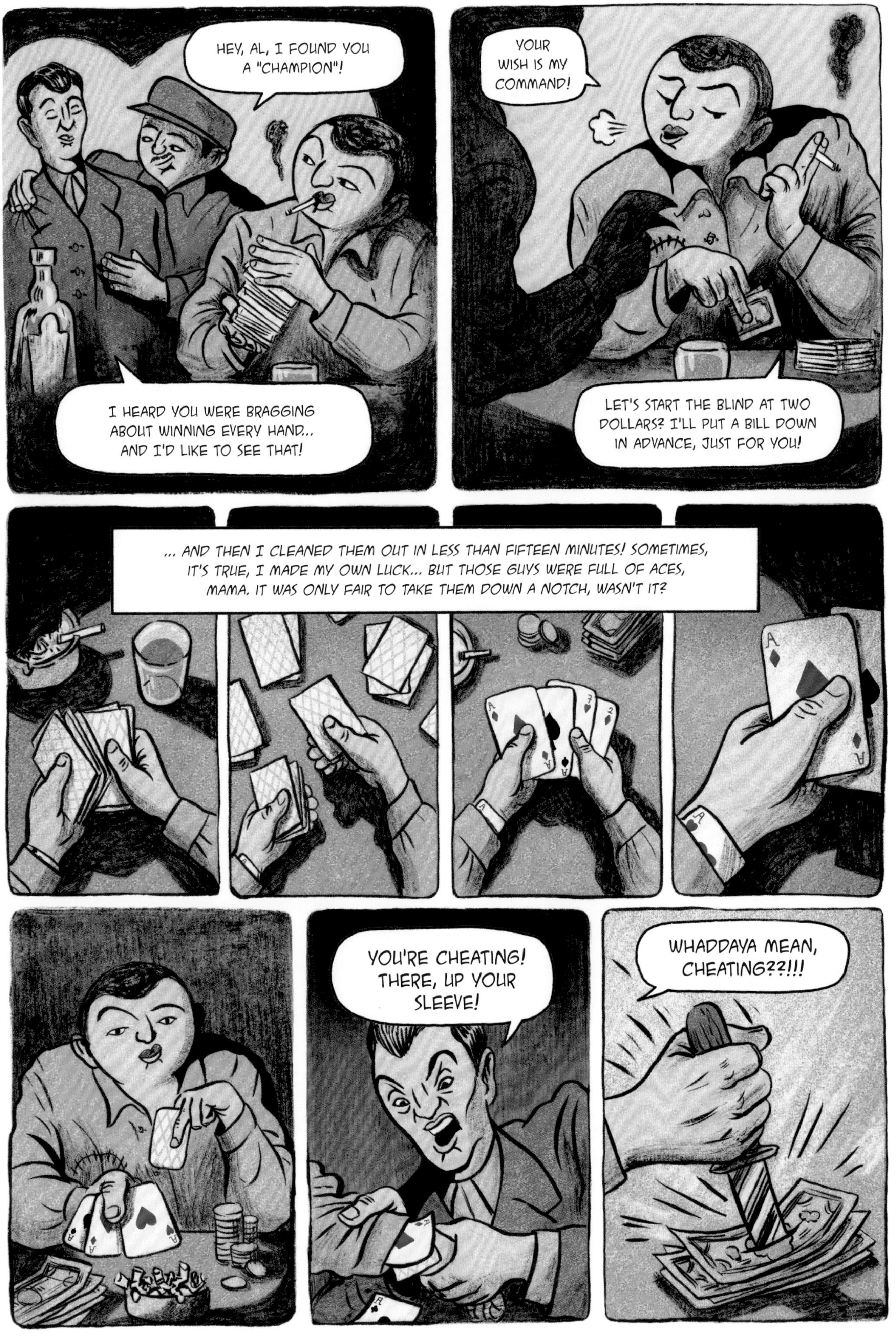
HEY, AL, I FOUND YOU A "CHAMPION"!
I HEARD YOU WERE BRAGGING ABOUT WINNING EVERY HAND... AND I'D LIKE TO SEE THAT!
YOUR WISH IS MY COMMAND!
LET'S START THE BLIND AT TWO DOLLARS? I'LL PUT A BILL DOWN IN ADVANCE, JUST FOR YOU!
... AND THEN I CLEANED THEM OUT IN LESS THAN FIFTEEN MINUTES! SOMETIMES, IT'S TRUE, I MADE MY OWN LUCK... BUT THOSE GUYS WERE FULL OF ACES, MAMA. IT WAS ONLY FAIR TO TAKE THEM DOWN A NOTCH, WASN'T IT?
YOU'RE CHEATING! THERE, UP YOUR SLEEVE!
WHADDAYA MEAN, CHEATING??!!!

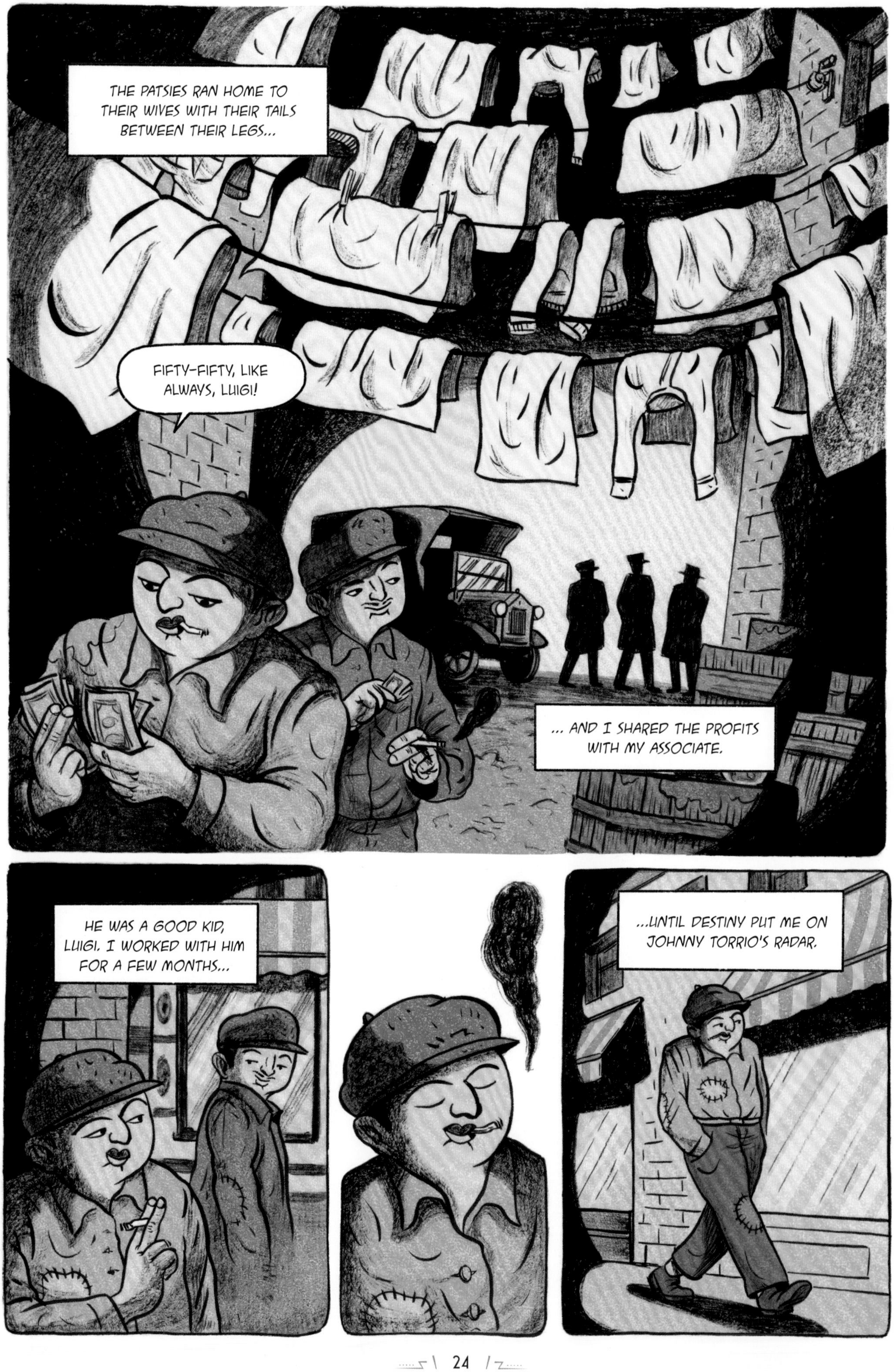
THE PATSIES RAN HOME TO THEIR WIVES WITH THEIR TAILS BETWEEN THEIR LEGS...
FIFTY-FIFTY, LIKE ALWAYS, LUIGI!
... AND I SHARED THE PROFITS WITH MY ASSOCIATE.
HE WAS A GOOD KID, LUIGI. I WORKED WITH HIM FOR A FEW MONTHS...
...UNTIL DESTINY PUT ME ON JOHNNY TORRIO'S RADAR.

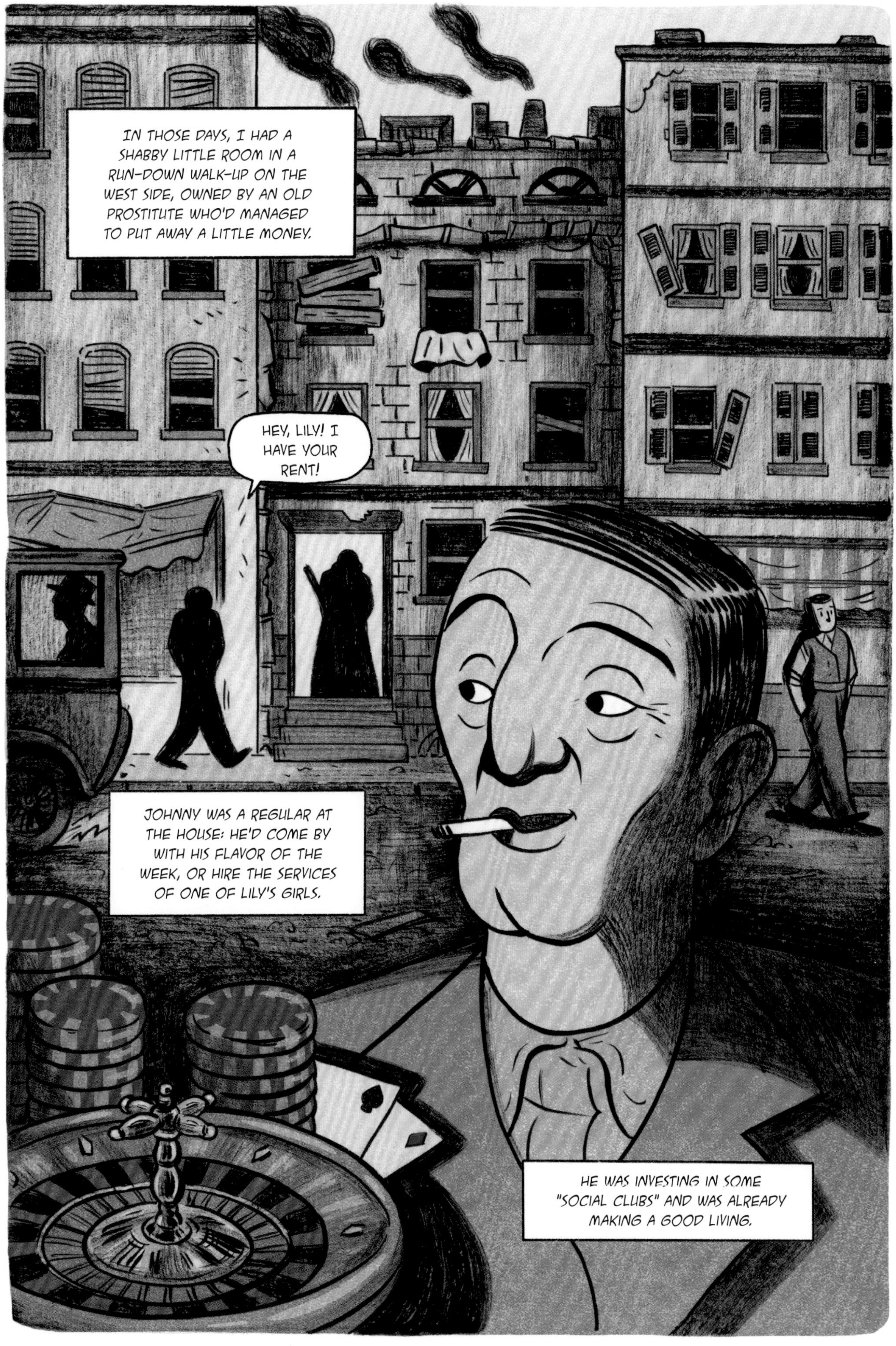
IN THOSE DAYS, I HAD A SHABBY LITTLE ROOM IN A RUN-DOWN WALK-UP ON THE WEST SIDE, OWNED BY AN OLD PROSTITUTE WHO'D MANAGED TO PUT AWAY A LITTLE MONEY.
HEY, LILY! I HAVE YOUR RENT!
JOHNNY WAS A REGULAR AT THE HOUSE: HE'D COME BY WITH HIS FLAVOR OF THE WEEK, OR HIRE THE SERVICES OF ONE OF LILY'S GIRLS.
HE WAS INVESTING IN SOME "SOCIAL CLUBS" AND WAS ALREADY MAKING A GOOD LIVING.

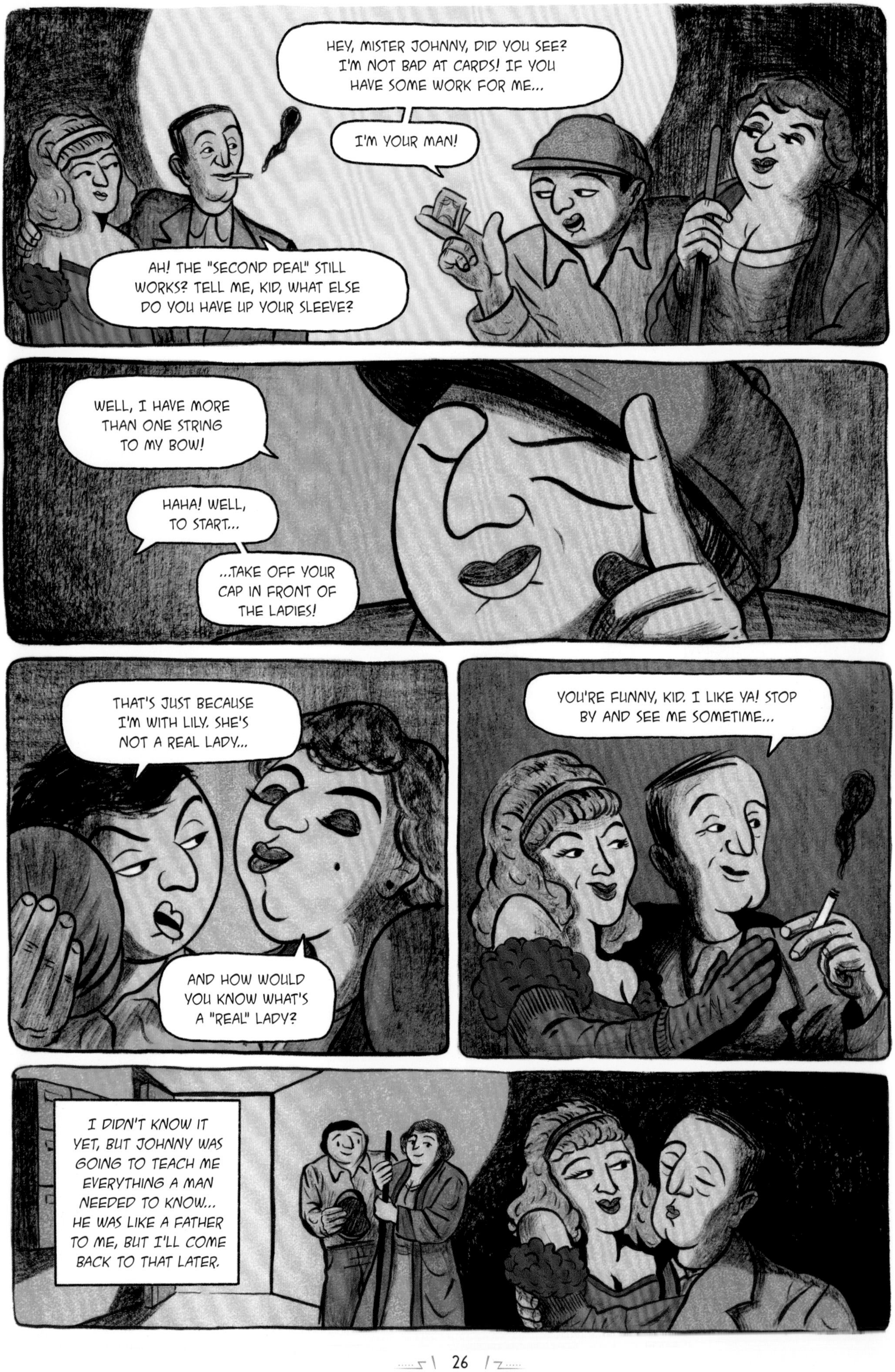
HEY, MISTER JOHNNY, DID YOU SEE? I'M NOT BAD AT CARDS! IF YOU HAVE SOME WORK FOR ME...
I'M YOUR MAN!
AH! THE "SECOND DEAL" STILL WORKS? TELL ME, KID, WHAT ELSE DO YOU HAVE UP YOUR SLEEVE?
WELL, I HAVE MORE THAN ONE STRING TO MY BOW!
HAHA! WELL, TO START...
...TAKE OFF YOUR CAP IN FRONT OF THE LADIES!
THAT'S JUST BECAUSE I'M WITH LILY. SHE'S NOT A REAL LADY...
AND HOW WOULD YOU KNOW WHAT'S A "REAL" LADY?
YOU'RE FUNNY, KID. I LIKE YA! STOP BY AND SEE ME SOMETIME...
I DIDN'T KNOW IT YET, BUT JOHNNY WAS GOING TO TEACH ME EVERYTHING A MAN NEEDED TO KNOW... HE WAS LIKE A FATHER TO ME, BUT I'LL COME BACK TO THAT LATER.

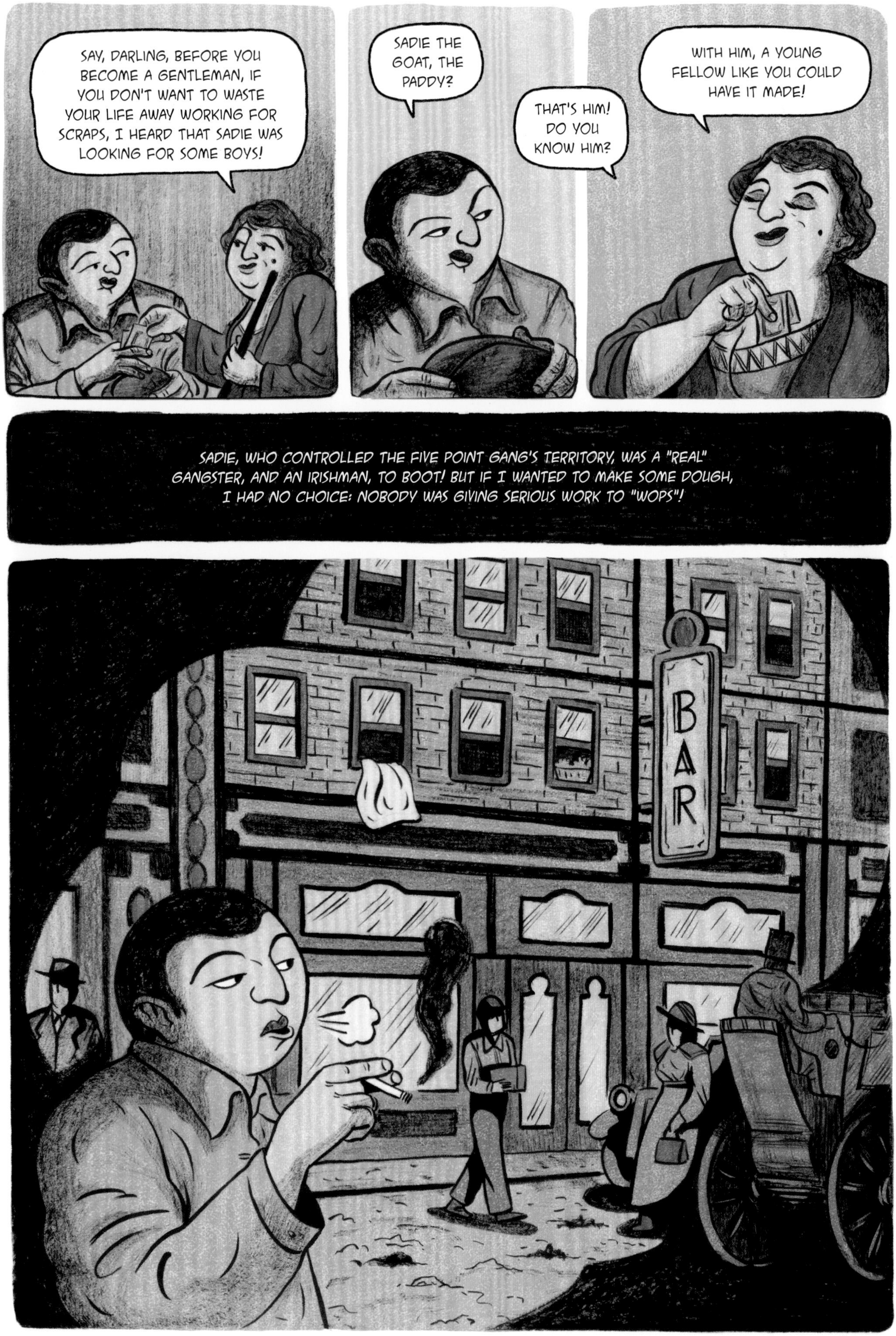
SAY, DARLING, BEFORE YOU BECOME A GENTLEMAN, IF YOU DON'T WANT TO WASTE YOUR LIFE AWAY WORKING FOR SCRAPS, I HEARD THAT SADIE WAS LOOKING FOR SOME BOYS!
SADIE THE GOAT, THE PADDY?
THAT'S HIM! DO YOU KNOW HIM?
WITH HIM, A YOUNG FELLOW LIKE YOU COULD HAVE IT MADE!
SADIE, WHO CONTROLLED THE FIVE POINT GANG'S TERRITORY, WAS A "REAL" GANGSTER, AND AN IRISHMAN, TO BOOT! BUT IF I WANTED TO MAKE SOME DOUGH, I HAD NO CHOICE: NOBODY WAS GIVING SERIOUS WORK TO "WOPS"!
BAR

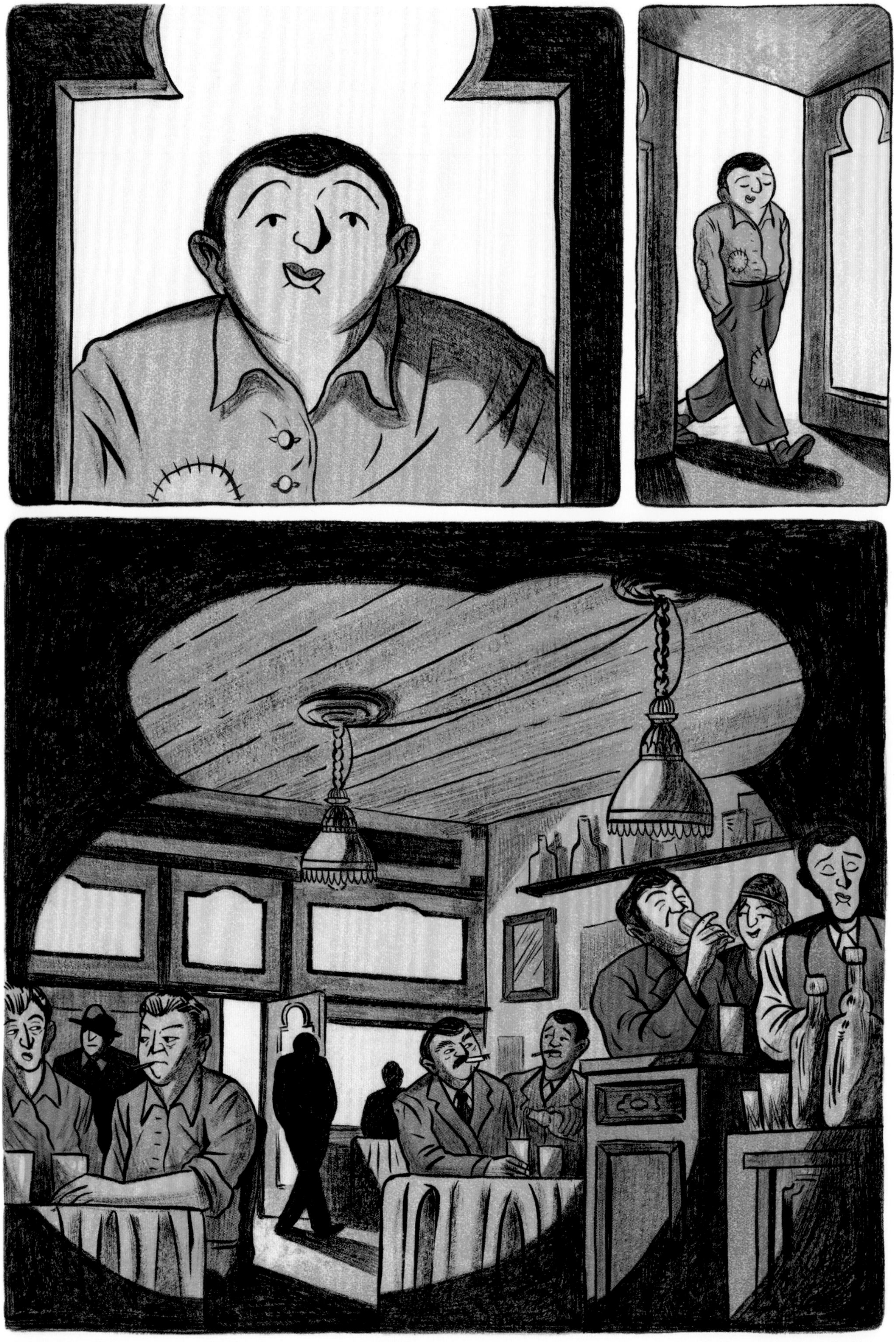

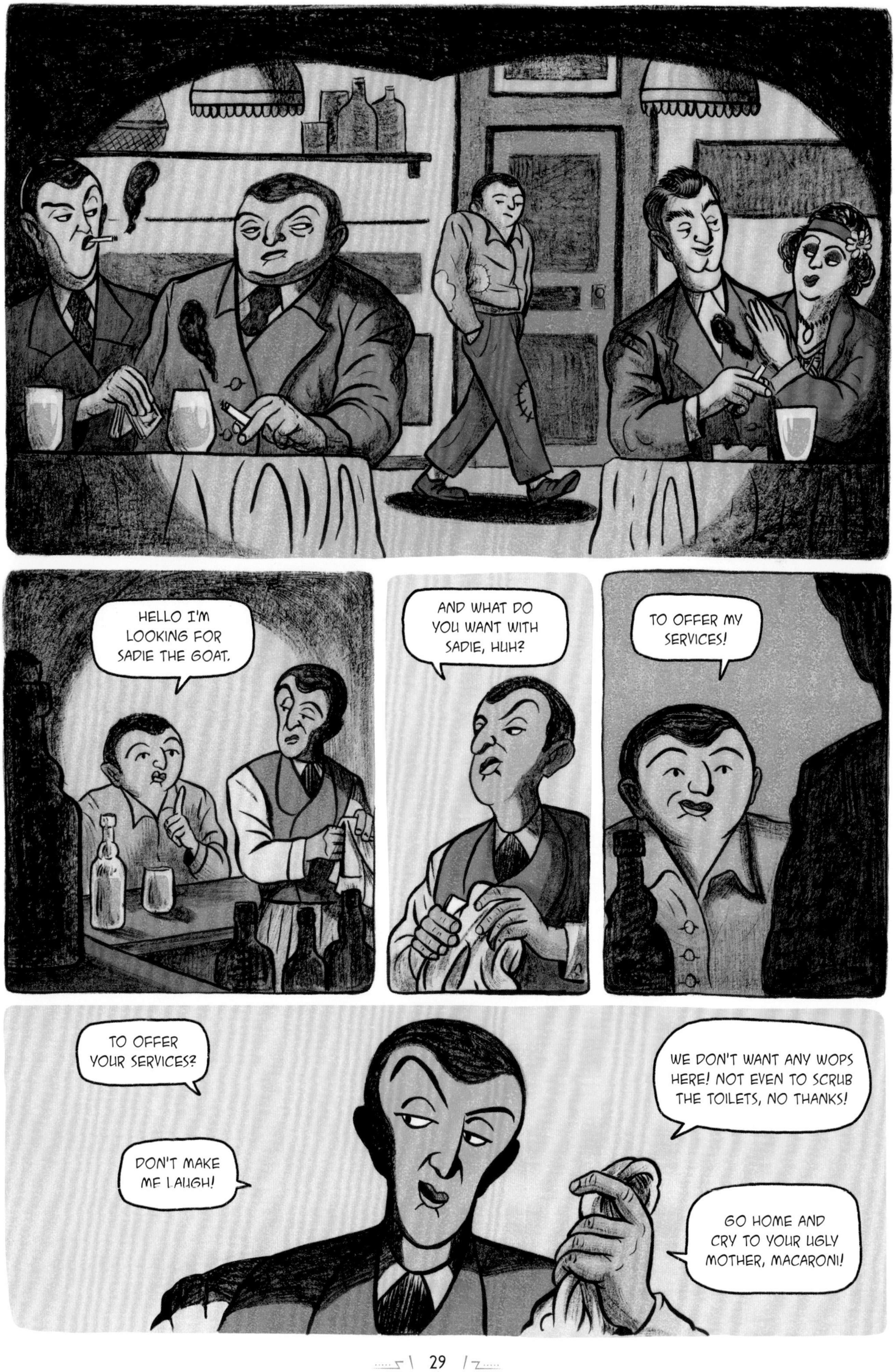
HELLO I'M LOOKING FOR SADIE THE GOAT.
AND WHAT DO YOU WANT WITH SADIE, HUH?
TO OFFER MY SERVICES!
TO OFFER YOUR SERVICES?
DON'T MAKE ME LAUGH!
WE DON'T WANT ANY WOPS HERE! NOT EVEN TO SCRUB THE TOILETS, NO THANKS!
GO HOME AND CRY TO YOUR UGLY MOTHER, MACARONI!

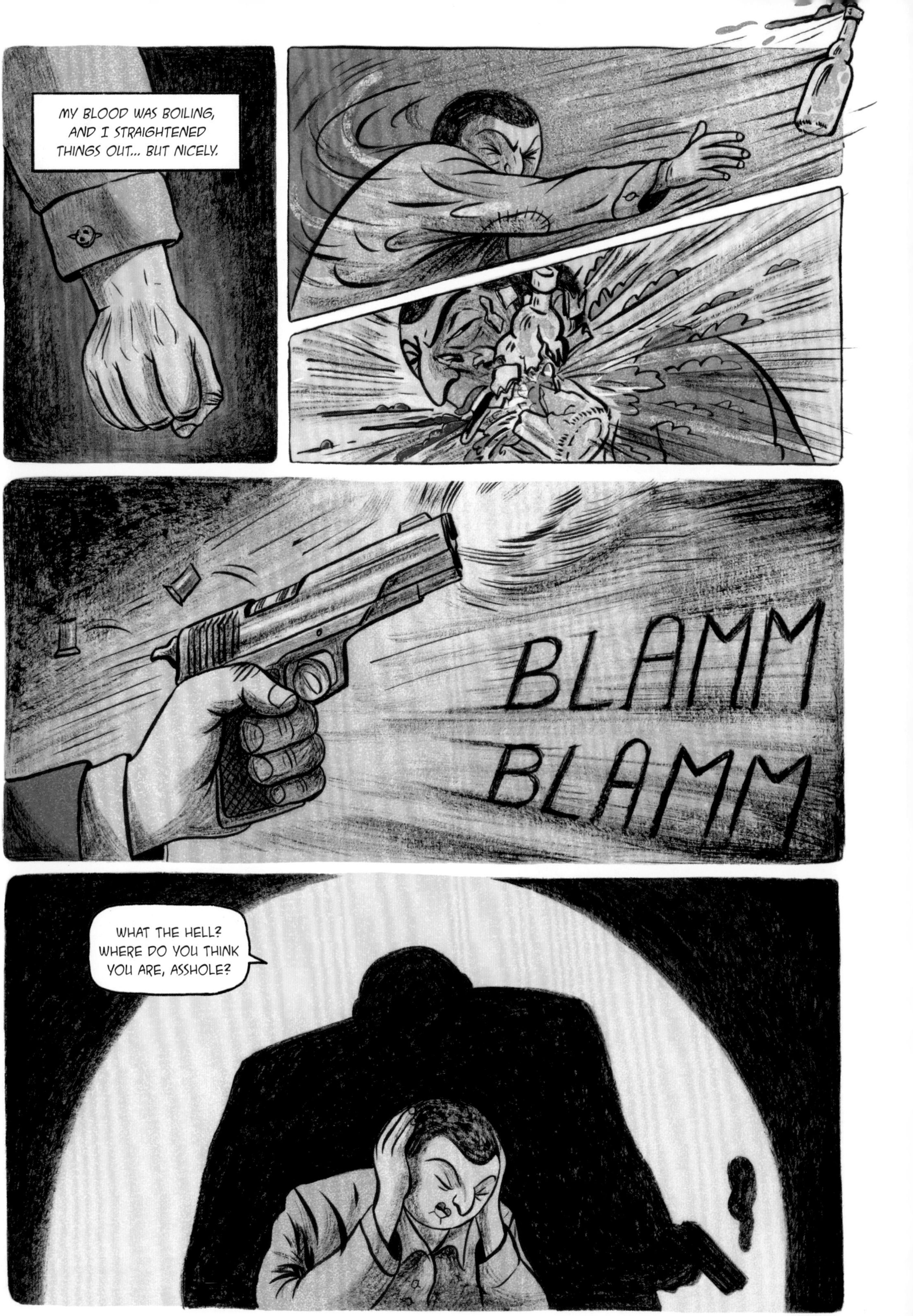
MY BLOOD WAS BOILING, AND I STRAIGHTENED THINGS OUT... BUT NICELY.
BLAMM BLAMM
WHAT THE HELL? WHERE DO YOU THINK YOU ARE, ASSHOLE?

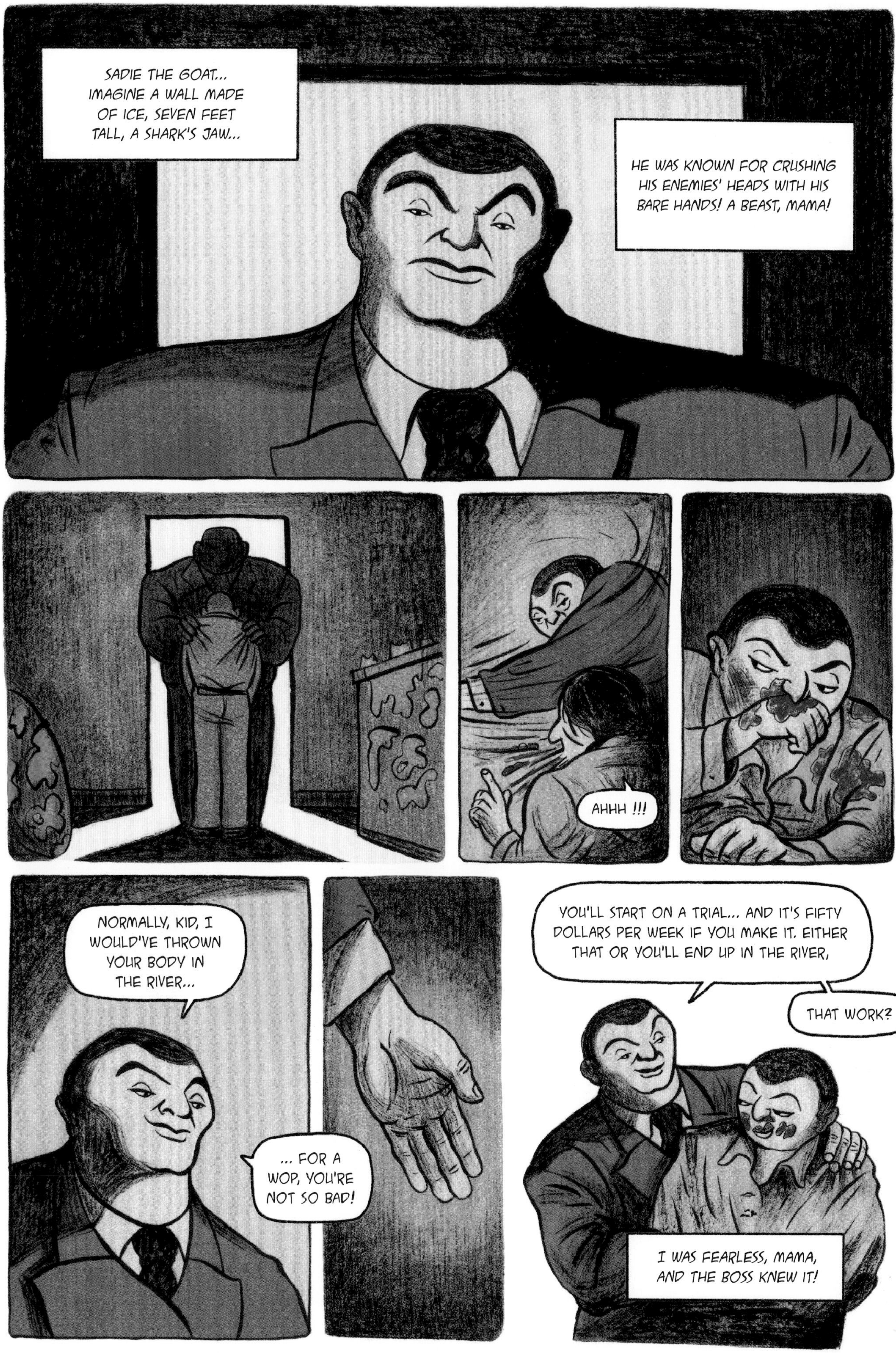
SADIE THE GOAT... IMAGINE A WALL MADE OF ICE, SEVEN FEET TALL, A SHARK'S JAW...
HE WAS KNOWN FOR CRUSHING HIS ENEMIES' HEADS WITH HIS BARE HANDS! A BEAST, MAMA!
AHHH !!!
NORMALLY, KID, I WOULD'VE THROWN YOUR BODY IN THE RIVER...
... FOR A WOP, YOU'RE NOT SO BAD!
YOU'LL START ON A TRIAL... AND IT'S FIFTY DOLLARS PER WEEK IF YOU MAKE IT. EITHER THAT OR YOU'LL END UP IN THE RIVER,
THAT WORK?
I WAS FEARLESS, MAMA, AND THE BOSS KNEW IT!

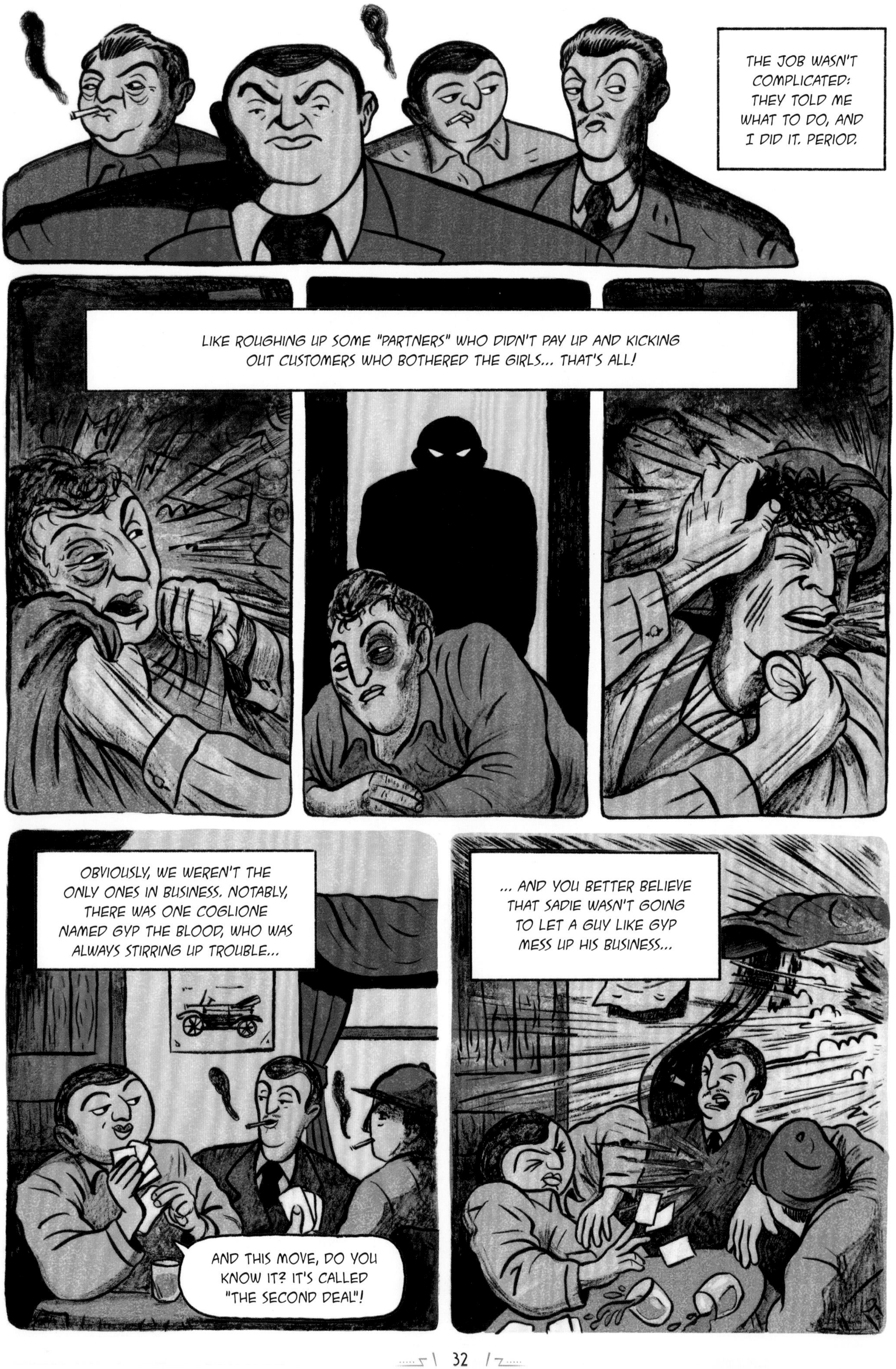
THE JOB WASN'T COMPLICATED: THEY TOLD ME WHAT TO DO, AND I DID IT. PERIOD.
LIKE ROUGHING UP SOME "PARTNERS" WHO DIDN'T PAY UP AND KICKING OUT CUSTOMERS WHO BOTHERED THE GIRLS... THAT'S ALL!
OBVIOUSLY, WE WEREN'T THE ONLY ONES IN BUSINESS. NOTABLY, THERE WAS ONE COGLIONE NAMED GYP THE BLOOD, WHO WAS ALWAYS STIRRING UP TROUBLE...
AND THIS MOVE, DO YOU KNOW IT? IT'S CALLED "THE SECOND DEAL"!
... AND YOU BETTER BELIEVE THAT SADIE WASN'T GOING TO LET A GUY LIKE GYP MESS UP HIS BUSINESS...

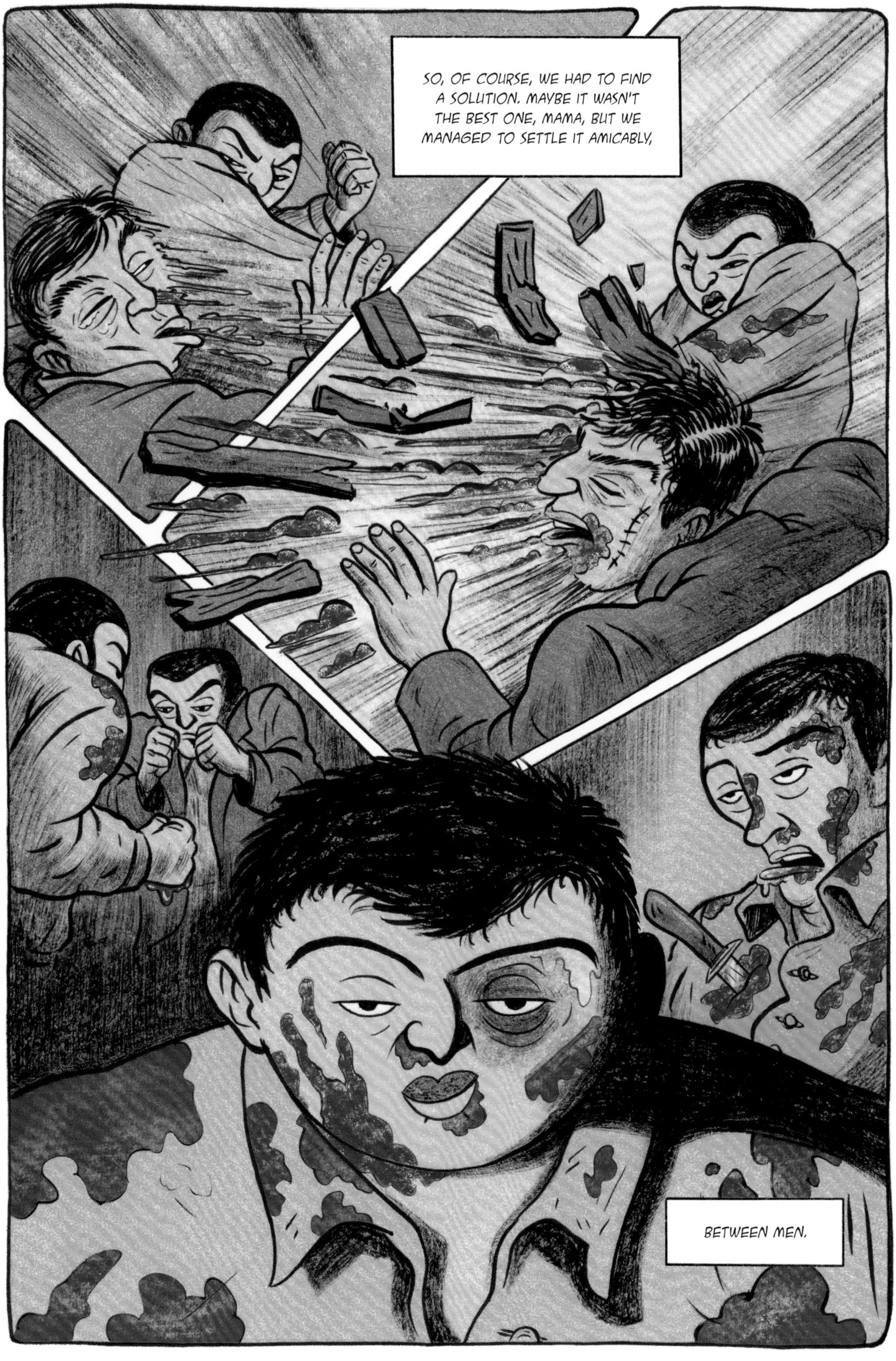
SO, OF COURSE, WE HAD TO FIND A SOLUTION. MAYBE IT WASN'T THE BEST ONE, MAMA, BUT WE MANAGED TO SETTLE IT AMICABLY,
BETWEEN MEN.

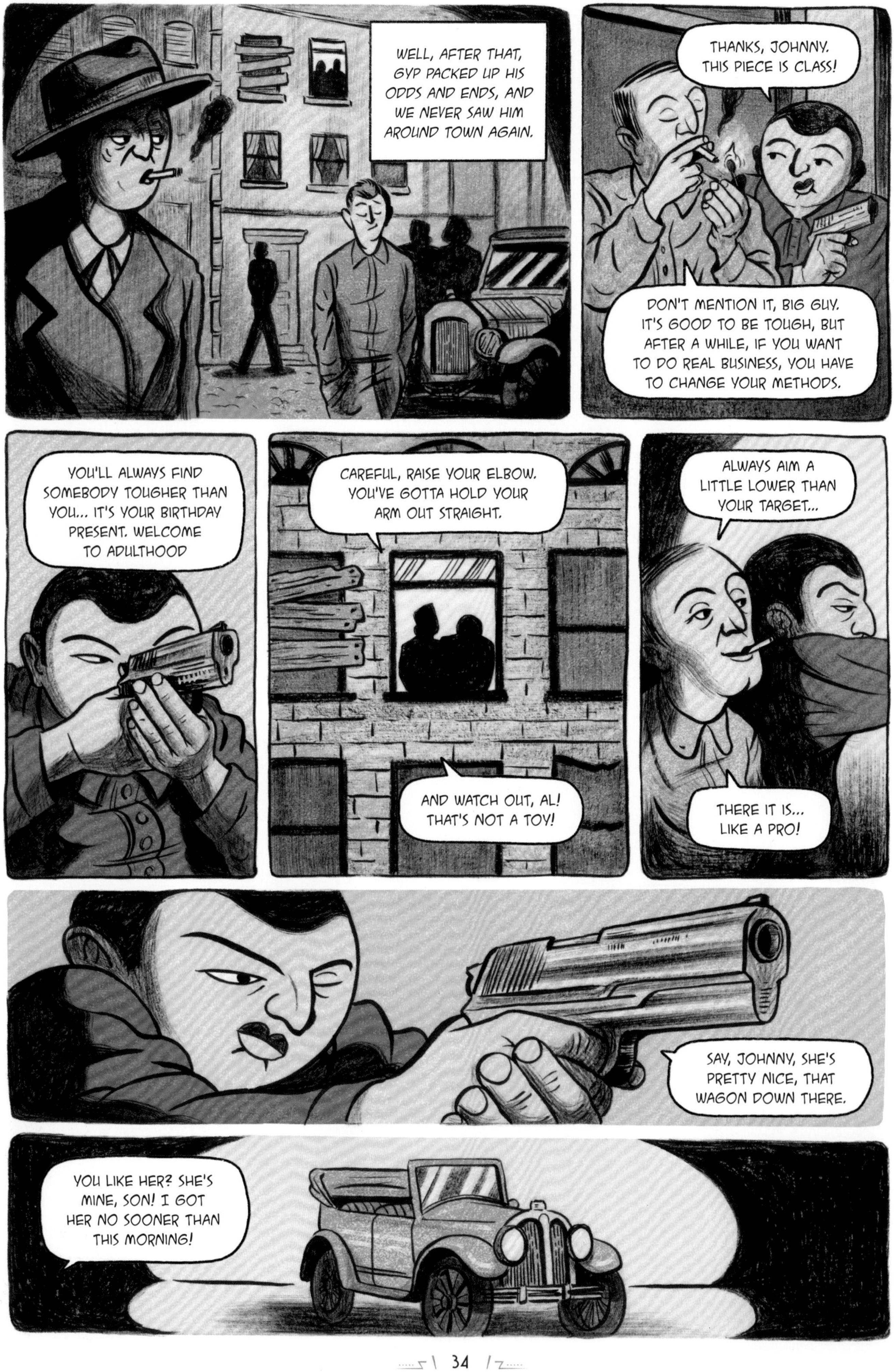
WELL, AFTER THAT, GYP PACKED UP HIS ODDS AND ENDS, AND WE NEVER SAW HIM AROUND TOWN AGAIN.
THANKS, JOHNNY. THIS PIECE IS CLASS!
DON'T MENTION IT, BIG GUY. IT'S GOOD TO BE TOUGH, BUT AFTER A WHILE, IF YOU WANT TO DO REAL BUSINESS, YOU HAVE TO CHANGE YOUR METHODS.
YOU'LL ALWAYS FIND SOMEBODY TOUGHER THAN YOU... IT'S YOUR BIRTHDAY PRESENT. WELCOME TO ADULTHOOD
CAREFUL, RAISE YOUR ELBOW. YOU'VE GOTTA HOLD YOUR ARM OUT STRAIGHT.
AND WATCH OUT, AL! THAT'S NOT A TOY!
ALWAYS AIM A LITTLE LOWER THAN YOUR TARGET...
THERE IT IS... LIKE A PRO!
SAY, JOHNNY, SHE'S PRETTY NICE, THAT WAGON DOWN THERE.
YOU LIKE HER? SHE'S MINE, SON! I GOT HER NO SOONER THAN THIS MORNING!

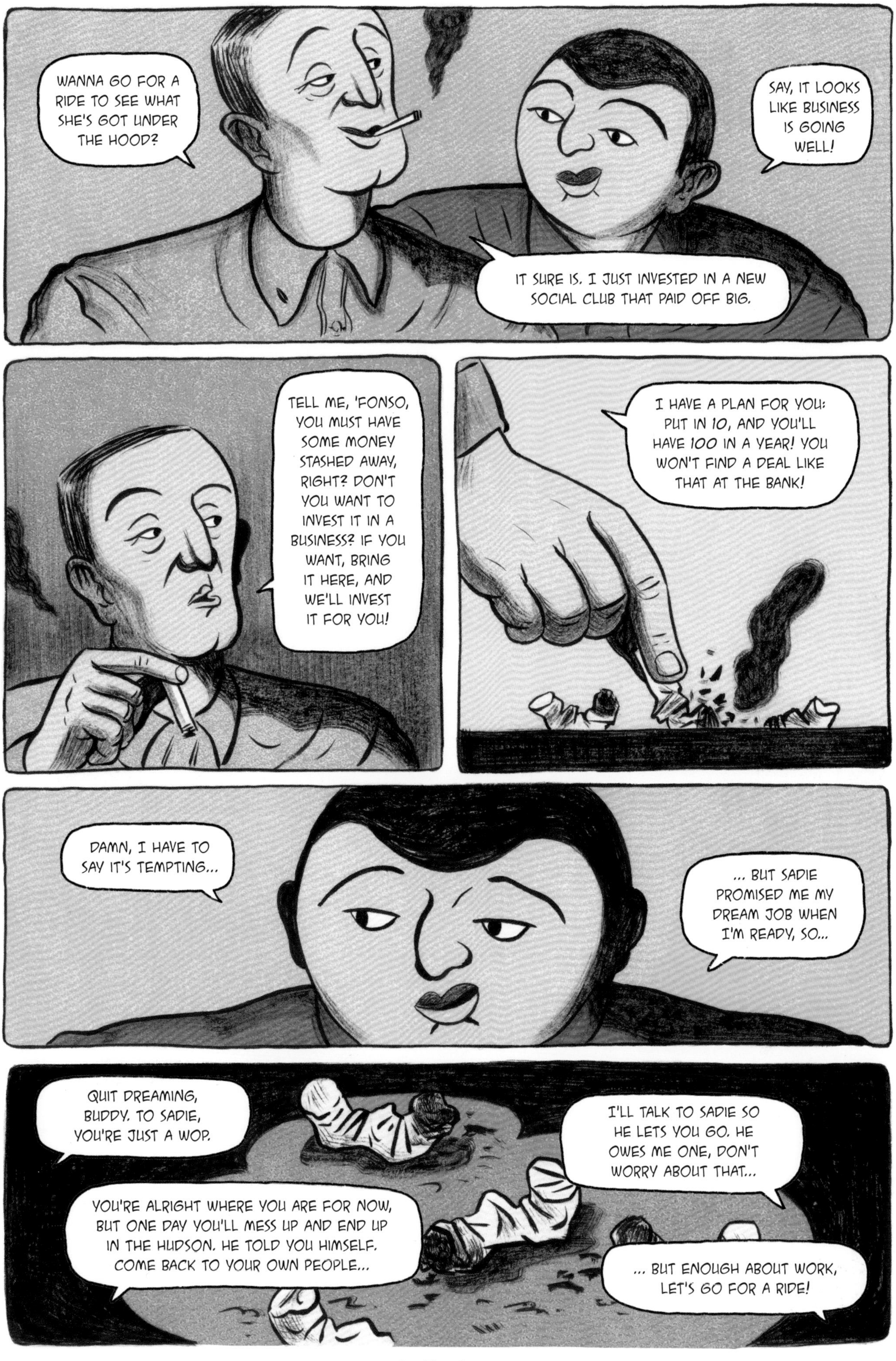
WANNA GO FOR A RIDE TO SEE WHAT SHE'S GOT UNDER THE HOOD?
SAY, IT LOOKS LIKE BUSINESS IS GOING WELL!
IT SURE IS. I JUST INVESTED IN A NEW SOCIAL CLUB THAT PAID OFF BIG.
TELL ME, 'FONSO, YOU MUST HAVE SOME MONEY STASHED AWAY, RIGHT? DON'T YOU WANT TO INVEST IT IN A BUSINESS? IF YOU WANT, BRING IT HERE, AND WE'LL INVEST IT FOR YOU!
I HAVE A PLAN FOR YOU: PUT IN 10, AND YOU'LL HAVE 100 IN A YEAR! YOU WON'T FIND A DEAL LIKE THAT AT THE BANK!
DAMN, I HAVE TO SAY IT'S TEMPTING...
... BUT SADIE PROMISED ME MY DREAM JOB WHEN I'M READY, SO...
QUIT DREAMING, BUDDY. TO SADIE, YOU'RE JUST A WOP.
I'LL TALK TO SADIE SO HE LETS YOU GO. HE OWES ME ONE, DON'T WORRY ABOUT THAT...
YOU'RE ALRIGHT WHERE YOU ARE FOR NOW, BUT ONE DAY YOU'LL MESS UP AND END UP IN THE HUDSON. HE TOLD YOU HIMSELF. COME BACK TO YOUR OWN PEOPLE...
... BUT ENOUGH ABOUT WORK, LET'S GO FOR A RIDE!

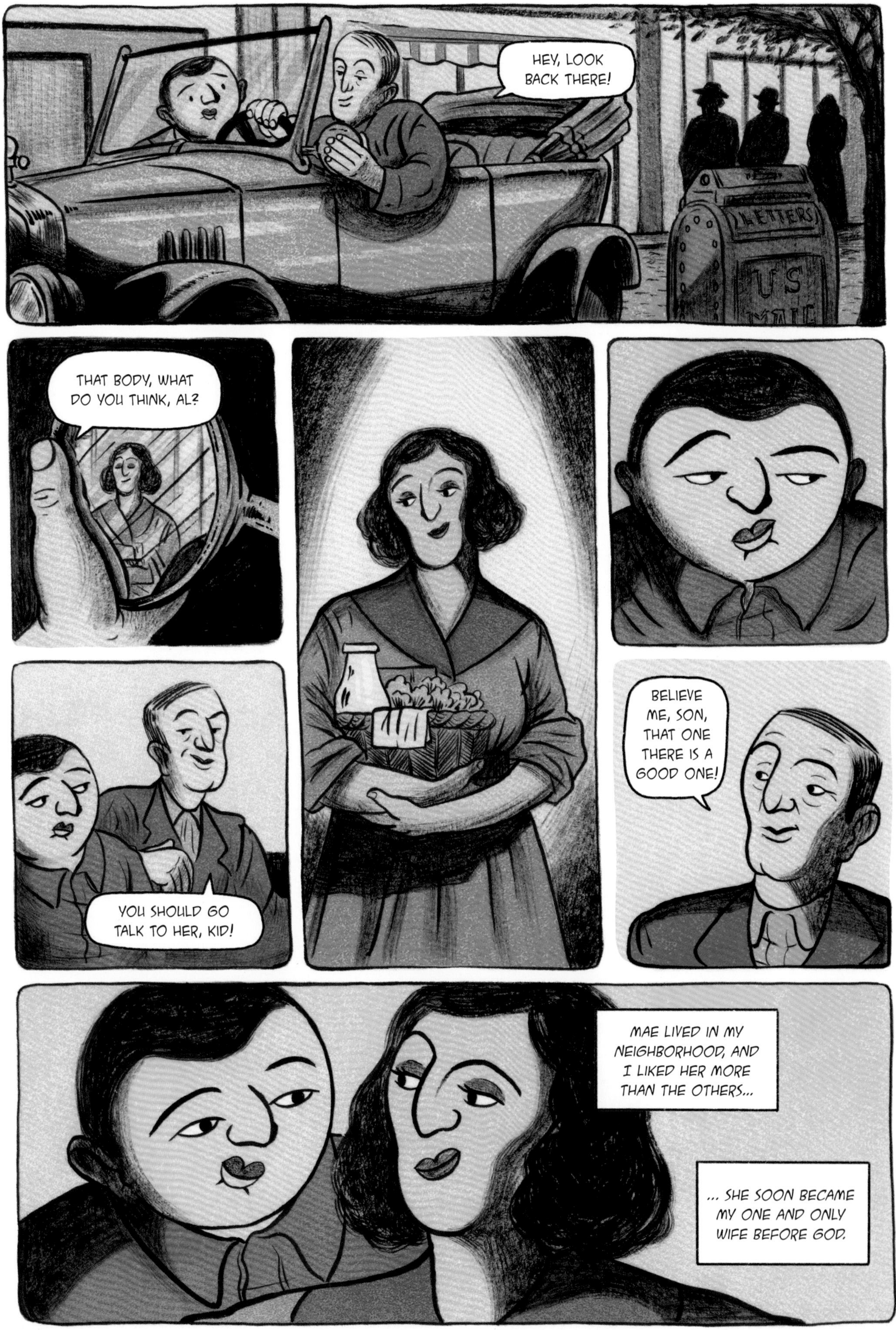
HEY, LOOK BACK THERE!
LETTERS
US
THAT BODY, WHAT DO YOU THINK, AL?
YOU SHOULD GO TALK TO HER, KID!
BELIEVE ME, SON, THAT ONE THERE IS A GOOD ONE!
MAE LIVED IN MY NEIGHBORHOOD, AND I LIKED HER MORE THAN THE OTHERS...
... SHE SOON BECAME MY ONE AND ONLY WIFE BEFORE GOD.

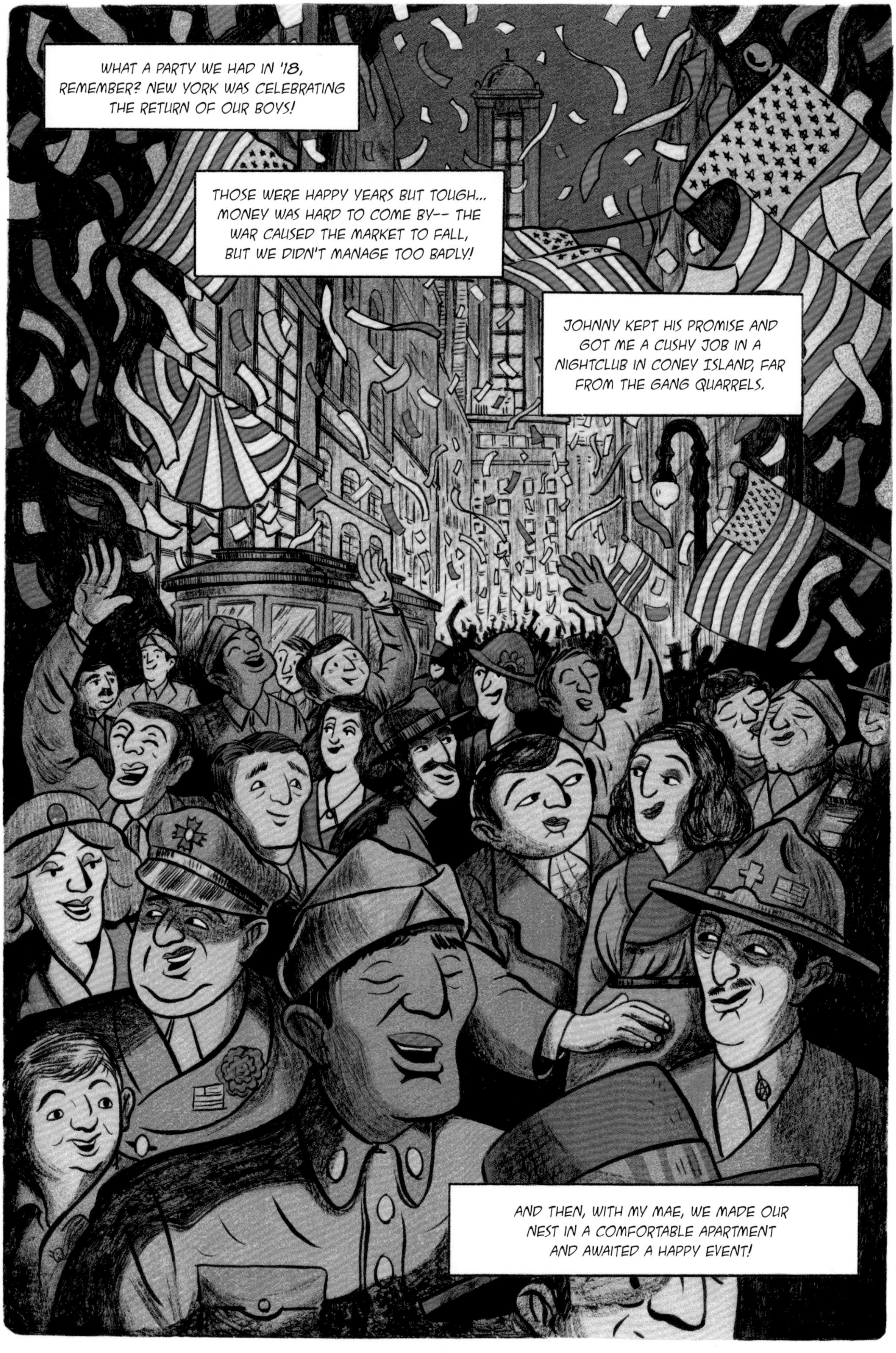
WHAT A PARTY WE HAD IN '18, REMEMBER? NEW YORK WAS CELEBRATING THE RETURN OF OUR BOYS!
THOSE WERE HAPPY YEARS BUT TOUGH... MONEY WAS HARD TO COME BY-- THE WAR CAUSED THE MARKET TO FALL, BUT WE DIDN'T MANAGE TOO BADLY!
JOHNNY KEPT HIS PROMISE AND GOT ME A CUSHY JOB IN A NIGHTCLUB IN CONEY ISLAND, FAR FROM THE GANG QUARRELS.
AND THEN, WITH MY MAE, WE MADE OUR NEST IN A COMFORTABLE APARTMENT AND AWAITED A HAPPY EVENT!

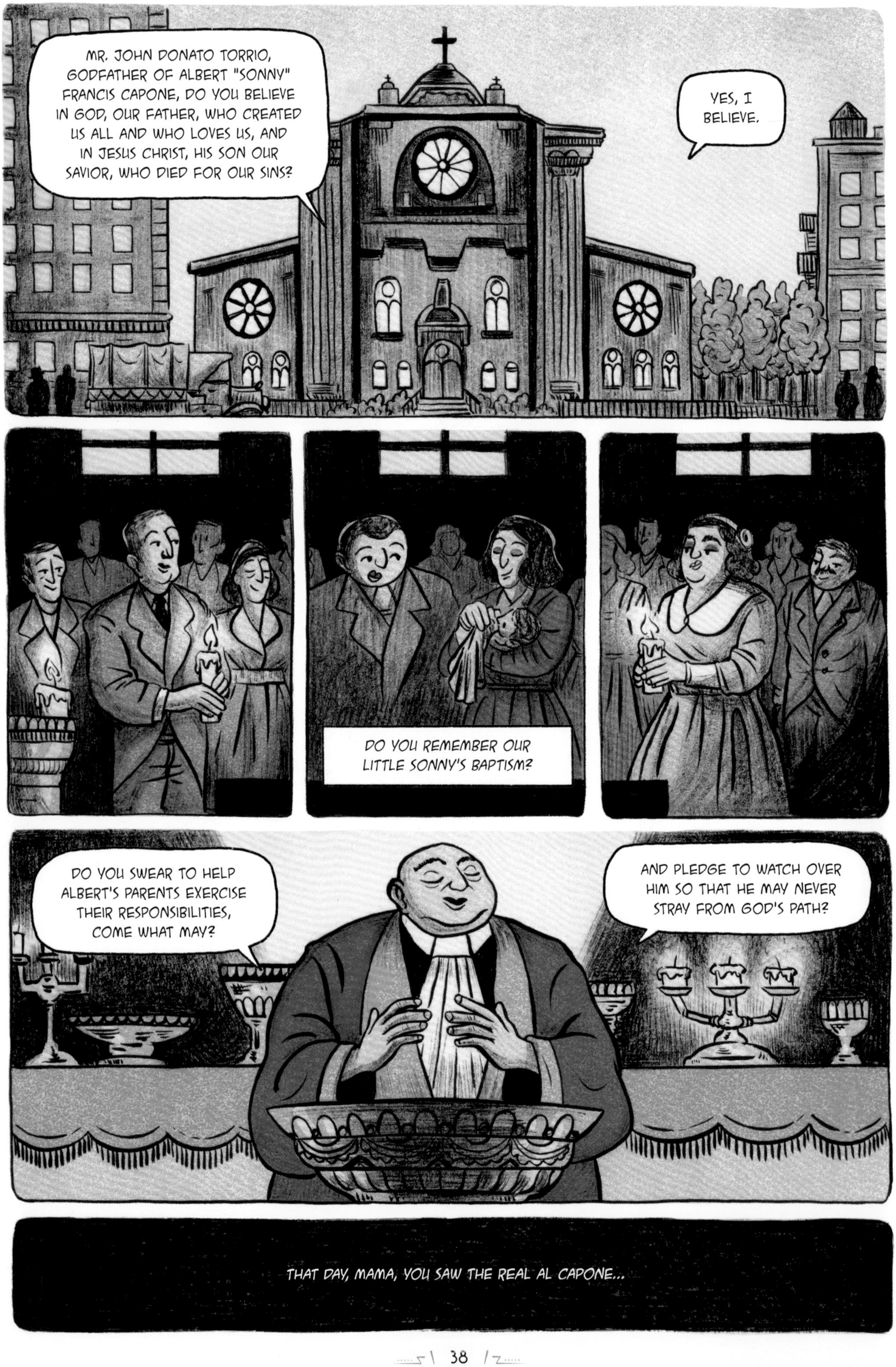
MR. JOHN DONATO TORRIO, GODFATHER OF ALBERT "SONNY" FRANCIS CAPONE, DO YOU BELIEVE IN GOD, OUR FATHER, WHO CREATED US ALL AND WHO LOVES US, AND IN JESUS CHRIST, HIS SON OUR SAVIOR, WHO DIED FOR OUR SINS?
YES, I BELIEVE.
DO YOU REMEMBER OUR LITTLE SONNY'S BAPTISM?
DO YOU SWEAR TO HELP ALBERT'S PARENTS EXERCISE THEIR RESPONSIBILITIES, COME WHAT MAY?
AND PLEDGE TO WATCH OVER HIM SO THAT HE MAY NEVER STRAY FROM GOD'S PATH?
THAT DAY, MAMA, YOU SAW THE REAL AL CAPONE...

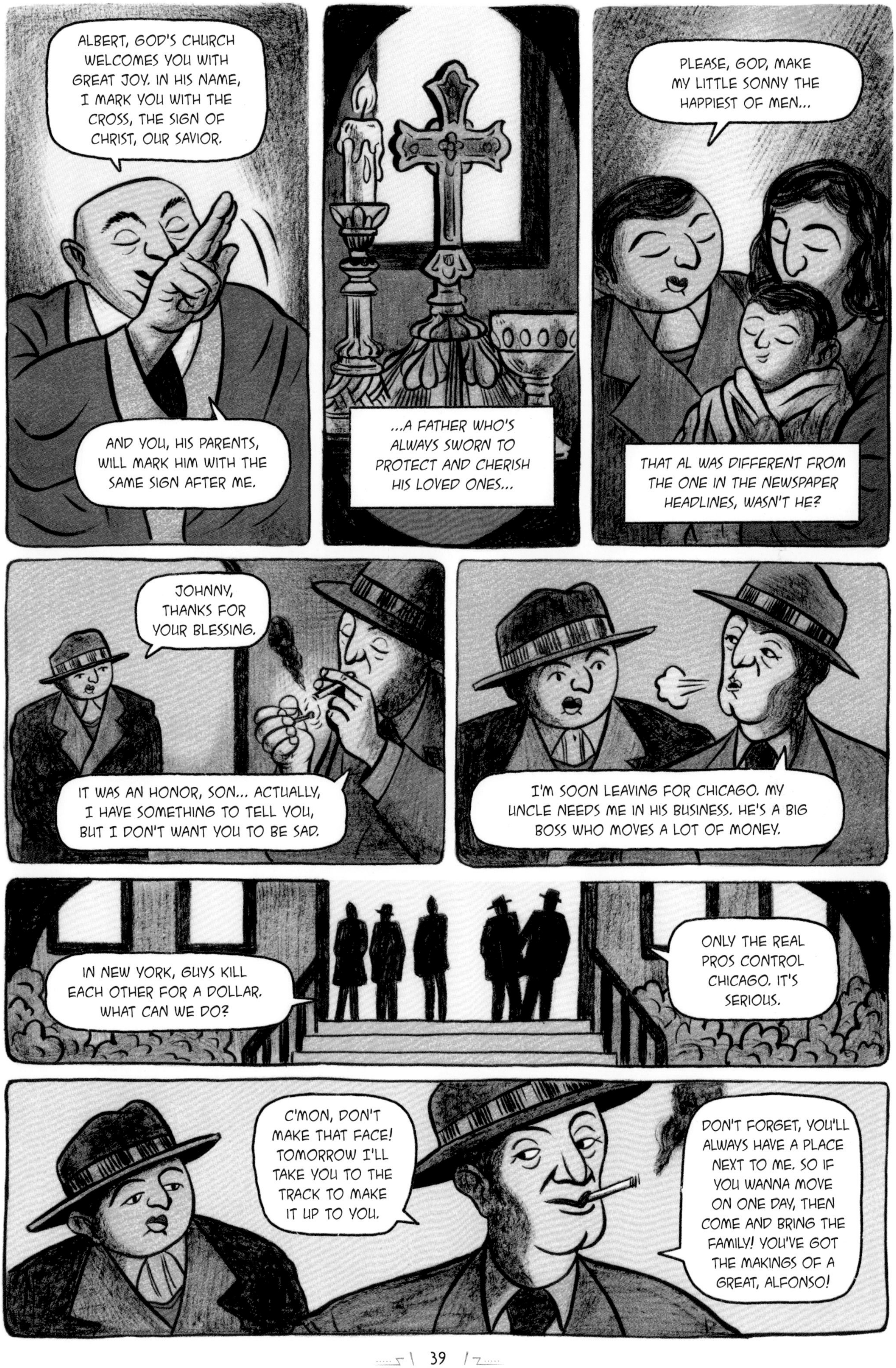
ALBERT, GOD'S CHURCH WELCOMES YOU WITH GREAT JOY. IN HIS NAME, I MARK YOU WITH THE CROSS, THE SIGN OF CHRIST, OUR SAVIOR.
AND YOU, HIS PARENTS, WILL MARK HIM WITH THE SAME SIGN AFTER ME.
...A FATHER WHO'S ALWAYS SWORN TO PROTECT AND CHERISH HIS LOVED ONES...
PLEASE, GOD, MAKE MY LITTLE SONNY THE HAPPIEST OF MEN...
THAT AL WAS DIFFERENT FROM THE ONE IN THE NEWSPAPER HEADLINES, WASN'T HE?
JOHNNY, THANKS FOR YOUR BLESSING.
IT WAS AN HONOR, SON... ACTUALLY, I HAVE SOMETHING TO TELL YOU, BUT I DON'T WANT YOU TO BE SAD.
I'M SOON LEAVING FOR CHICAGO. MY UNCLE NEEDS ME IN HIS BUSINESS. HE'S A BIG BOSS WHO MOVES A LOT OF MONEY.
IN NEW YORK, GUYS KILL EACH OTHER FOR A DOLLAR. WHAT CAN WE DO?
ONLY THE REAL PROS CONTROL CHICAGO. IT'S SERIOUS.
C'MON, DON'T MAKE THAT FACE! TOMORROW I'LL TAKE YOU TO THE TRACK TO MAKE IT UP TO YOU.
DON'T FORGET, YOU'LL ALWAYS HAVE A PLACE NEXT TO ME. SO IF YOU WANNA MOVE ON ONE DAY, THEN COME AND BRING THE FAMILY! YOU'VE GOT THE MAKINGS OF A GREAT, ALFONSO!

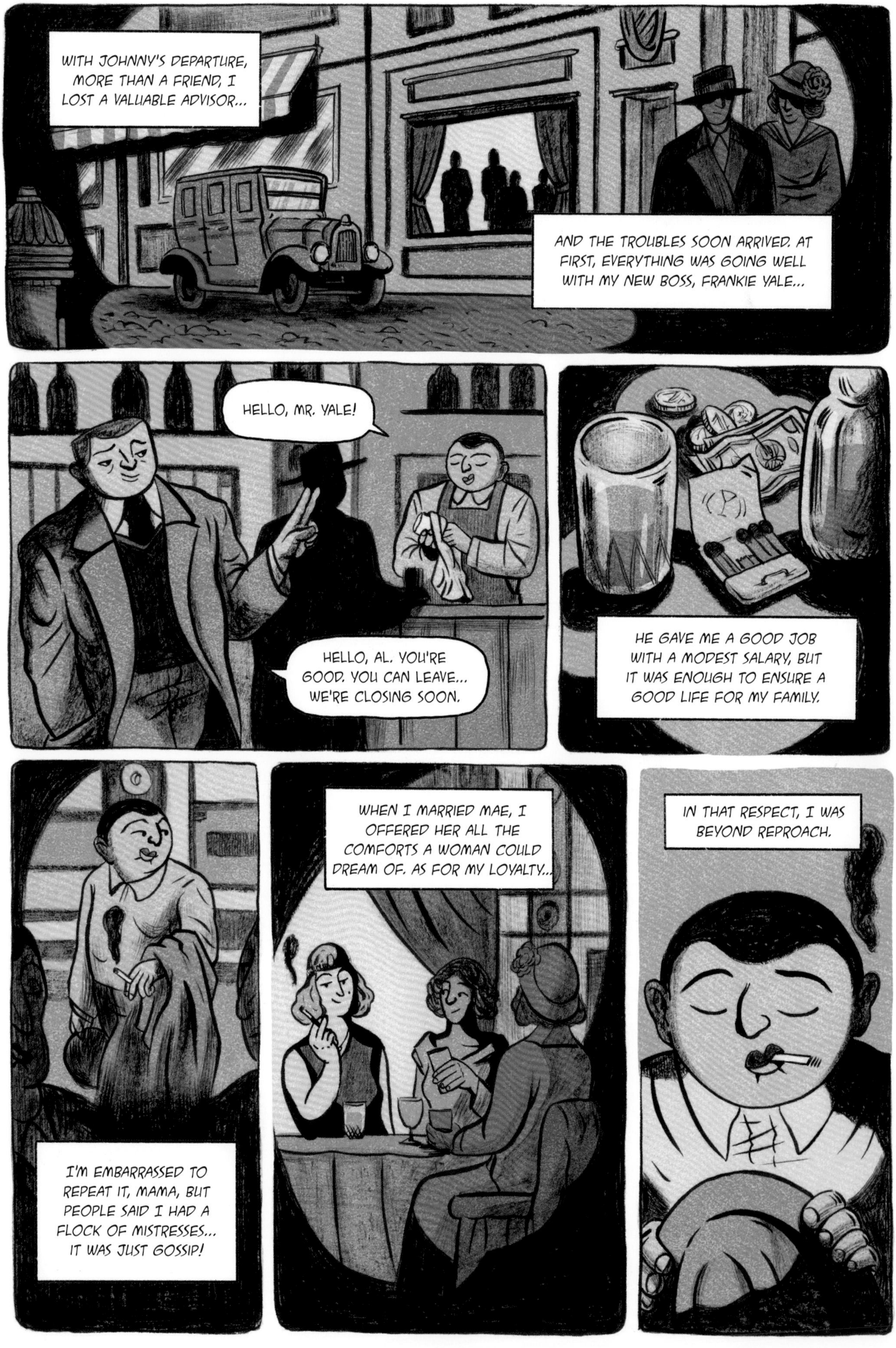
WITH JOHNNY'S DEPARTURE, MORE THAN A FRIEND, I LOST A VALUABLE ADVISOR...
AND THE TROUBLES SOON ARRIVED. AT FIRST, EVERYTHING WAS GOING WELL WITH MY NEW BOSS, FRANKIE YALE...
HELLO, MR. YALE!
HELLO, AL. YOU'RE GOOD. YOU CAN LEAVE... WE'RE CLOSING SOON.
HE GAVE ME A GOOD JOB WITH A MODEST SALARY, BUT IT WAS ENOUGH TO ENSURE A GOOD LIFE FOR MY FAMILY.
I'M EMBARRASSED TO REPEAT IT, MAMA, BUT PEOPLE SAID I HAD A FLOCK OF MISTRESSES... IT WAS JUST GOSSIP!
WHEN I MARRIED MAE, I OFFERED HER ALL THE COMFORTS A WOMAN COULD DREAM OF. AS FOR MY LOYALTY...
IN THAT RESPECT, I WAS BEYOND REPROACH.

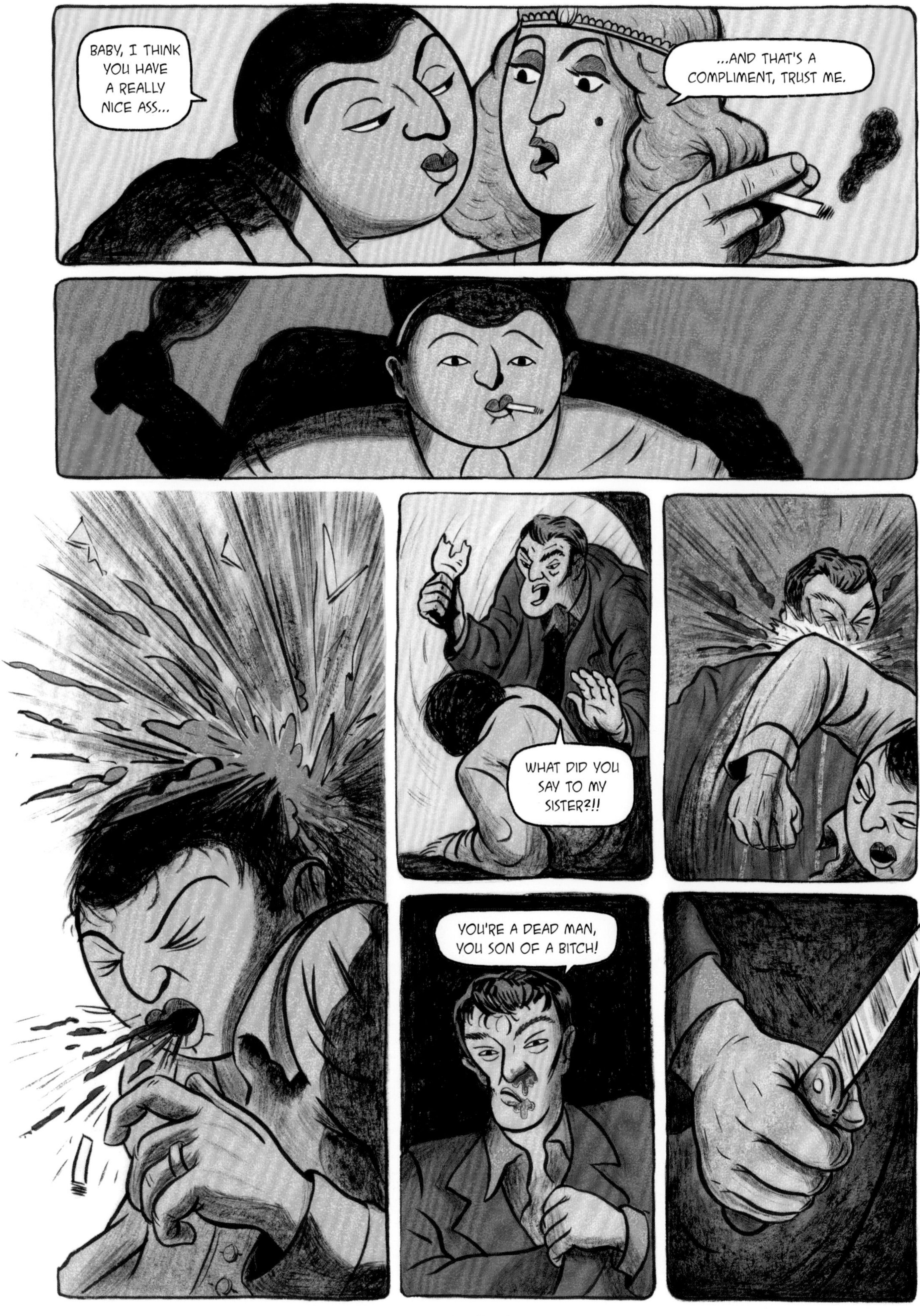
BABY, I THINK YOU HAVE A REALLY NICE ASS...
...AND THAT'S A COMPLIMENT, TRUST ME.
WHAT DID YOU SAY TO MY SISTER?!!
YOU'RE A DEAD MAN, YOU SON OF A BITCH!

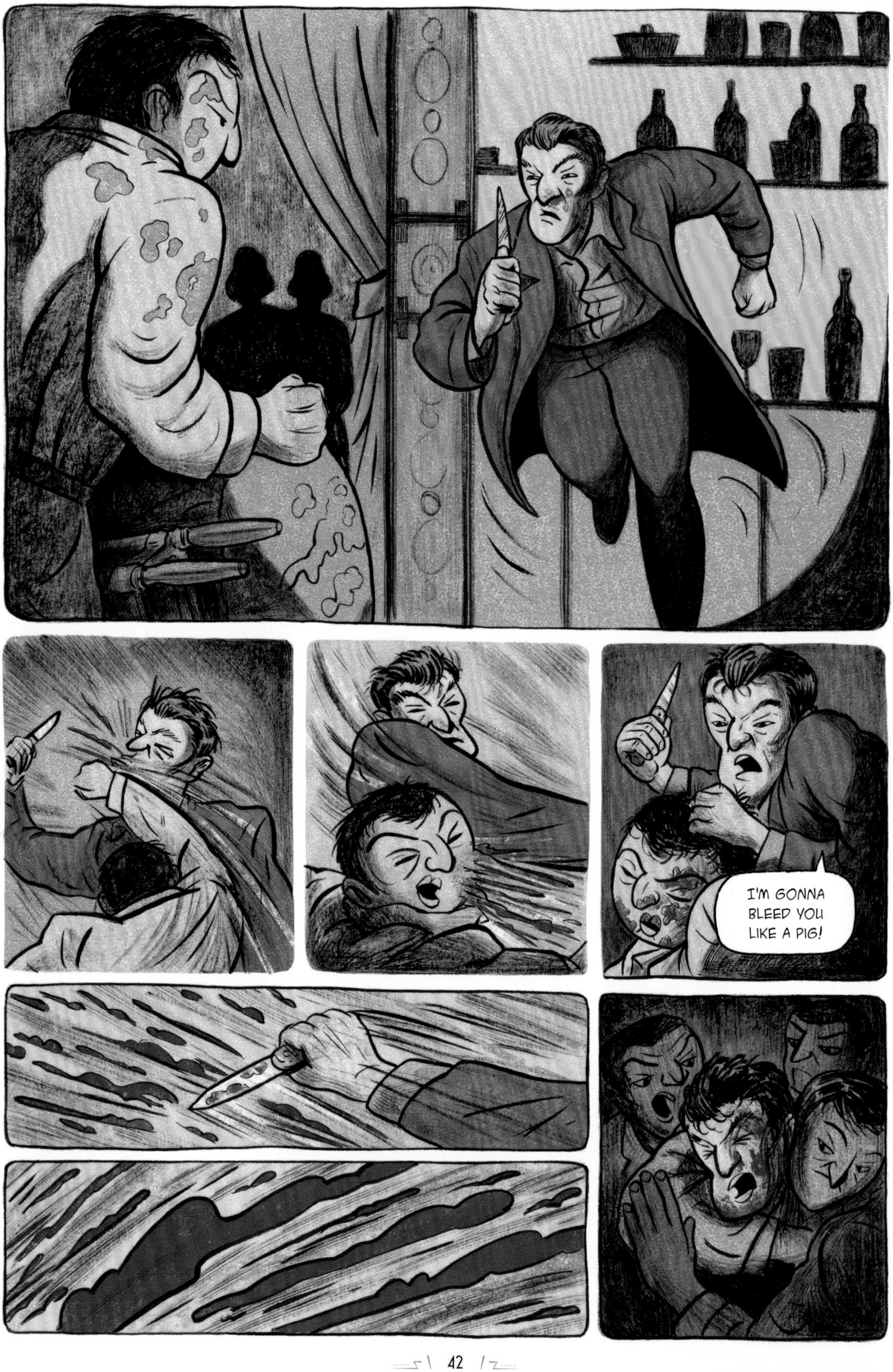
I'M GONNA BLEED YOU LIKE A PIG!

I HELD MY OWN, BUT WORKING IN A CLUB WAS STILL DANGEROUS... I WAS CONSTANTLY SURROUNDED BY CROOKS...

...ALL READY TO POUNCE ON ME AND SLASH MY FACE AT THE SLIGHTEST GLANCE...

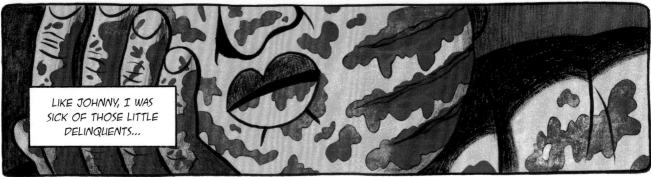

LIKE JOHNNY, I WAS SICK OF THOSE LITTLE DELINQUENTS...

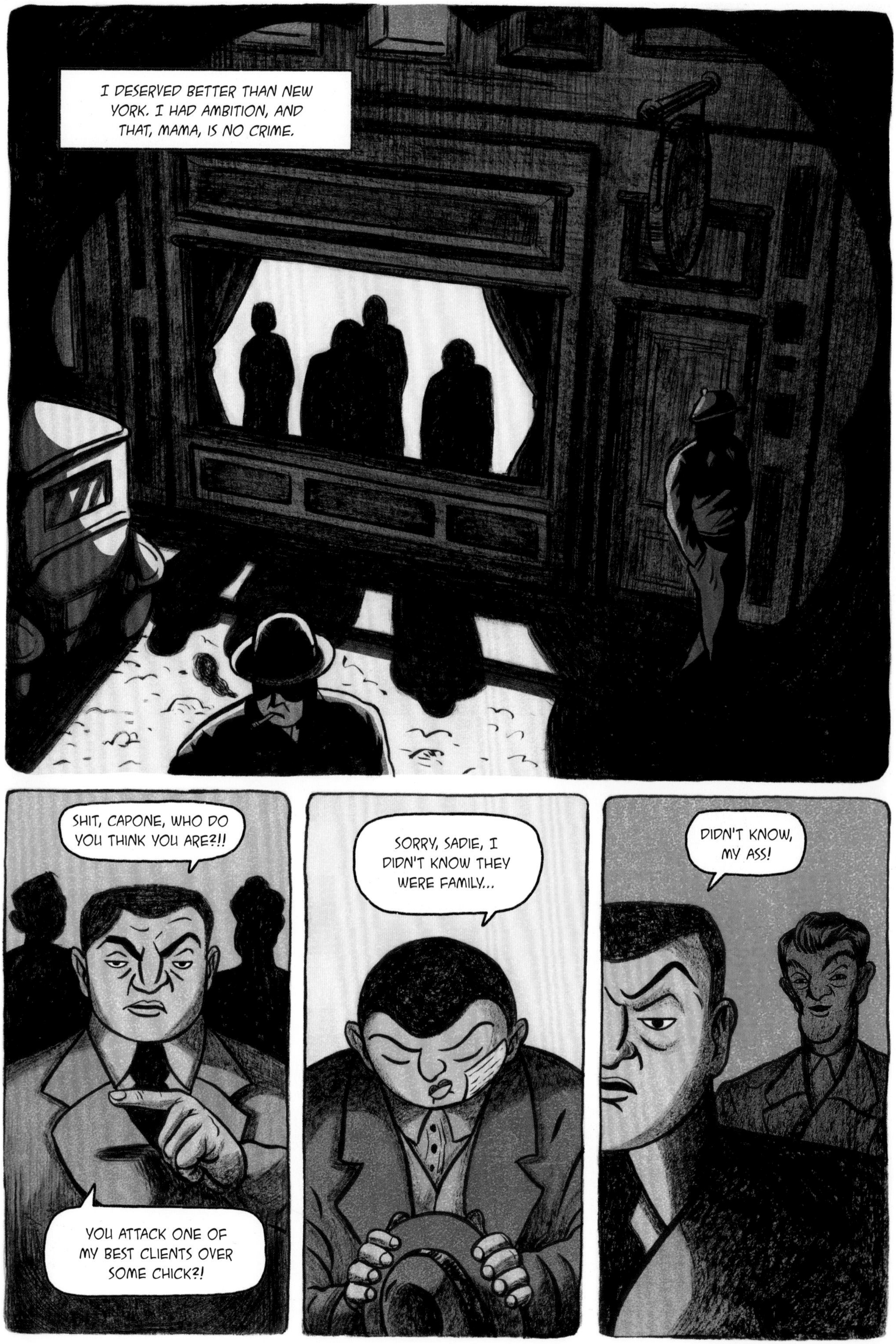
I DESERVED BETTER THAN NEW YORK. I HAD AMBITION, AND THAT, MAMA, IS NO CRIME.
SHIT, CAPONE, WHO DO YOU THINK YOU ARE?!!
YOU ATTACK ONE OF MY BEST CLIENTS OVER SOME CHICK?!
SORRY, SADIE, I DIDN'T KNOW THEY WERE FAMILY...
DIDN'T KNOW, MY ASS!

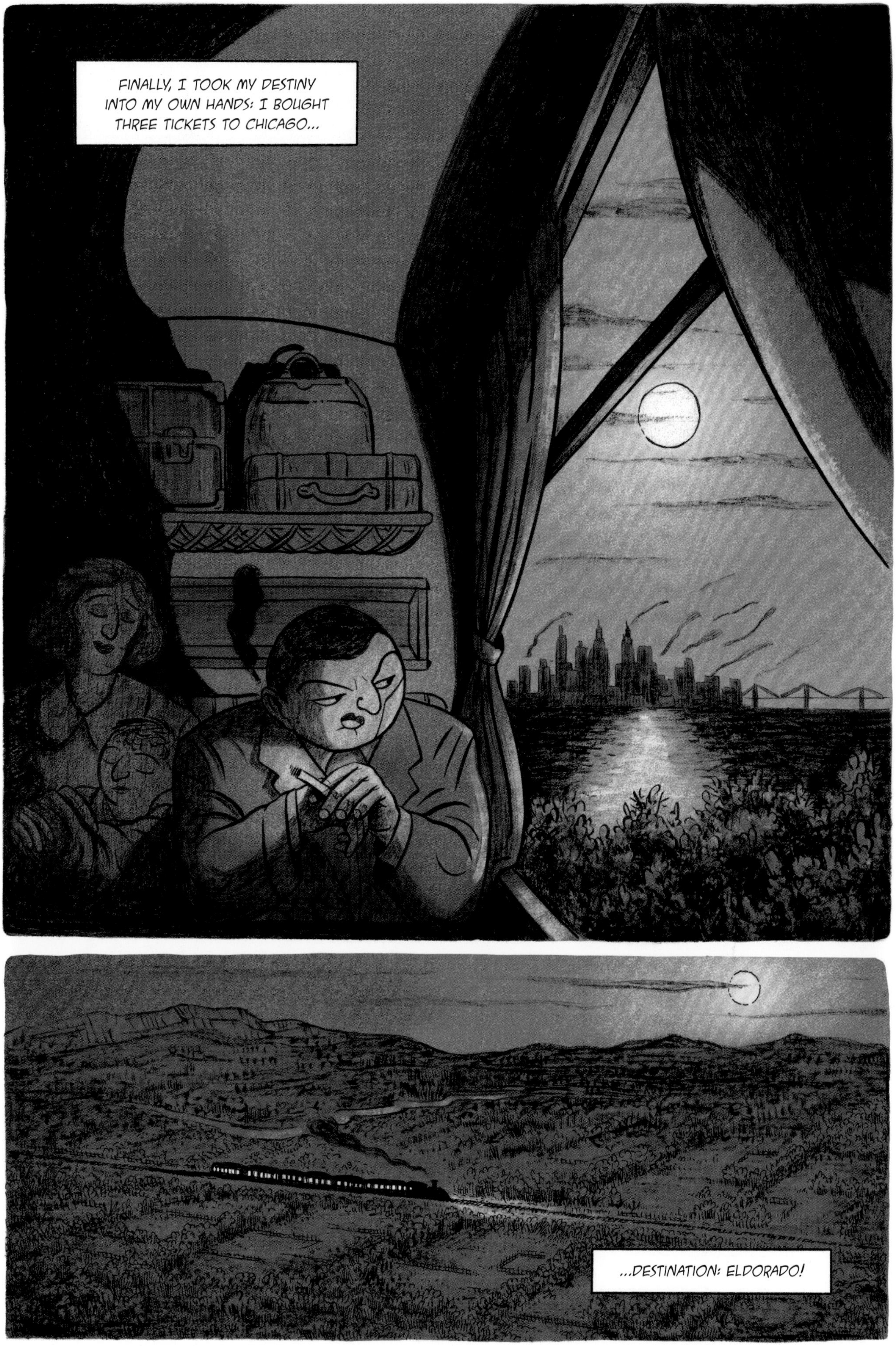
FINALLY, I TOOK MY DESTINY INTO MY OWN HANDS: I BOUGHT THREE TICKETS TO CHICAGO...
...DESTINATION: ELDORADO!

CHAPTER 2

Scarface

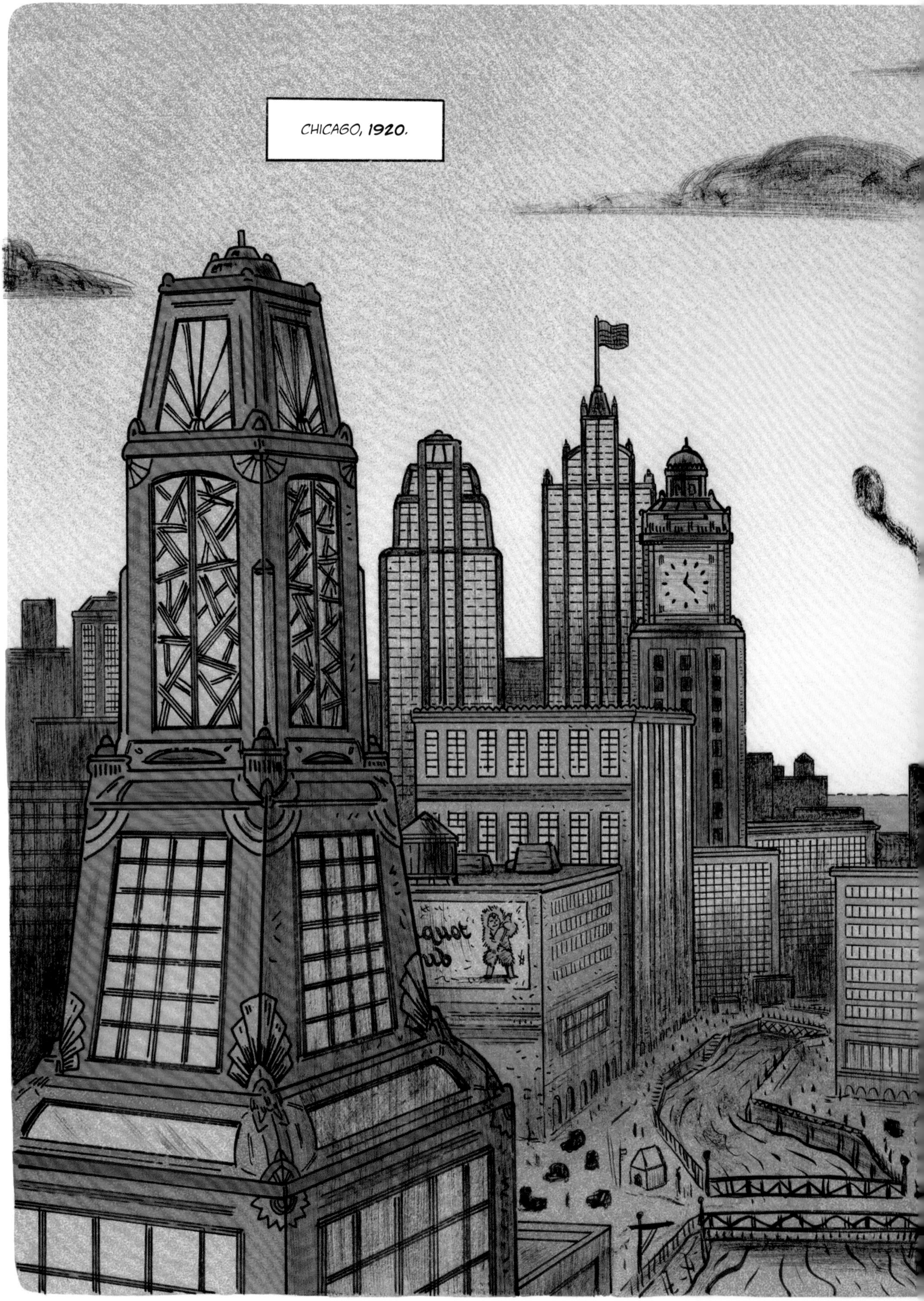
CHICAGO, 1920.

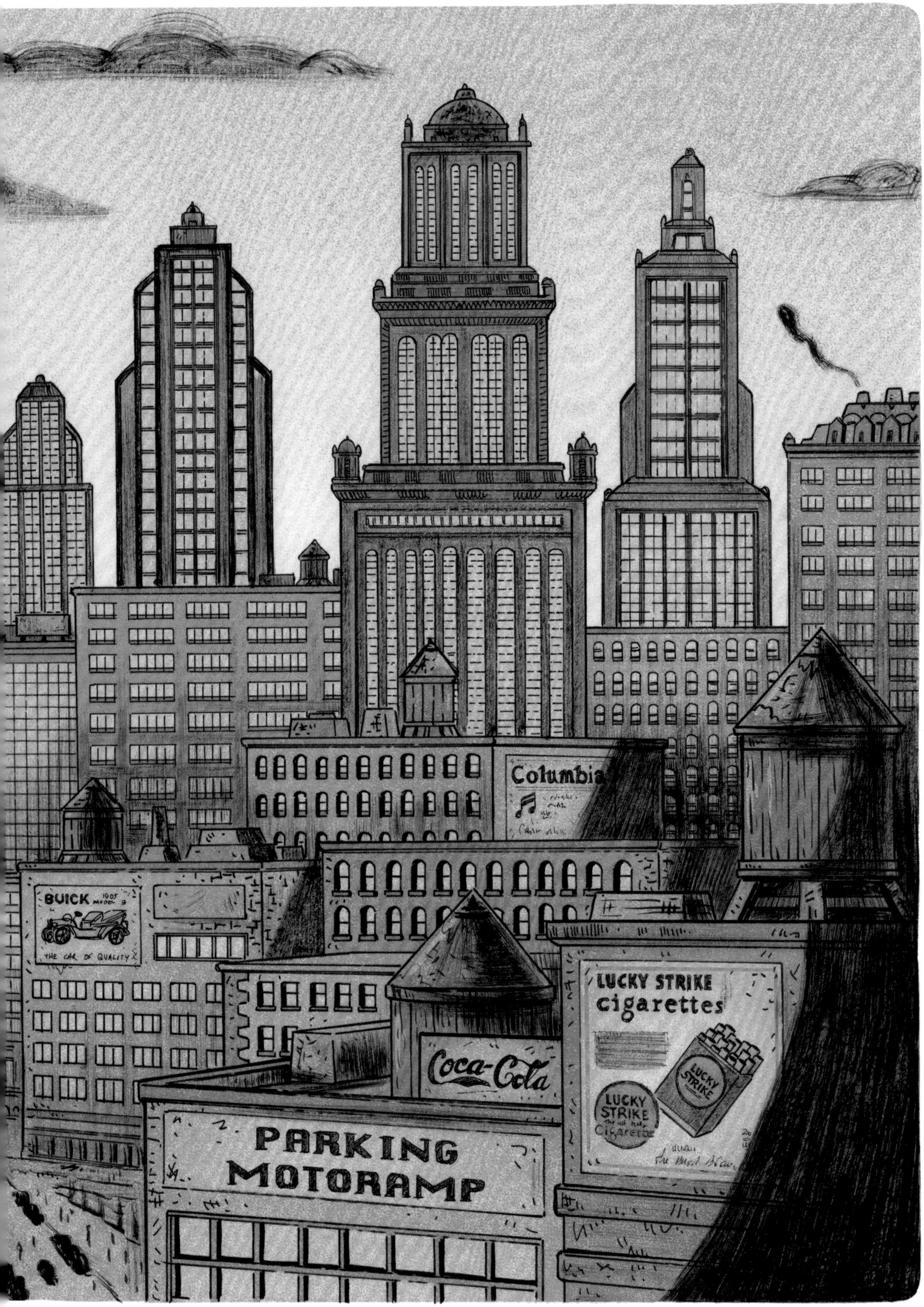
Columbia
BUICK
THE CAR OF QUALITY
LUCKY STRIKE
cigarettes
LUCKY STRIKE
LUCKY STRIKE
Cigarettes
Coca-Cola
PARKING
MOTORAMP

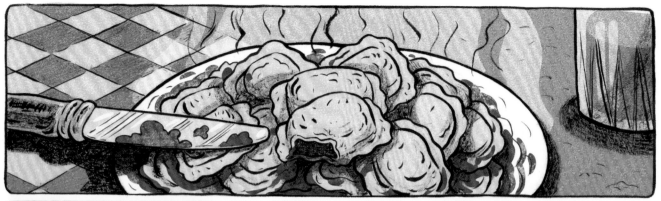

LET'S GET RIGHT TO IT, JOHNNY. WHO HAVE YOU BROUGHT ME HERE?

A FRIEND FROM NEW YORK, TONTON JIM.

HE'S LOOKING FOR WORK. HE'S A TRUE NEAPOLITAN, TRUSTWORTHY.

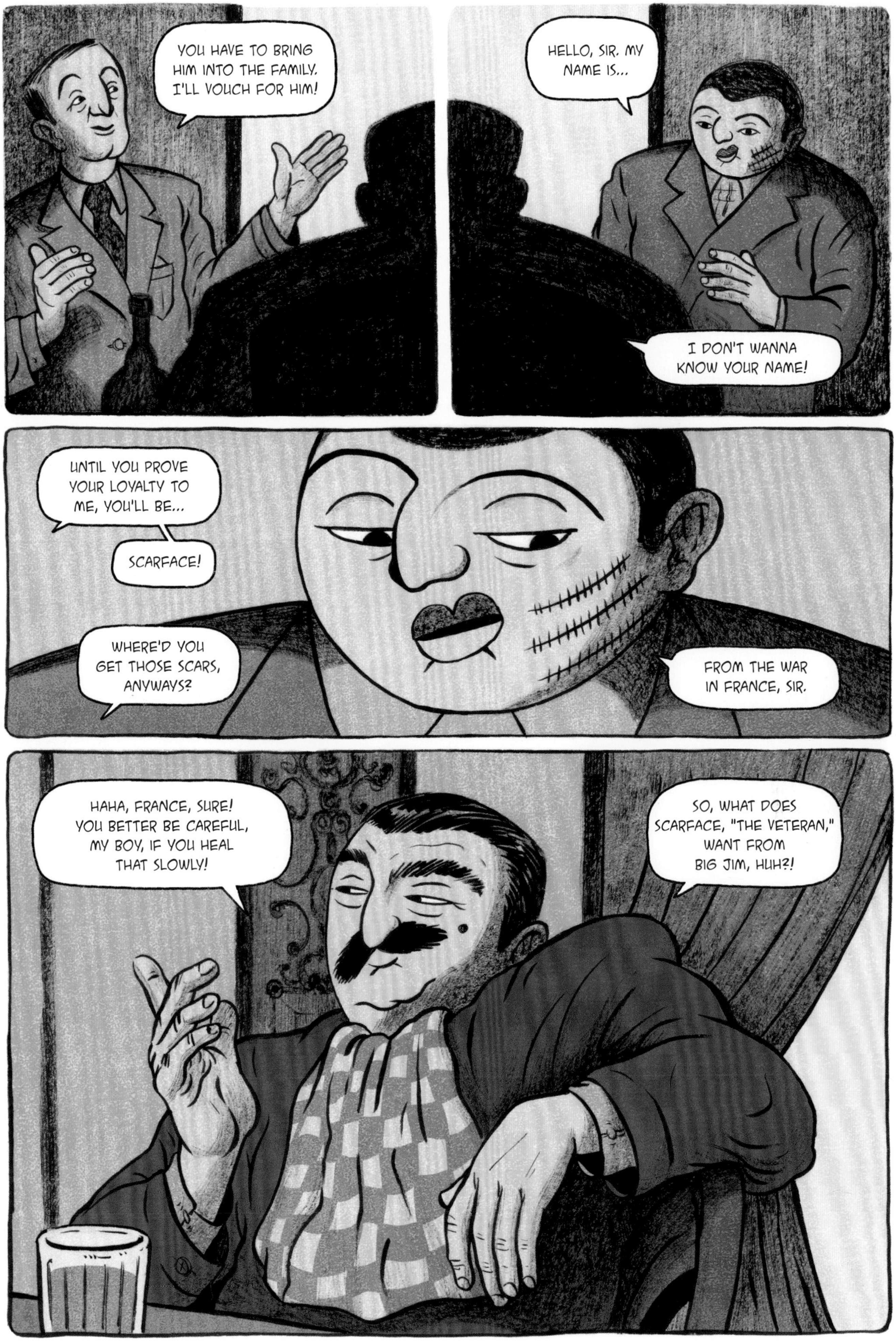
YOU HAVE TO BRING HIM INTO THE FAMILY. I'LL VOUCH FOR HIM!
HELLO, SIR. MY NAME IS...
I DON'T WANNA KNOW YOUR NAME!
UNTIL YOU PROVE YOUR LOYALTY TO ME, YOU'LL BE...
SCARFACE!
WHERE'D YOU GET THOSE SCARS, ANYWAYS?
FROM THE WAR IN FRANCE, SIR.
HAHA, FRANCE, SURE! YOU BETTER BE CAREFUL, MY BOY, IF YOU HEAL THAT SLOWLY!
SO, WHAT DOES SCARFACE, "THE VETERAN," WANT FROM BIG JIM, HUH?!

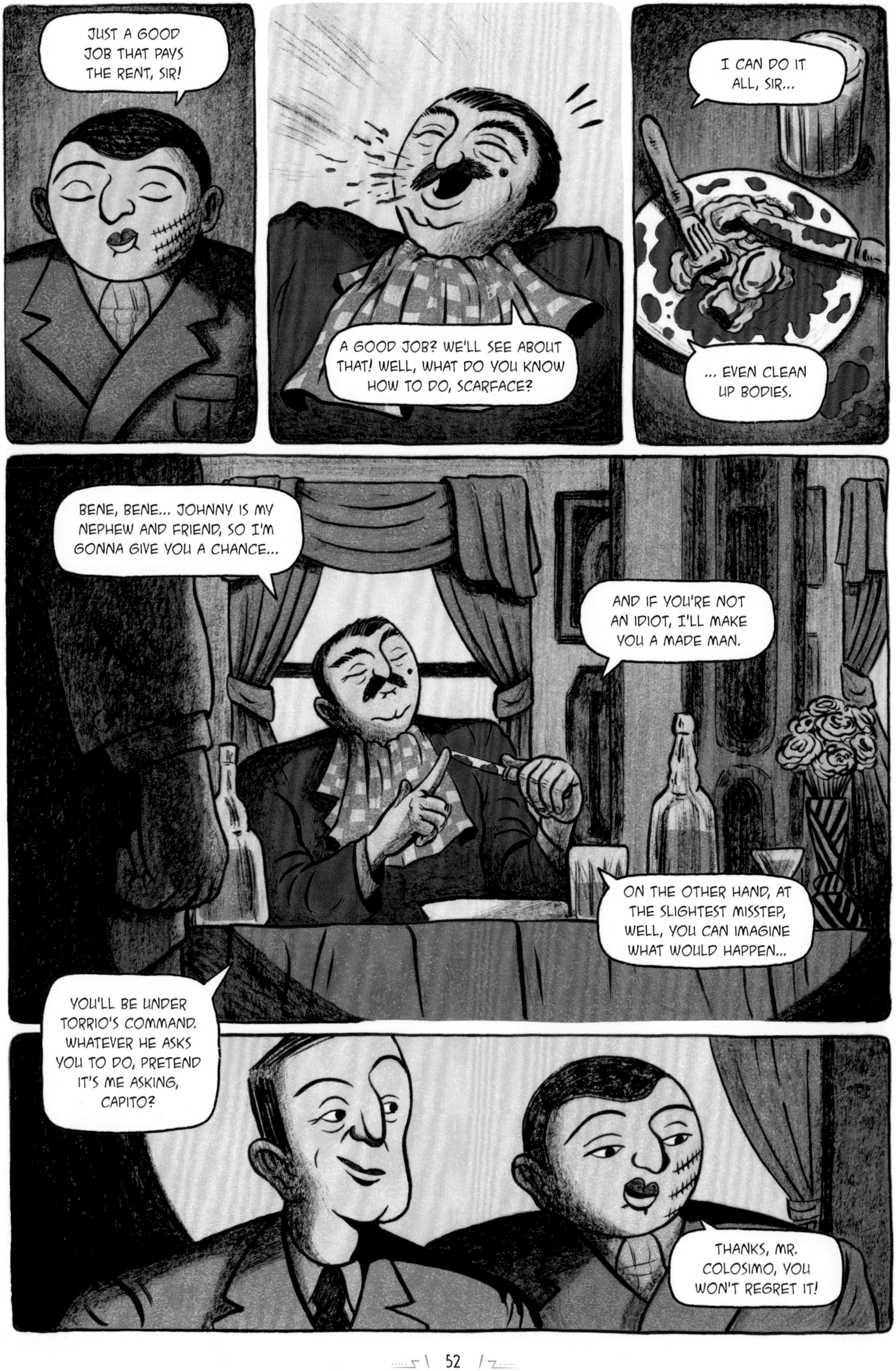
JUST A GOOD JOB THAT PAYS THE RENT, SIR!
A GOOD JOB? WE'LL SEE ABOUT THAT! WELL, WHAT DO YOU KNOW HOW TO DO, SCARFACE?
I CAN DO IT ALL, SIR...
... EVEN CLEAN UP BODIES.
BENE, BENE... JOHNNY IS MY NEPHEW AND FRIEND, SO I'M GONNA GIVE YOU A CHANCE...
AND IF YOU'RE NOT AN IDIOT, I'LL MAKE YOU A MADE MAN.
ON THE OTHER HAND, AT THE SLIGHTEST MISSTEP, WELL, YOU CAN IMAGINE WHAT WOULD HAPPEN...
YOU'LL BE UNDER TORRIO'S COMMAND. WHATEVER HE ASKS YOU TO DO, PRETEND IT'S ME ASKING, CAPITO?
THANKS, MR. COLOSIMO, YOU WON'T REGRET IT!

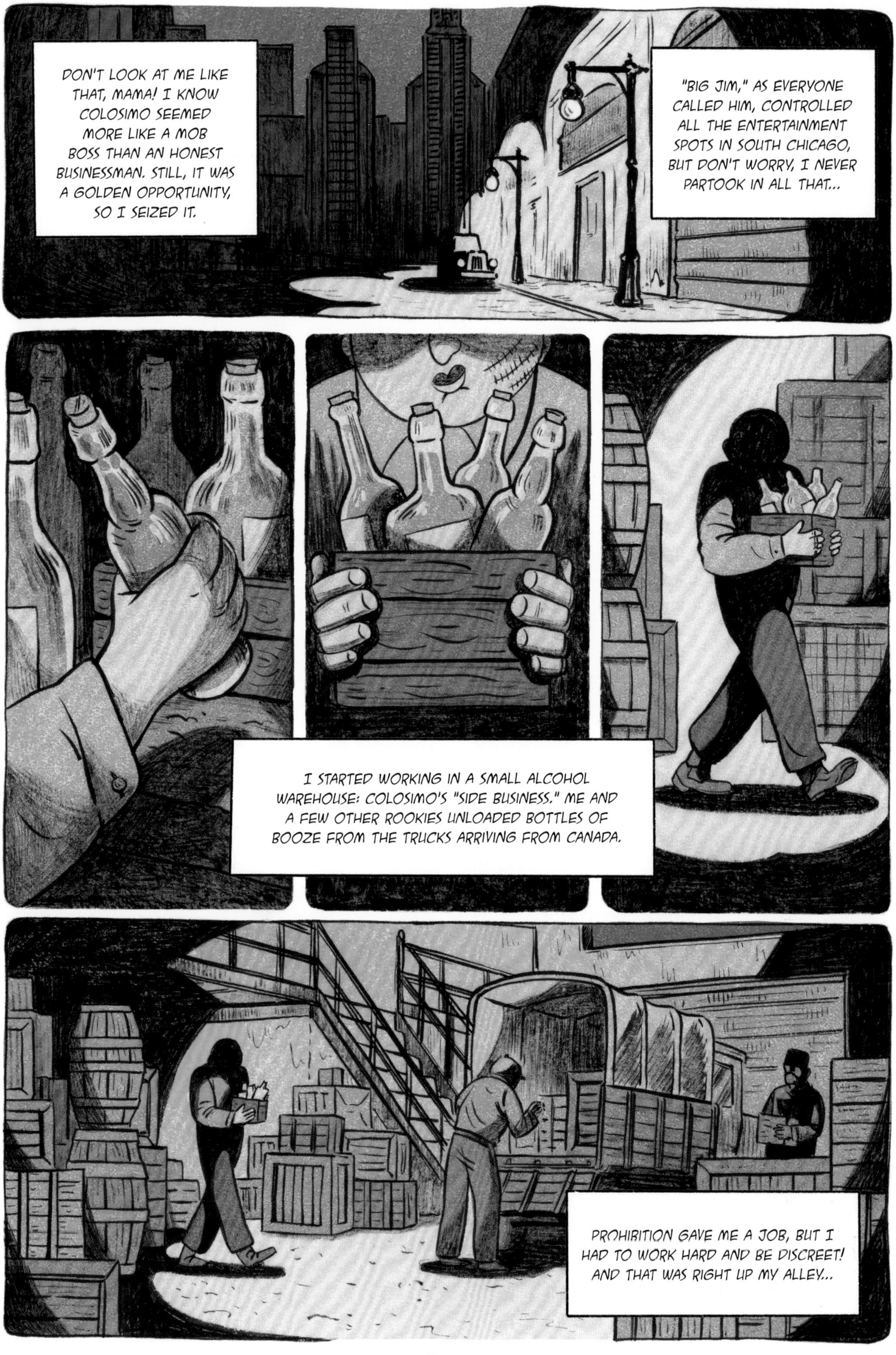
DON'T LOOK AT ME LIKE THAT, MAMA! I KNOW COLOSIMO SEEMED MORE LIKE A MOB BOSS THAN AN HONEST BUSINESSMAN. STILL, IT WAS A GOLDEN OPPORTUNITY, SO I SEIZED IT.
"BIG JIM," AS EVERYONE CALLED HIM, CONTROLLED ALL THE ENTERTAINMENT SPOTS IN SOUTH CHICAGO, BUT DON'T WORRY, I NEVER PARTOOK IN ALL THAT...
I STARTED WORKING IN A SMALL ALCOHOL WAREHOUSE: COLOSIMO'S "SIDE BUSINESS." ME AND A FEW OTHER ROOKIES UNLOADED BOTTLES OF BOOZE FROM THE TRUCKS ARRIVING FROM CANADA.
PROHIBITION GAVE ME A JOB, BUT I HAD TO WORK HARD AND BE DISCREET! AND THAT WAS RIGHT UP MY ALLEY...

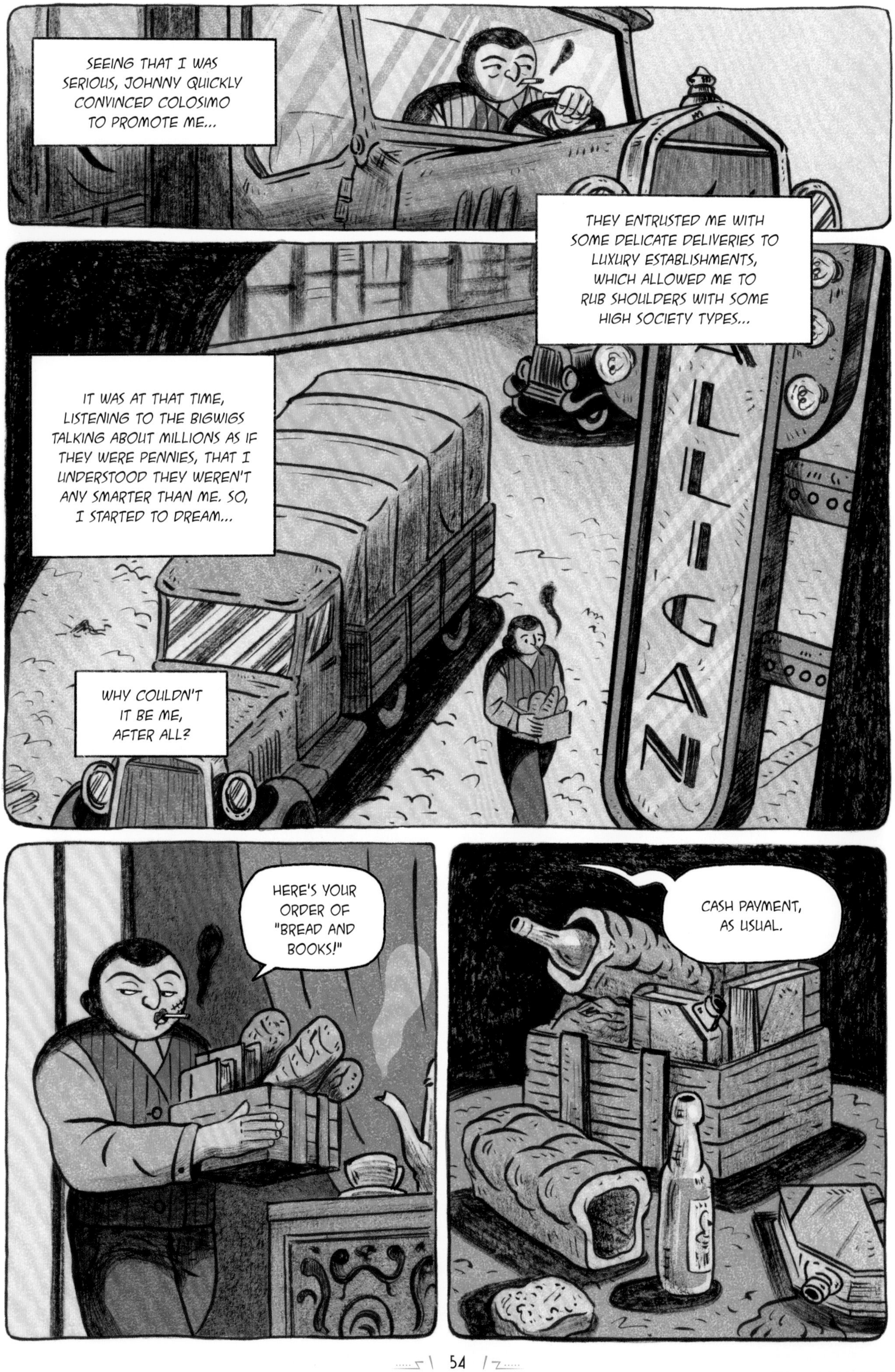
SEEING THAT I WAS SERIOUS, JOHNNY QUICKLY CONVINCED COLOSIMO TO PROMOTE ME...
THEY ENTRUSTED ME WITH SOME DELICATE DELIVERIES TO LUXURY ESTABLISHMENTS, WHICH ALLOWED ME TO RUB SHOULDERS WITH SOME HIGH SOCIETY TYPES...
IT WAS AT THAT TIME, LISTENING TO THE BIGWIGS TALKING ABOUT MILLIONS AS IF THEY WERE PENNIES, THAT I UNDERSTOOD THEY WEREN'T ANY SMARTER THAN ME. SO, I STARTED TO DREAM...
WHY COULDN'T IT BE ME, AFTER ALL?
HERE'S YOUR ORDER OF "BREAD AND BOOKS!"
CASH PAYMENT, AS USUAL.

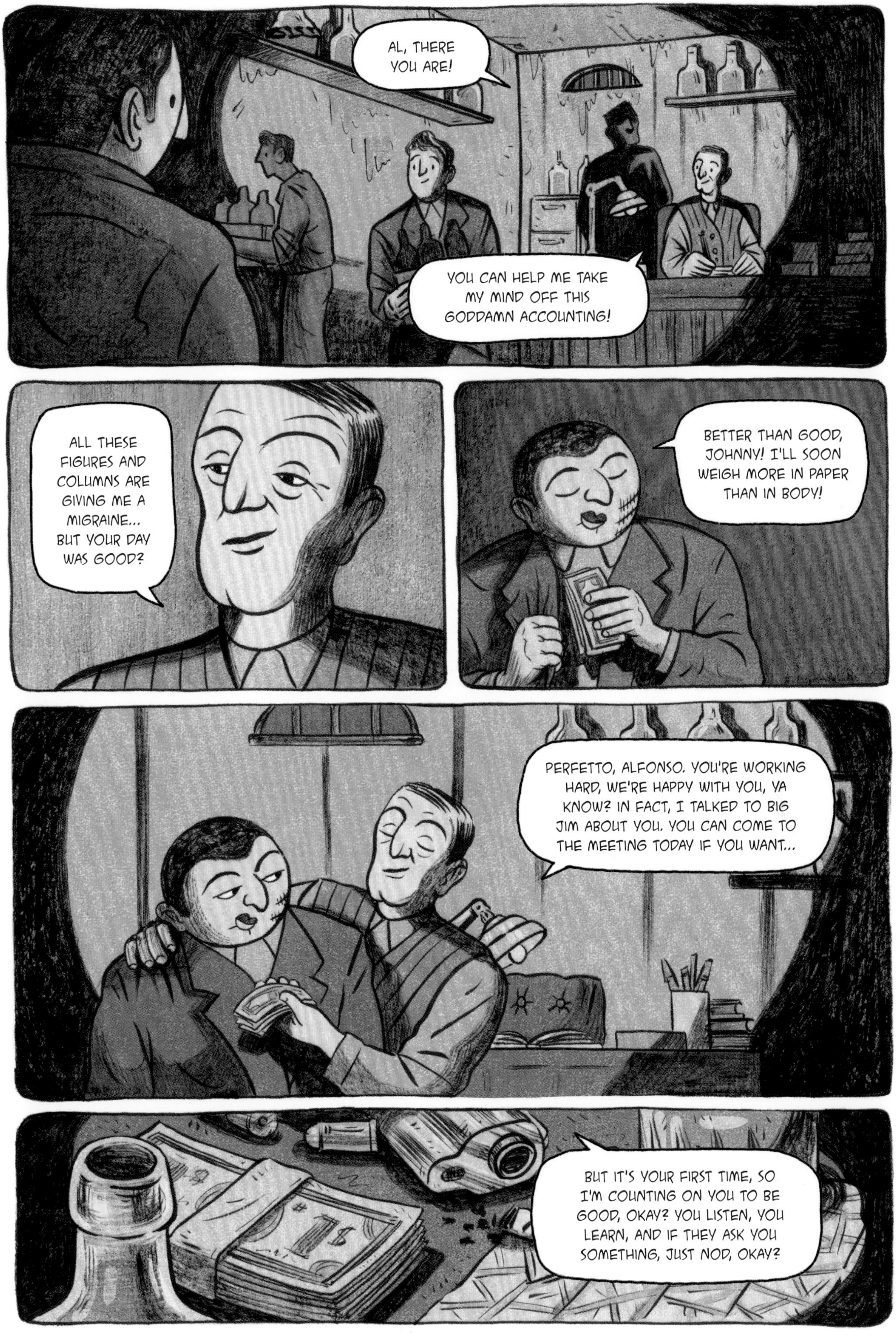
AL, THERE YOU ARE!
YOU CAN HELP ME TAKE MY MIND OFF THIS GODDAMN ACCOUNTING!
ALL THESE FIGURES AND COLUMNS ARE GIVING ME A MIGRAINE... BUT YOUR DAY WAS GOOD?
BETTER THAN GOOD, JOHNNY! I'LL SOON WEIGH MORE IN PAPER THAN IN BODY!
PERFETTO, ALFONSO. YOU'RE WORKING HARD, WE'RE HAPPY WITH YOU, YA KNOW? IN FACT, I TALKED TO BIG JIM ABOUT YOU. YOU CAN COME TO THE MEETING TODAY IF YOU WANT...
BUT IT'S YOUR FIRST TIME, SO I'M COUNTING ON YOU TO BE GOOD, OKAY? YOU LISTEN, YOU LEARN, AND IF THEY ASK YOU SOMETHING, JUST NOD, OKAY?

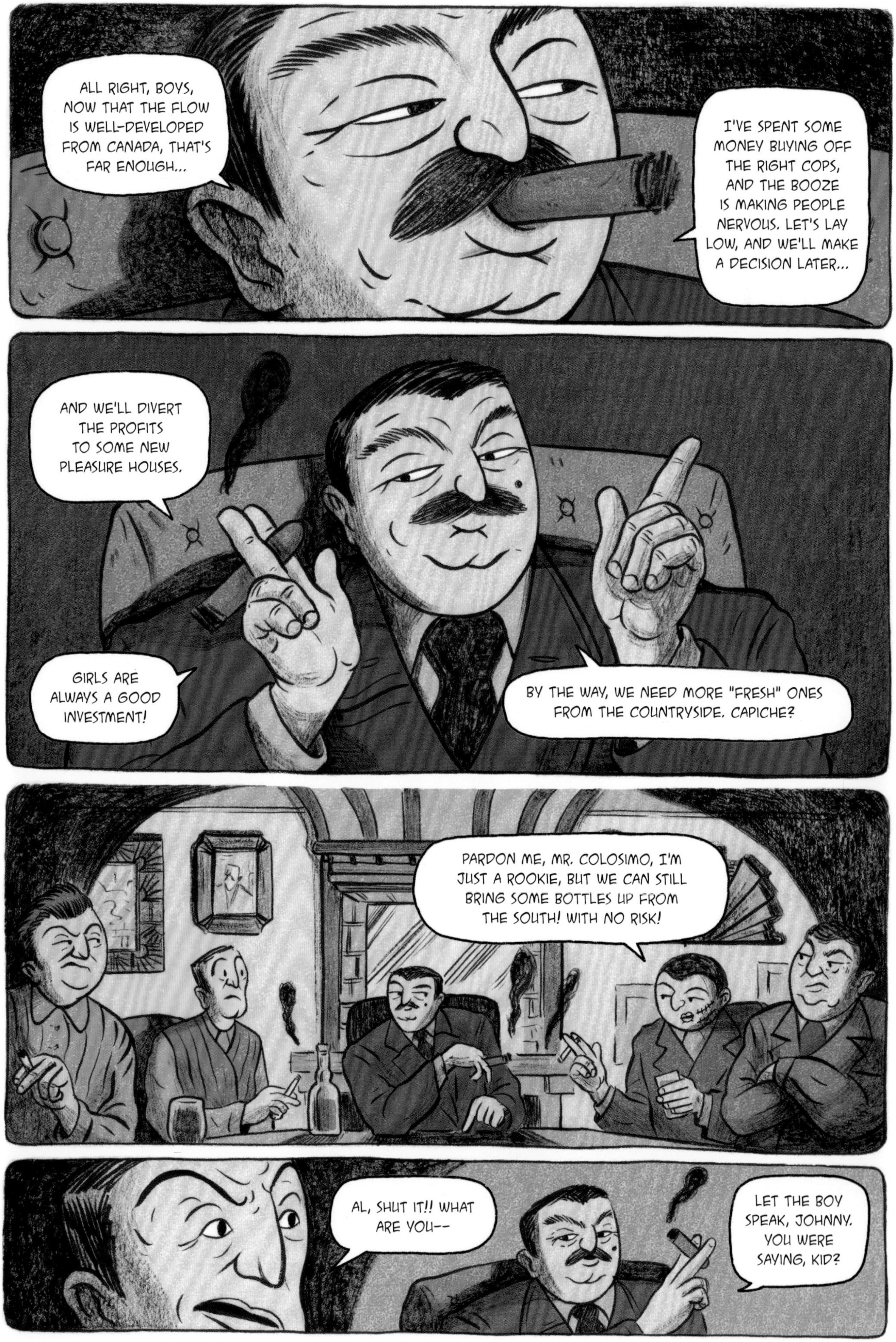

ALL RIGHT, BOYS, NOW THAT THE FLOW IS WELL-DEVELOPED FROM CANADA, THAT'S FAR ENOUGH...
I'VE SPENT SOME MONEY BUYING OFF THE RIGHT COPS, AND THE BOOZE IS MAKING PEOPLE NERVOUS. LET'S LAY LOW, AND WE'LL MAKE A DECISION LATER...
AND WE'LL DIVERT THE PROFITS TO SOME NEW PLEASURE HOUSES.
GIRLS ARE ALWAYS A GOOD INVESTMENT!
BY THE WAY, WE NEED MORE "FRESH" ONES FROM THE COUNTRYSIDE. CAPICHE?
PARDON ME, MR. COLOSIMO, I'M JUST A ROOKIE, BUT WE CAN STILL BRING SOME BOTTLES UP FROM THE SOUTH! WITH NO RISK!
AL, SHUT IT!! WHAT ARE YOU--
LET THE BOY SPEAK, JOHNNY. YOU WERE SAYING, KID?

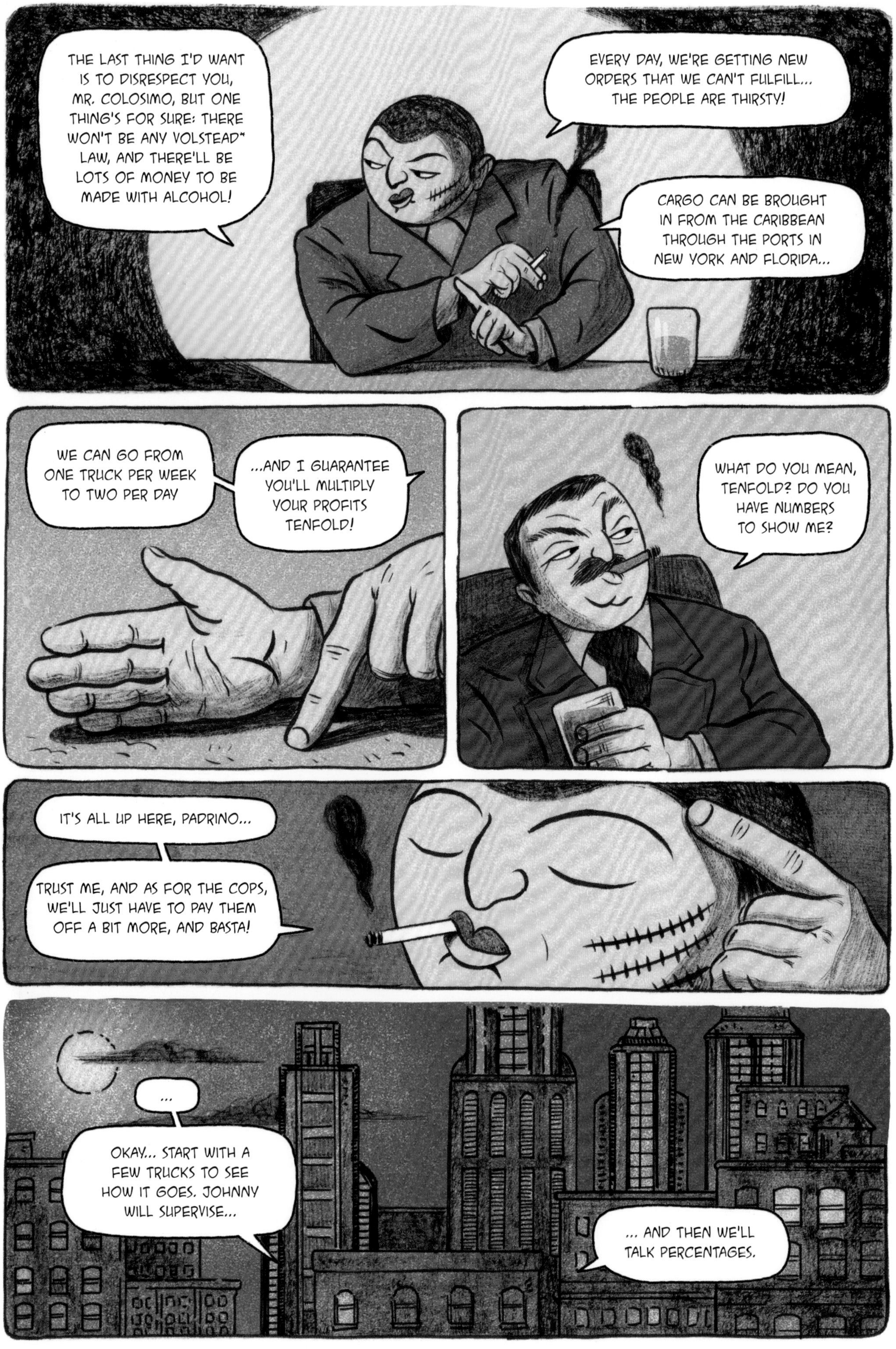
THE LAST THING I'D WANT IS TO DISRESPECT YOU, MR. COLOSIMO, BUT ONE THING'S FOR SURE: THERE WON'T BE ANY VOLSTEAD* LAW, AND THERE'LL BE LOTS OF MONEY TO BE MADE WITH ALCOHOL!
EVERY DAY, WE'RE GETTING NEW ORDERS THAT WE CAN'T FULFILL... THE PEOPLE ARE THIRSTY!
CARGO CAN BE BROUGHT IN FROM THE CARIBBEAN THROUGH THE PORTS IN NEW YORK AND FLORIDA...
WE CAN GO FROM ONE TRUCK PER WEEK TO TWO PER DAY
...AND I GUARANTEE YOU'LL MULTIPLY YOUR PROFITS TENFOLD!
WHAT DO YOU MEAN, TENFOLD? DO YOU HAVE NUMBERS TO SHOW ME?
IT'S ALL UP HERE, PADRINO...
TRUST ME, AND AS FOR THE COPS, WE'LL JUST HAVE TO PAY THEM OFF A BIT MORE, AND BASTA!
...
OKAY... START WITH A FEW TRUCKS TO SEE HOW IT GOES. JOHNNY WILL SUPERVISE...
... AND THEN WE'LL TALK PERCENTAGES.

*COMPLEMENTARY LAW TO THE XIIITH AMENDMENT OF THE CONSTITUTION PROHIBITING THE PRODUCTION AND SALE OF ALCOHOL.

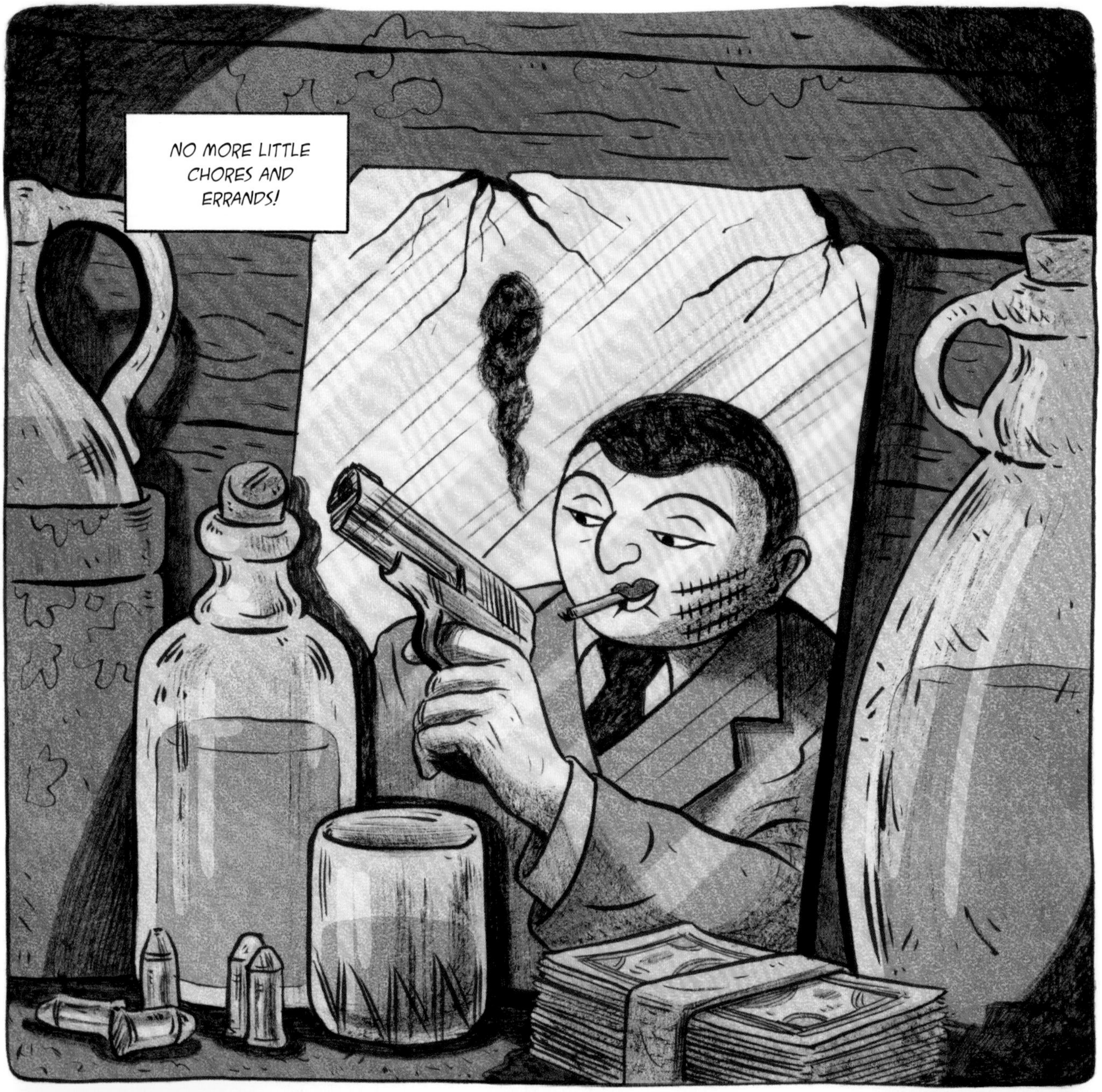
NO MORE LITTLE CHORES AND ERRANDS!

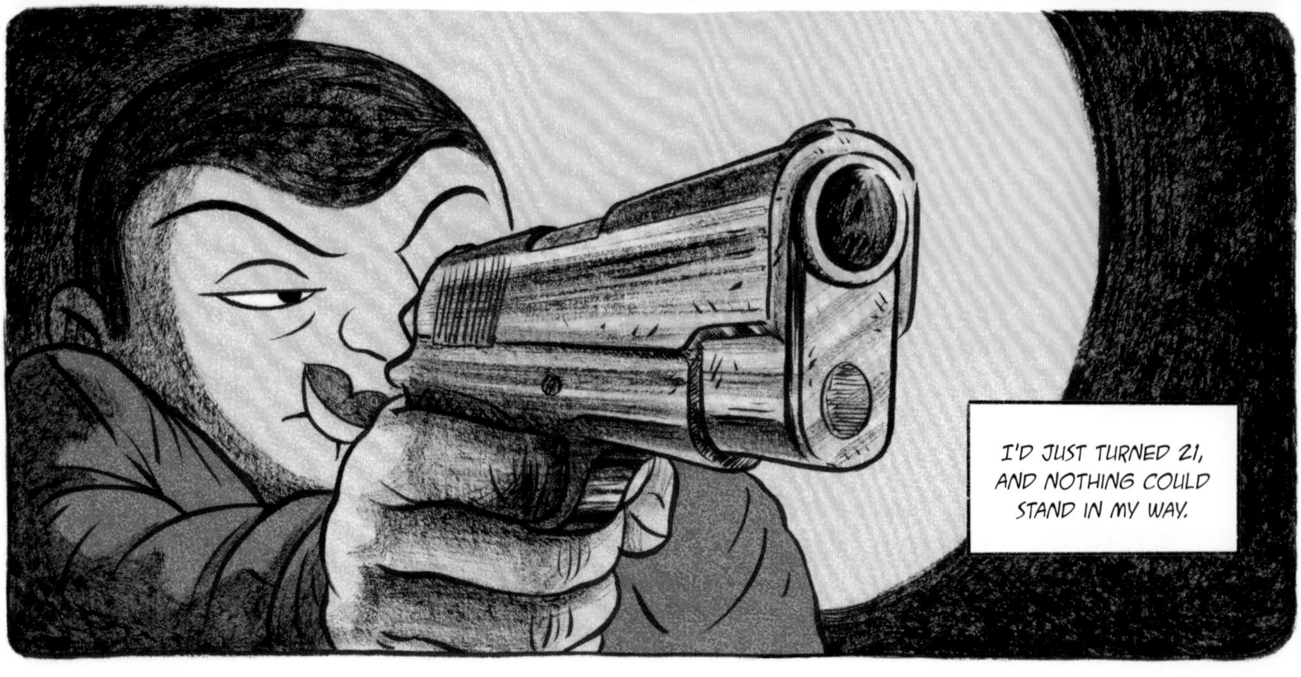
I'D JUST TURNED 21, AND NOTHING COULD STAND IN MY WAY.

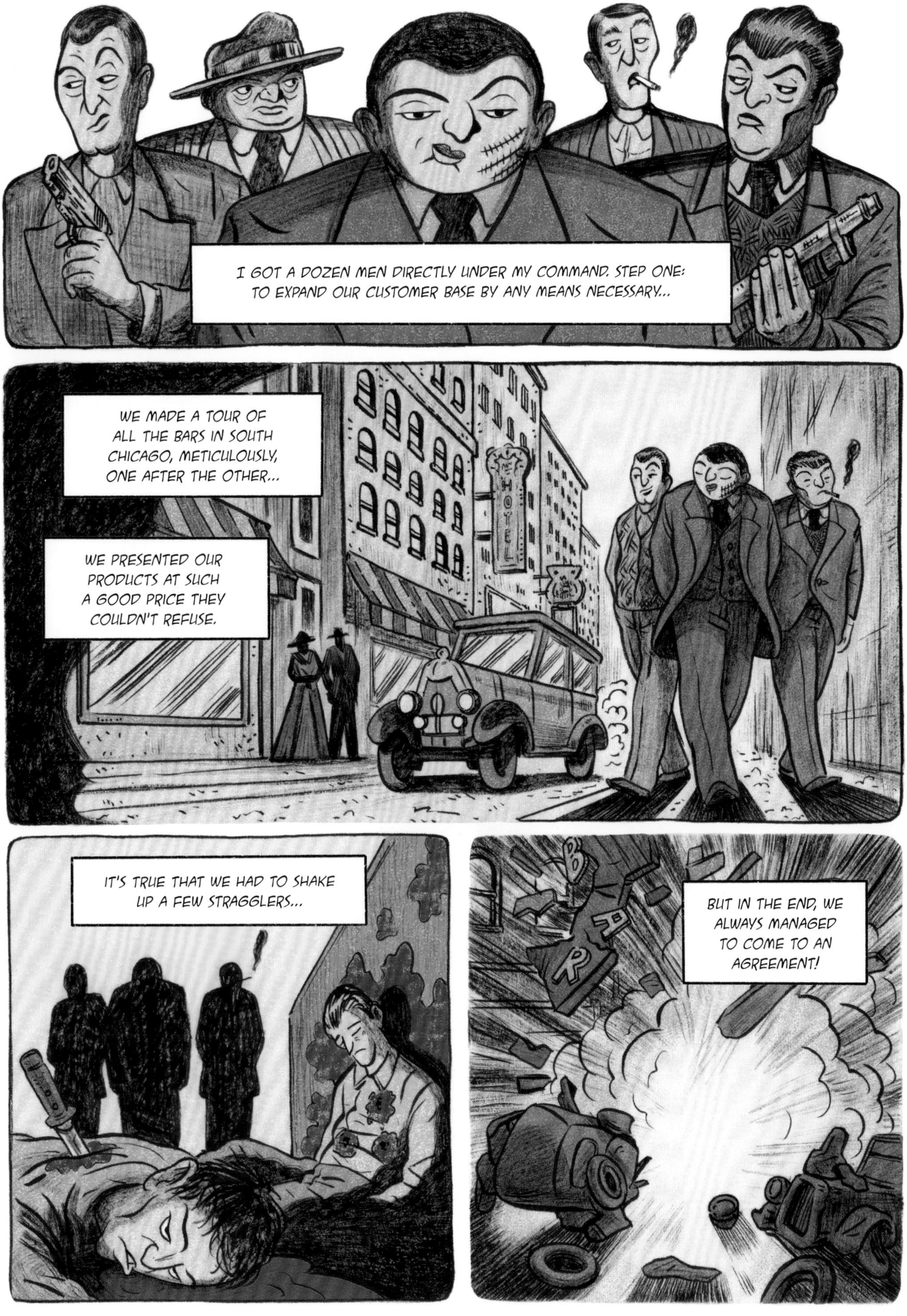
I GOT A DOZEN MEN DIRECTLY UNDER MY COMMAND. STEP ONE: TO EXPAND OUR CUSTOMER BASE BY ANY MEANS NECESSARY...
WE MADE A TOUR OF ALL THE BARS IN SOUTH CHICAGO, METICULOUSLY, ONE AFTER THE OTHER...
WE PRESENTED OUR PRODUCTS AT SUCH A GOOD PRICE THEY COULDN'T REFUSE.
HOTEL
IT'S TRUE THAT WE HAD TO SHAKE UP A FEW STRAGGLERS...
BUT IN THE END, WE ALWAYS MANAGED TO COME TO AN AGREEMENT!

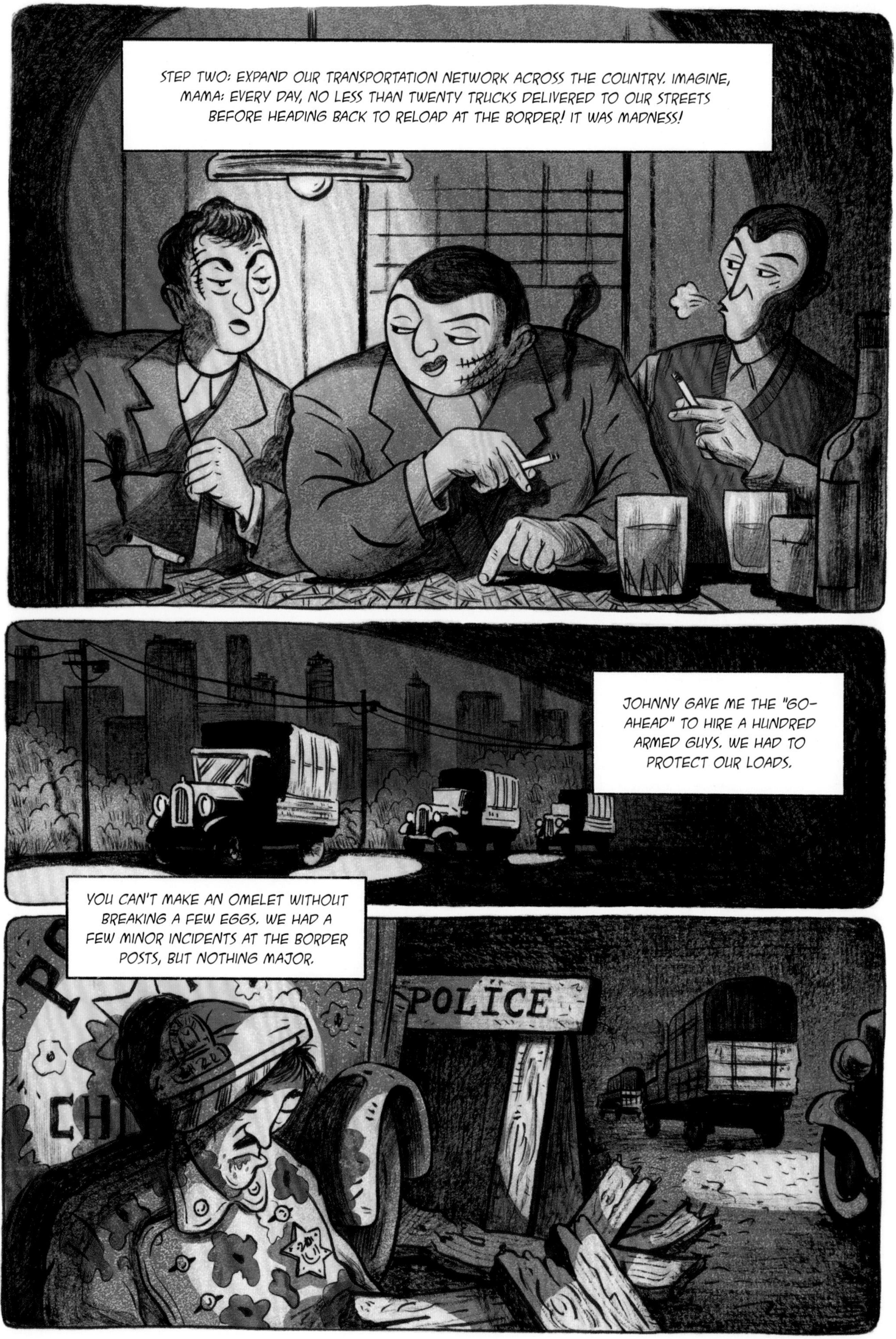
STEP TWO: EXPAND OUR TRANSPORTATION NETWORK ACROSS THE COUNTRY. IMAGINE, MAMA: EVERY DAY, NO LESS THAN TWENTY TRUCKS DELIVERED TO OUR STREETS BEFORE HEADING BACK TO RELOAD AT THE BORDER! IT WAS MADNESS!
JOHNNY GAVE ME THE "GO-AHEAD" TO HIRE A HUNDRED ARMED GUYS. WE HAD TO PROTECT OUR LOADS.
YOU CAN'T MAKE AN OMELET WITHOUT BREAKING A FEW EGGS. WE HAD A FEW MINOR INCIDENTS AT THE BORDER POSTS, BUT NOTHING MAJOR.
POLICE

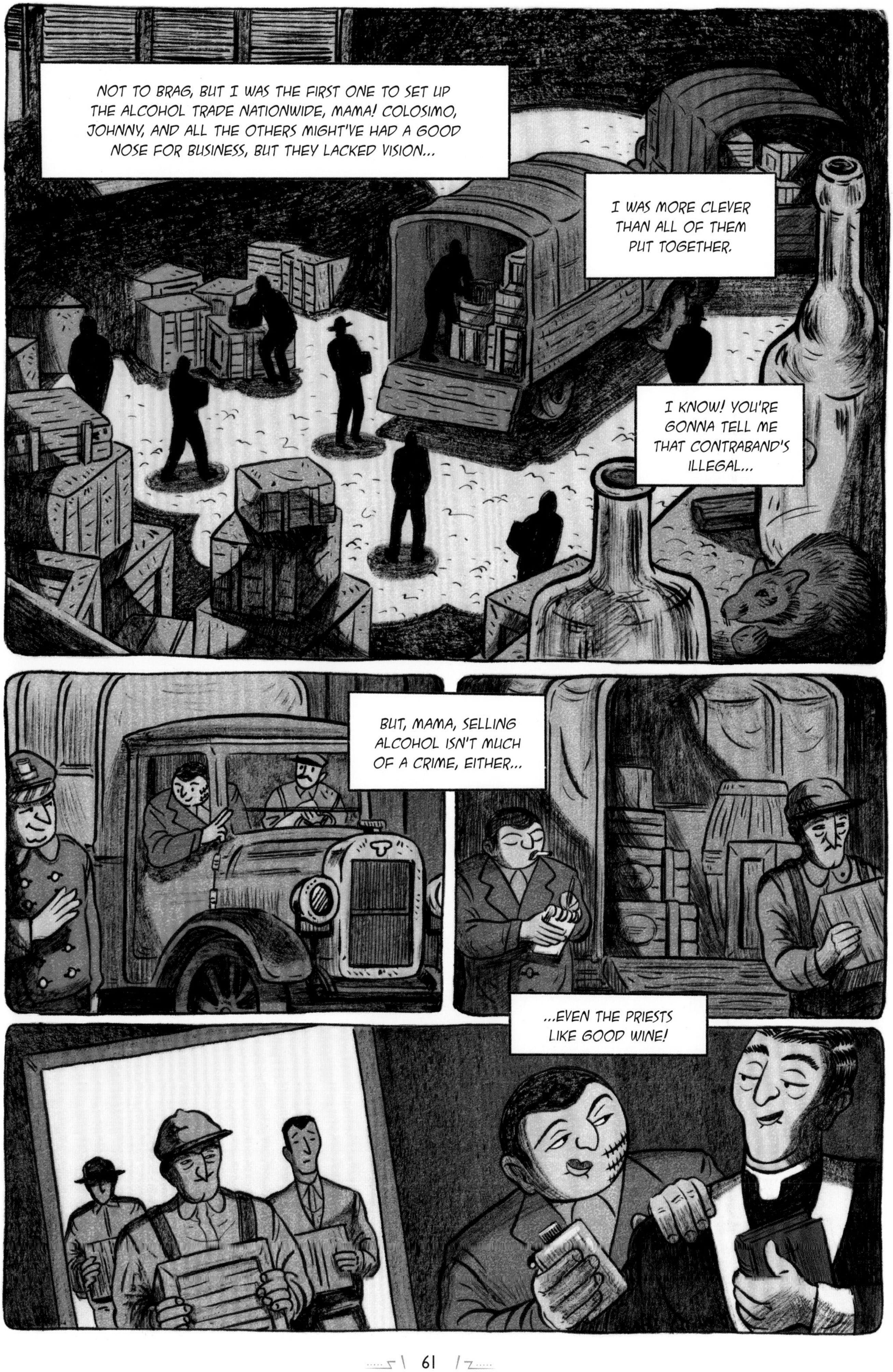
NOT TO BRAG, BUT I WAS THE FIRST ONE TO SET UP THE ALCOHOL TRADE NATIONWIDE, MAMA! COLOSIMO, JOHNNY, AND ALL THE OTHERS MIGHT'VE HAD A GOOD NOSE FOR BUSINESS, BUT THEY LACKED VISION...
I WAS MORE CLEVER THAN ALL OF THEM PUT TOGETHER.
I KNOW! YOU'RE GONNA TELL ME THAT CONTRABAND'S ILLEGAL...
BUT, MAMA, SELLING ALCOHOL ISN'T MUCH OF A CRIME, EITHER...
...EVEN THE PRIESTS LIKE GOOD WINE!

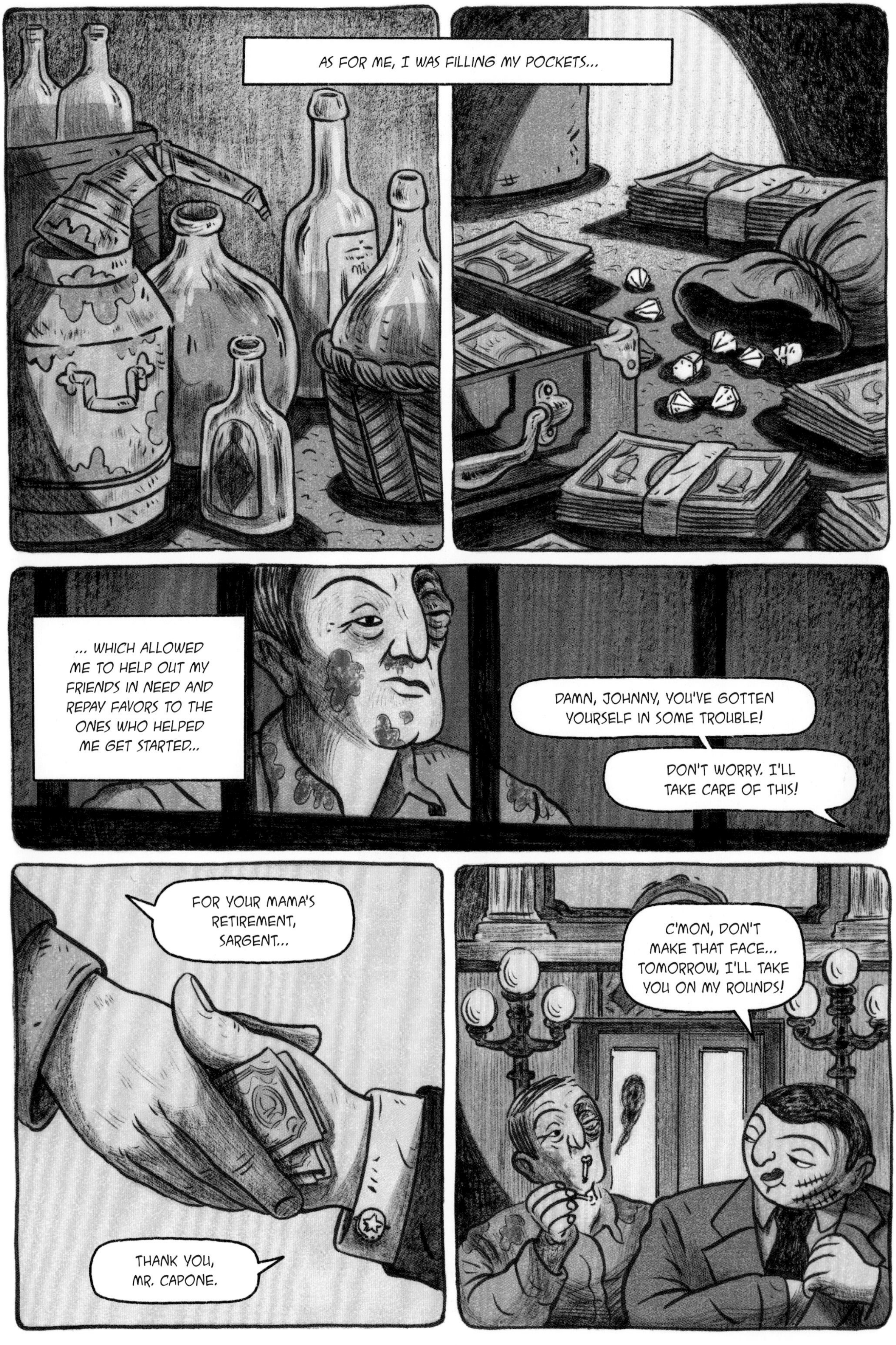

AS FOR ME, I WAS FILLING MY POCKETS...
... WHICH ALLOWED ME TO HELP OUT MY FRIENDS IN NEED AND REPAY FAVORS TO THE ONES WHO HELPED ME GET STARTED...
DAMN, JOHNNY, YOU'VE GOTTEN YOURSELF IN SOME TROUBLE!
DON'T WORRY. I'LL TAKE CARE OF THIS!
FOR YOUR MAMA'S RETIREMENT, SARGENT...
THANK YOU, MR. CAPONE.
C'MON, DON'T MAKE THAT FACE... TOMORROW, I'LL TAKE YOU ON MY ROUNDS!

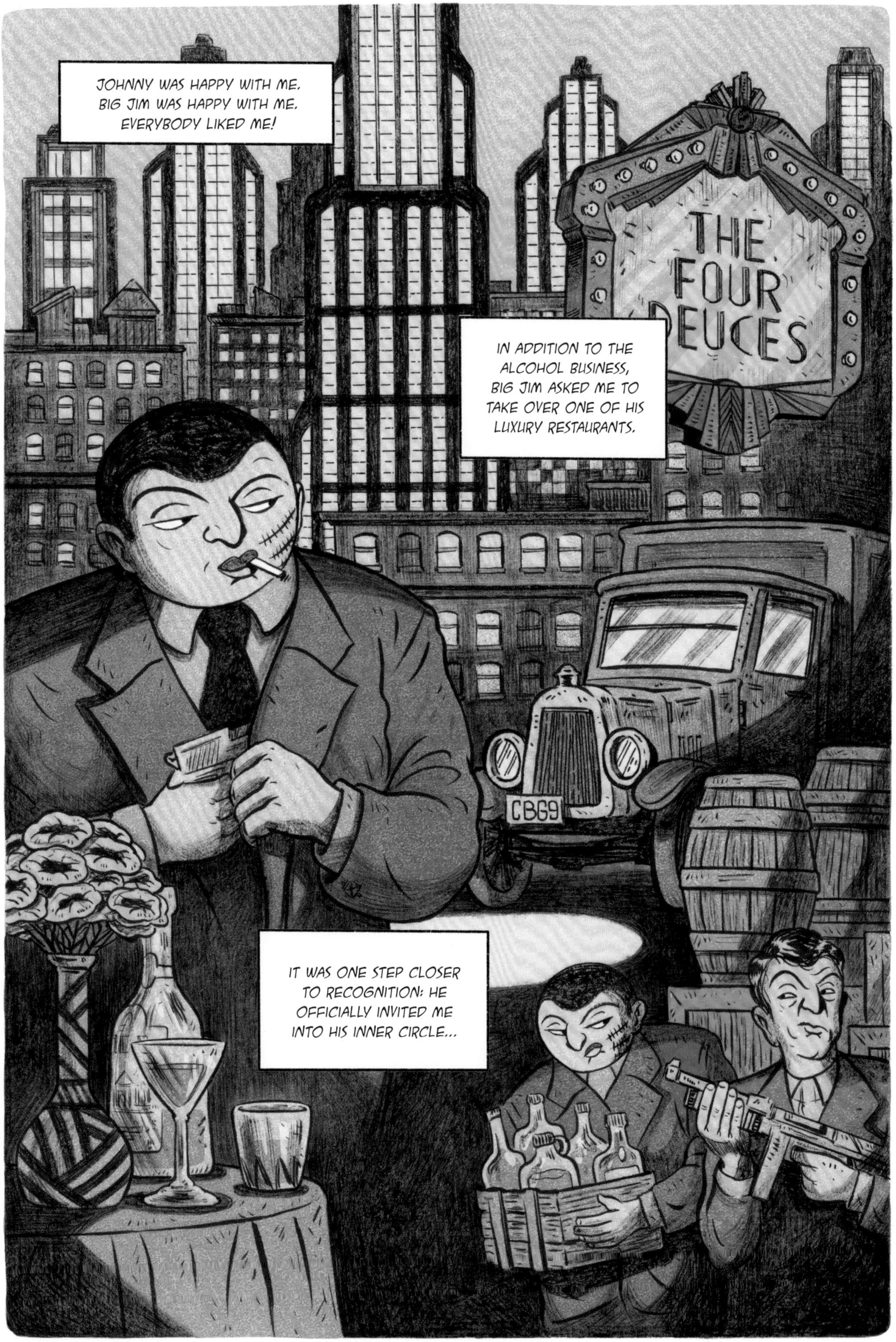
JOHNNY WAS HAPPY WITH ME. BIG JIM WAS HAPPY WITH ME. EVERYBODY LIKED ME!
THE FOUR DEUCES
IN ADDITION TO THE ALCOHOL BUSINESS, BIG JIM ASKED ME TO TAKE OVER ONE OF HIS LUXURY RESTAURANTS.
CBG9
IT WAS ONE STEP CLOSER TO RECOGNITION: HE OFFICIALLY INVITED ME INTO HIS INNER CIRCLE...

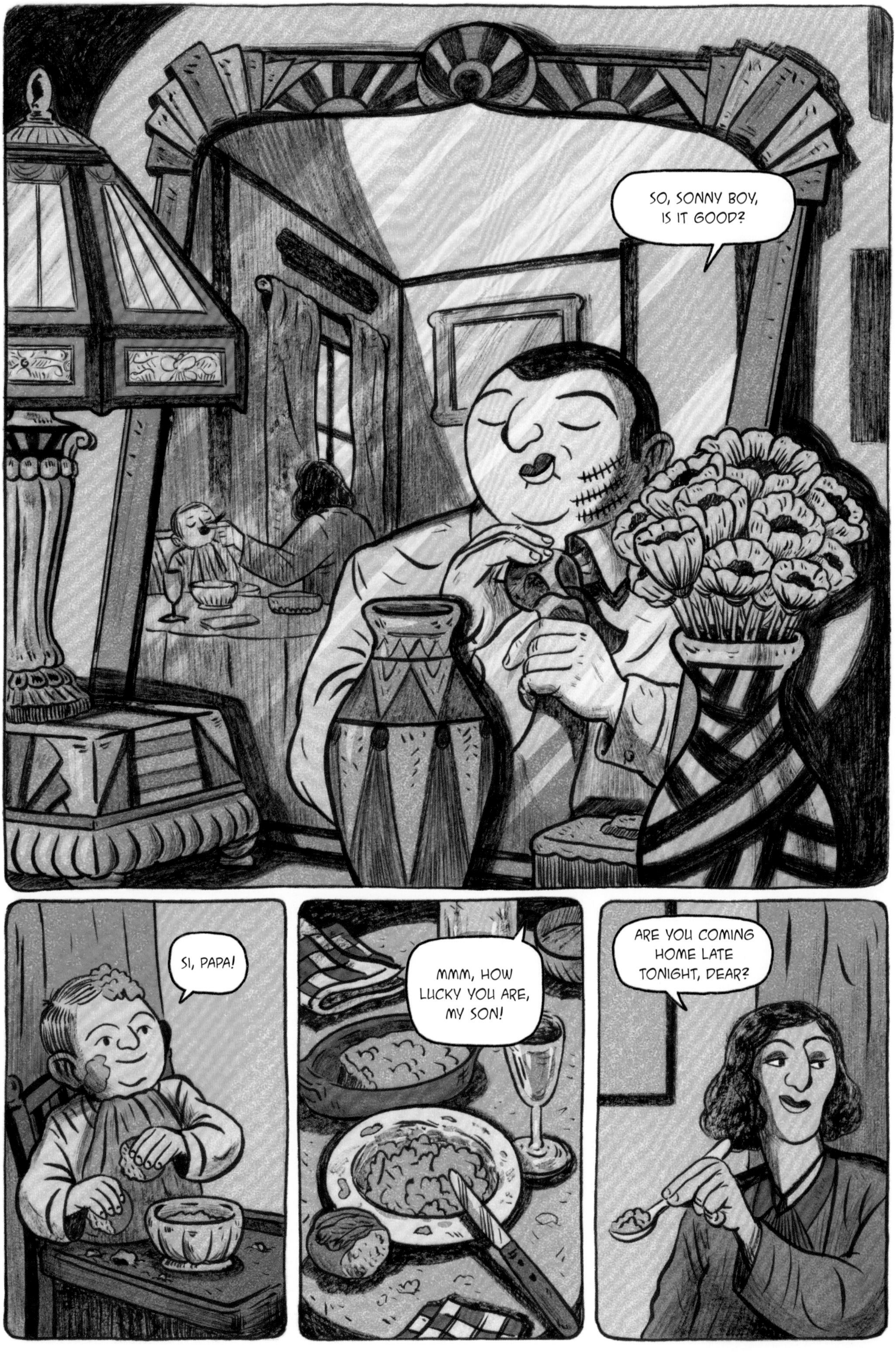
SO, SONNY BOY, IS IT GOOD?
SI, PAPA!
MMM, HOW LUCKY YOU ARE, MY SON!
ARE YOU COMING HOME LATE TONIGHT, DEAR?

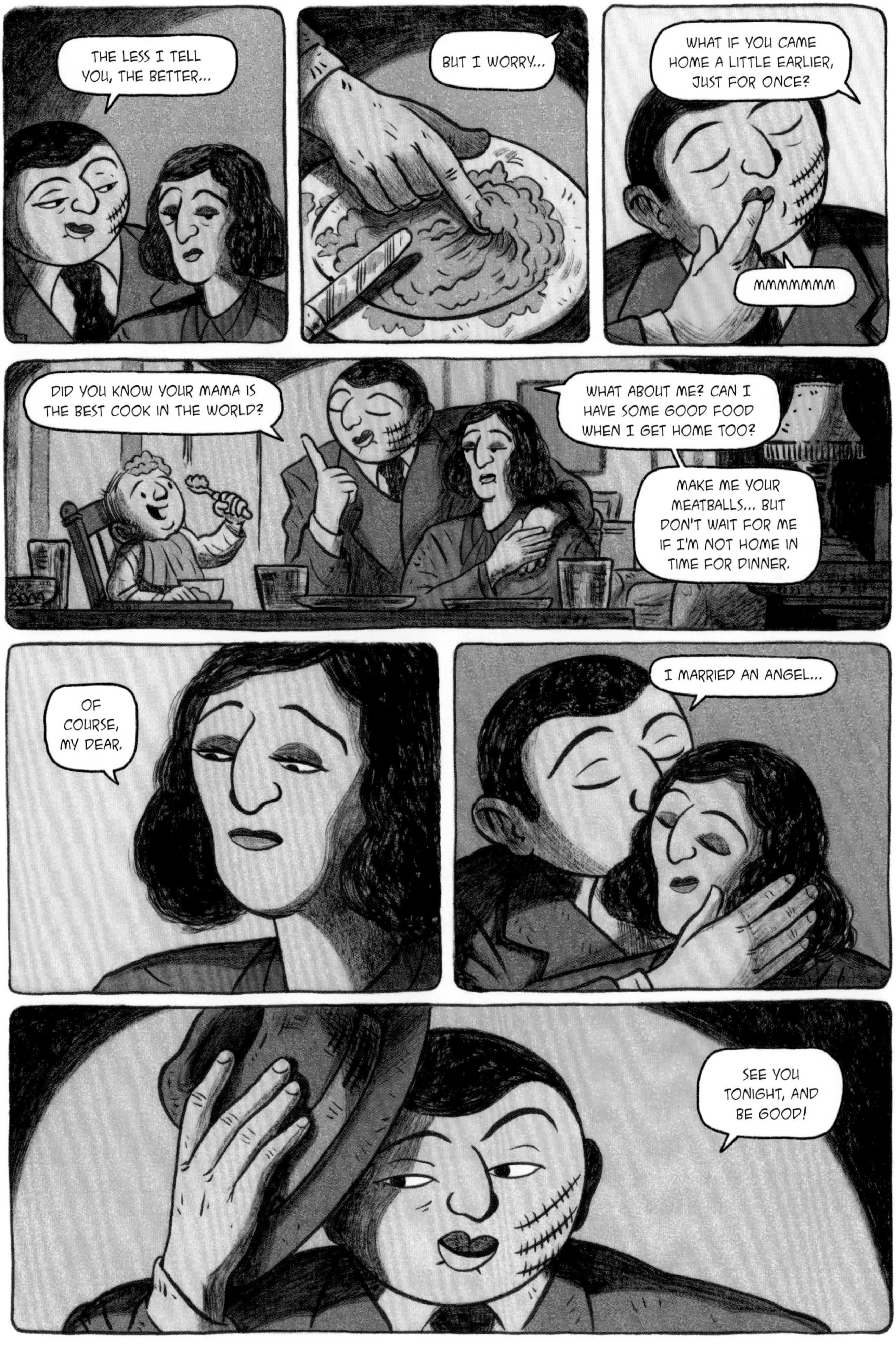
THE LESS I TELL YOU, THE BETTER...
BUT I WORRY...
WHAT IF YOU CAME HOME A LITTLE EARLIER, JUST FOR ONCE?
MMMMMMM
DID YOU KNOW YOUR MAMA IS THE BEST COOK IN THE WORLD?
WHAT ABOUT ME? CAN I HAVE SOME GOOD FOOD WHEN I GET HOME TOO?
MAKE ME YOUR MEATBALLS... BUT DON'T WAIT FOR ME IF I'M NOT HOME IN TIME FOR DINNER.
OF COURSE, MY DEAR.
I MARRIED AN ANGEL...
SEE YOU TONIGHT, AND BE GOOD!

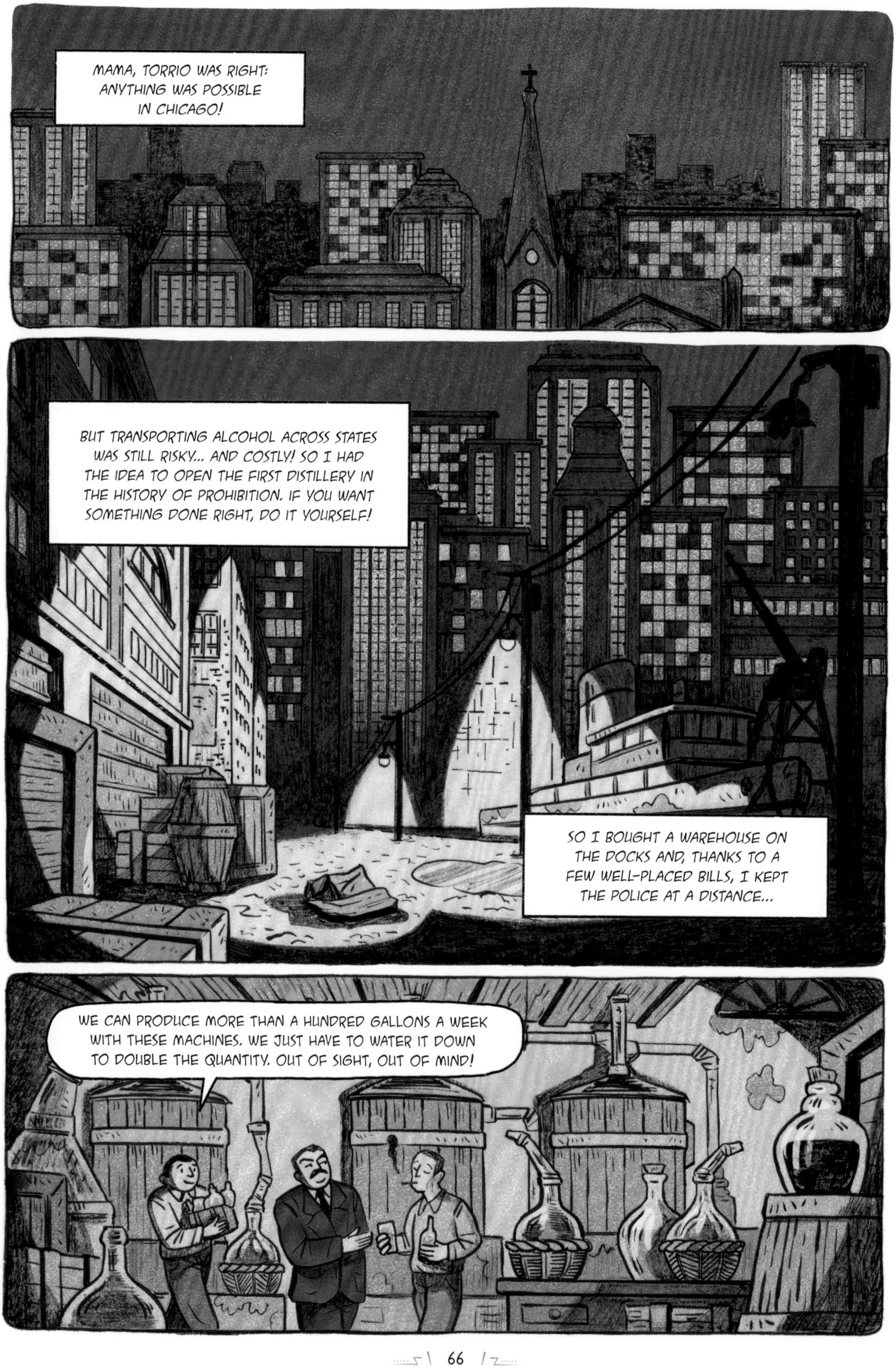
MAMA, TORRIO WAS RIGHT: ANYTHING WAS POSSIBLE IN CHICAGO!
BUT TRANSPORTING ALCOHOL ACROSS STATES WAS STILL RISKY... AND COSTLY! SO I HAD THE IDEA TO OPEN THE FIRST DISTILLERY IN THE HISTORY OF PROHIBITION. IF YOU WANT SOMETHING DONE RIGHT, DO IT YOURSELF!
SO I BOUGHT A WAREHOUSE ON THE DOCKS AND, THANKS TO A FEW WELL-PLACED BILLS, I KEPT THE POLICE AT A DISTANCE...
WE CAN PRODUCE MORE THAN A HUNDRED GALLONS A WEEK WITH THESE MACHINES. WE JUST HAVE TO WATER IT DOWN TO DOUBLE THE QUANTITY. OUT OF SIGHT, OUT OF MIND!

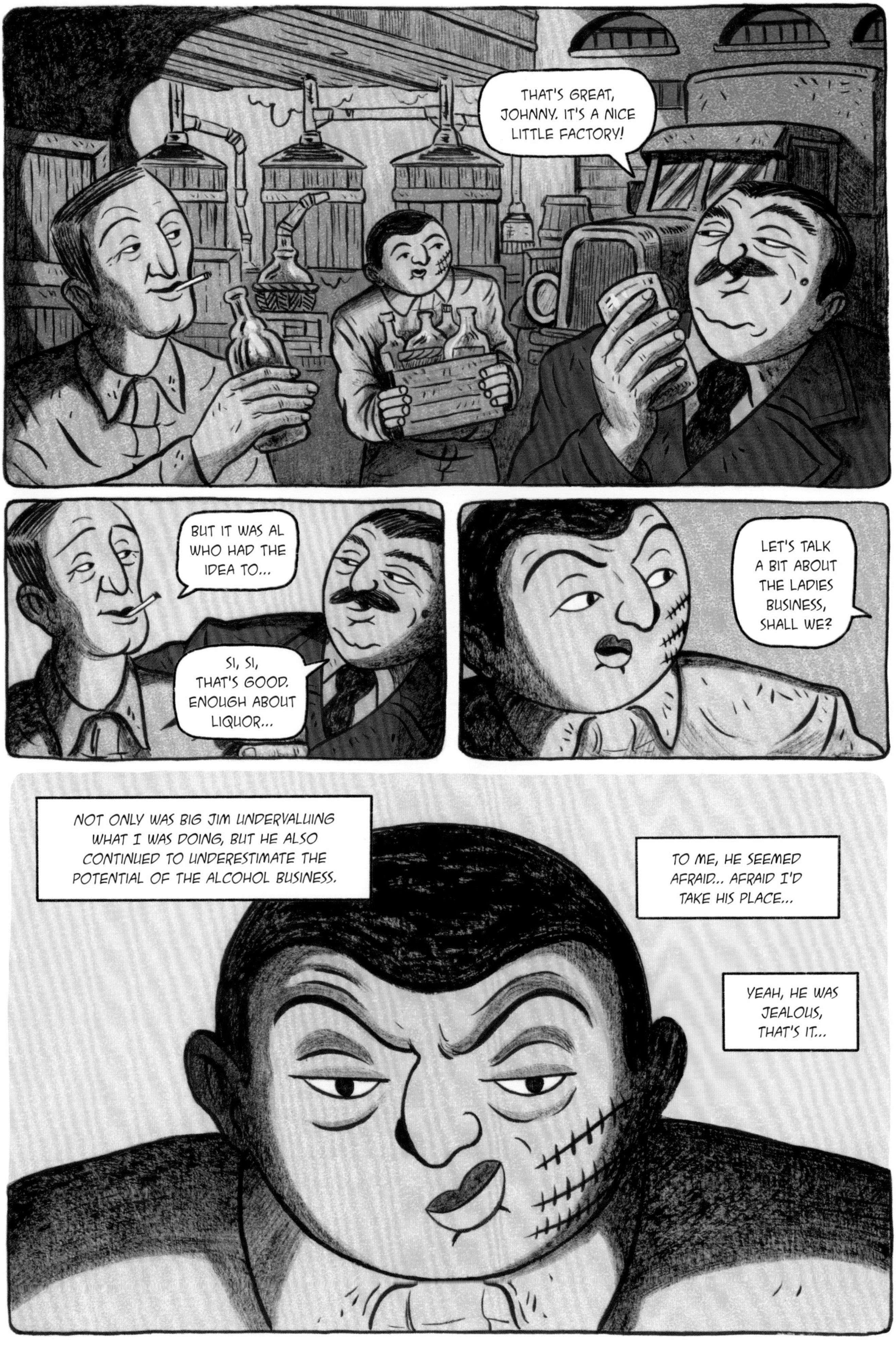
THAT'S GREAT, JOHNNY. IT'S A NICE LITTLE FACTORY!
BUT IT WAS AL WHO HAD THE IDEA TO...
SI, SI, THAT'S GOOD. ENOUGH ABOUT LIQUOR...
LET'S TALK A BIT ABOUT THE LADIES BUSINESS, SHALL WE?
NOT ONLY WAS BIG JIM UNDERVALUING WHAT I WAS DOING, BUT HE ALSO CONTINUED TO UNDERESTIMATE THE POTENTIAL OF THE ALCOHOL BUSINESS.
TO ME, HE SEEMED AFRAID... AFRAID I'D TAKE HIS PLACE...
YEAH, HE WAS JEALOUS, THAT'S IT...

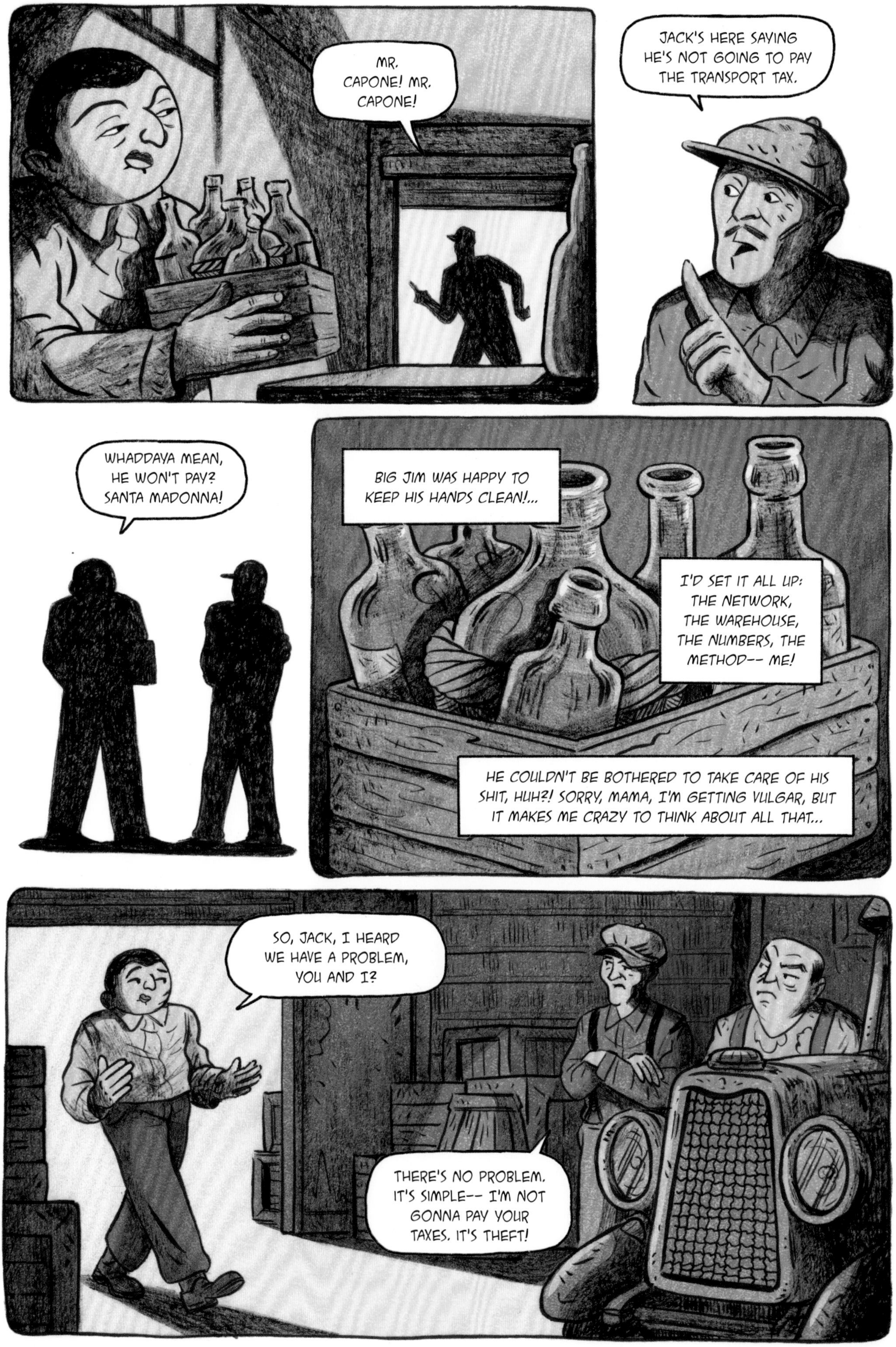
MR. CAPONE! MR. CAPONE!
JACK'S HERE SAYING HE'S NOT GOING TO PAY THE TRANSPORT TAX.
WHADDAYA MEAN, HE WON'T PAY? SANTA MADONNA!
BIG JIM WAS HAPPY TO KEEP HIS HANDS CLEAN!...
I'D SET IT ALL UP: THE NETWORK, THE WAREHOUSE, THE NUMBERS, THE METHOD-- ME!
HE COULDN'T BE BOTHERED TO TAKE CARE OF HIS SHIT, HUH?! SORRY, MAMA, I'M GETTING VULGAR, BUT IT MAKES ME CRAZY TO THINK ABOUT ALL THAT...
SO, JACK, I HEARD WE HAVE A PROBLEM, YOU AND I?
THERE'S NO PROBLEM. IT'S SIMPLE-- I'M NOT GONNA PAY YOUR TAXES. IT'S THEFT!

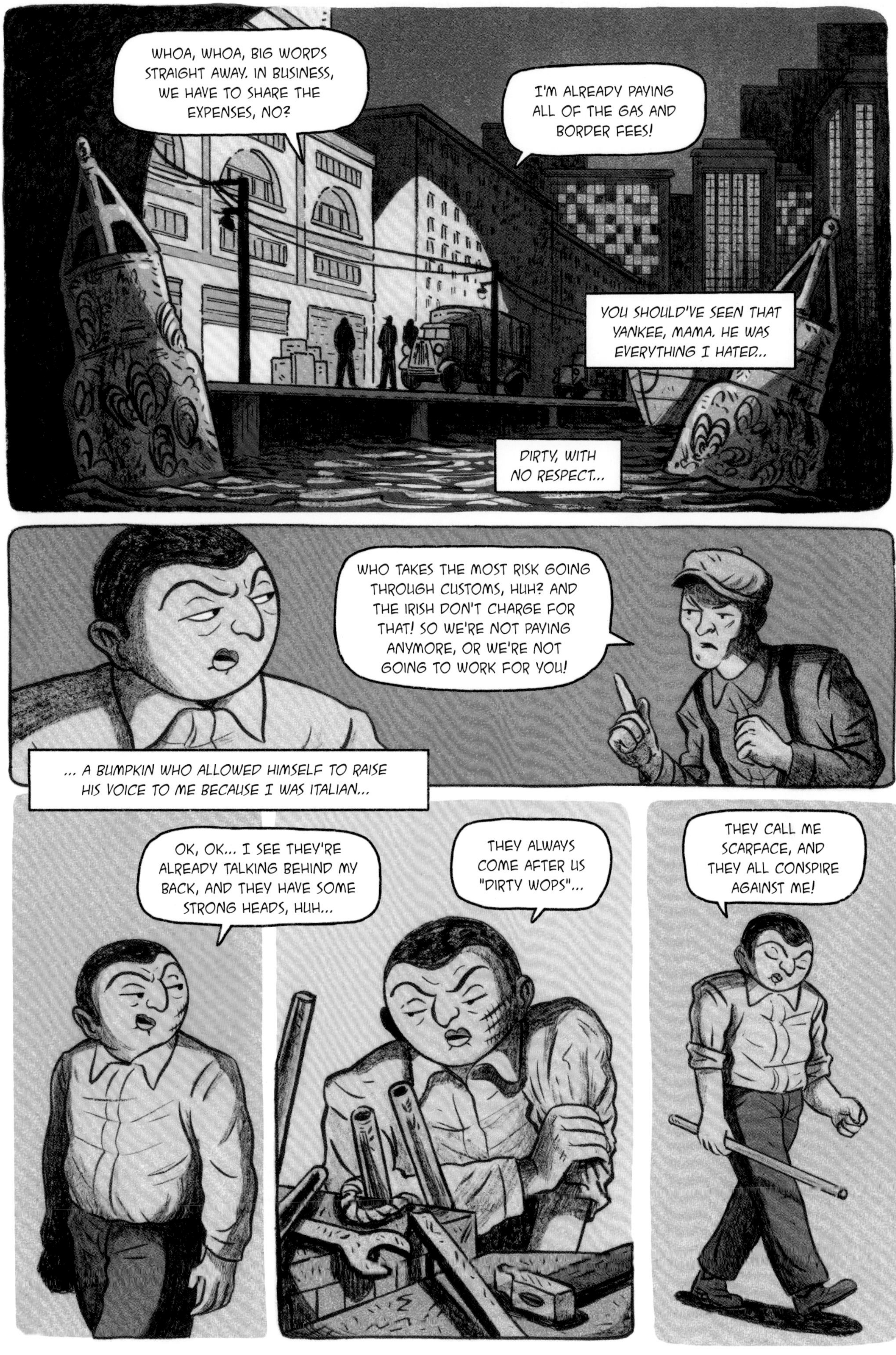
WHOA, WHOA, BIG WORDS STRAIGHT AWAY. IN BUSINESS, WE HAVE TO SHARE THE EXPENSES, NO?
I'M ALREADY PAYING ALL OF THE GAS AND BORDER FEES!
YOU SHOULD'VE SEEN THAT YANKEE, MAMA. HE WAS EVERYTHING I HATED...
DIRTY, WITH NO RESPECT...
WHO TAKES THE MOST RISK GOING THROUGH CUSTOMS, HUH? AND THE IRISH DON'T CHARGE FOR THAT! SO WE'RE NOT PAYING ANYMORE, OR WE'RE NOT GOING TO WORK FOR YOU!
... A BUMPKIN WHO ALLOWED HIMSELF TO RAISE HIS VOICE TO ME BECAUSE I WAS ITALIAN...
OK, OK... I SEE THEY'RE ALREADY TALKING BEHIND MY BACK, AND THEY HAVE SOME STRONG HEADS, HUH...
THEY ALWAYS COME AFTER US "DIRTY WOPS"...
THEY CALL ME SCARFACE, AND THEY ALL CONSPIRE AGAINST ME!

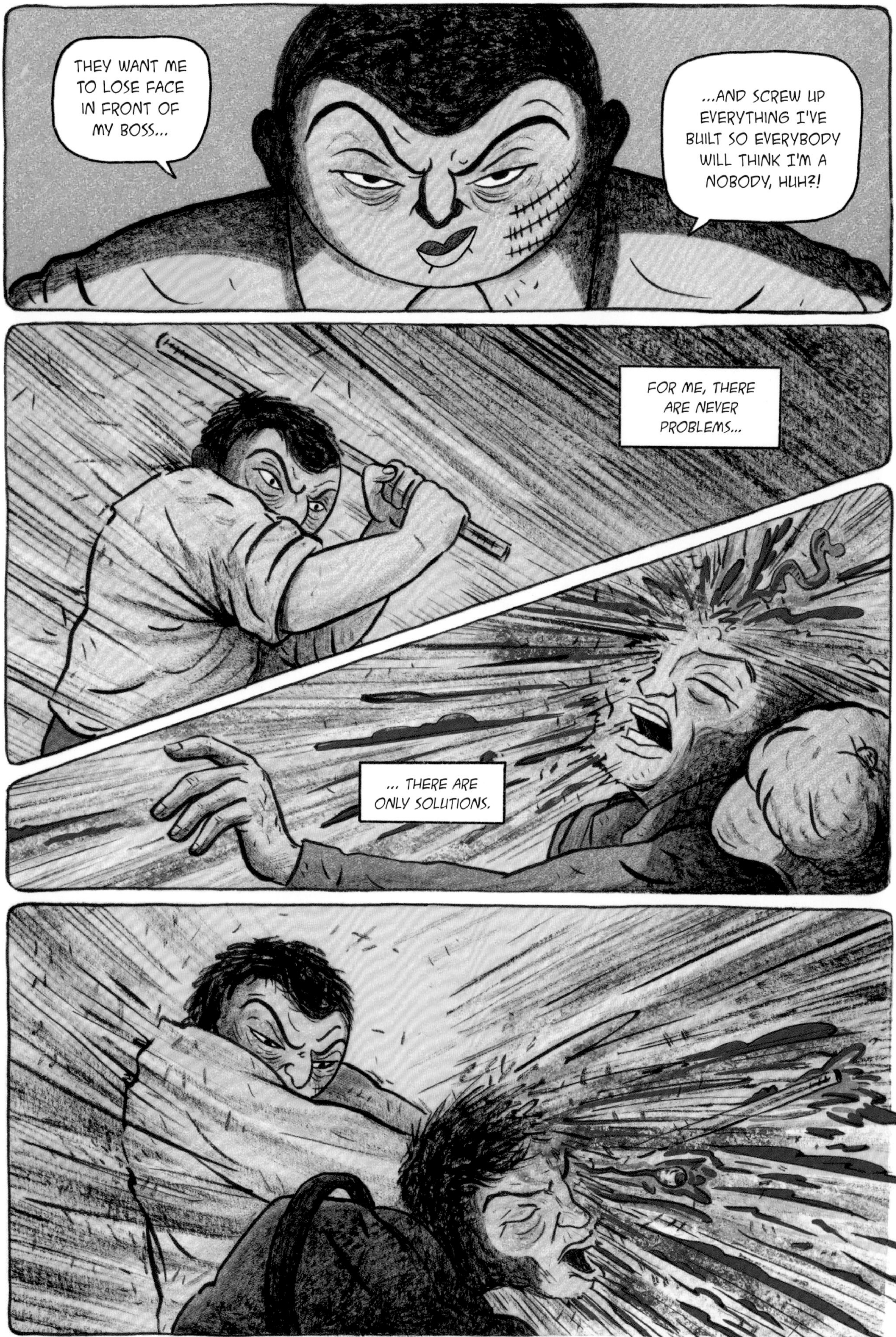
THEY WANT ME TO LOSE FACE IN FRONT OF MY BOSS...
...AND SCREW UP EVERYTHING I'VE BUILT SO EVERYBODY WILL THINK I'M A NOBODY, HUH?!
FOR ME, THERE ARE NEVER PROBLEMS...
... THERE ARE ONLY SOLUTIONS.

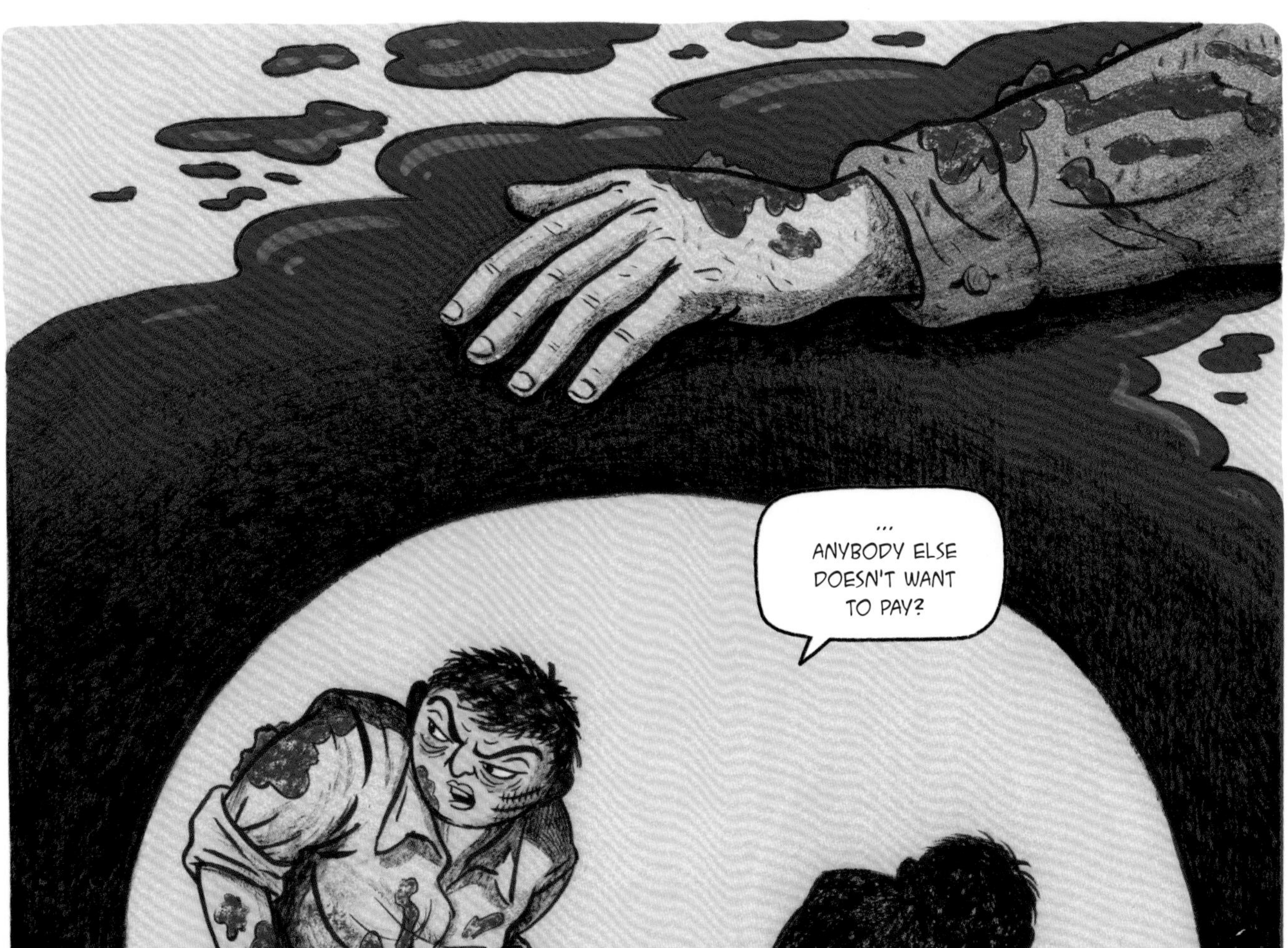
... ANYBODY ELSE DOESN'T WANT TO PAY?

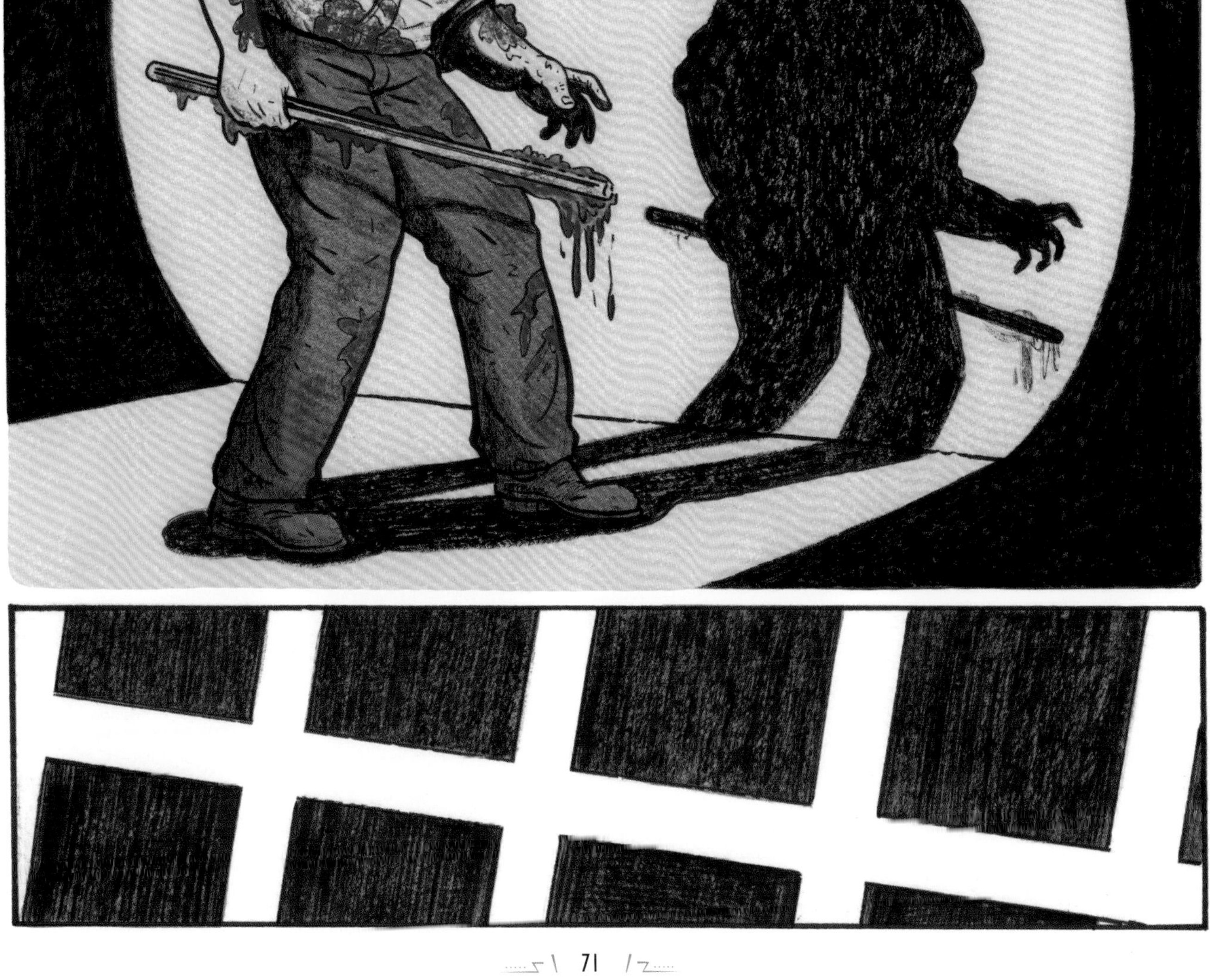

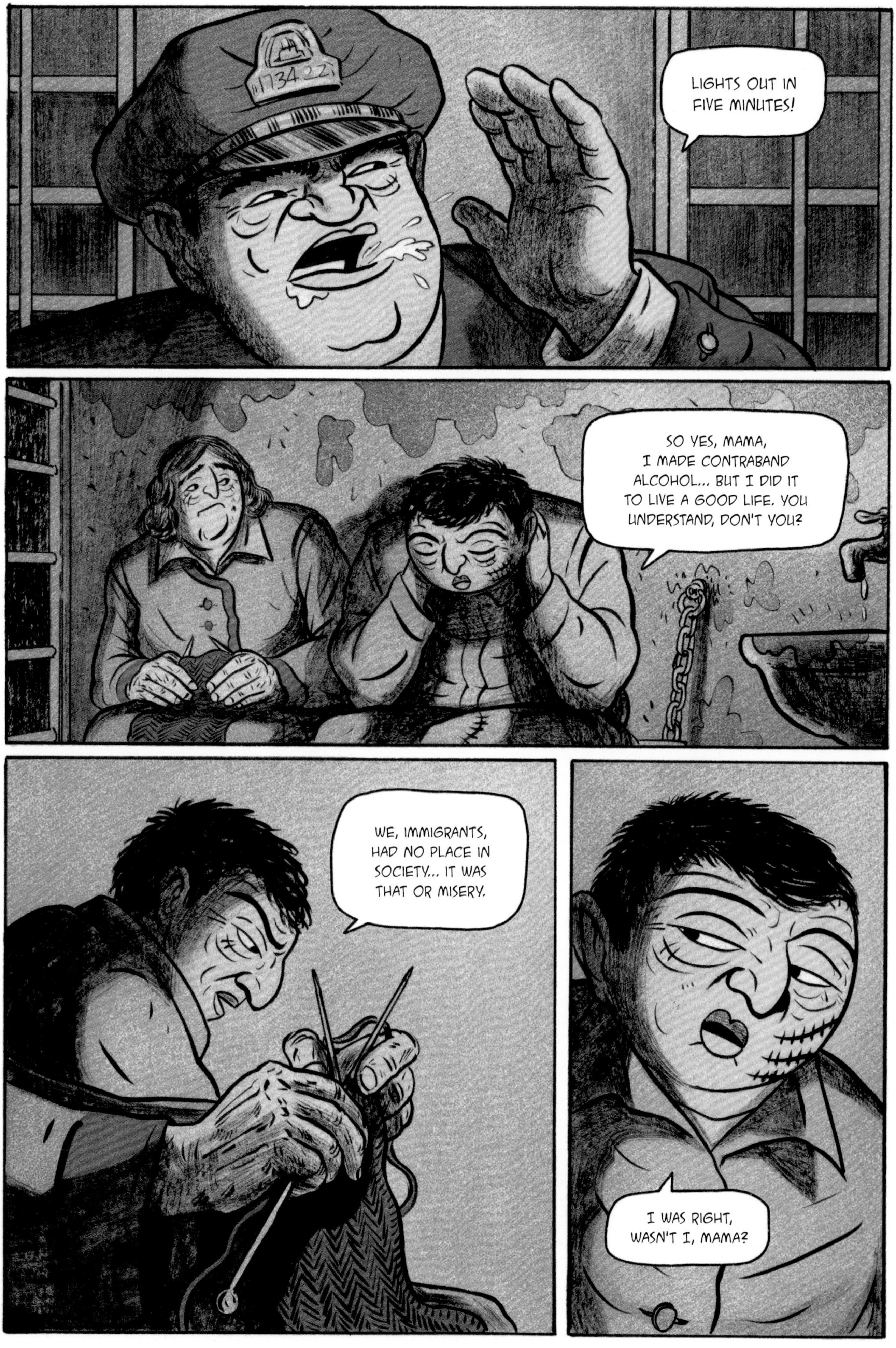
LIGHTS OUT IN FIVE MINUTES!
SO YES, MAMA, I MADE CONTRABAND ALCOHOL... BUT I DID IT TO LIVE A GOOD LIFE. YOU UNDERSTAND, DON'T YOU?
WE, IMMIGRANTS, HAD NO PLACE IN SOCIETY... IT WAS THAT OR MISERY.
I WAS RIGHT, WASN'T I, MAMA?

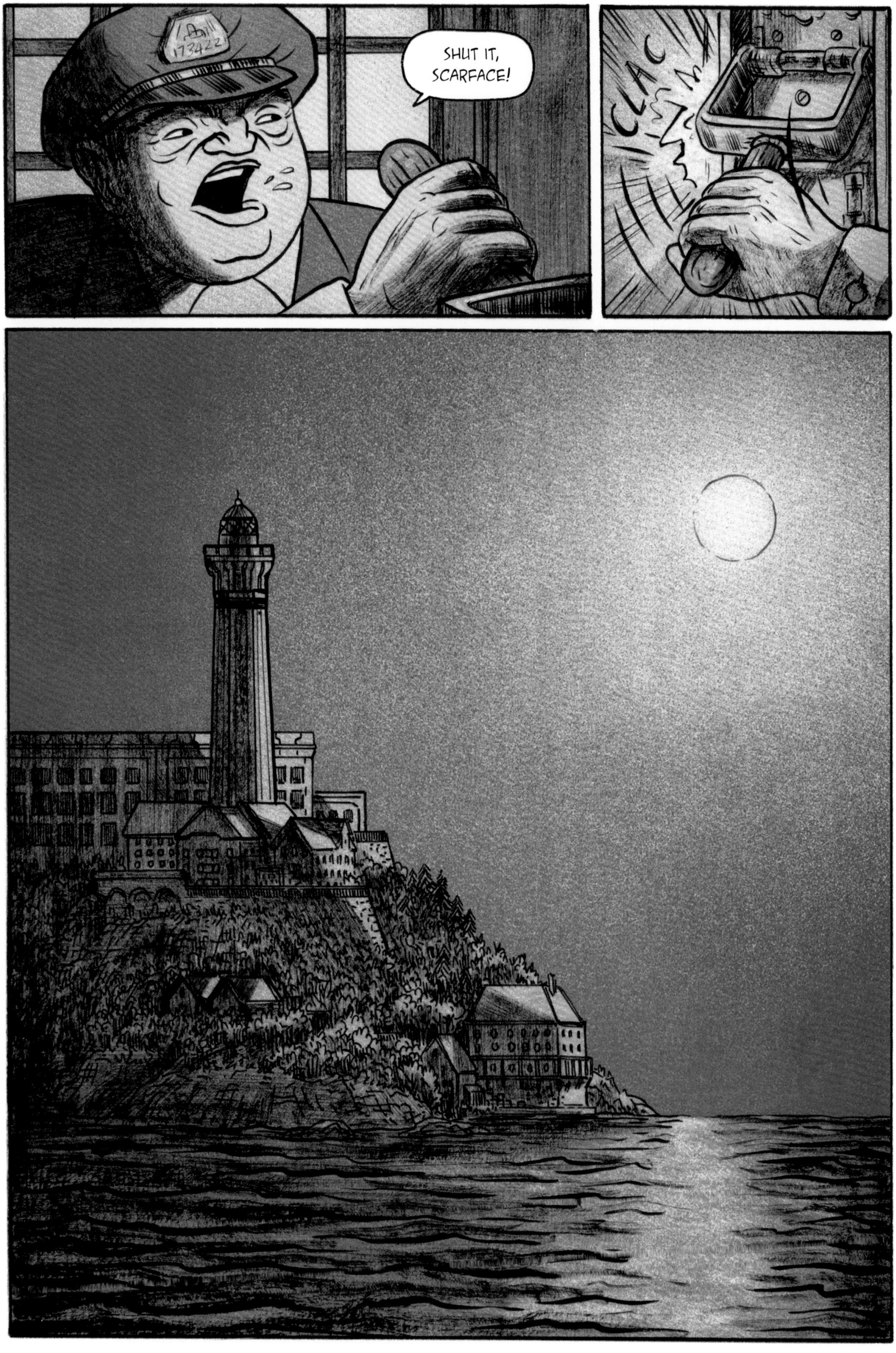
SHUT IT, SCARFACE!
CLAC

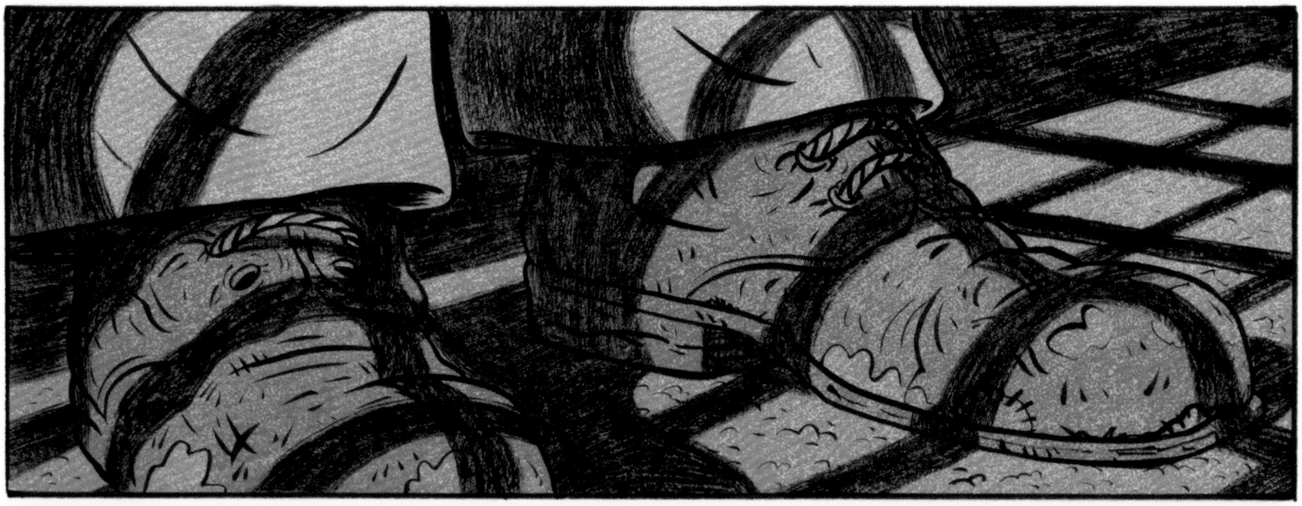

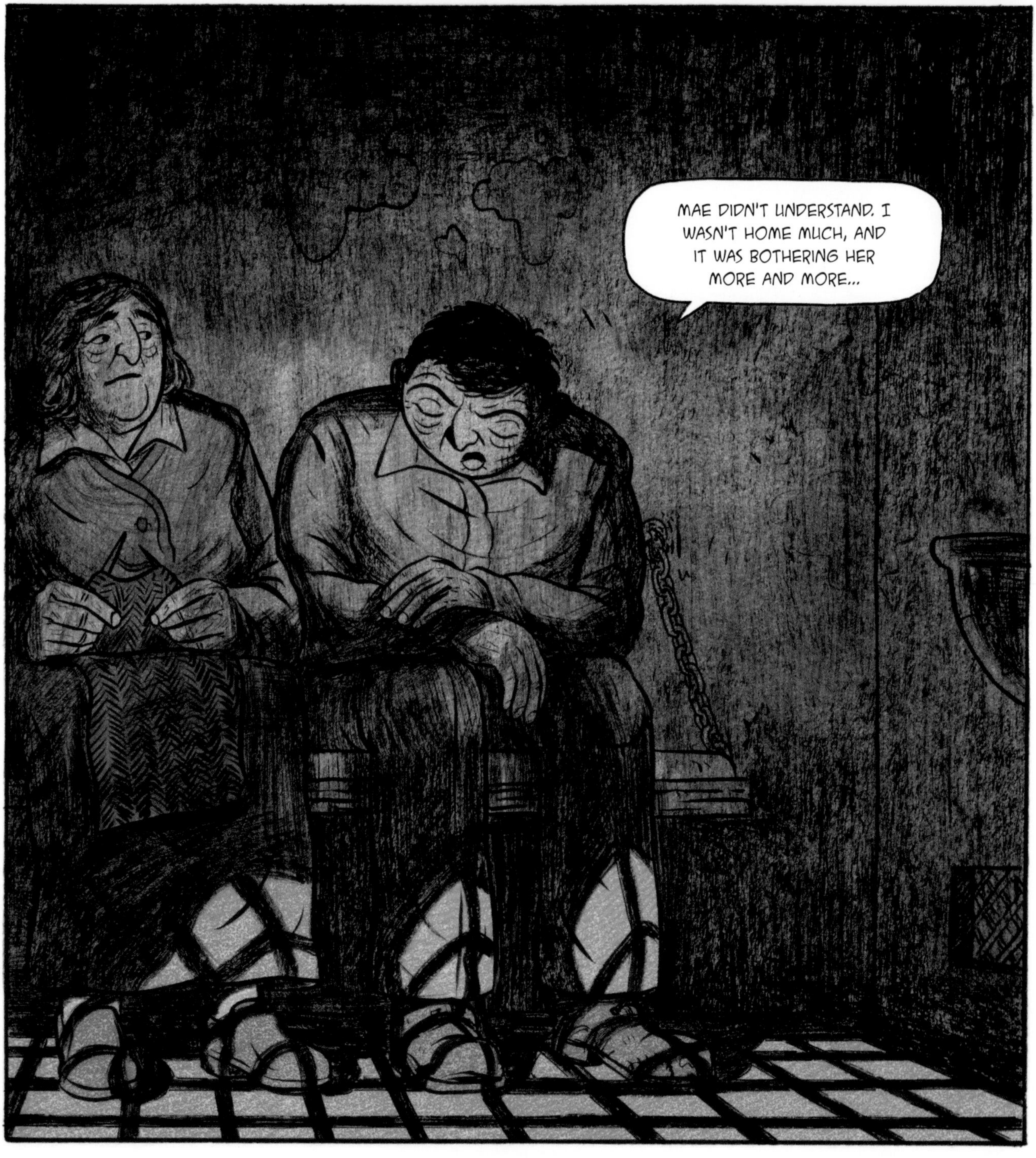
MAE DIDN'T UNDERSTAND. I WASN'T HOME MUCH, AND IT WAS BOTHERING HER MORE AND MORE...

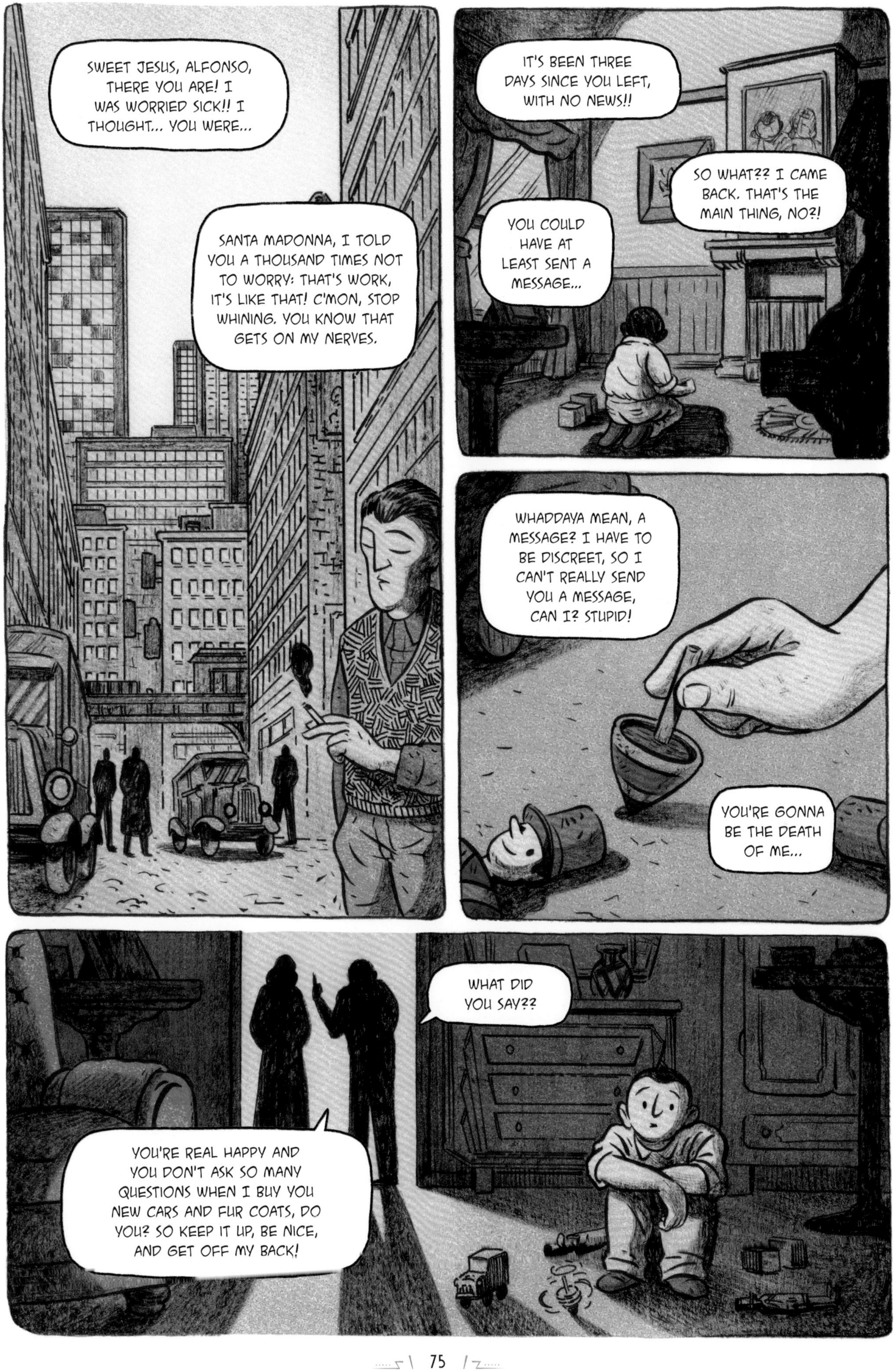

SWEET JESUS, ALFONSO, THERE YOU ARE! I WAS WORRIED SICK!! I THOUGHT... YOU WERE...
SANTA MADONNA, I TOLD YOU A THOUSAND TIMES NOT TO WORRY: THAT'S WORK, IT'S LIKE THAT! C'MON, STOP WHINING. YOU KNOW THAT GETS ON MY NERVES.
IT'S BEEN THREE DAYS SINCE YOU LEFT, WITH NO NEWS!!
YOU COULD HAVE AT LEAST SENT A MESSAGE...
SO WHAT?? I CAME BACK. THAT'S THE MAIN THING, NO?!
WHADDAYA MEAN, A MESSAGE? I HAVE TO BE DISCREET, SO I CAN'T REALLY SEND YOU A MESSAGE, CAN I? STUPID!
YOU'RE GONNA BE THE DEATH OF ME...
WHAT DID YOU SAY??
YOU'RE REAL HAPPY AND YOU DON'T ASK SO MANY QUESTIONS WHEN I BUY YOU NEW CARS AND FUR COATS, DO YOU? SO KEEP IT UP, BE NICE, AND GET OFF MY BACK!

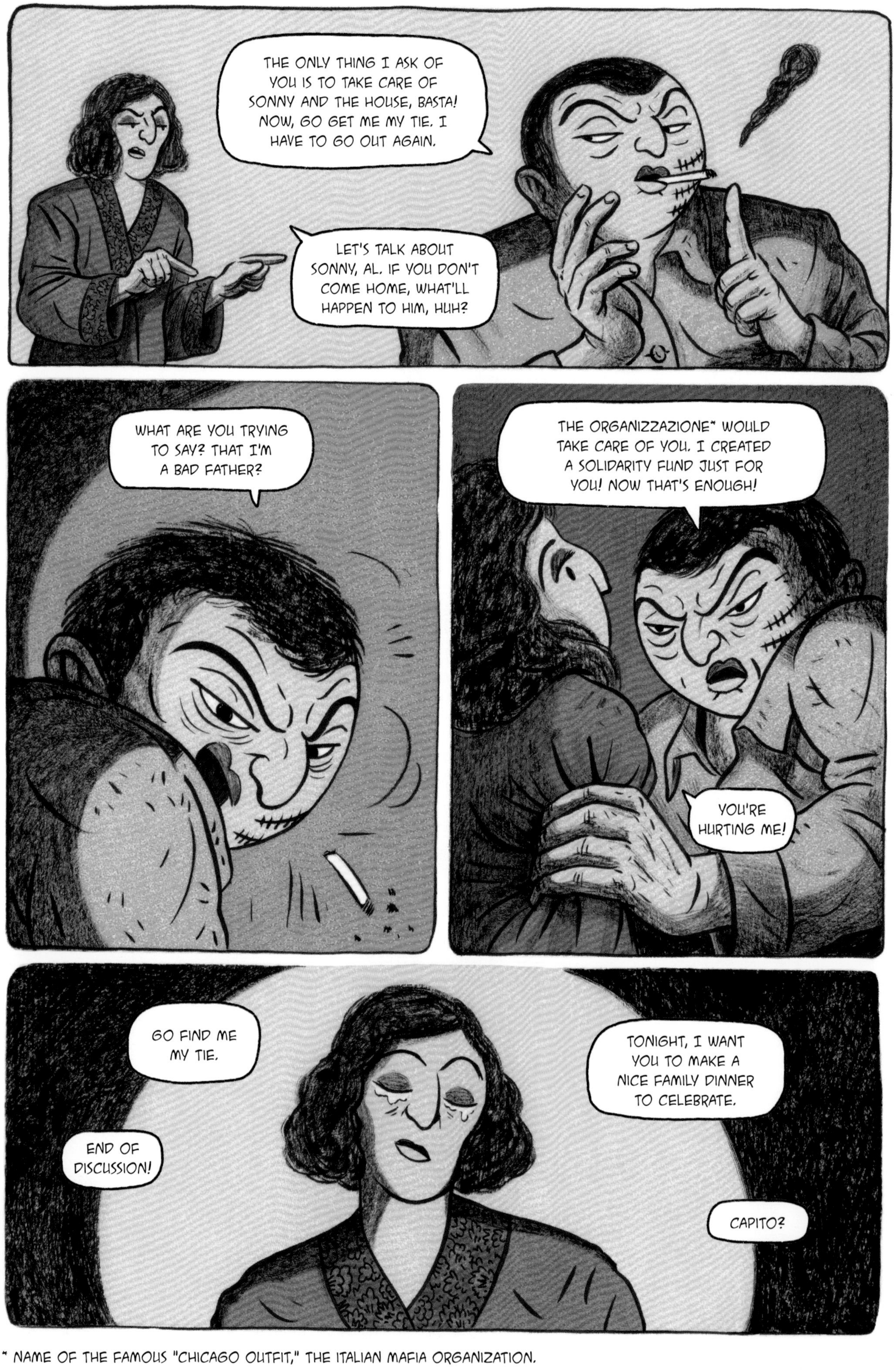
THE ONLY THING I ASK OF YOU IS TO TAKE CARE OF SONNY AND THE HOUSE, BASTA! NOW, GO GET ME MY TIE. I HAVE TO GO OUT AGAIN.
LET'S TALK ABOUT SONNY, AL. IF YOU DON'T COME HOME, WHAT'LL HAPPEN TO HIM, HUH?
WHAT ARE YOU TRYING TO SAY? THAT I'M A BAD FATHER?
THE ORGANIZZAZIONE* WOULD TAKE CARE OF YOU. I CREATED A SOLIDARITY FUND JUST FOR YOU! NOW THAT'S ENOUGH!
YOU'RE HURTING ME!
GO FIND ME MY TIE.
END OF DISCUSSION!
TONIGHT, I WANT YOU TO MAKE A NICE FAMILY DINNER TO CELEBRATE.
CAPITO?

* NAME OF THE FAMOUS "CHICAGO OUTFIT," THE ITALIAN MAFIA ORGANIZATION.

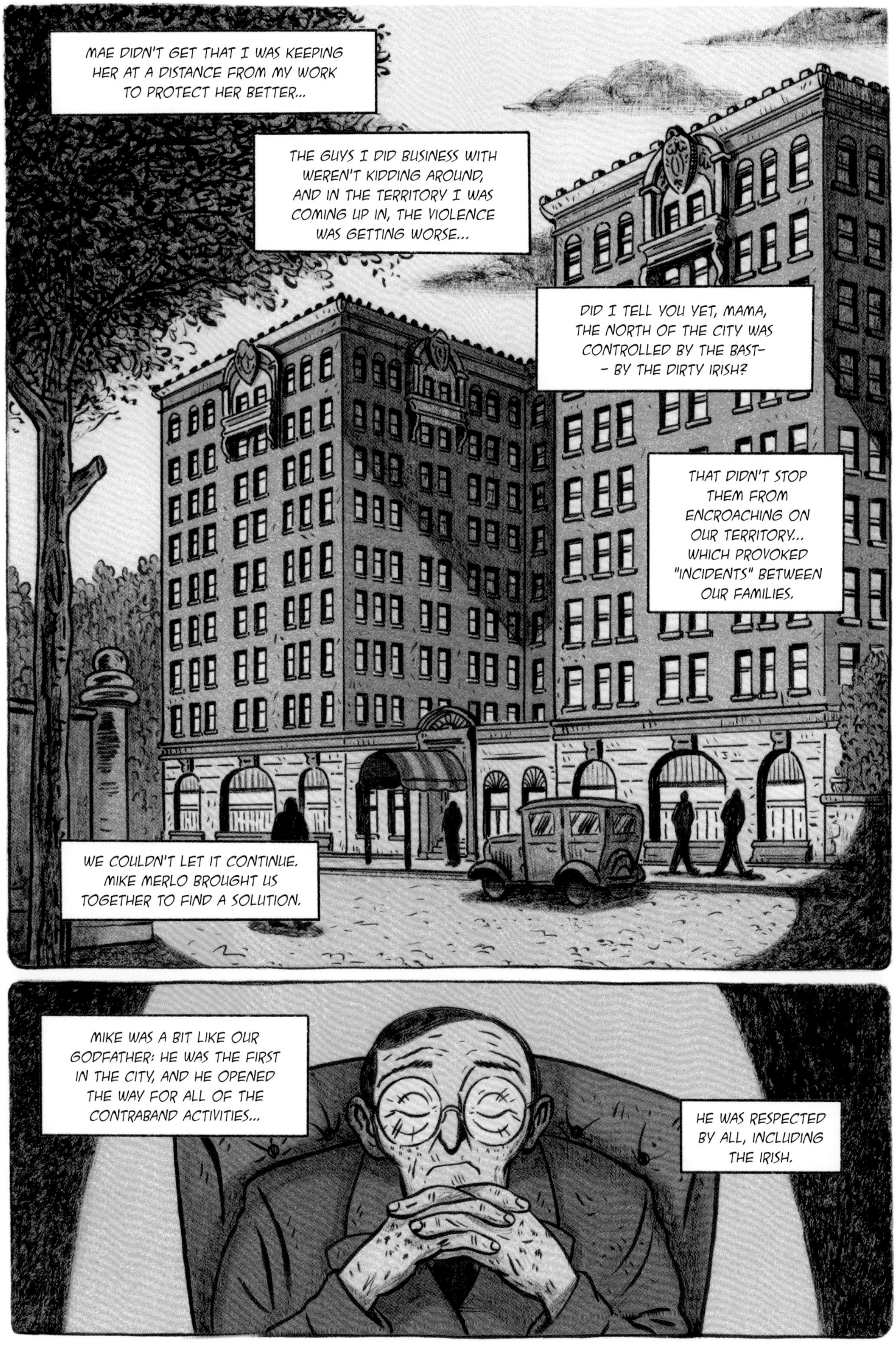
MAE DIDN'T GET THAT I WAS KEEPING HER AT A DISTANCE FROM MY WORK TO PROTECT HER BETTER...
THE GUYS I DID BUSINESS WITH WEREN'T KIDDING AROUND, AND IN THE TERRITORY I WAS COMING UP IN, THE VIOLENCE WAS GETTING WORSE...
DID I TELL YOU YET, MAMA, THE NORTH OF THE CITY WAS CONTROLLED BY THE BAST– – BY THE DIRTY IRISH?
THAT DIDN'T STOP THEM FROM ENCROACHING ON OUR TERRITORY... WHICH PROVOKED "INCIDENTS" BETWEEN OUR FAMILIES.
WE COULDN'T LET IT CONTINUE. MIKE MERLO BROUGHT US TOGETHER TO FIND A SOLUTION.
MIKE WAS A BIT LIKE OUR GODFATHER: HE WAS THE FIRST IN THE CITY, AND HE OPENED THE WAY FOR ALL OF THE CONTRABAND ACTIVITIES...
HE WAS RESPECTED BY ALL, INCLUDING THE IRISH.

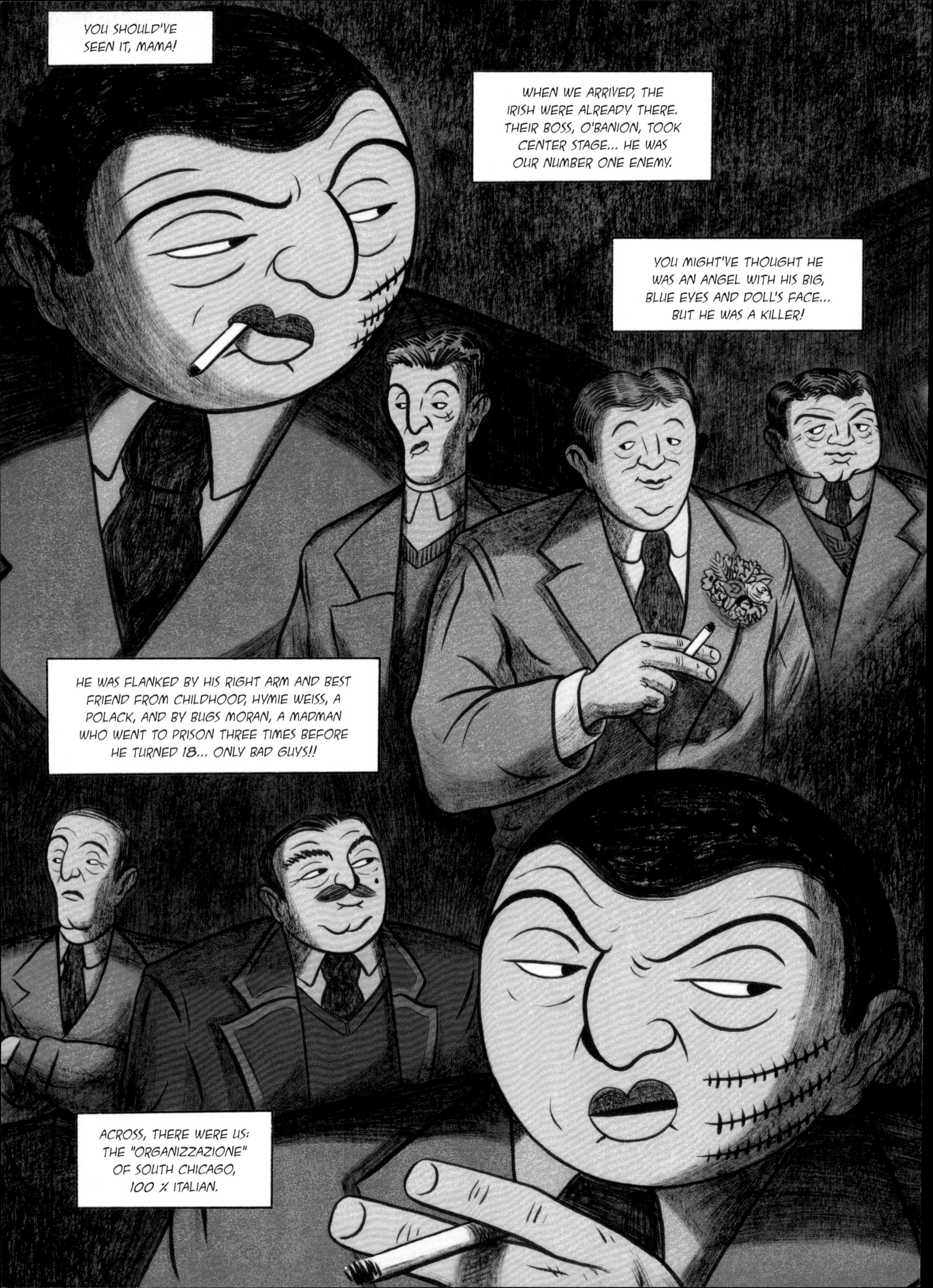
YOU SHOULD'VE SEEN IT, MAMA!
WHEN WE ARRIVED, THE IRISH WERE ALREADY THERE. THEIR BOSS, O'BANION, TOOK CENTER STAGE... HE WAS OUR NUMBER ONE ENEMY.
YOU MIGHT'VE THOUGHT HE WAS AN ANGEL WITH HIS BIG, BLUE EYES AND DOLL'S FACE... BUT HE WAS A KILLER!
HE WAS FLANKED BY HIS RIGHT ARM AND BEST FRIEND FROM CHILDHOOD, HYMIE WEISS, A POLACK, AND BY BUGS MORAN, A MADMAN WHO WENT TO PRISON THREE TIMES BEFORE HE TURNED 18... ONLY BAD GUYS!!
ACROSS, THERE WERE US: THE "ORGANIZZAZIONE" OF SOUTH CHICAGO, 100 % ITALIAN.

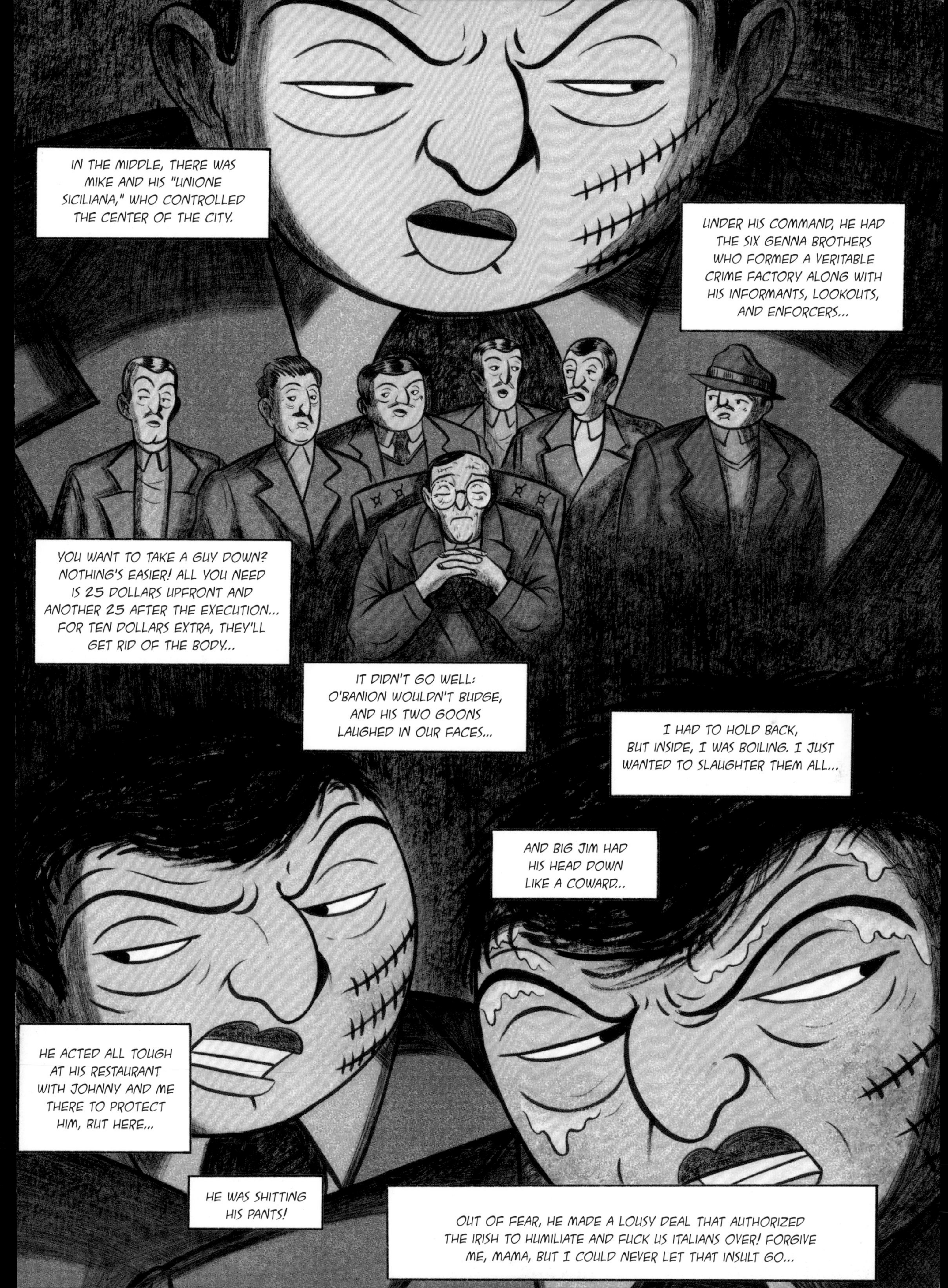
IN THE MIDDLE, THERE WAS MIKE AND HIS "UNIONE SICILIANA," WHO CONTROLLED THE CENTER OF THE CITY.
UNDER HIS COMMAND, HE HAD THE SIX GENNA BROTHERS WHO FORMED A VERITABLE CRIME FACTORY ALONG WITH HIS INFORMANTS, LOOKOUTS, AND ENFORCERS...
YOU WANT TO TAKE A GUY DOWN? NOTHING'S EASIER! ALL YOU NEED IS 25 DOLLARS UPFRONT AND ANOTHER 25 AFTER THE EXECUTION... FOR TEN DOLLARS EXTRA, THEY'LL GET RID OF THE BODY...
IT DIDN'T GO WELL: O'BANION WOULDN'T BUDGE, AND HIS TWO GOONS LAUGHED IN OUR FACES...
I HAD TO HOLD BACK, BUT INSIDE, I WAS BOILING. I JUST WANTED TO SLAUGHTER THEM ALL...
AND BIG JIM HAD HIS HEAD DOWN LIKE A COWARD...
HE ACTED ALL TOUGH AT HIS RESTAURANT WITH JOHNNY AND ME THERE TO PROTECT HIM, BUT HERE...
HE WAS SHITTING HIS PANTS!
OUT OF FEAR, HE MADE A LOUSY DEAL THAT AUTHORIZED THE IRISH TO HUMILIATE AND FUCK US ITALIANS OVER! FORGIVE ME, MAMA, BUT I COULD NEVER LET THAT INSULT GO...

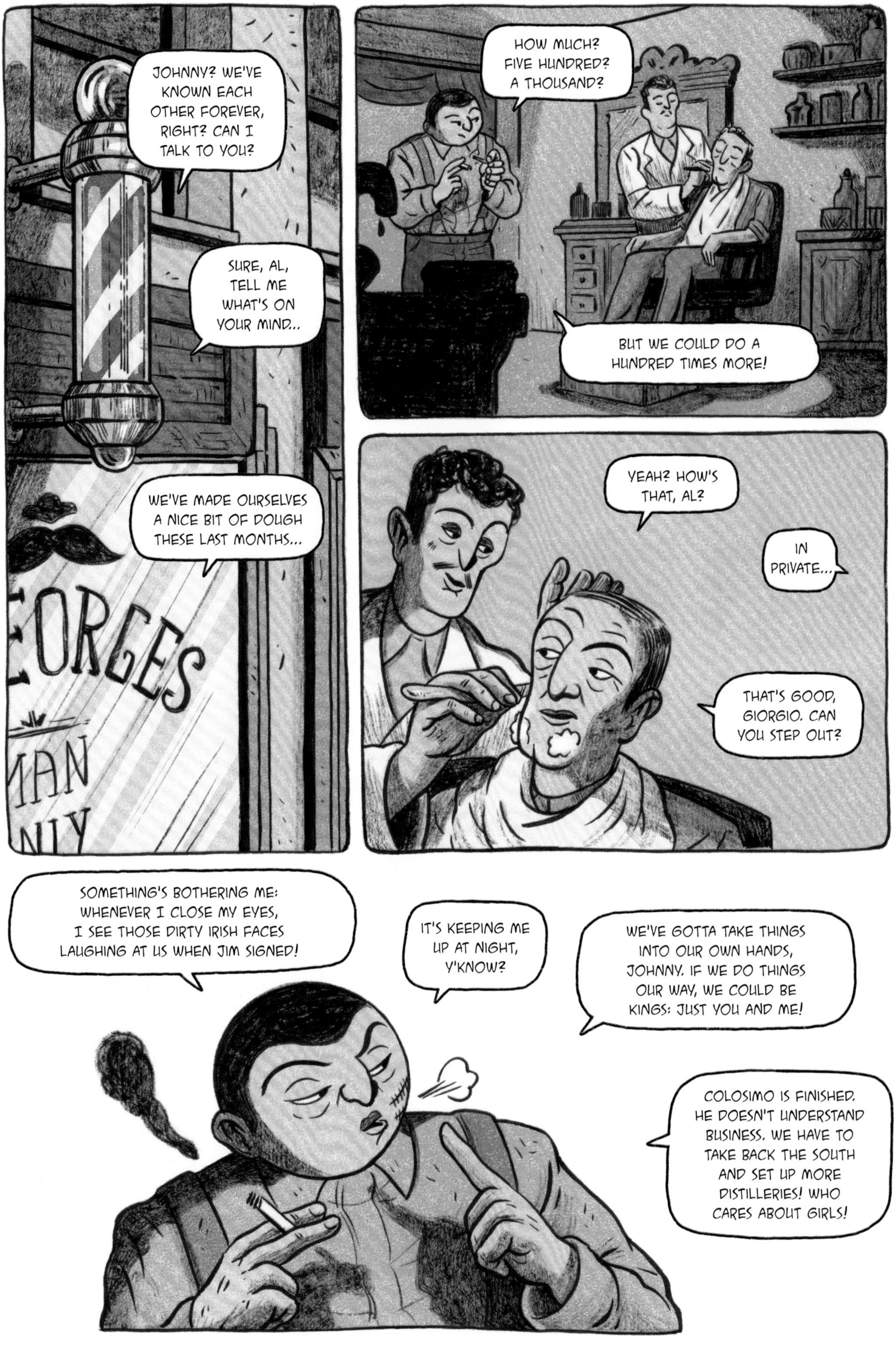
JOHNNY? WE'VE KNOWN EACH OTHER FOREVER, RIGHT? CAN I TALK TO YOU?
SURE, AL, TELL ME WHAT'S ON YOUR MIND...
WE'VE MADE OURSELVES A NICE BIT OF DOUGH THESE LAST MONTHS...
EORGES
MAN
NLY
HOW MUCH? FIVE HUNDRED? A THOUSAND?
BUT WE COULD DO A HUNDRED TIMES MORE!
YEAH? HOW'S THAT, AL?
IN PRIVATE...
THAT'S GOOD, GIORGIO. CAN YOU STEP OUT?
SOMETHING'S BOTHERING ME: WHENEVER I CLOSE MY EYES, I SEE THOSE DIRTY IRISH FACES LAUGHING AT US WHEN JIM SIGNED!
IT'S KEEPING ME UP AT NIGHT, Y'KNOW?
WE'VE GOTTA TAKE THINGS INTO OUR OWN HANDS, JOHNNY. IF WE DO THINGS OUR WAY, WE COULD BE KINGS: JUST YOU AND ME!
COLOSIMO IS FINISHED. HE DOESN'T UNDERSTAND BUSINESS. WE HAVE TO TAKE BACK THE SOUTH AND SET UP MORE DISTILLERIES! WHO CARES ABOUT GIRLS!

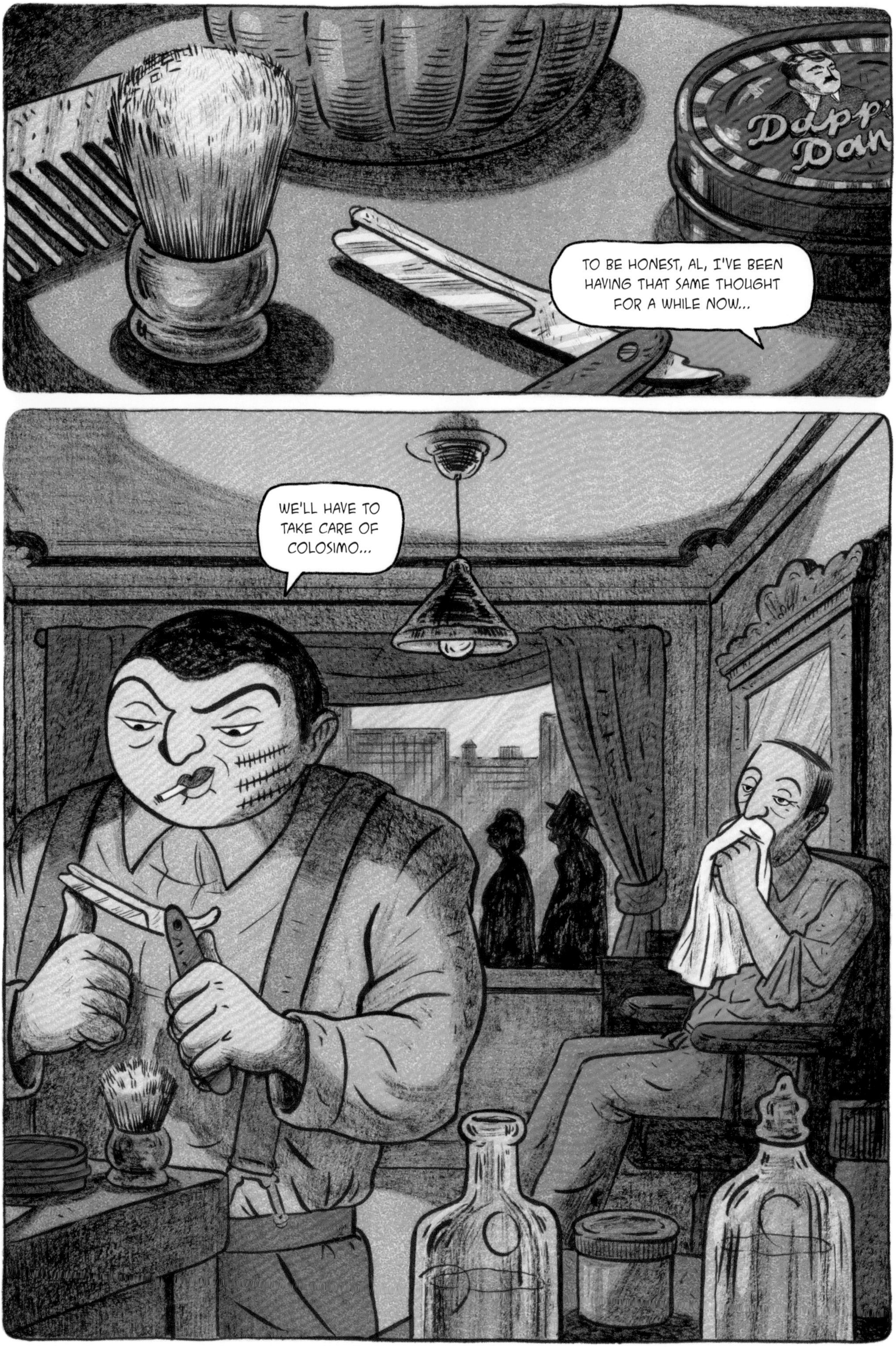
TO BE HONEST, AL, I'VE BEEN HAVING THAT SAME THOUGHT FOR A WHILE NOW...
WE'LL HAVE TO TAKE CARE OF COLOSIMO...

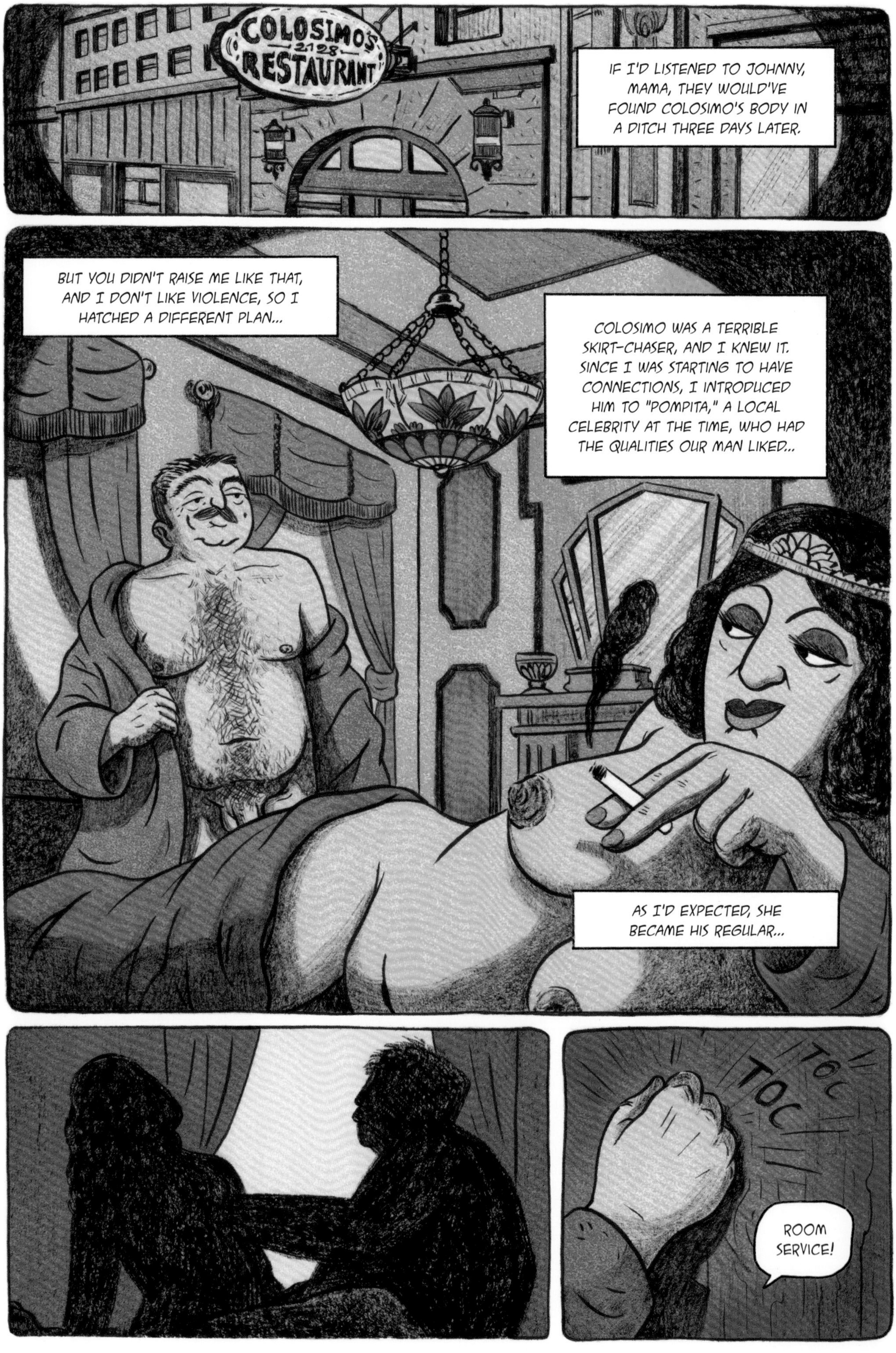
COLOSIMO'S
2128
RESTAURANT
IF I'D LISTENED TO JOHNNY, MAMA, THEY WOULD'VE FOUND COLOSIMO'S BODY IN A DITCH THREE DAYS LATER.
BUT YOU DIDN'T RAISE ME LIKE THAT, AND I DON'T LIKE VIOLENCE, SO I HATCHED A DIFFERENT PLAN...
COLOSIMO WAS A TERRIBLE SKIRT-CHASER, AND I KNEW IT. SINCE I WAS STARTING TO HAVE CONNECTIONS, I INTRODUCED HIM TO "POMPITA," A LOCAL CELEBRITY AT THE TIME, WHO HAD THE QUALITIES OUR MAN LIKED...
AS I'D EXPECTED, SHE BECAME HIS REGULAR...
TOC TOC
ROOM SERVICE!

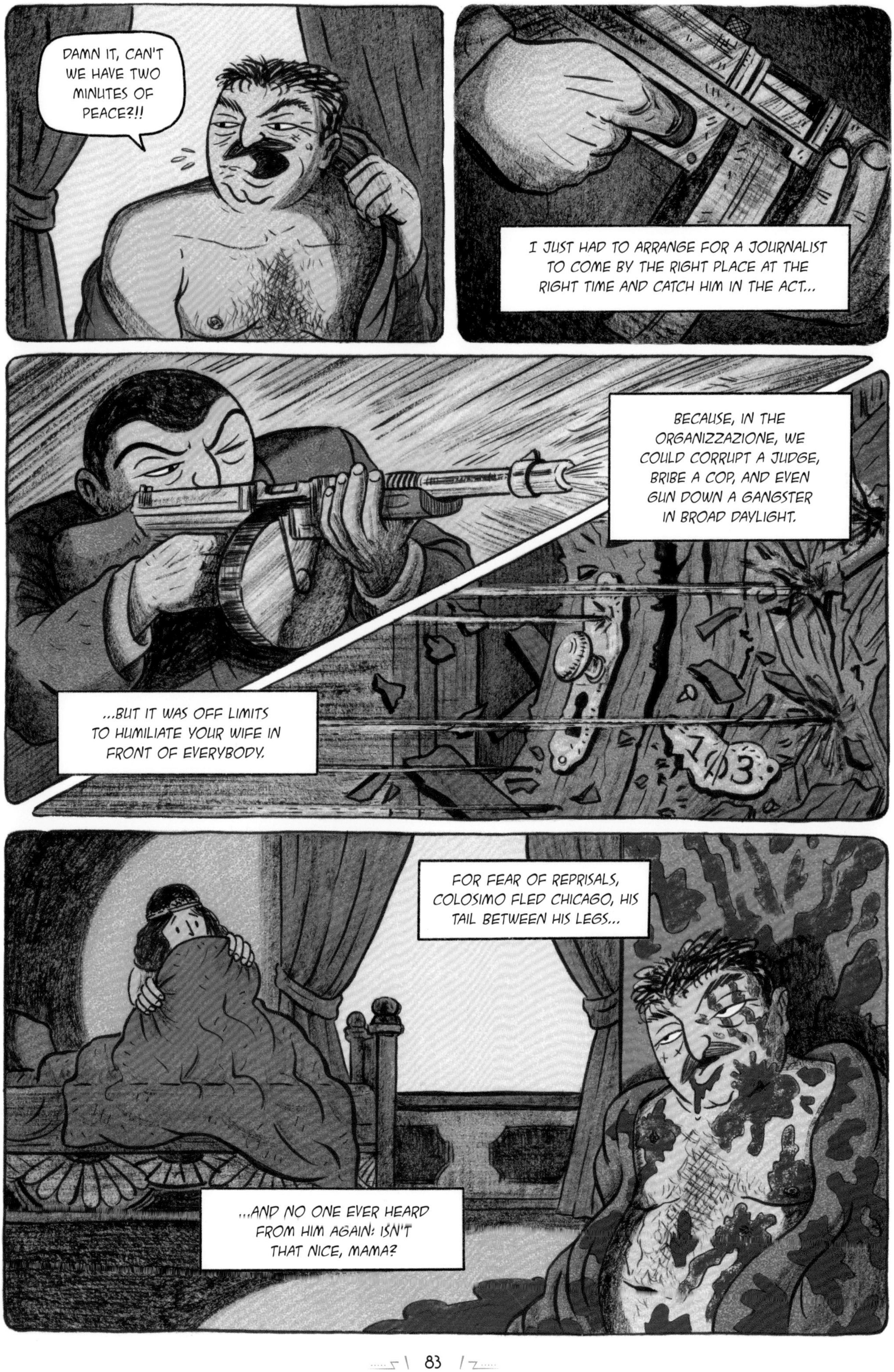
DAMN IT, CAN'T WE HAVE TWO MINUTES OF PEACE?!!
I JUST HAD TO ARRANGE FOR A JOURNALIST TO COME BY THE RIGHT PLACE AT THE RIGHT TIME AND CATCH HIM IN THE ACT...
BECAUSE, IN THE ORGANIZZAZIONE, WE COULD CORRUPT A JUDGE, BRIBE A COP, AND EVEN GUN DOWN A GANGSTER IN BROAD DAYLIGHT.
...BUT IT WAS OFF LIMITS TO HUMILIATE YOUR WIFE IN FRONT OF EVERYBODY.
FOR FEAR OF REPRISALS, COLOSIMO FLED CHICAGO, HIS TAIL BETWEEN HIS LEGS...
...AND NO ONE EVER HEARD FROM HIM AGAIN: ISN'T THAT NICE, MAMA?

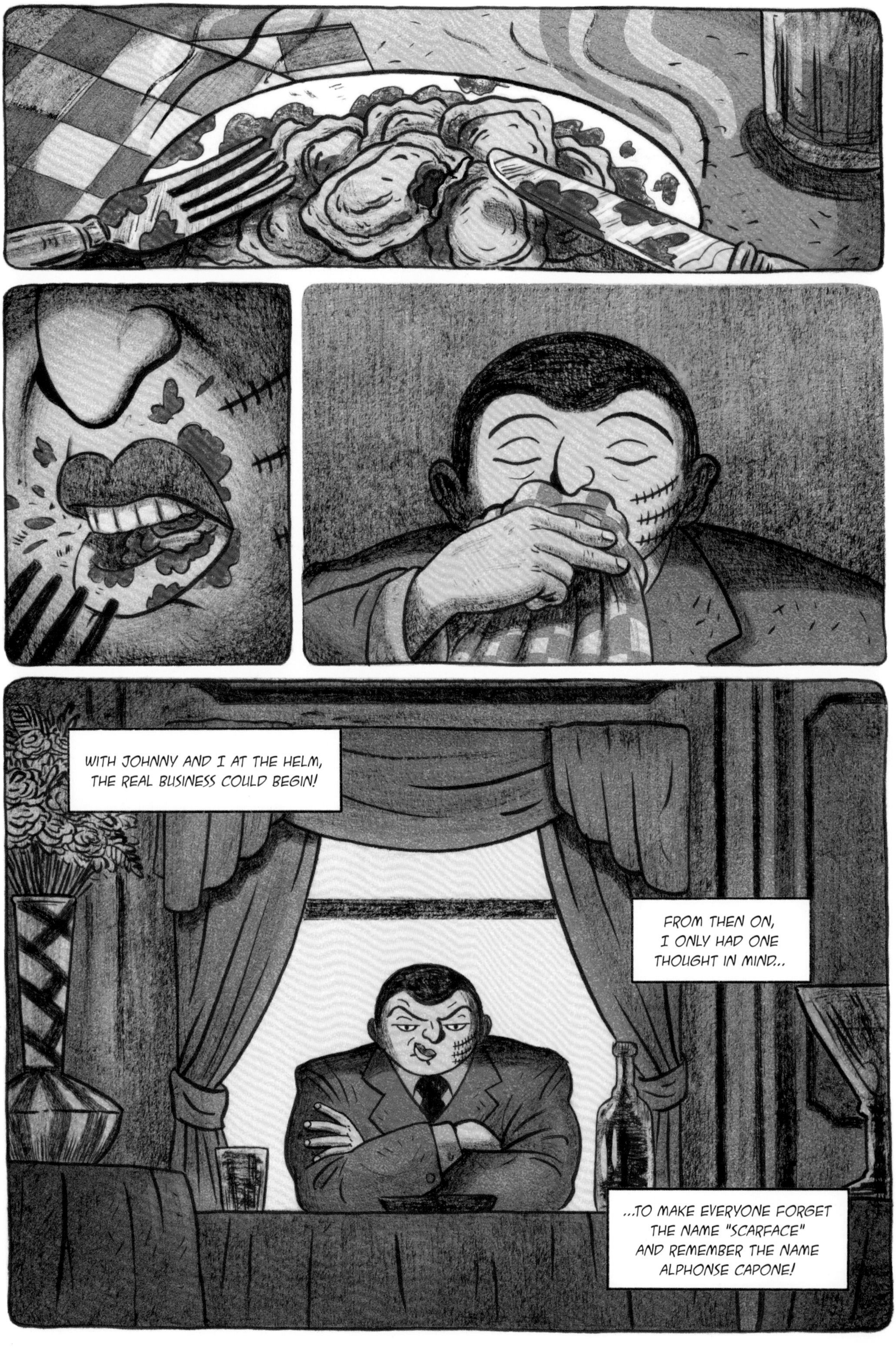
WITH JOHNNY AND I AT THE HELM, THE REAL BUSINESS COULD BEGIN!
FROM THEN ON, I ONLY HAD ONE THOUGHT IN MIND...
...TO MAKE EVERYONE FORGET THE NAME "SCARFACE" AND REMEMBER THE NAME ALPHONSE CAPONE!

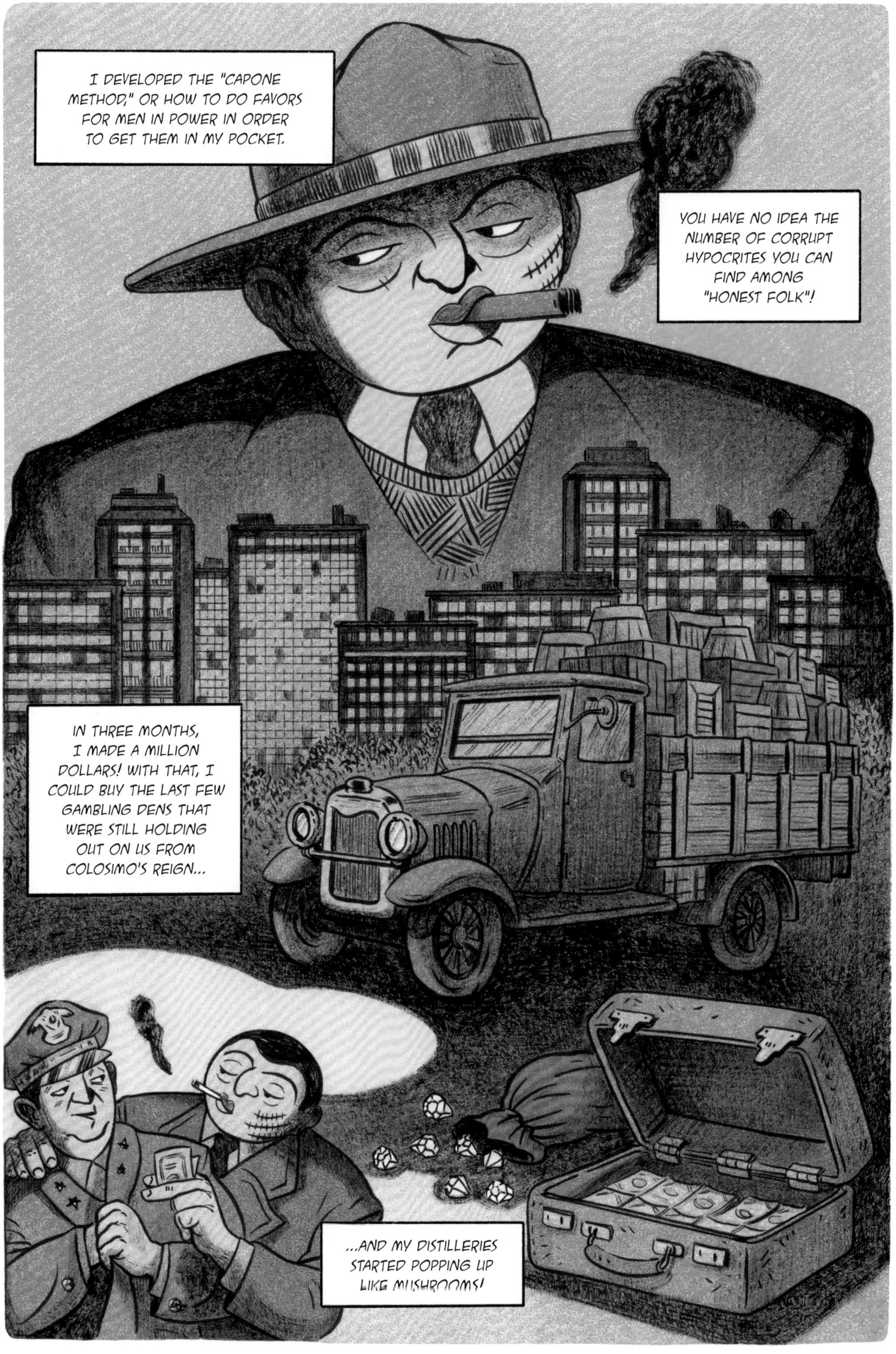
I DEVELOPED THE "CAPONE METHOD," OR HOW TO DO FAVORS FOR MEN IN POWER IN ORDER TO GET THEM IN MY POCKET.
YOU HAVE NO IDEA THE NUMBER OF CORRUPT HYPOCRITES YOU CAN FIND AMONG "HONEST FOLK"!
IN THREE MONTHS, I MADE A MILLION DOLLARS! WITH THAT, I COULD BUY THE LAST FEW GAMBLING DENS THAT WERE STILL HOLDING OUT ON US FROM COLOSIMO'S REIGN...
...AND MY DISTILLERIES STARTED POPPING UP LIKE MUSHROOMS!

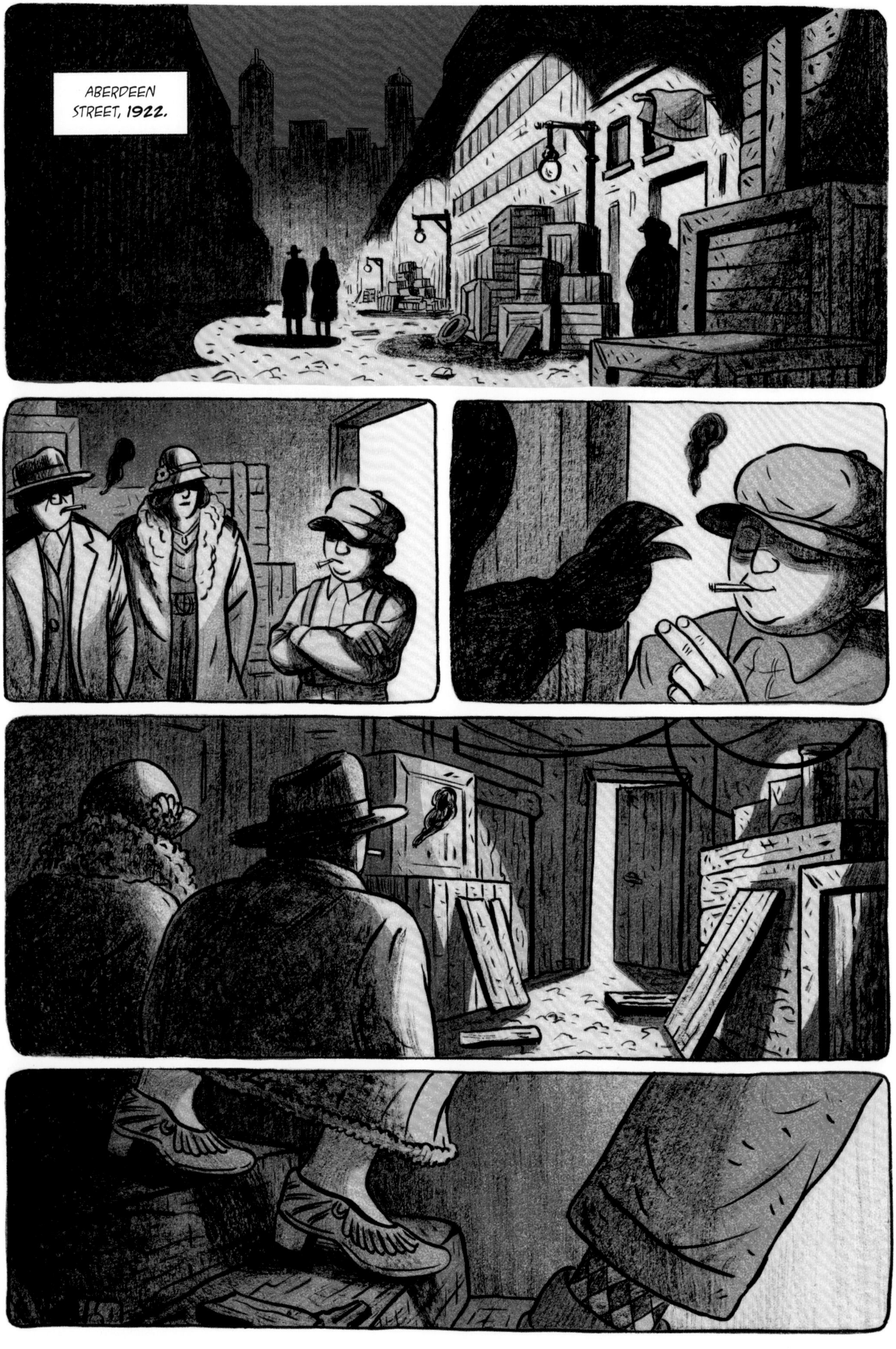
ABERDEEN
STREET, 1922.

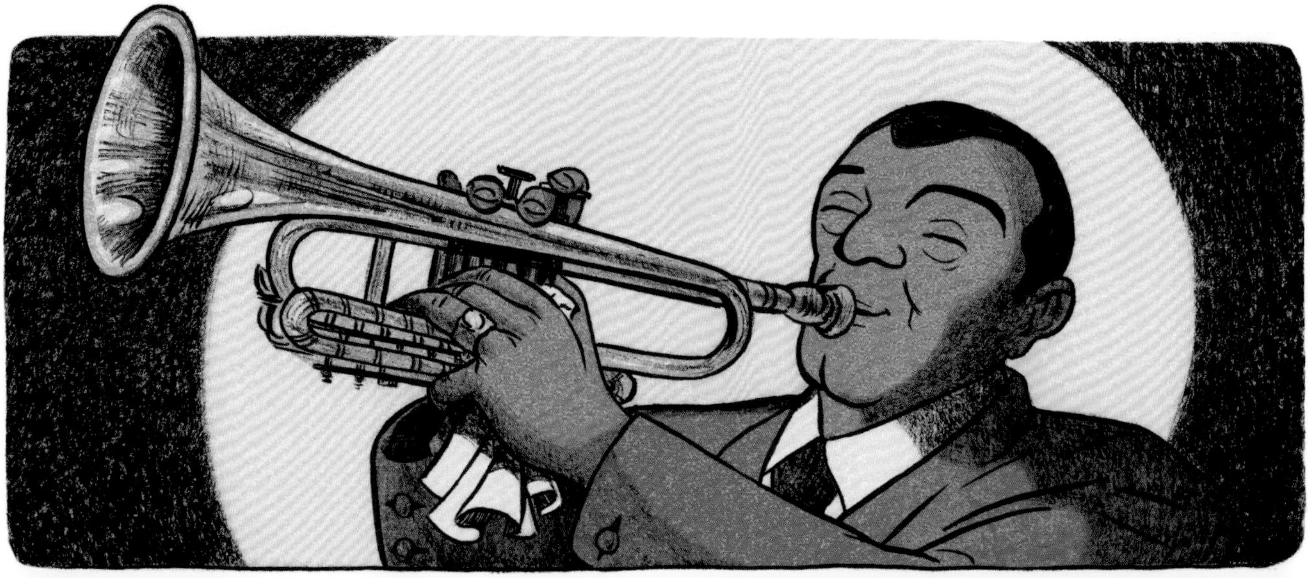

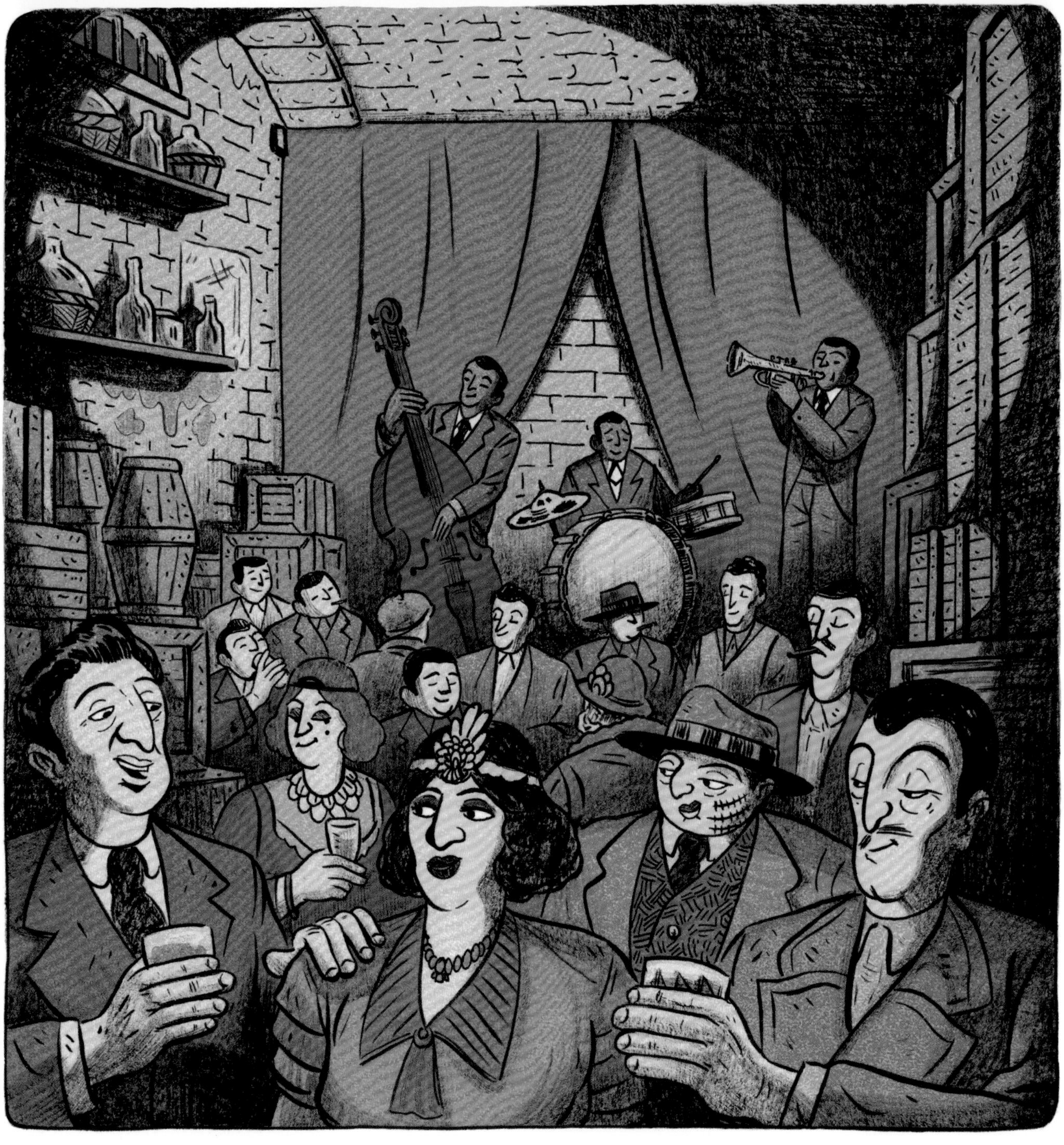

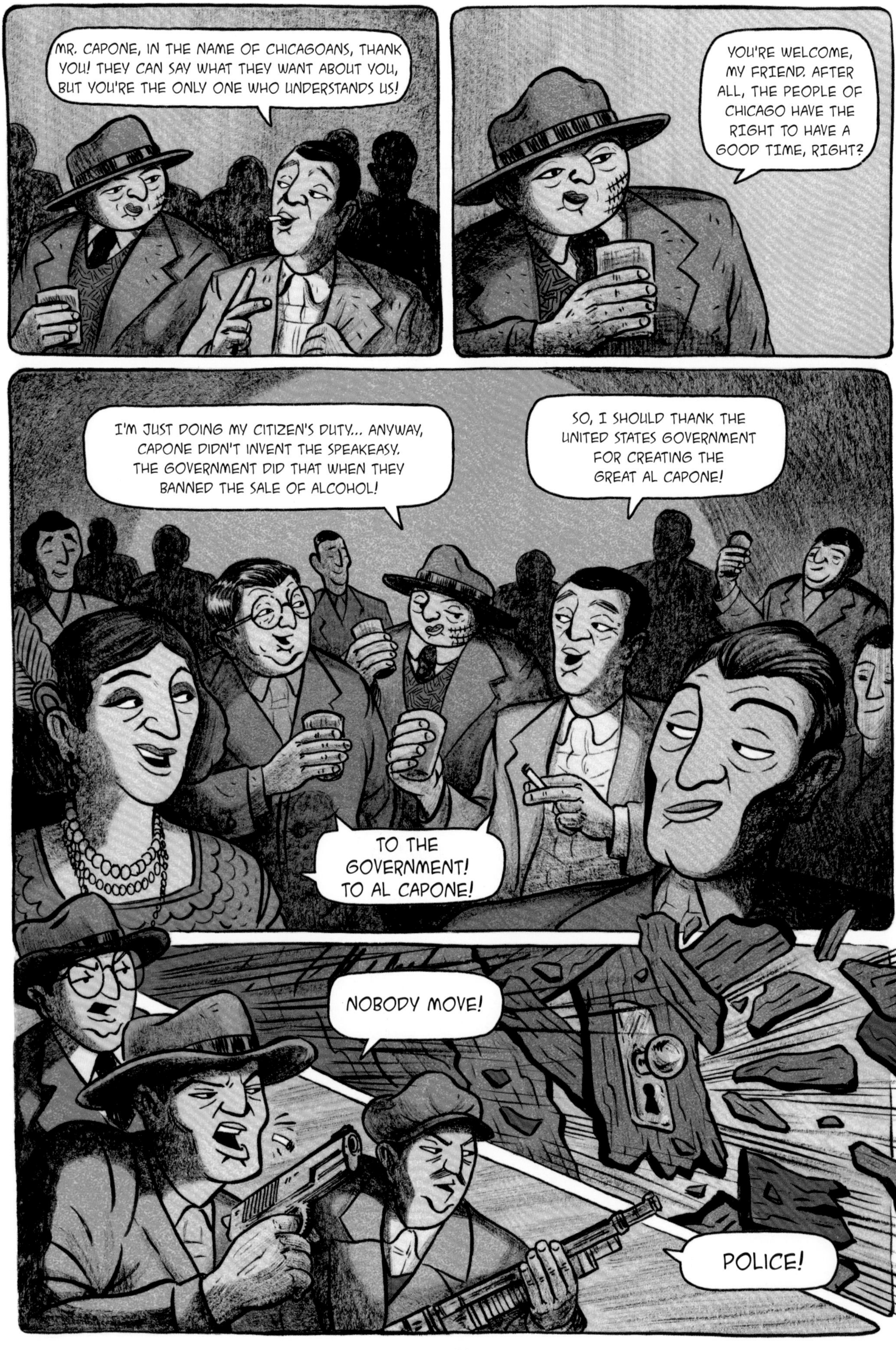
MR. CAPONE, IN THE NAME OF CHICAGOANS, THANK YOU! THEY CAN SAY WHAT THEY WANT ABOUT YOU, BUT YOU'RE THE ONLY ONE WHO UNDERSTANDS US!
YOU'RE WELCOME, MY FRIEND. AFTER ALL, THE PEOPLE OF CHICAGO HAVE THE RIGHT TO HAVE A GOOD TIME, RIGHT?
I'M JUST DOING MY CITIZEN'S DUTY... ANYWAY, CAPONE DIDN'T INVENT THE SPEAKEASY. THE GOVERNMENT DID THAT WHEN THEY BANNED THE SALE OF ALCOHOL!
SO, I SHOULD THANK THE UNITED STATES GOVERNMENT FOR CREATING THE GREAT AL CAPONE!
TO THE GOVERNMENT! TO AL CAPONE!
NOBODY MOVE!
POLICE!

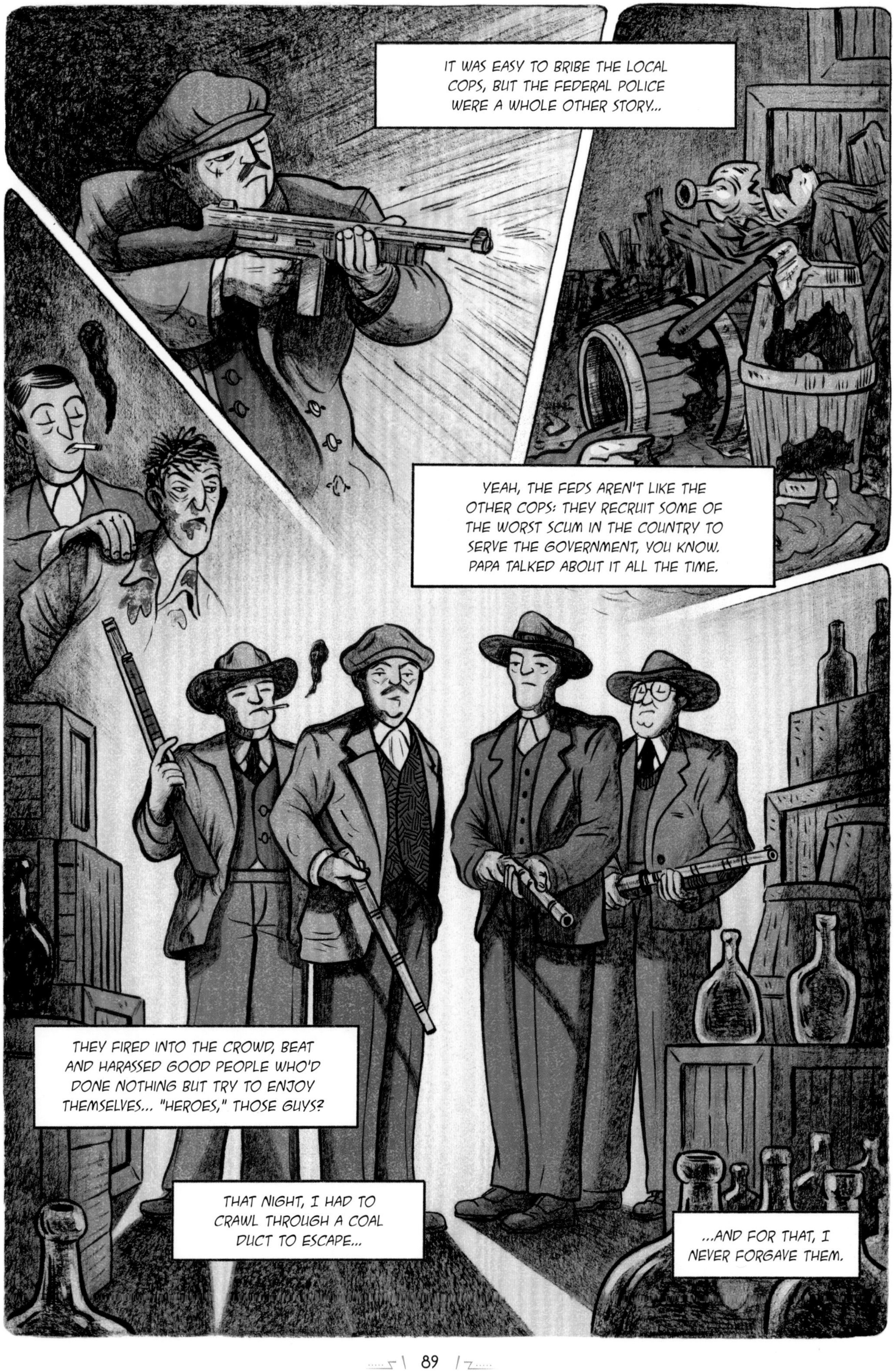
IT WAS EASY TO BRIBE THE LOCAL COPS, BUT THE FEDERAL POLICE WERE A WHOLE OTHER STORY...
YEAH, THE FEDS AREN'T LIKE THE OTHER COPS: THEY RECRUIT SOME OF THE WORST SCUM IN THE COUNTRY TO SERVE THE GOVERNMENT, YOU KNOW. PAPA TALKED ABOUT IT ALL THE TIME.
THEY FIRED INTO THE CROWD, BEAT AND HARASSED GOOD PEOPLE WHO'D DONE NOTHING BUT TRY TO ENJOY THEMSELVES... "HEROES," THOSE GUYS?
THAT NIGHT, I HAD TO CRAWL THROUGH A COAL DUCT TO ESCAPE...
...AND FOR THAT, I NEVER FORGAVE THEM.

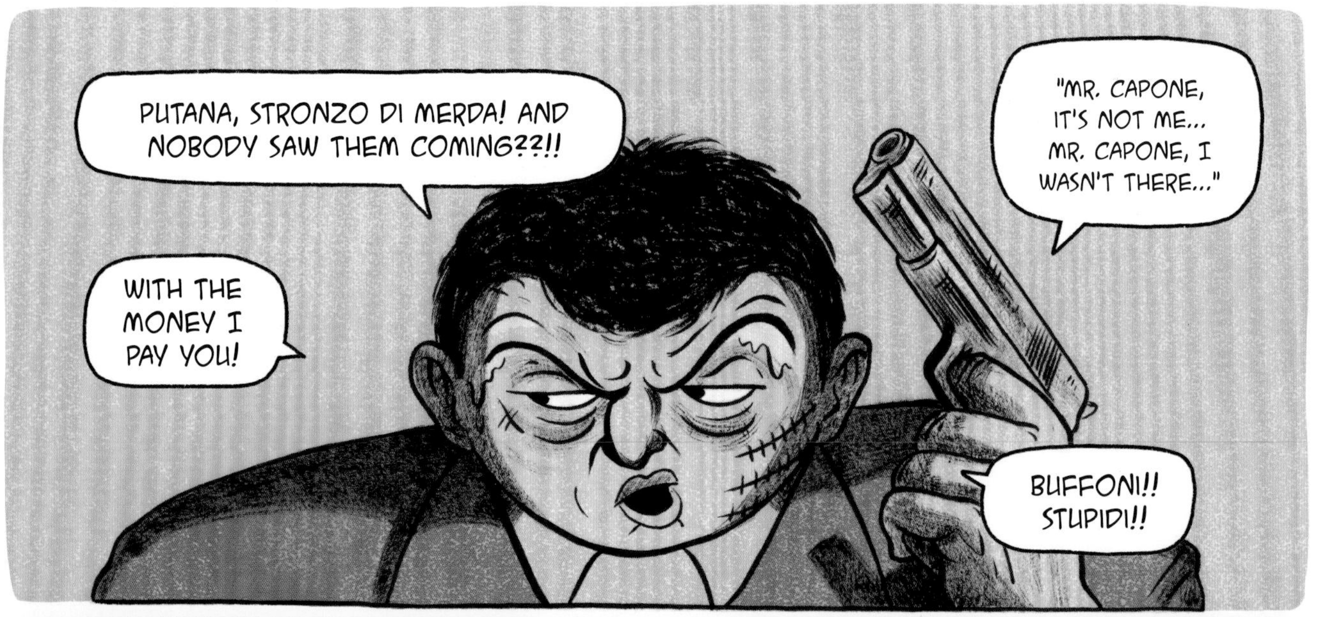
PUTANA, STRONZO DI MERDA! AND NOBODY SAW THEM COMING??!!
WITH THE MONEY I PAY YOU!
"MR. CAPONE, IT'S NOT ME... MR. CAPONE, I WASN'T THERE..."
BUFFONI!! STUPIDI!!

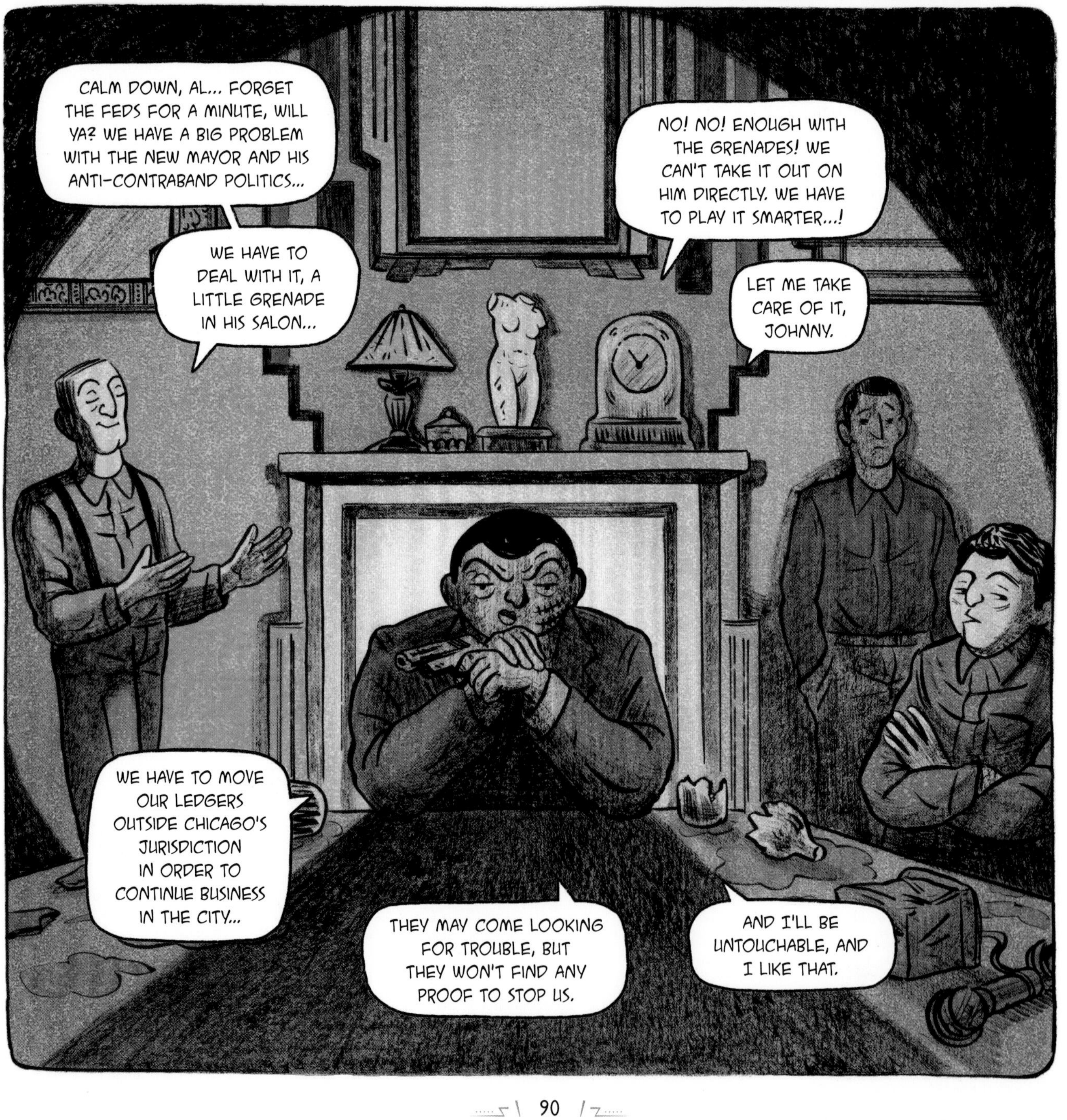
CALM DOWN, AL... FORGET THE FEDS FOR A MINUTE, WILL YA? WE HAVE A BIG PROBLEM WITH THE NEW MAYOR AND HIS ANTI-CONTRABAND POLITICS...
WE HAVE TO DEAL WITH IT, A LITTLE GRENADE IN HIS SALON...
NO! NO! ENOUGH WITH THE GRENADES! WE CAN'T TAKE IT OUT ON HIM DIRECTLY. WE HAVE TO PLAY IT SMARTER...!
LET ME TAKE CARE OF IT, JOHNNY.
WE HAVE TO MOVE OUR LEDGERS OUTSIDE CHICAGO'S JURISDICTION IN ORDER TO CONTINUE BUSINESS IN THE CITY...
THEY MAY COME LOOKING FOR TROUBLE, BUT THEY WON'T FIND ANY PROOF TO STOP US.
AND I'LL BE UNTOUCHABLE, AND I LIKE THAT.

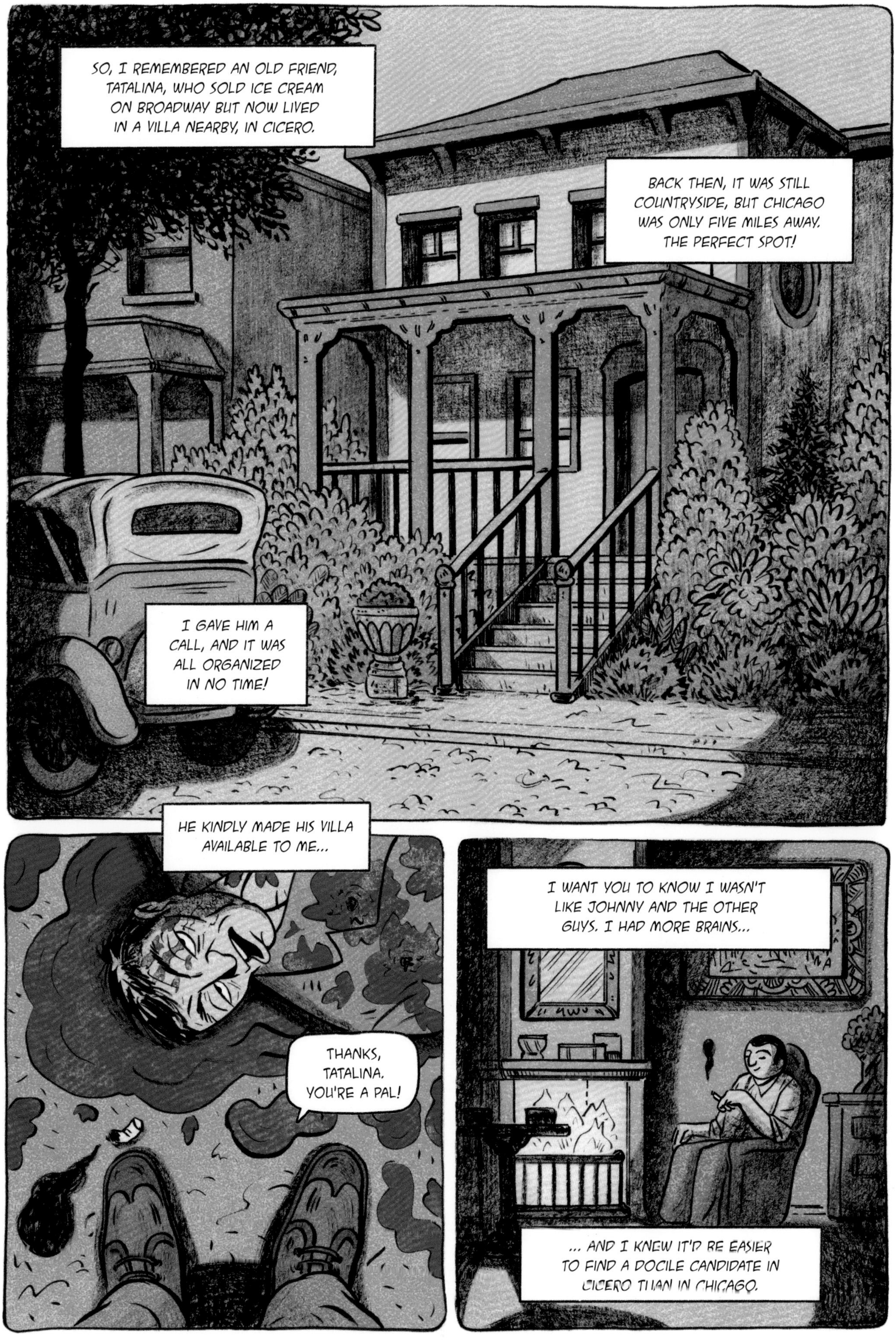
SO, I REMEMBERED AN OLD FRIEND, TATALINA, WHO SOLD ICE CREAM ON BROADWAY BUT NOW LIVED IN A VILLA NEARBY, IN CICERO.
BACK THEN, IT WAS STILL COUNTRYSIDE, BUT CHICAGO WAS ONLY FIVE MILES AWAY. THE PERFECT SPOT!
I GAVE HIM A CALL, AND IT WAS ALL ORGANIZED IN NO TIME!
HE KINDLY MADE HIS VILLA AVAILABLE TO ME...
THANKS, TATALINA. YOU'RE A PAL!
I WANT YOU TO KNOW I WASN'T LIKE JOHNNY AND THE OTHER GUYS. I HAD MORE BRAINS...
... AND I KNEW IT'D BE EASIER TO FIND A DOCILE CANDIDATE IN CICERO THAN IN CHICAGO.

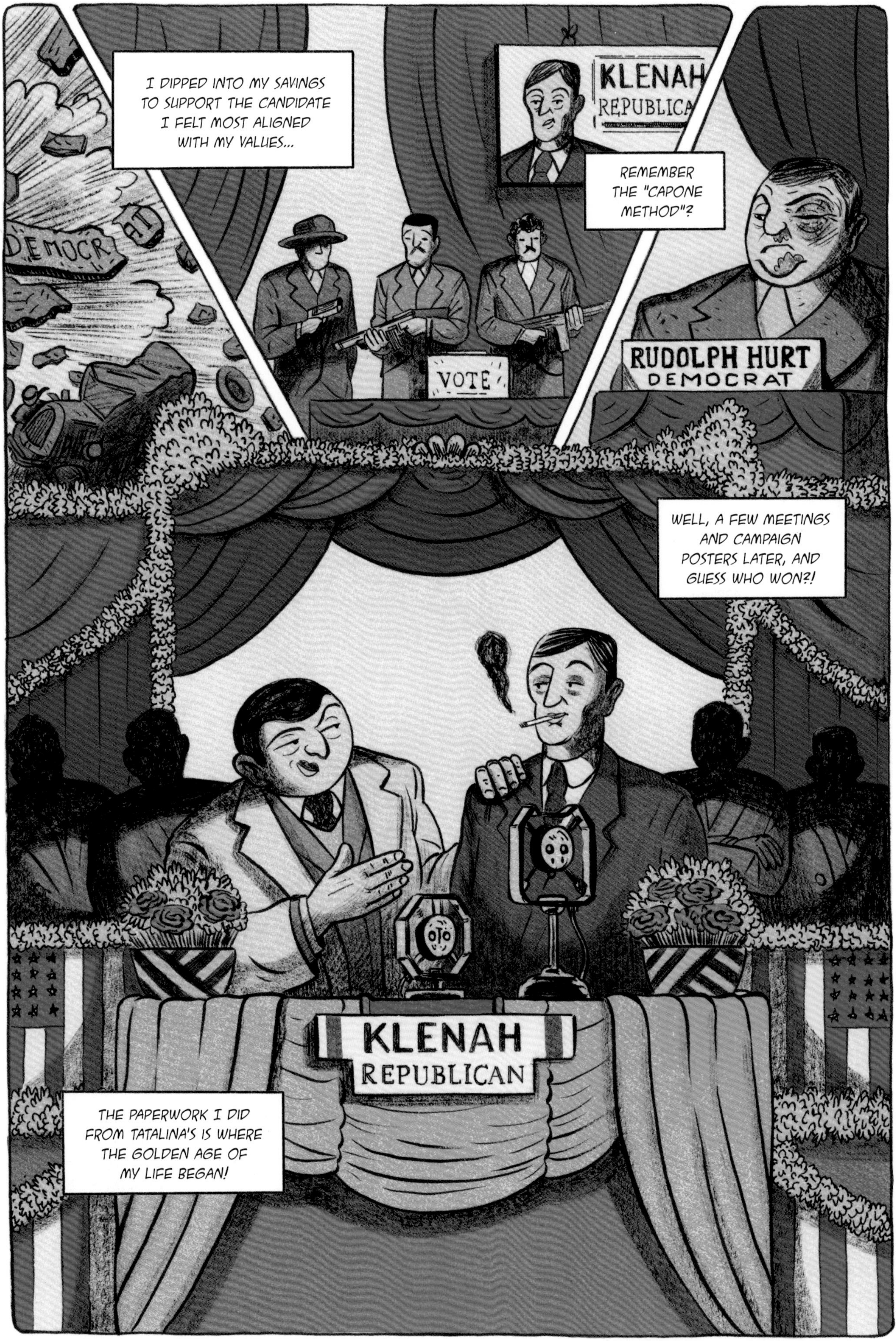
I DIPPED INTO MY SAVINGS TO SUPPORT THE CANDIDATE I FELT MOST ALIGNED WITH MY VALUES...
DEMOCR
KLENAH
REPUBLICA
VOTE
REMEMBER THE "CAPONE METHOD"?
RUDOLPH HURT
DEMOCRAT
WELL, A FEW MEETINGS AND CAMPAIGN POSTERS LATER, AND GUESS WHO WON?!
KLENAH
REPUBLICAN
THE PAPERWORK I DID FROM TATALINA'S IS WHERE THE GOLDEN AGE OF MY LIFE BEGAN!

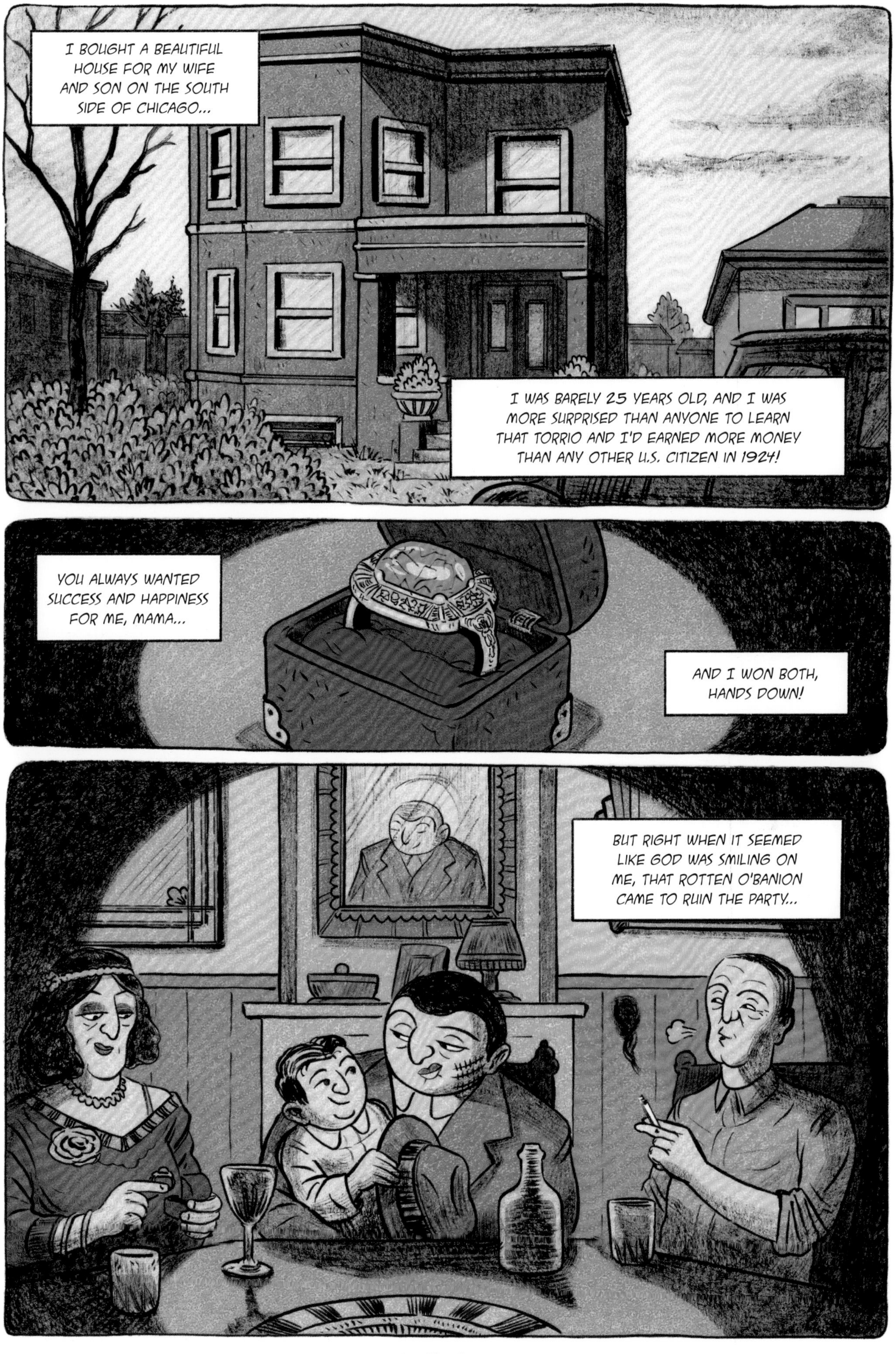
I BOUGHT A BEAUTIFUL HOUSE FOR MY WIFE AND SON ON THE SOUTH SIDE OF CHICAGO...
I WAS BARELY 25 YEARS OLD, AND I WAS MORE SURPRISED THAN ANYONE TO LEARN THAT TORRIO AND I'D EARNED MORE MONEY THAN ANY OTHER U.S. CITIZEN IN 1924!
YOU ALWAYS WANTED SUCCESS AND HAPPINESS FOR ME, MAMA...
AND I WON BOTH, HANDS DOWN!
BUT RIGHT WHEN IT SEEMED LIKE GOD WAS SMILING ON ME, THAT ROTTEN O'BANION CAME TO RUIN THE PARTY...

CHAPTER 3

The King of Chicago

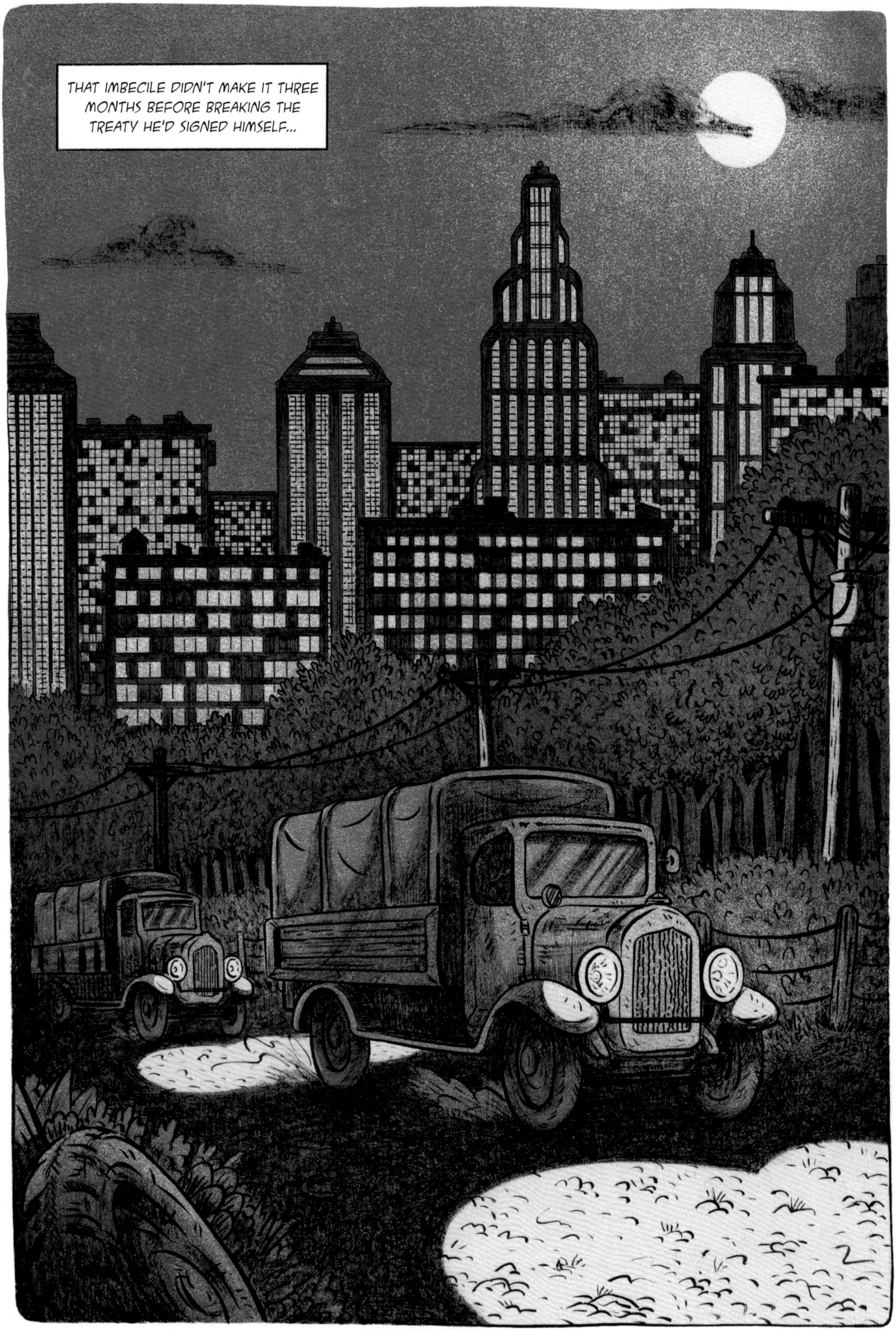
THAT IMBECILE DIDN'T MAKE IT THREE MONTHS BEFORE BREAKING THE TREATY HE'D SIGNED HIMSELF...

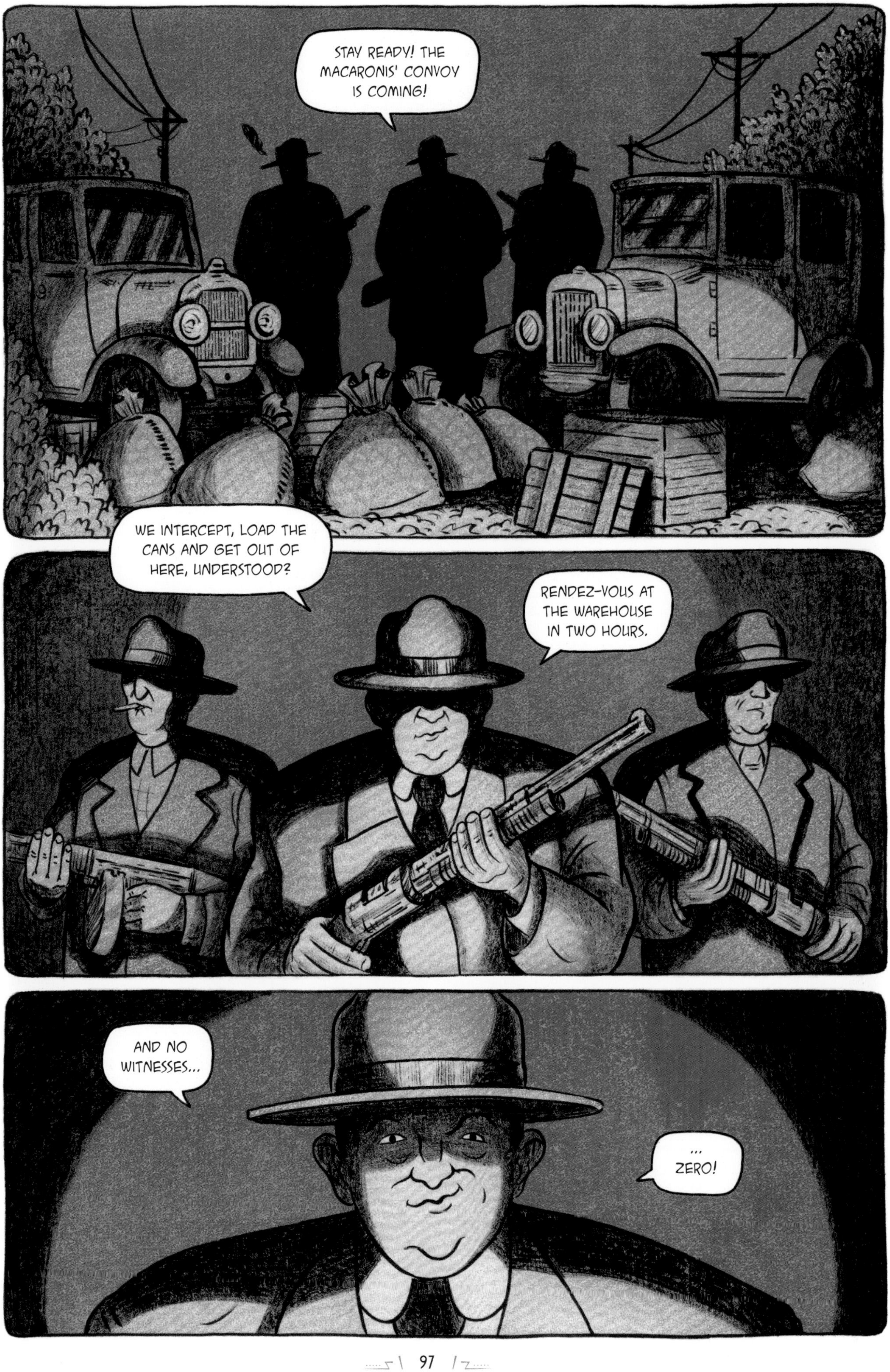
STAY READY! THE MACARONIS' CONVOY IS COMING!
WE INTERCEPT, LOAD THE CANS AND GET OUT OF HERE, UNDERSTOOD?
RENDEZ-VOUS AT THE WAREHOUSE IN TWO HOURS.
AND NO WITNESSES...
... ZERO!

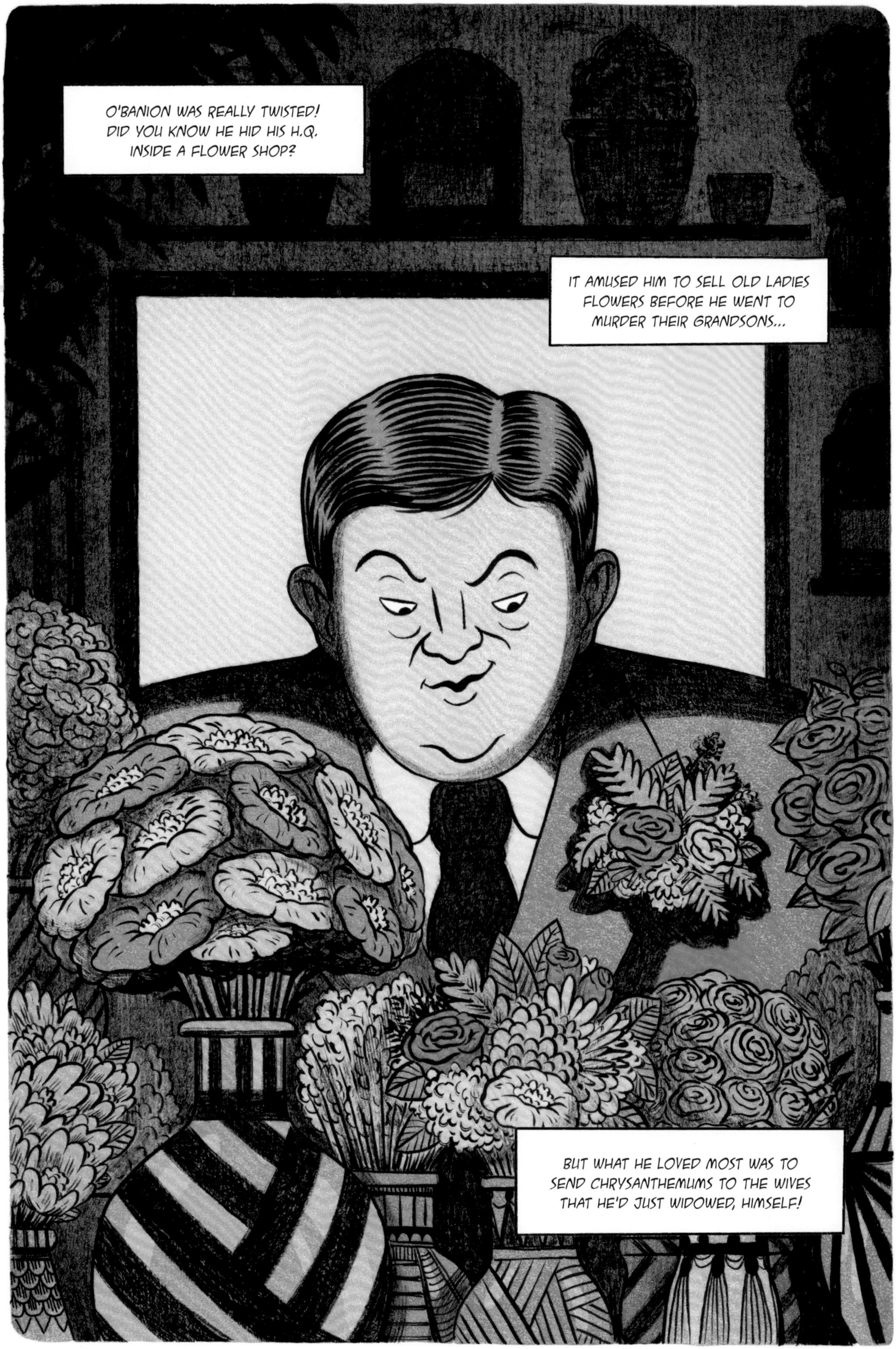
O'BANION WAS REALLY TWISTED! DID YOU KNOW HE HID HIS H.Q. INSIDE A FLOWER SHOP?
IT AMUSED HIM TO SELL OLD LADIES FLOWERS BEFORE HE WENT TO MURDER THEIR GRANDSONS...
BUT WHAT HE LOVED MOST WAS TO SEND CHRYSANTHEMUMS TO THE WIVES THAT HE'D JUST WIDOWED, HIMSELF!

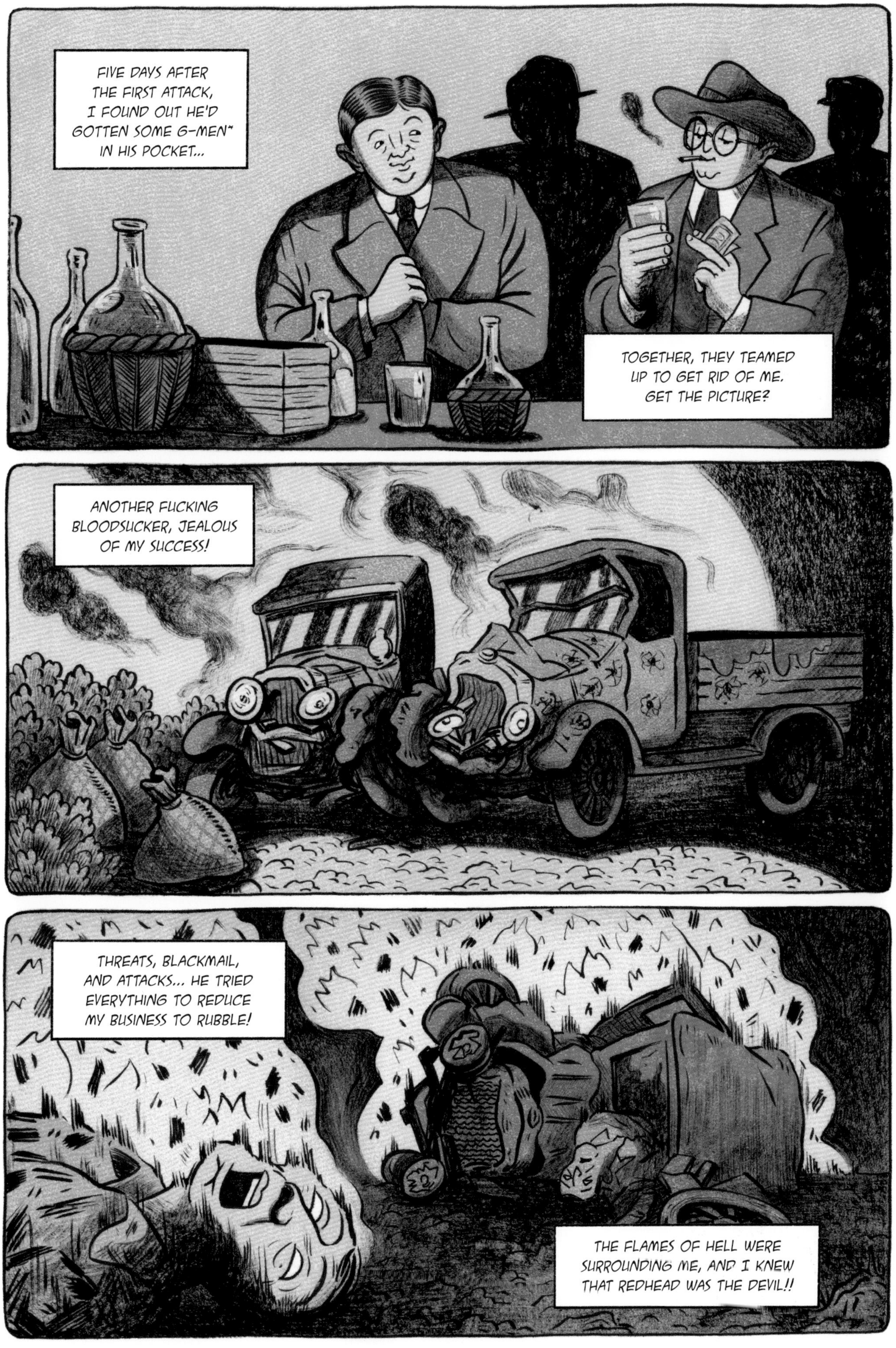
FIVE DAYS AFTER THE FIRST ATTACK, I FOUND OUT HE'D GOTTEN SOME G-MEN* IN HIS POCKET...
TOGETHER, THEY TEAMED UP TO GET RID OF ME. GET THE PICTURE?
ANOTHER FUCKING BLOODSUCKER, JEALOUS OF MY SUCCESS!
THREATS, BLACKMAIL, AND ATTACKS... HE TRIED EVERYTHING TO REDUCE MY BUSINESS TO RUBBLE!
THE FLAMES OF HELL WERE SURROUNDING ME, AND I KNEW THAT REDHEAD WAS THE DEVIL!!

*SLANG TERM FOR AMERICAN SPECIAL AGENTS BETWEEN THE 1930S AND 1950S, ESPECIALLY FBI AGENTS.

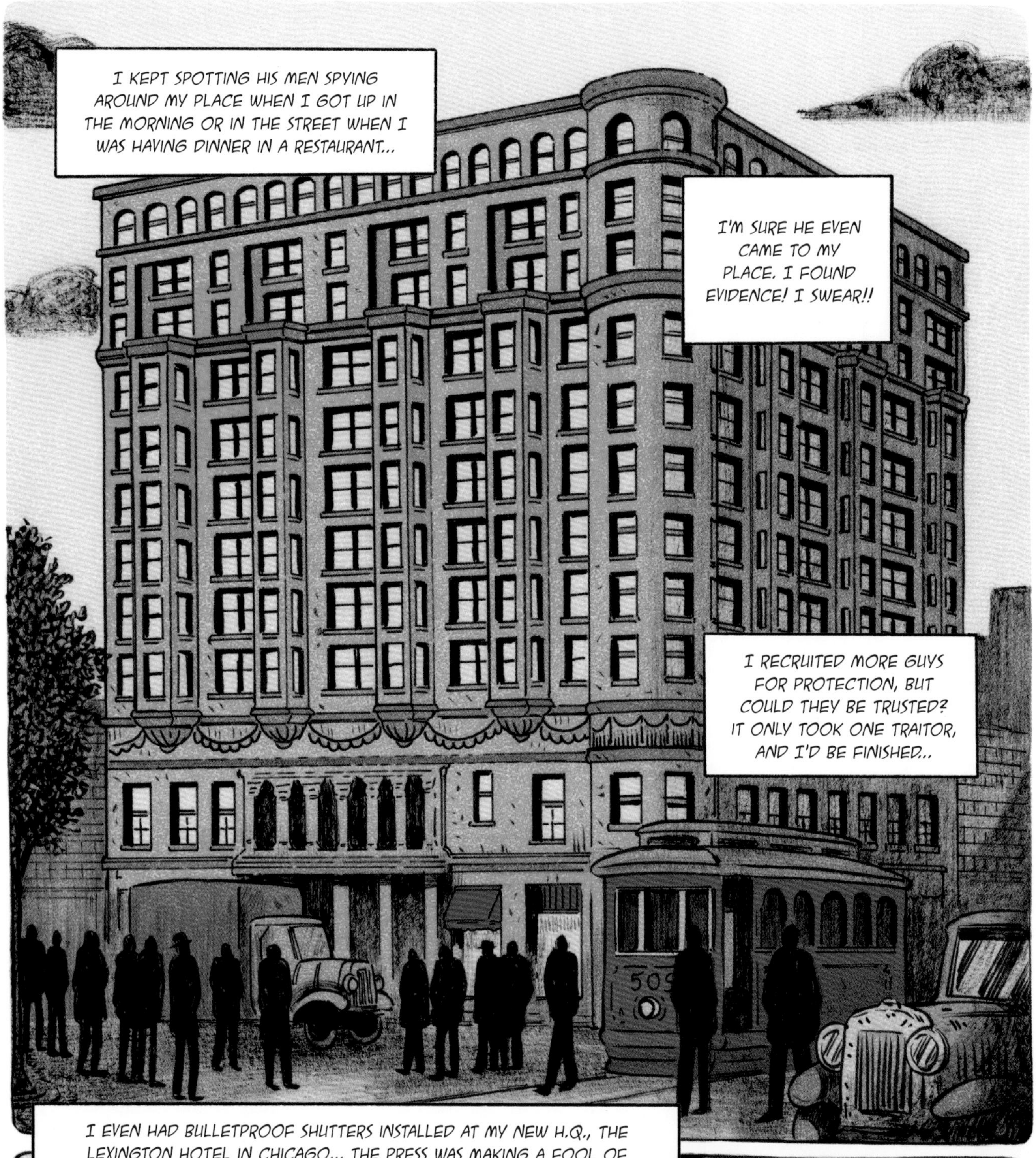
I KEPT SPOTTING HIS MEN SPYING AROUND MY PLACE WHEN I GOT UP IN THE MORNING OR IN THE STREET WHEN I WAS HAVING DINNER IN A RESTAURANT...
I'M SURE HE EVEN CAME TO MY PLACE. I FOUND EVIDENCE! I SWEAR!!
I RECRUITED MORE GUYS FOR PROTECTION, BUT COULD THEY BE TRUSTED? IT ONLY TOOK ONE TRAITOR, AND I'D BE FINISHED...
509

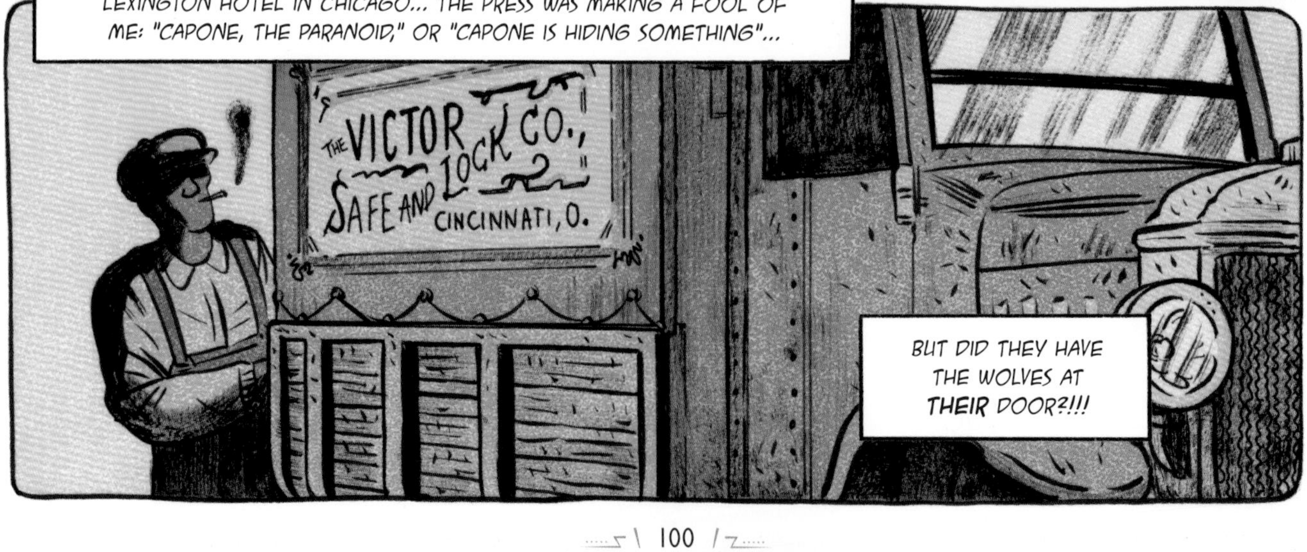
I EVEN HAD BULLETPROOF SHUTTERS INSTALLED AT MY NEW H.Q., THE LEXINGTON HOTEL IN CHICAGO... THE PRESS WAS MAKING A FOOL OF ME: "CAPONE, THE PARANOID," OR "CAPONE IS HIDING SOMETHING"...
THE VICTOR SAFE AND LOCK CO., CINCINNATI, O.
BUT DID THEY HAVE THE WOLVES AT **THEIR** DOOR?!!!

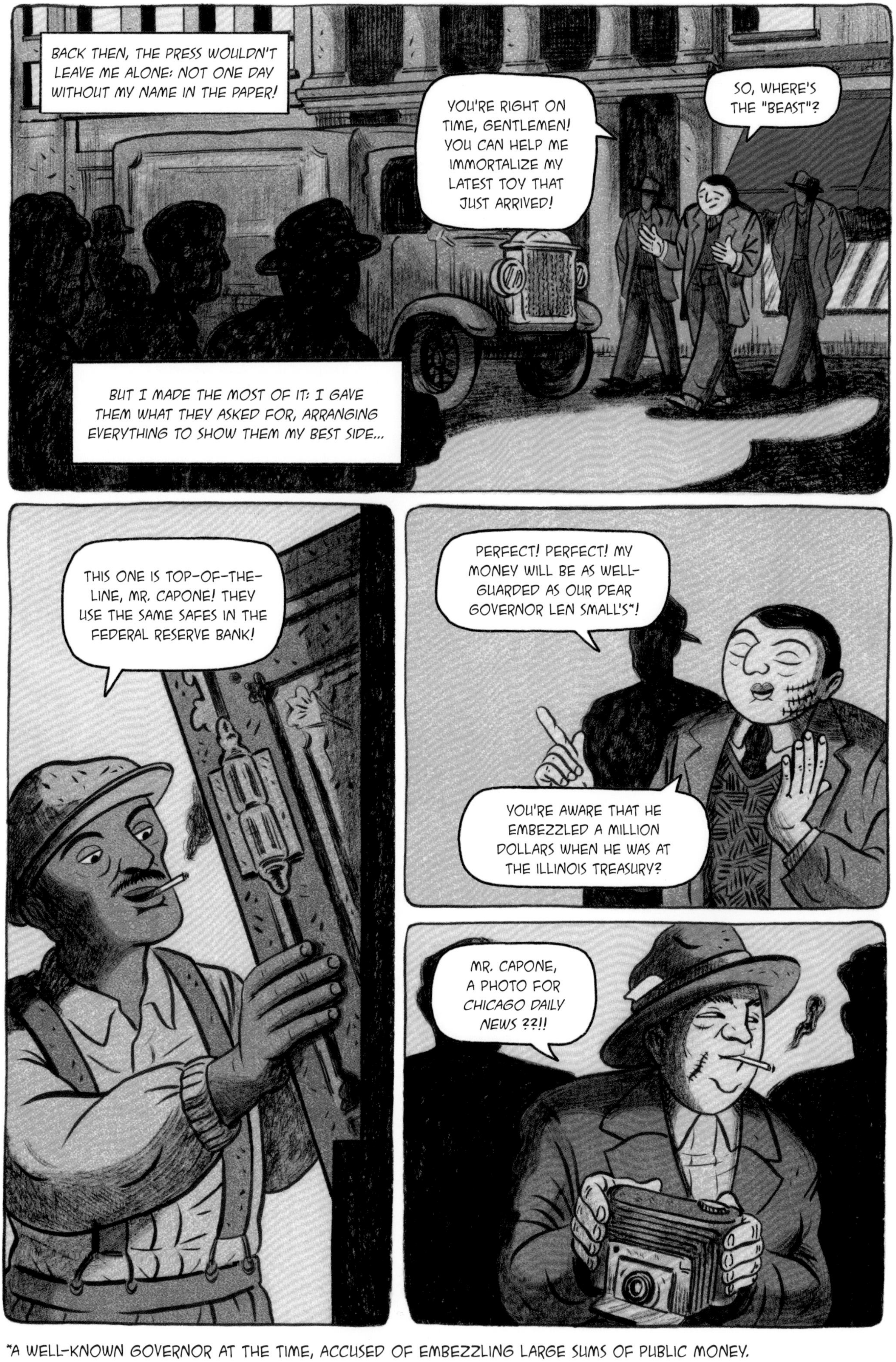
BACK THEN, THE PRESS WOULDN'T LEAVE ME ALONE: NOT ONE DAY WITHOUT MY NAME IN THE PAPER!
YOU'RE RIGHT ON TIME, GENTLEMEN! YOU CAN HELP ME IMMORTALIZE MY LATEST TOY THAT JUST ARRIVED!
SO, WHERE'S THE "BEAST"?
BUT I MADE THE MOST OF IT: I GAVE THEM WHAT THEY ASKED FOR, ARRANGING EVERYTHING TO SHOW THEM MY BEST SIDE...
THIS ONE IS TOP-OF-THE-LINE, MR. CAPONE! THEY USE THE SAME SAFES IN THE FEDERAL RESERVE BANK!
PERFECT! PERFECT! MY MONEY WILL BE AS WELL-GUARDED AS OUR DEAR GOVERNOR LEN SMALL'S*!
YOU'RE AWARE THAT HE EMBEZZLED A MILLION DOLLARS WHEN HE WAS AT THE ILLINOIS TREASURY?
MR. CAPONE, A PHOTO FOR CHICAGO DAILY NEWS ??!!

*A WELL-KNOWN GOVERNOR AT THE TIME, ACCUSED OF EMBEZZLING LARGE SUMS OF PUBLIC MONEY.

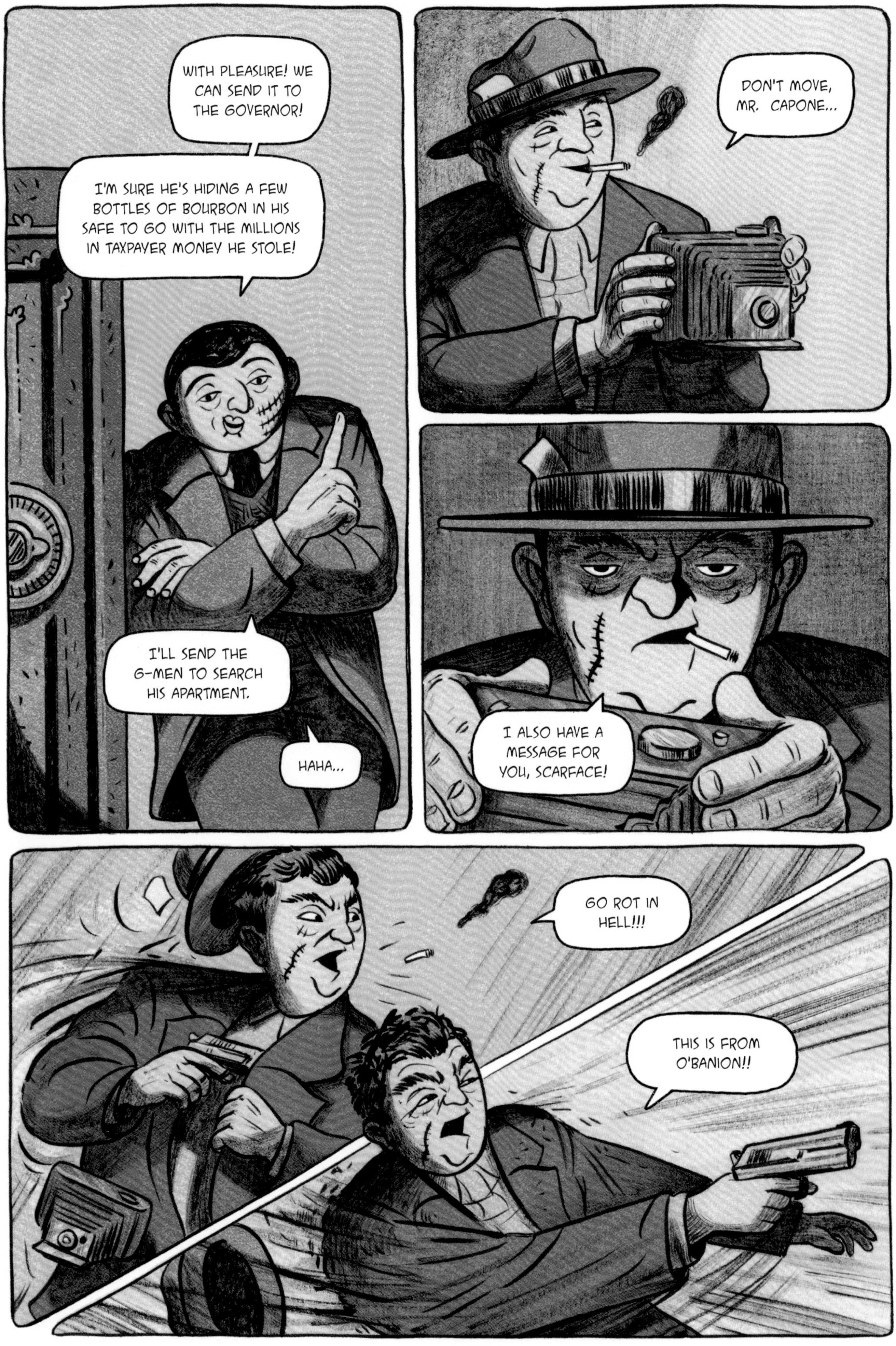
WITH PLEASURE! WE CAN SEND IT TO THE GOVERNOR!
I'M SURE HE'S HIDING A FEW BOTTLES OF BOURBON IN HIS SAFE TO GO WITH THE MILLIONS IN TAXPAYER MONEY HE STOLE!
I'LL SEND THE G-MEN TO SEARCH HIS APARTMENT.
HAHA...
DON'T MOVE, MR. CAPONE...
I ALSO HAVE A MESSAGE FOR YOU, SCARFACE!
GO ROT IN HELL!!!
THIS IS FROM O'BANION!!

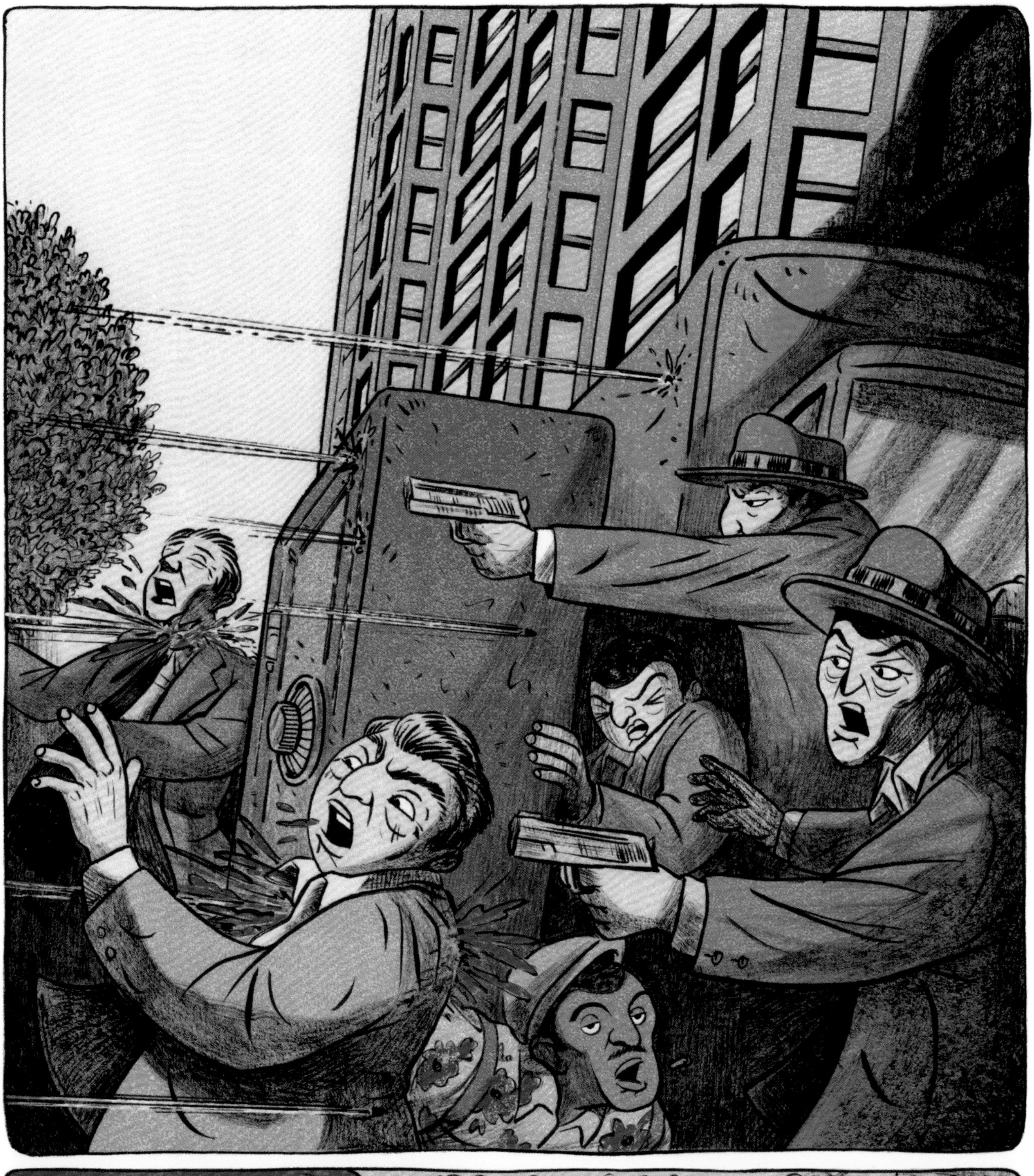

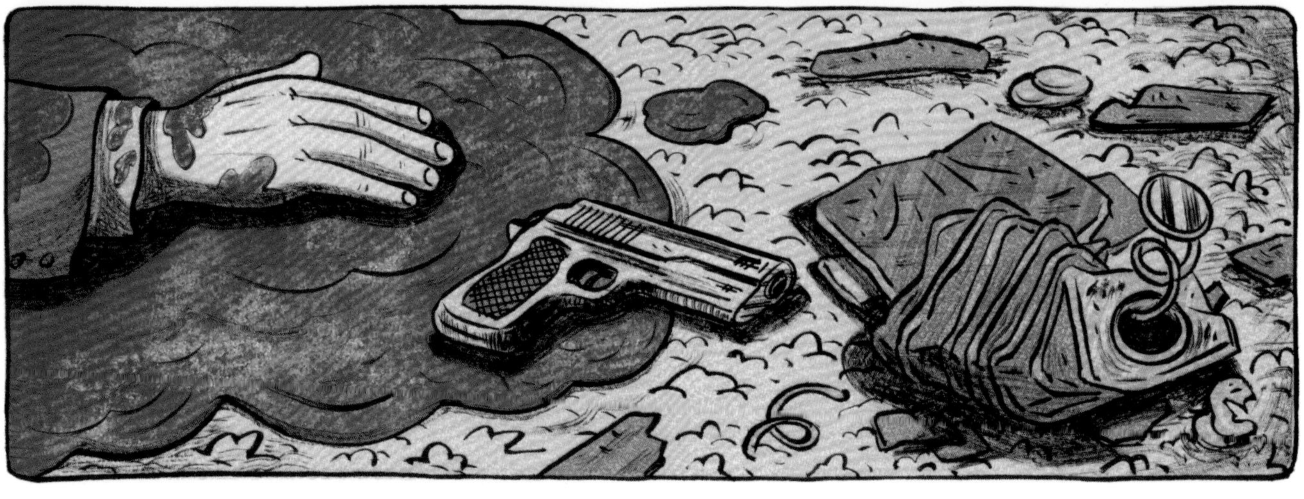

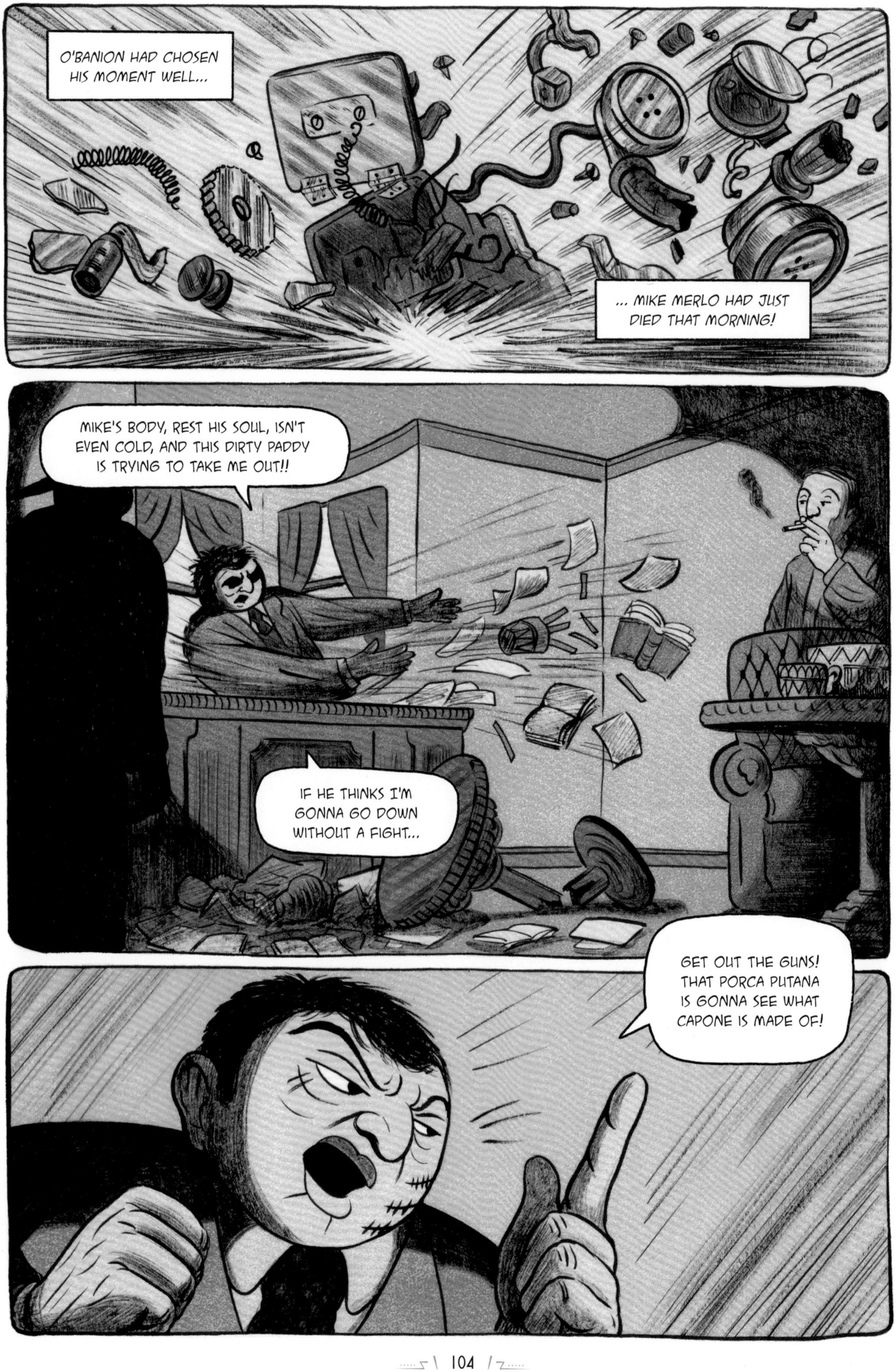
O'BANION HAD CHOSEN HIS MOMENT WELL...
... MIKE MERLO HAD JUST DIED THAT MORNING!
MIKE'S BODY, REST HIS SOUL, ISN'T EVEN COLD, AND THIS DIRTY PADDY IS TRYING TO TAKE ME OUT!!
IF HE THINKS I'M GONNA GO DOWN WITHOUT A FIGHT...
GET OUT THE GUNS! THAT PORCA PUTANA IS GONNA SEE WHAT CAPONE IS MADE OF!

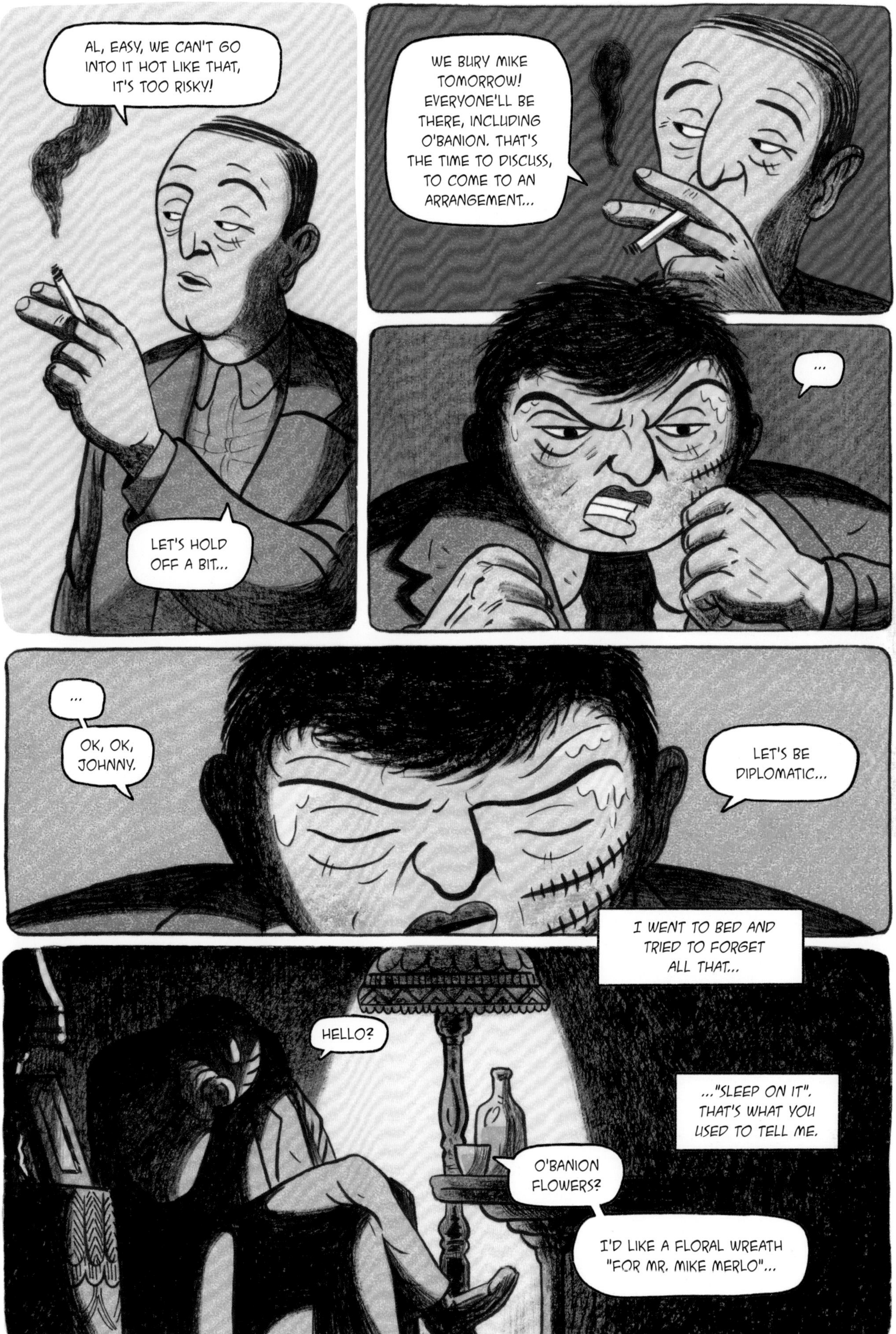
AL, EASY, WE CAN'T GO INTO IT HOT LIKE THAT, IT'S TOO RISKY!
LET'S HOLD OFF A BIT...
WE BURY MIKE TOMORROW! EVERYONE'LL BE THERE, INCLUDING O'BANION. THAT'S THE TIME TO DISCUSS, TO COME TO AN ARRANGEMENT...
...
...
OK, OK, JOHNNY.
LET'S BE DIPLOMATIC...
I WENT TO BED AND TRIED TO FORGET ALL THAT...
HELLO?
..."SLEEP ON IT". THAT'S WHAT YOU USED TO TELL ME.
O'BANION FLOWERS?
I'D LIKE A FLORAL WREATH "FOR MR. MIKE MERLO"...

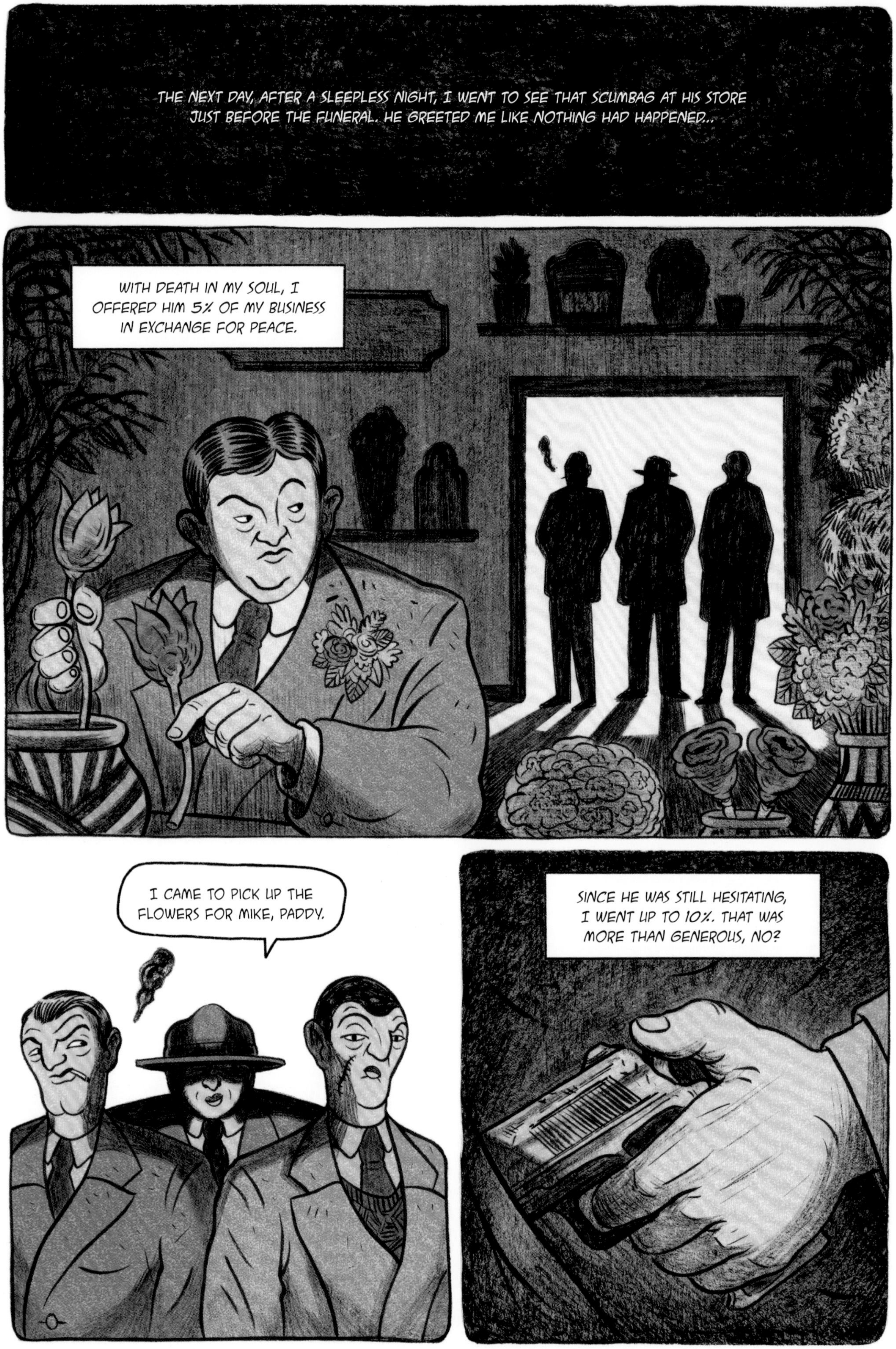
THE NEXT DAY, AFTER A SLEEPLESS NIGHT, I WENT TO SEE THAT SCUMBAG AT HIS STORE JUST BEFORE THE FUNERAL. HE GREETED ME LIKE NOTHING HAD HAPPENED...
WITH DEATH IN MY SOUL, I OFFERED HIM 5% OF MY BUSINESS IN EXCHANGE FOR PEACE.
I CAME TO PICK UP THE FLOWERS FOR MIKE, PADDY.
SINCE HE WAS STILL HESITATING, I WENT UP TO 10%. THAT WAS MORE THAN GENEROUS, NO?

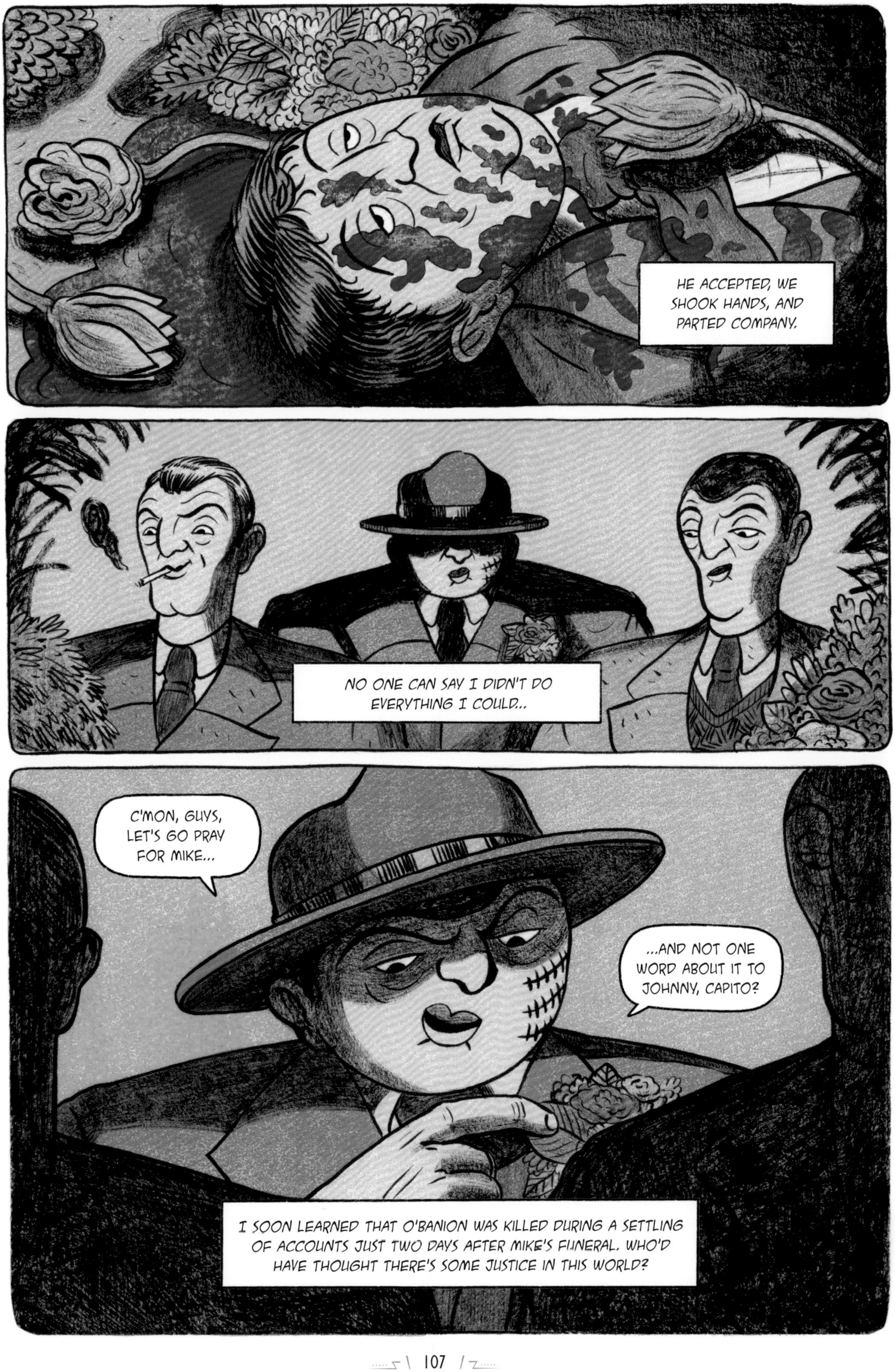
HE ACCEPTED, WE SHOOK HANDS, AND PARTED COMPANY.
NO ONE CAN SAY I DIDN'T DO EVERYTHING I COULD...
C'MON, GUYS, LET'S GO PRAY FOR MIKE...
...AND NOT ONE WORD ABOUT IT TO JOHNNY, CAPITO?
I SOON LEARNED THAT O'BANION WAS KILLED DURING A SETTLING OF ACCOUNTS JUST TWO DAYS AFTER MIKE'S FUNERAL. WHO'D HAVE THOUGHT THERE'S SOME JUSTICE IN THIS WORLD?

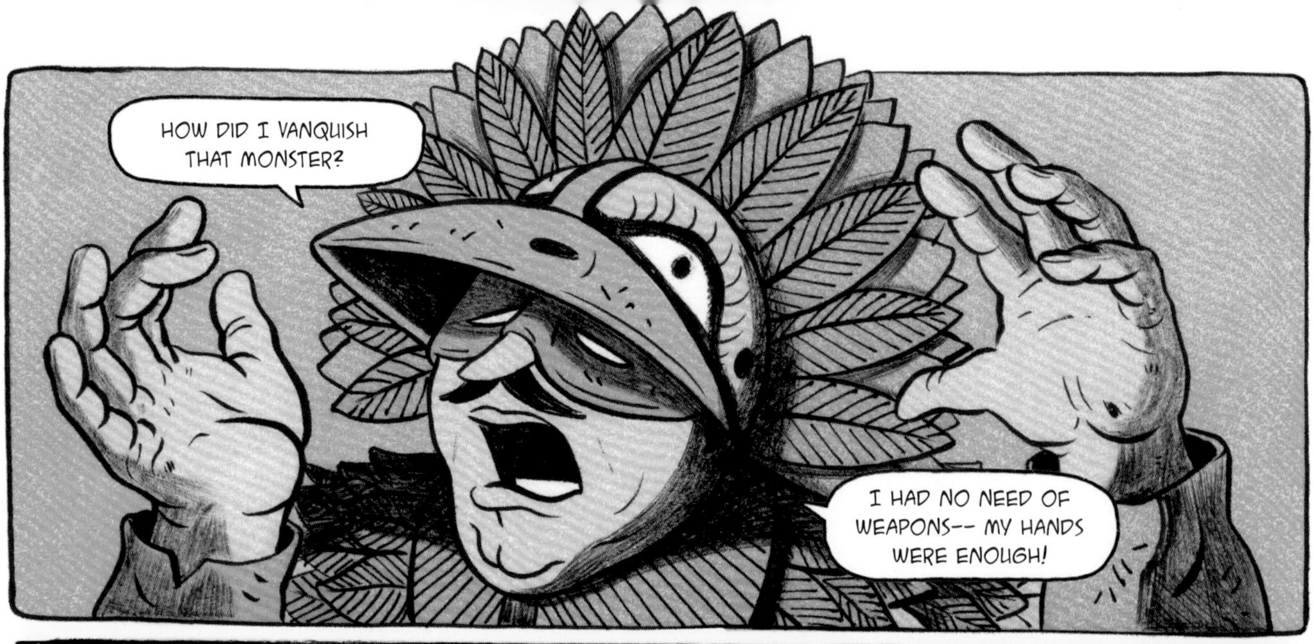
HOW DID I VANQUISH THAT MONSTER?
I HAD NO NEED OF WEAPONS-- MY HANDS WERE ENOUGH!

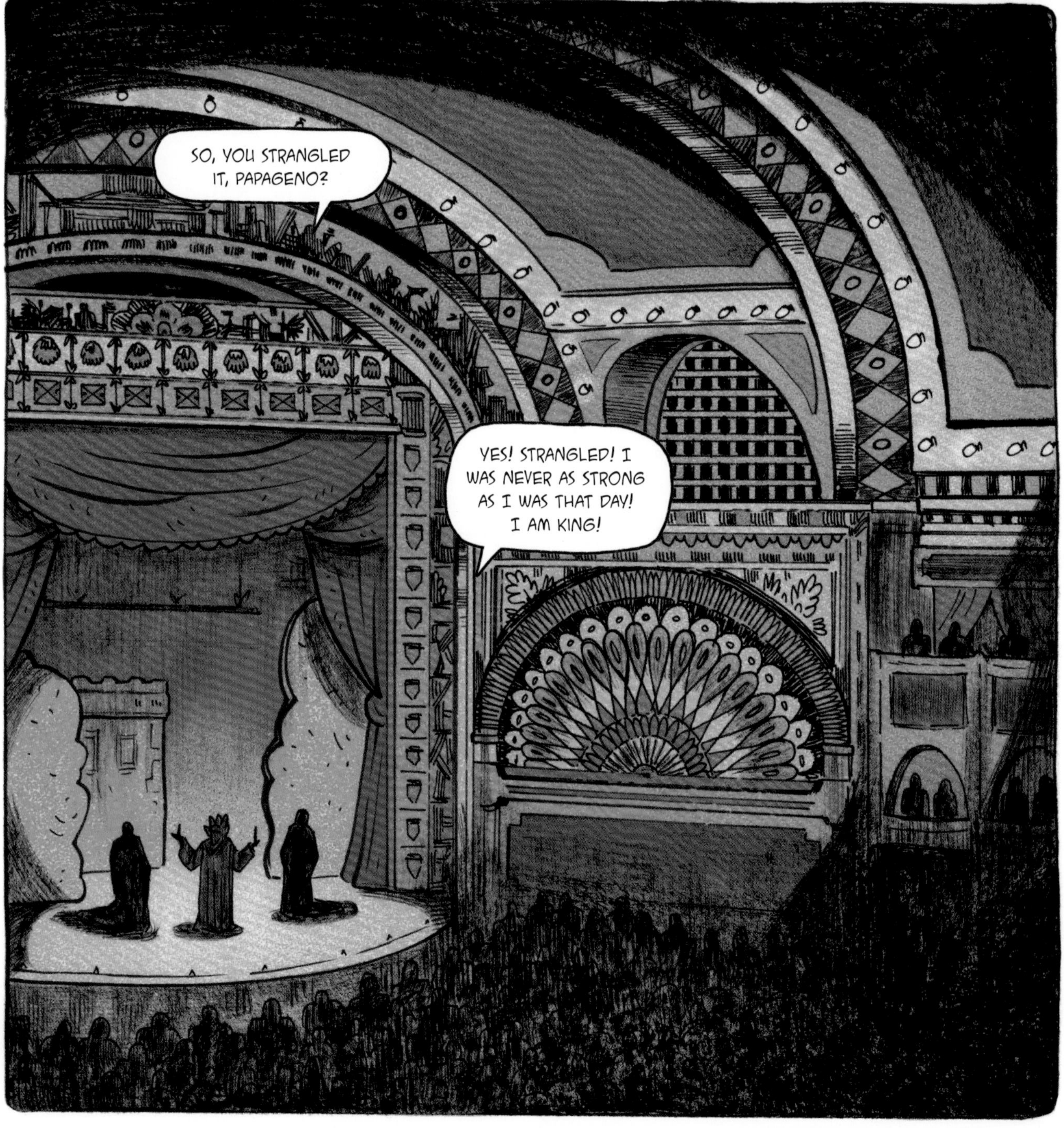
SO, YOU STRANGLED IT, PAPAGENO?
YES! STRANGLED! I WAS NEVER AS STRONG AS I WAS THAT DAY! I AM KING!

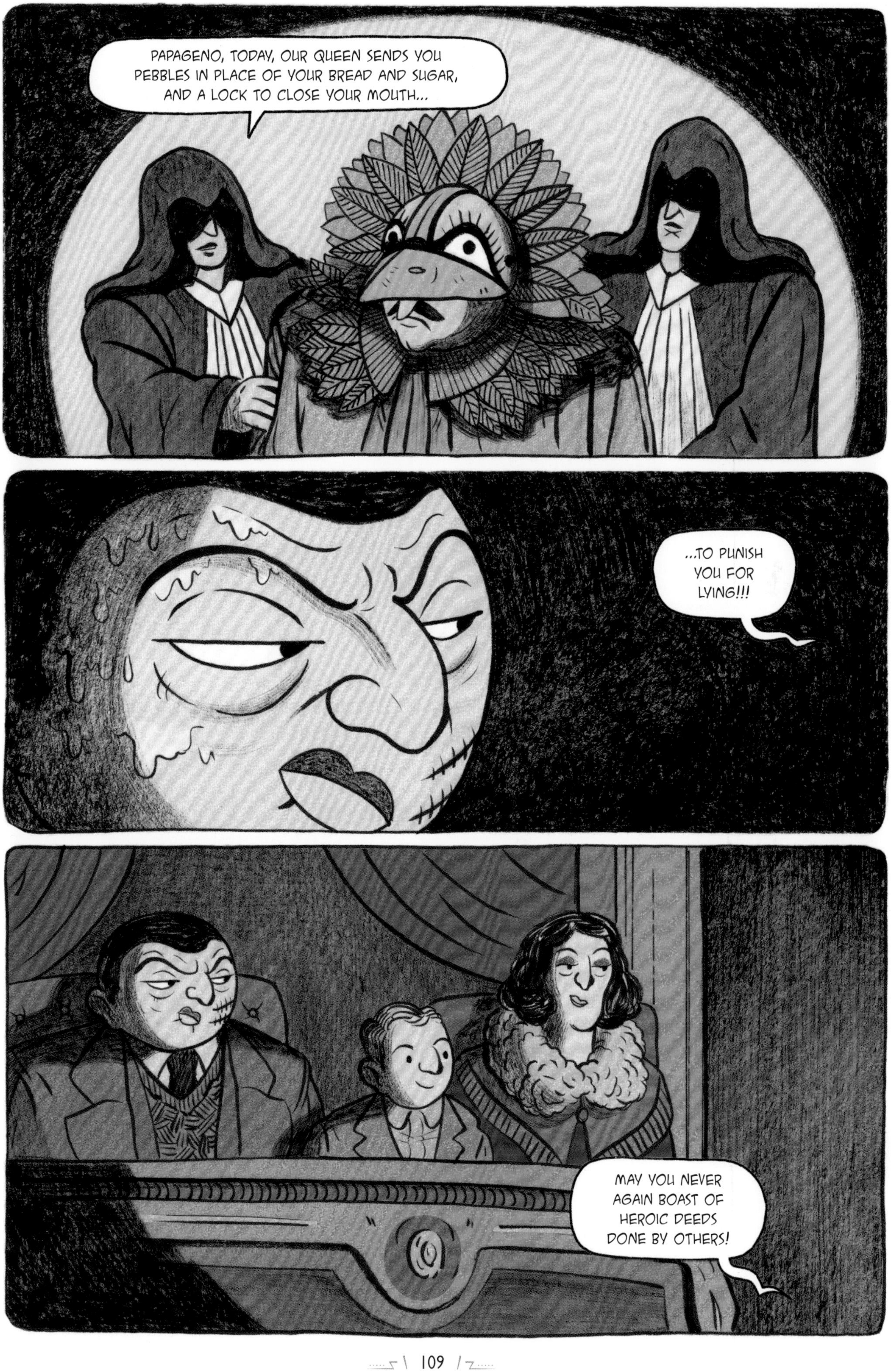
PAPAGENO, TODAY, OUR QUEEN SENDS YOU PEBBLES IN PLACE OF YOUR BREAD AND SUGAR, AND A LOCK TO CLOSE YOUR MOUTH...
...TO PUNISH YOU FOR LYING!!!
MAY YOU NEVER AGAIN BOAST OF HEROIC DEEDS DONE BY OTHERS!

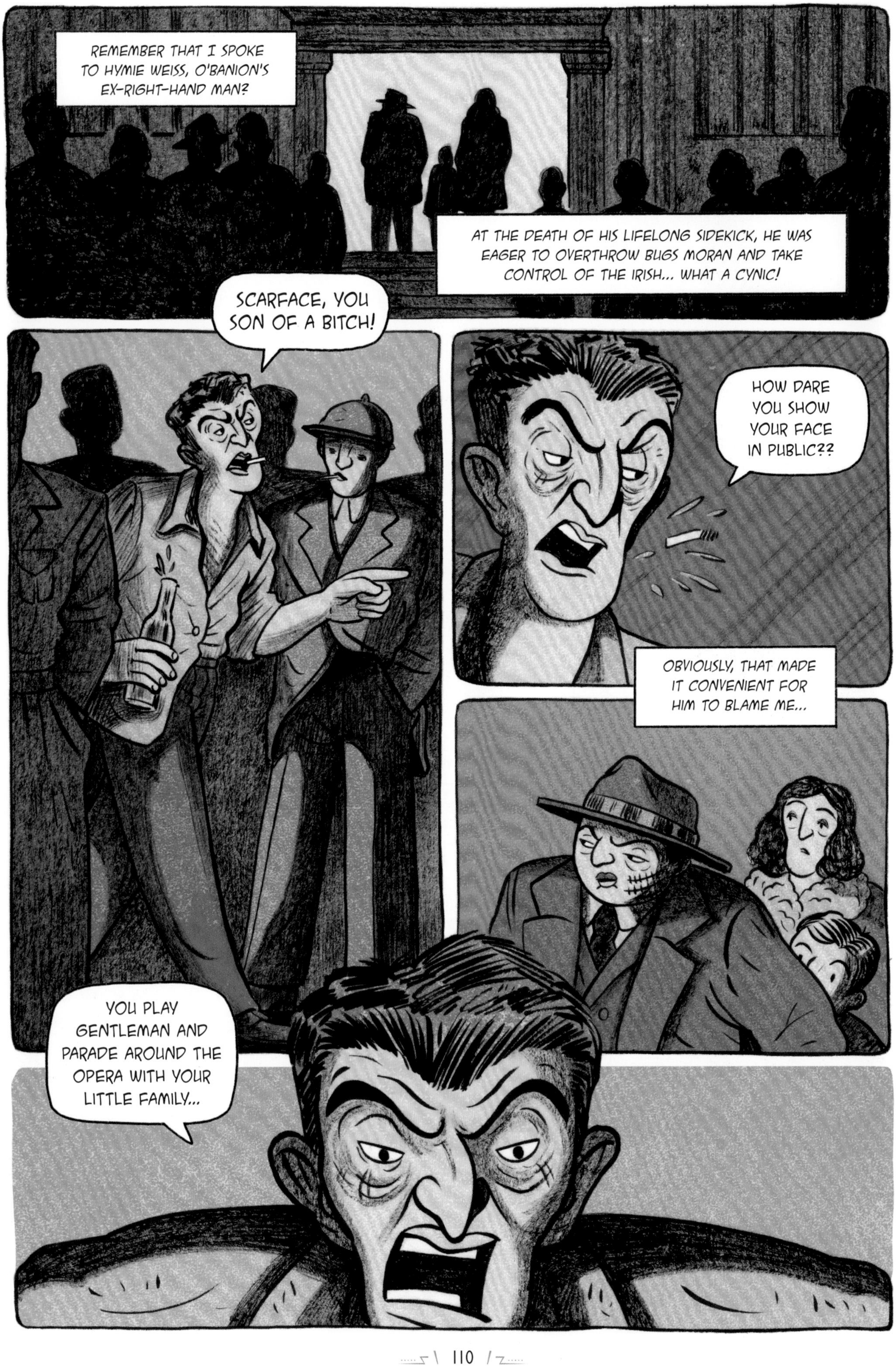
REMEMBER THAT I SPOKE TO HYMIE WEISS, O'BANION'S EX-RIGHT-HAND MAN?
AT THE DEATH OF HIS LIFELONG SIDEKICK, HE WAS EAGER TO OVERTHROW BUGS MORAN AND TAKE CONTROL OF THE IRISH... WHAT A CYNIC!
SCARFACE, YOU SON OF A BITCH!
HOW DARE YOU SHOW YOUR FACE IN PUBLIC??
OBVIOUSLY, THAT MADE IT CONVENIENT FOR HIM TO BLAME ME...
YOU PLAY GENTLEMAN AND PARADE AROUND THE OPERA WITH YOUR LITTLE FAMILY...

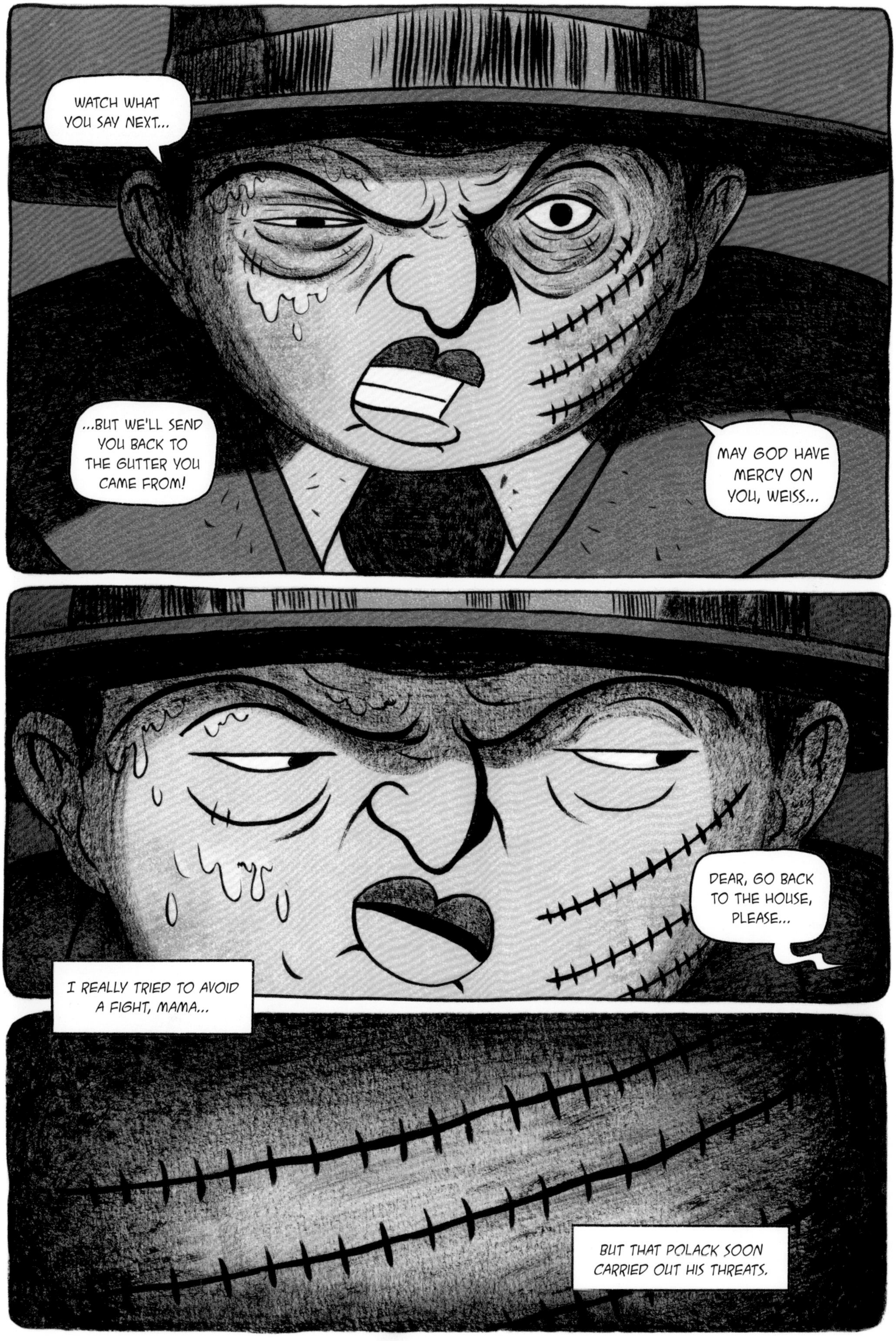
WATCH WHAT YOU SAY NEXT...
...BUT WE'LL SEND YOU BACK TO THE GUTTER YOU CAME FROM!
MAY GOD HAVE MERCY ON YOU, WEISS...
DEAR, GO BACK TO THE HOUSE, PLEASE...
I REALLY TRIED TO AVOID A FIGHT, MAMA...
BUT THAT POLACK SOON CARRIED OUT HIS THREATS.

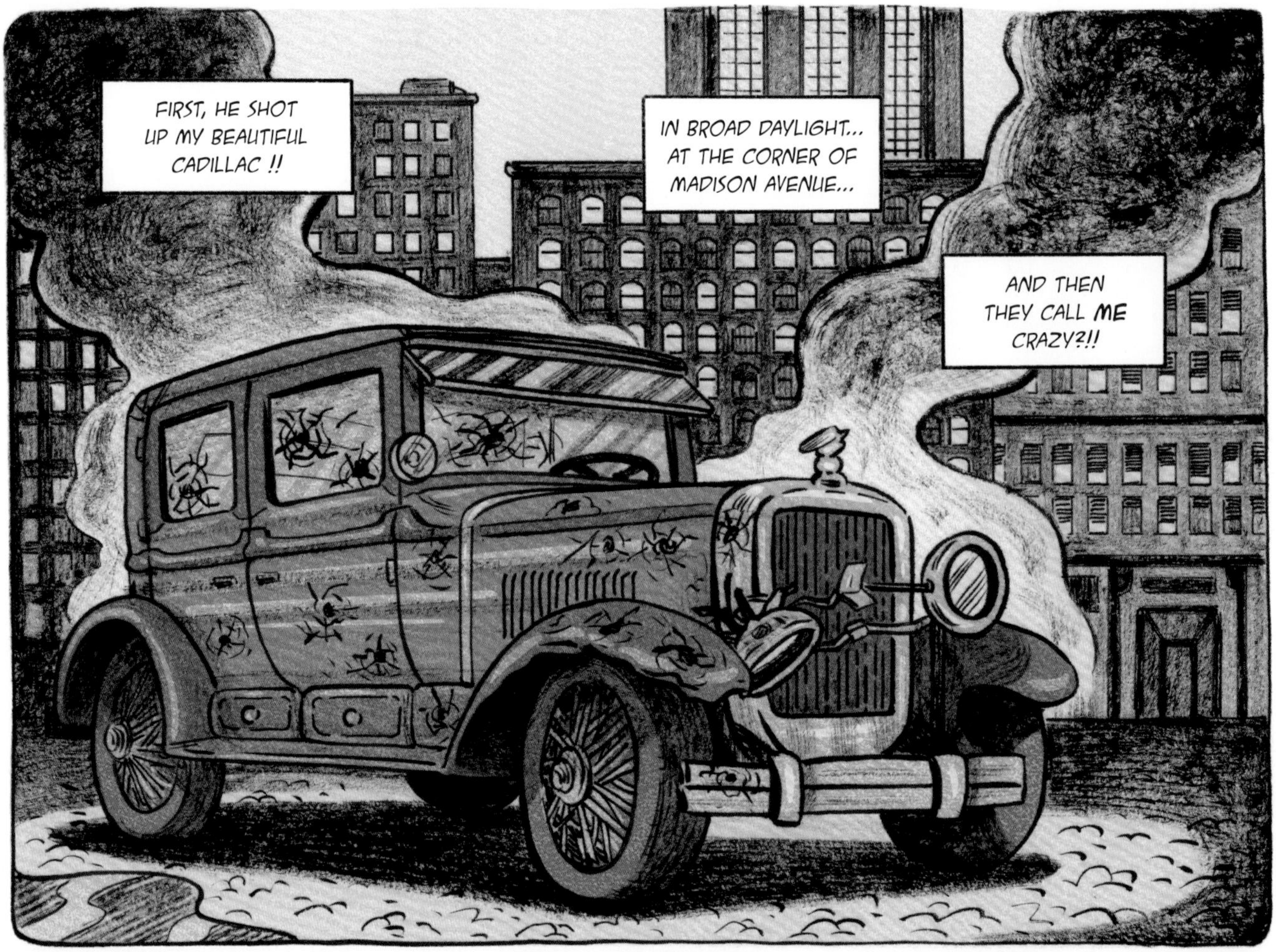
FIRST, HE SHOT UP MY BEAUTIFUL CADILLAC !!
IN BROAD DAYLIGHT... AT THE CORNER OF MADISON AVENUE...
AND THEN THEY CALL ME CRAZY?!!

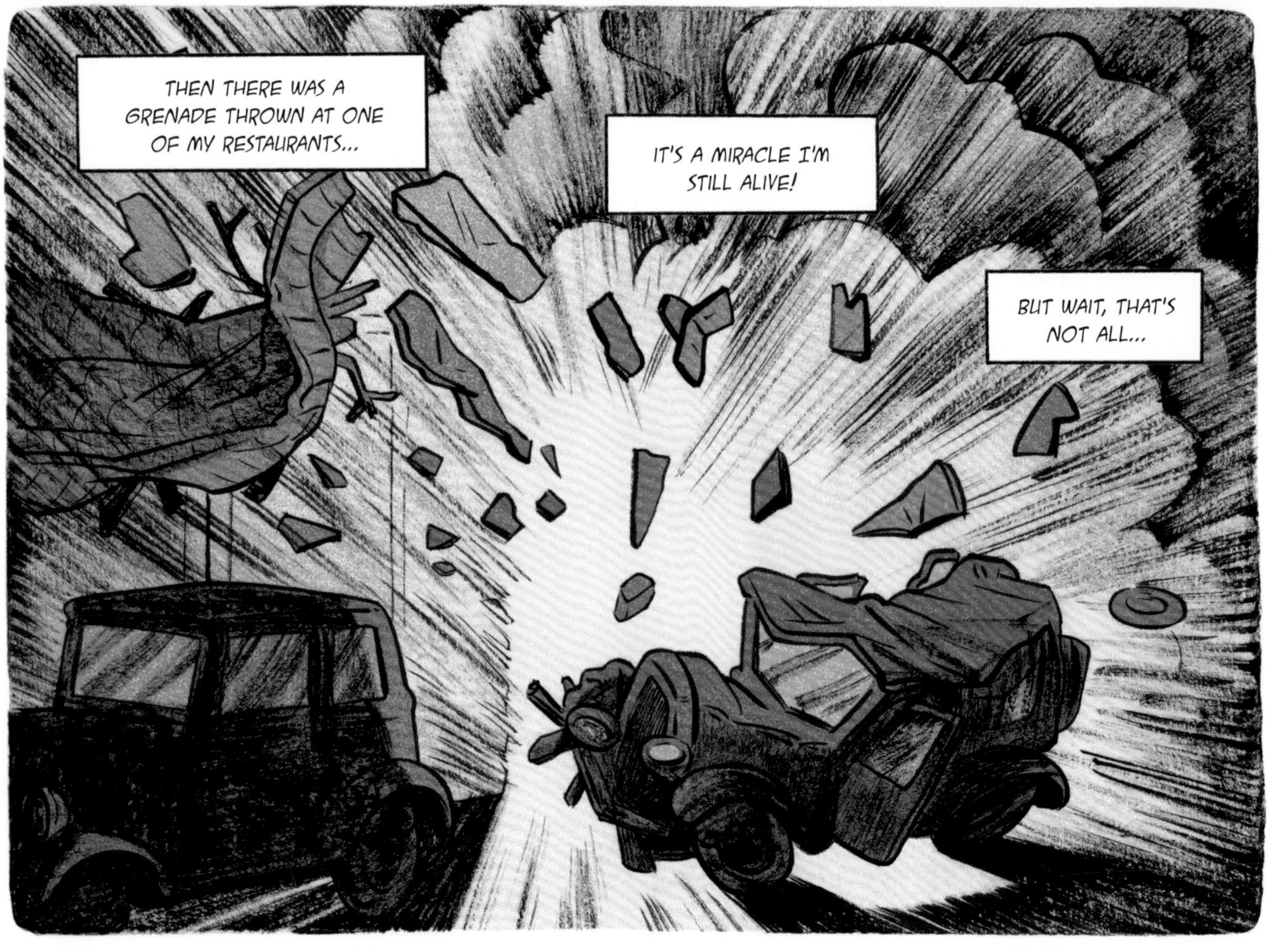
THEN THERE WAS A GRENADE THROWN AT ONE OF MY RESTAURANTS...
IT'S A MIRACLE I'M STILL ALIVE!
BUT WAIT, THAT'S NOT ALL...

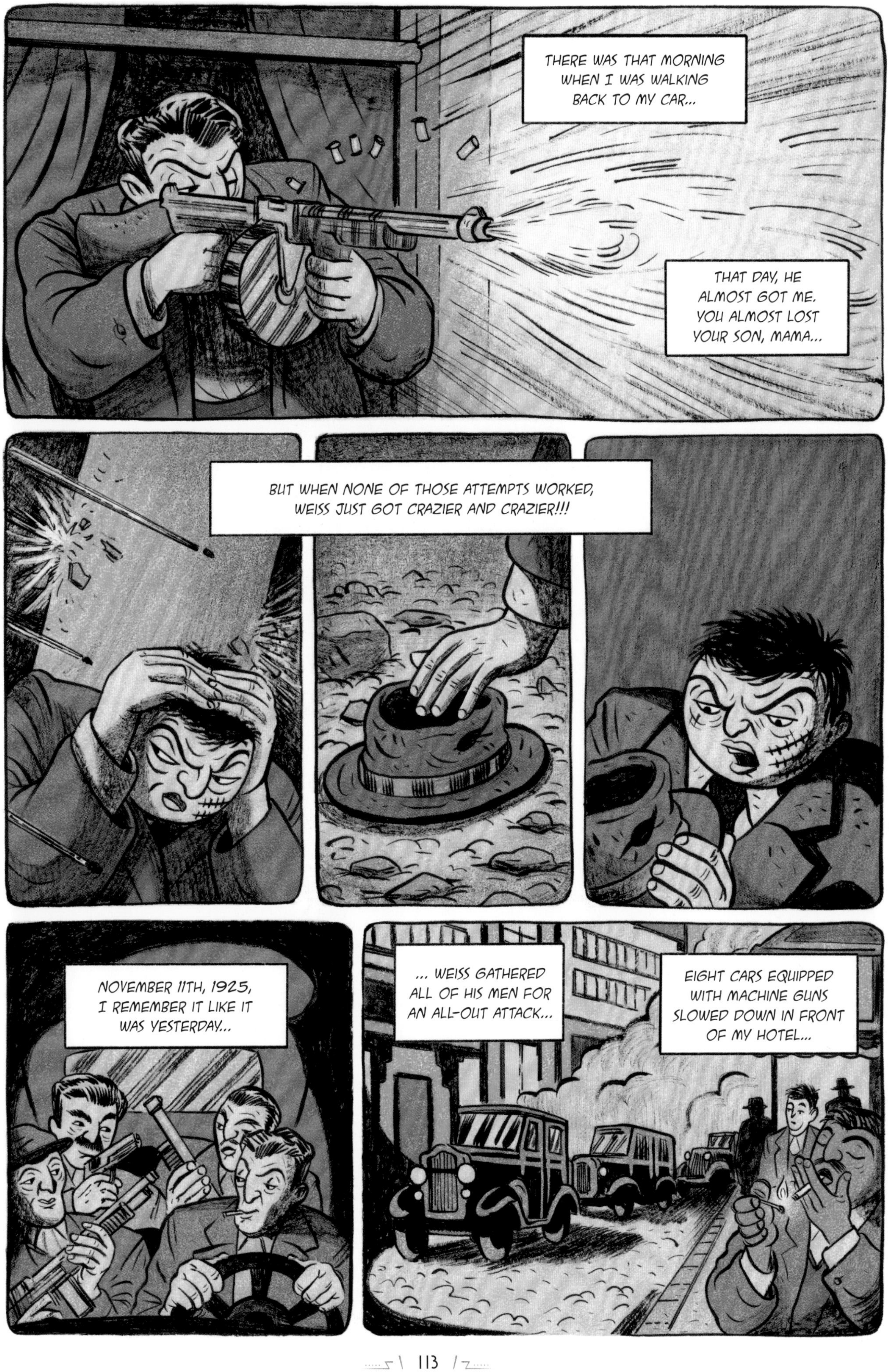
THERE WAS THAT MORNING WHEN I WAS WALKING BACK TO MY CAR...
THAT DAY, HE ALMOST GOT ME. YOU ALMOST LOST YOUR SON, MAMA...
BUT WHEN NONE OF THOSE ATTEMPTS WORKED, WEISS JUST GOT CRAZIER AND CRAZIER!!!
NOVEMBER 11TH, 1925, I REMEMBER IT LIKE IT WAS YESTERDAY...
... WEISS GATHERED ALL OF HIS MEN FOR AN ALL-OUT ATTACK...
EIGHT CARS EQUIPPED WITH MACHINE GUNS SLOWED DOWN IN FRONT OF MY HOTEL...

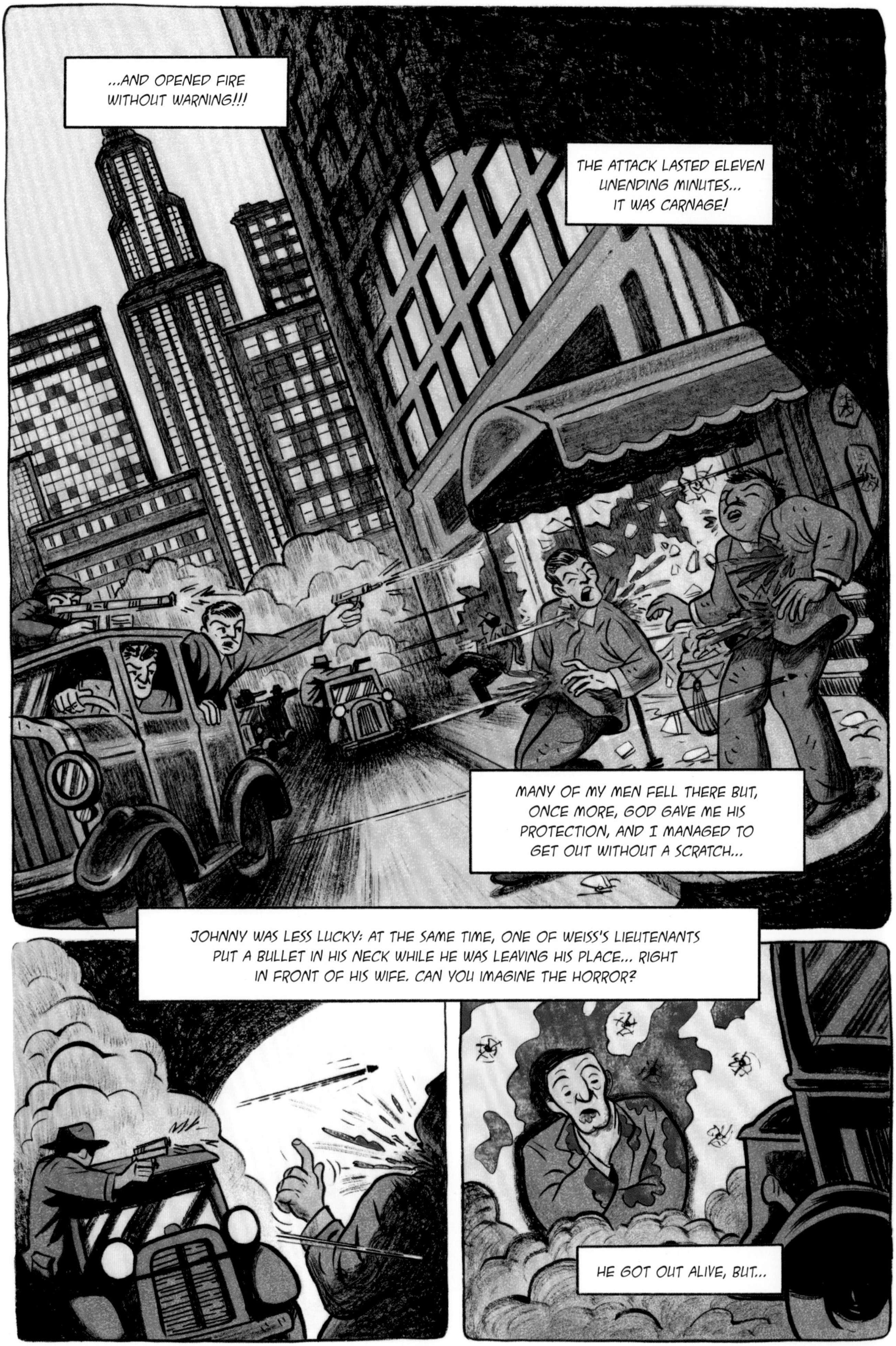
...AND OPENED FIRE WITHOUT WARNING!!!
THE ATTACK LASTED ELEVEN UNENDING MINUTES... IT WAS CARNAGE!
MANY OF MY MEN FELL THERE BUT, ONCE MORE, GOD GAVE ME HIS PROTECTION, AND I MANAGED TO GET OUT WITHOUT A SCRATCH...
JOHNNY WAS LESS LUCKY: AT THE SAME TIME, ONE OF WEISS'S LIEUTENANTS PUT A BULLET IN HIS NECK WHILE HE WAS LEAVING HIS PLACE... RIGHT IN FRONT OF HIS WIFE. CAN YOU IMAGINE THE HORROR?
HE GOT OUT ALIVE, BUT...

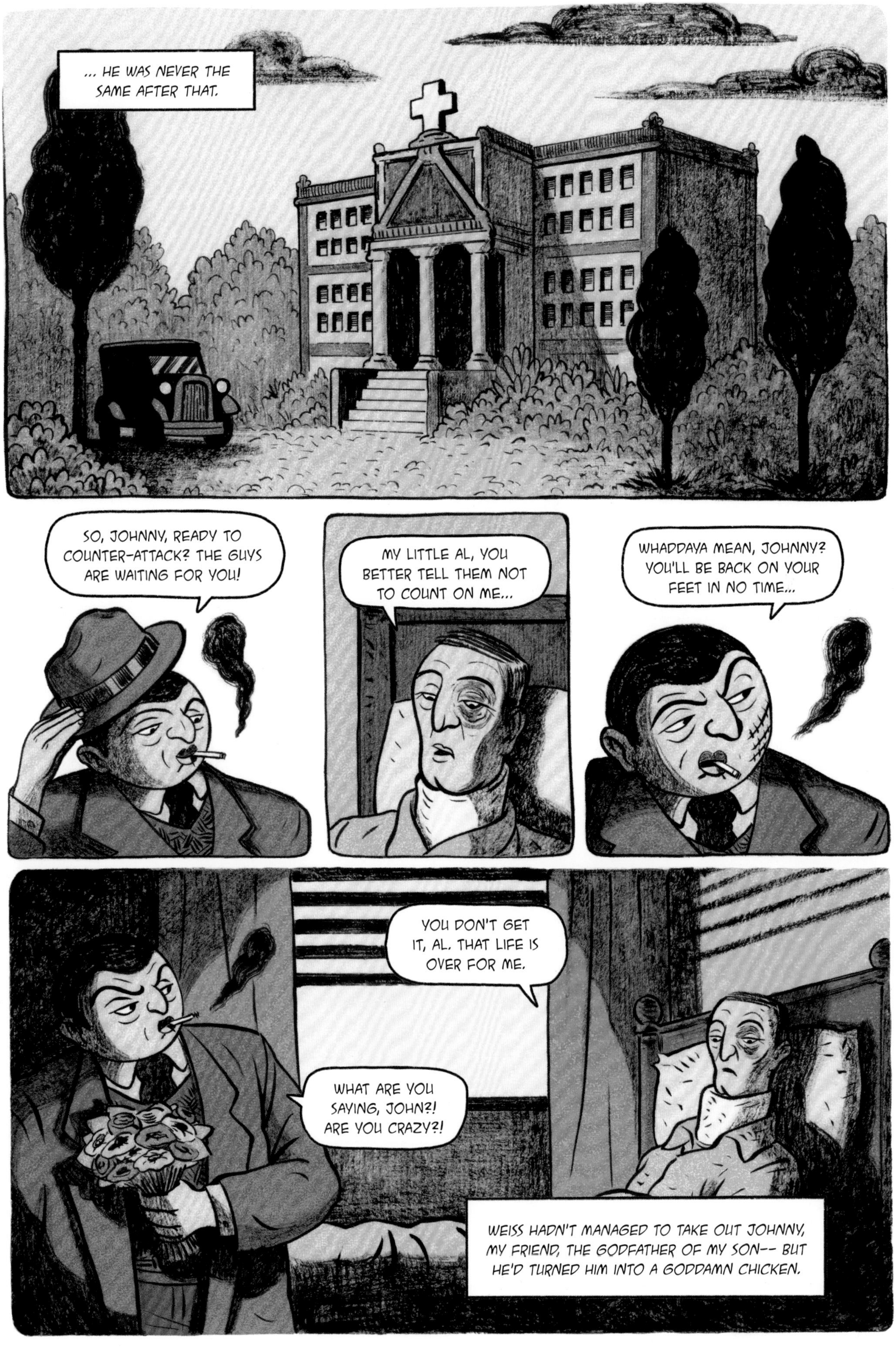
... HE WAS NEVER THE SAME AFTER THAT.
SO, JOHNNY, READY TO COUNTER-ATTACK? THE GUYS ARE WAITING FOR YOU!
MY LITTLE AL, YOU BETTER TELL THEM NOT TO COUNT ON ME...
WHADDAYA MEAN, JOHNNY? YOU'LL BE BACK ON YOUR FEET IN NO TIME...
YOU DON'T GET IT, AL. THAT LIFE IS OVER FOR ME.
WHAT ARE YOU SAYING, JOHN?! ARE YOU CRAZY?!
WEISS HADN'T MANAGED TO TAKE OUT JOHNNY, MY FRIEND, THE GODFATHER OF MY SON-- BUT HE'D TURNED HIM INTO A GODDAMN CHICKEN.

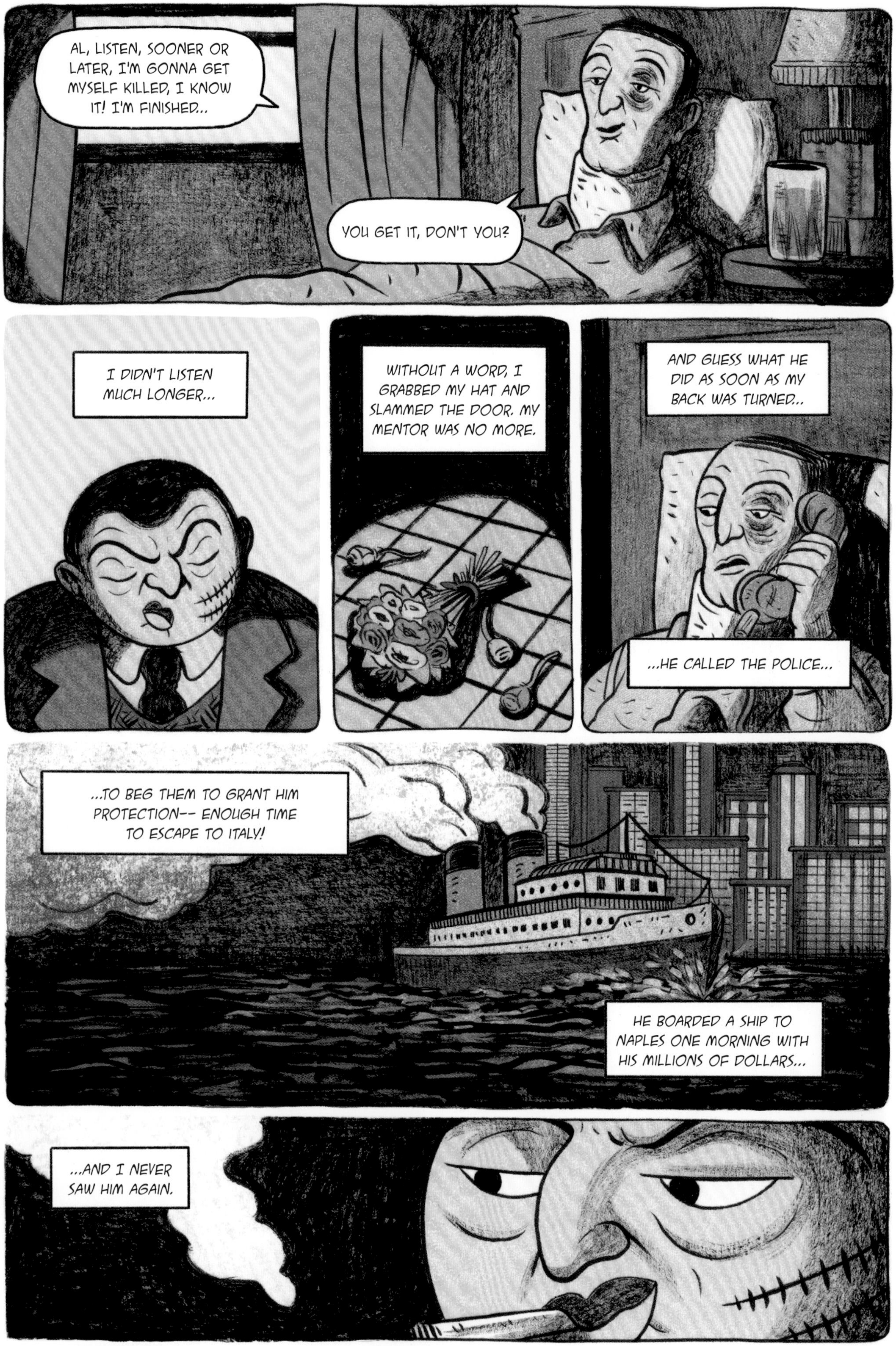
AL, LISTEN, SOONER OR LATER, I'M GONNA GET MYSELF KILLED, I KNOW IT! I'M FINISHED...
YOU GET IT, DON'T YOU?
I DIDN'T LISTEN MUCH LONGER...
WITHOUT A WORD, I GRABBED MY HAT AND SLAMMED THE DOOR. MY MENTOR WAS NO MORE.
AND GUESS WHAT HE DID AS SOON AS MY BACK WAS TURNED...
...HE CALLED THE POLICE...
...TO BEG THEM TO GRANT HIM PROTECTION-- ENOUGH TIME TO ESCAPE TO ITALY!
HE BOARDED A SHIP TO NAPLES ONE MORNING WITH HIS MILLIONS OF DOLLARS...
...AND I NEVER SAW HIM AGAIN.

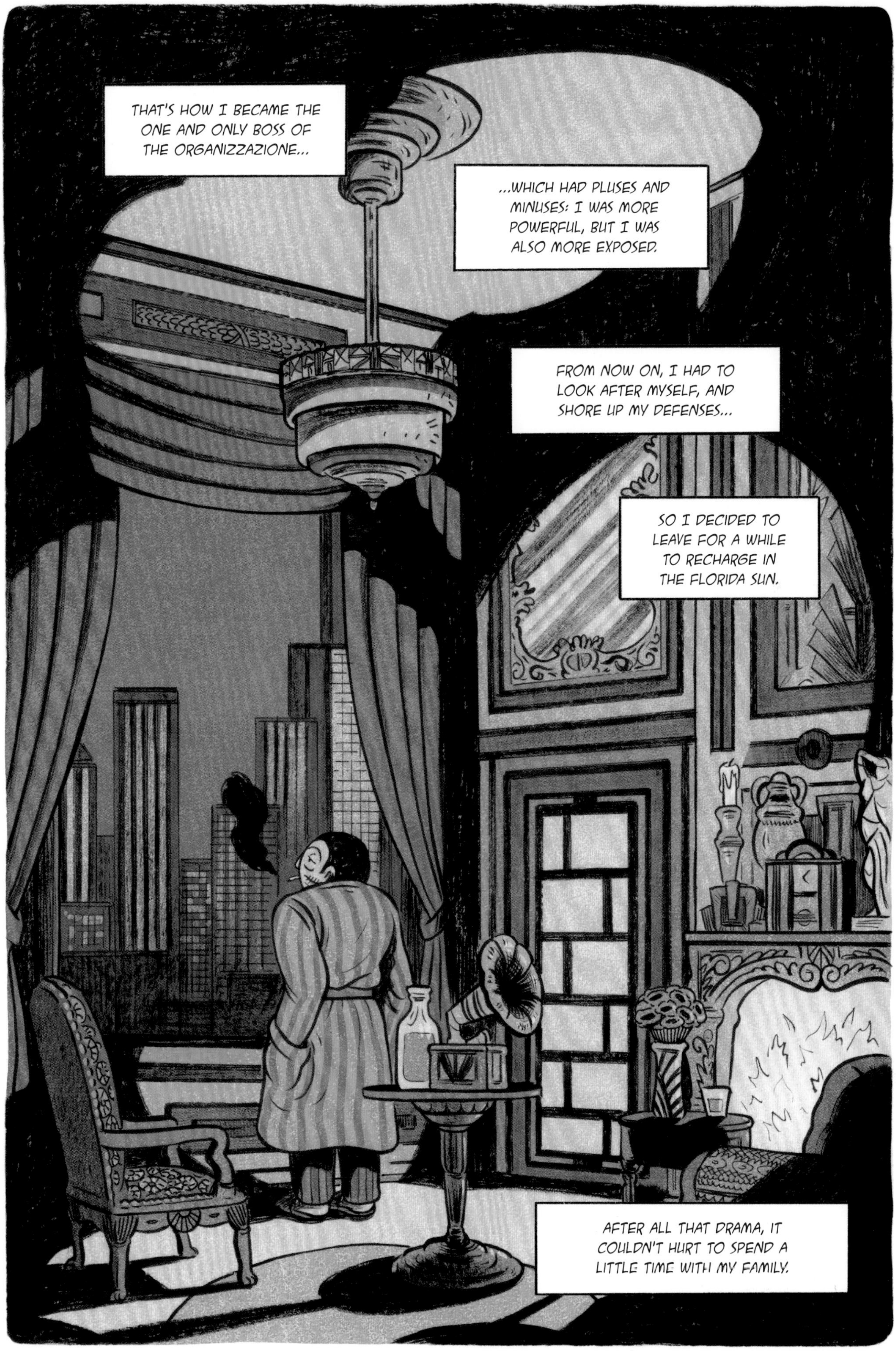
THAT'S HOW I BECAME THE ONE AND ONLY BOSS OF THE ORGANIZZAZIONE...
...WHICH HAD PLUSES AND MINUSES: I WAS MORE POWERFUL, BUT I WAS ALSO MORE EXPOSED.
FROM NOW ON, I HAD TO LOOK AFTER MYSELF, AND SHORE UP MY DEFENSES...
SO I DECIDED TO LEAVE FOR A WHILE TO RECHARGE IN THE FLORIDA SUN.
AFTER ALL THAT DRAMA, IT COULDN'T HURT TO SPEND A LITTLE TIME WITH MY FAMILY.

CHAPTER 4

The Great Capone

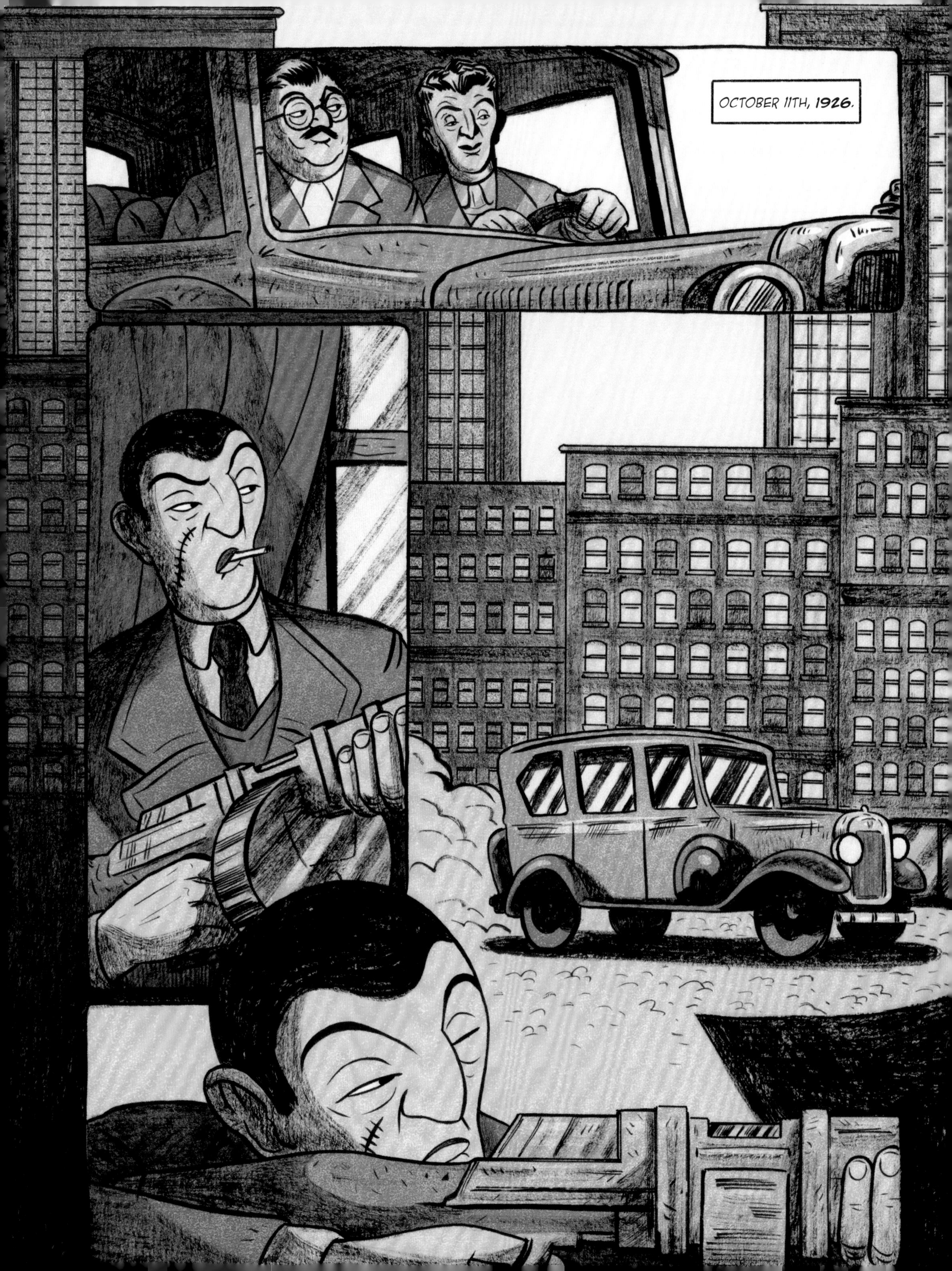
OCTOBER 11TH, 1926.

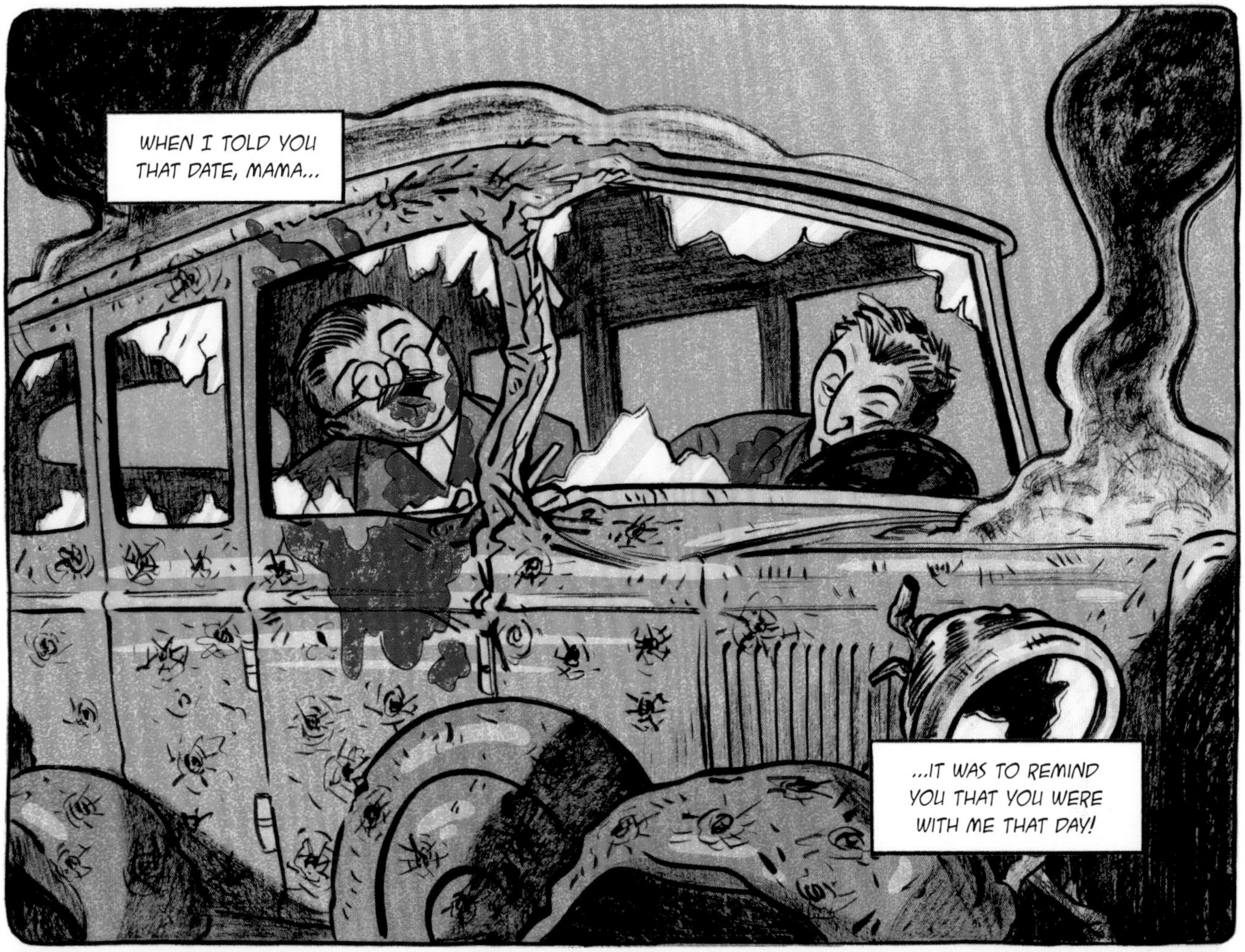
WHEN I TOLD YOU THAT DATE, MAMA...
...IT WAS TO REMIND YOU THAT YOU WERE WITH ME THAT DAY!

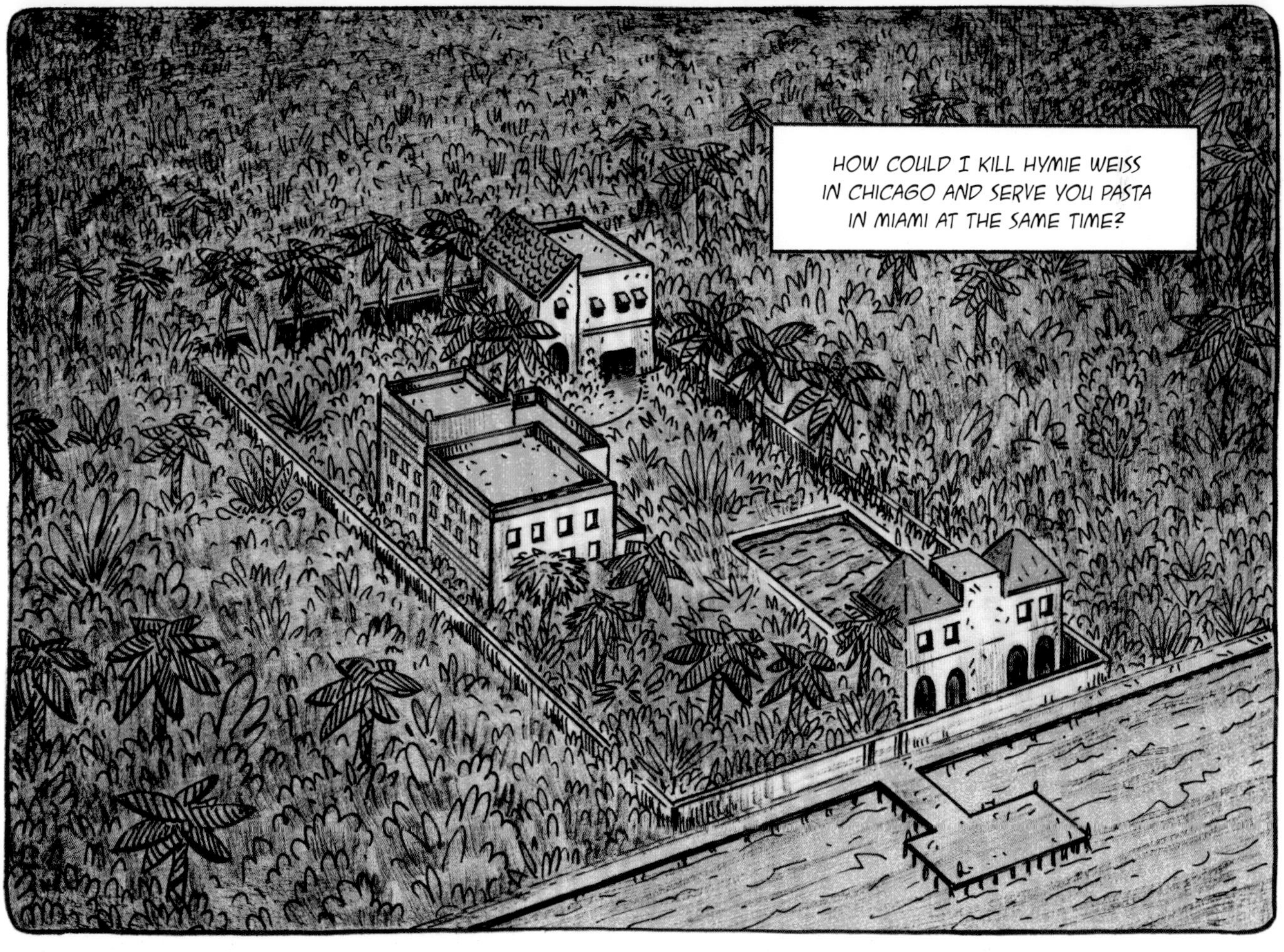
HOW COULD I KILL HYMIE WEISS IN CHICAGO AND SERVE YOU PASTA IN MIAMI AT THE SAME TIME?

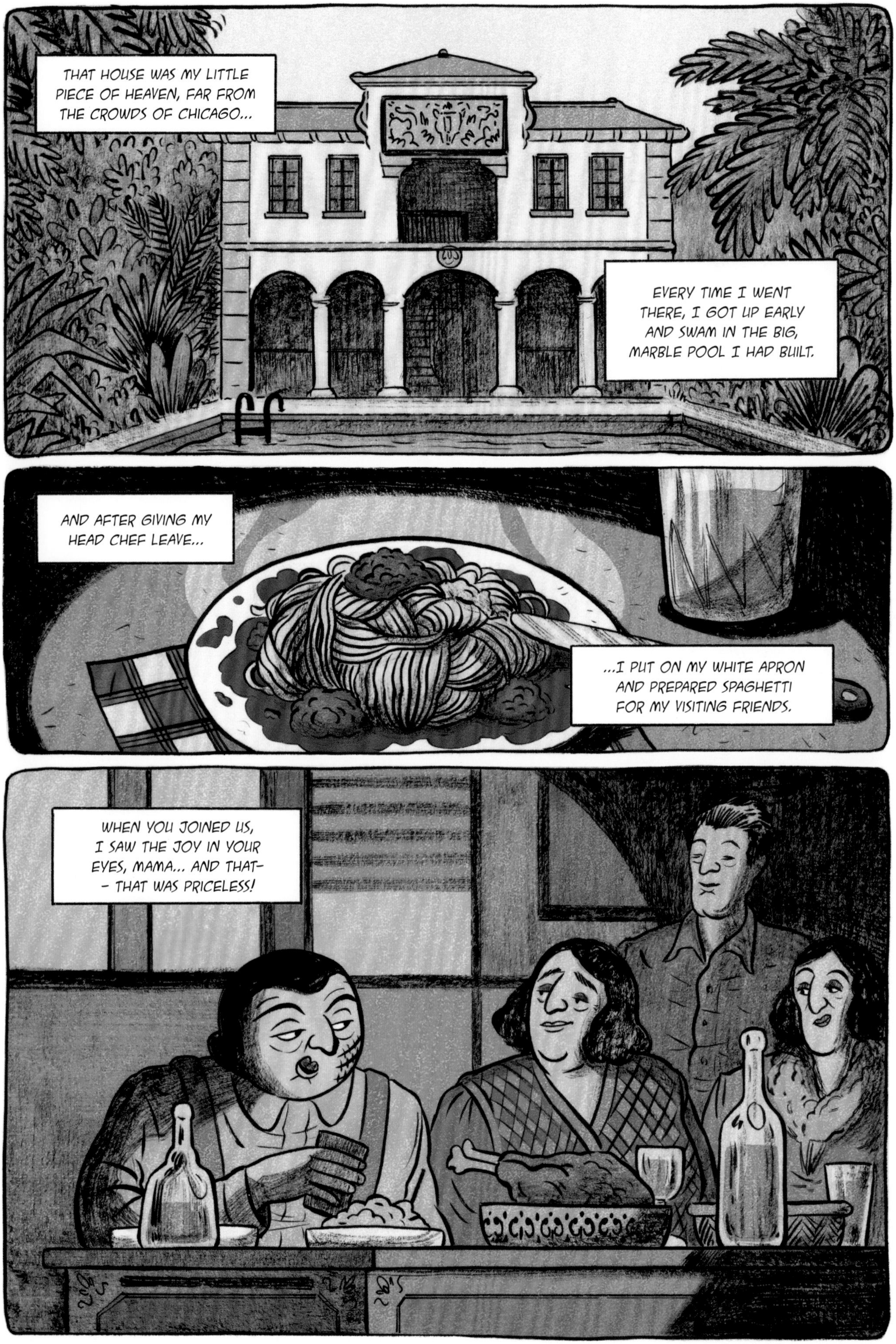
THAT HOUSE WAS MY LITTLE PIECE OF HEAVEN, FAR FROM THE CROWDS OF CHICAGO...
EVERY TIME I WENT THERE, I GOT UP EARLY AND SWAM IN THE BIG, MARBLE POOL I HAD BUILT.
AND AFTER GIVING MY HEAD CHEF LEAVE...
...I PUT ON MY WHITE APRON AND PREPARED SPAGHETTI FOR MY VISITING FRIENDS.
WHEN YOU JOINED US, I SAW THE JOY IN YOUR EYES, MAMA... AND THAT- - THAT WAS PRICELESS!

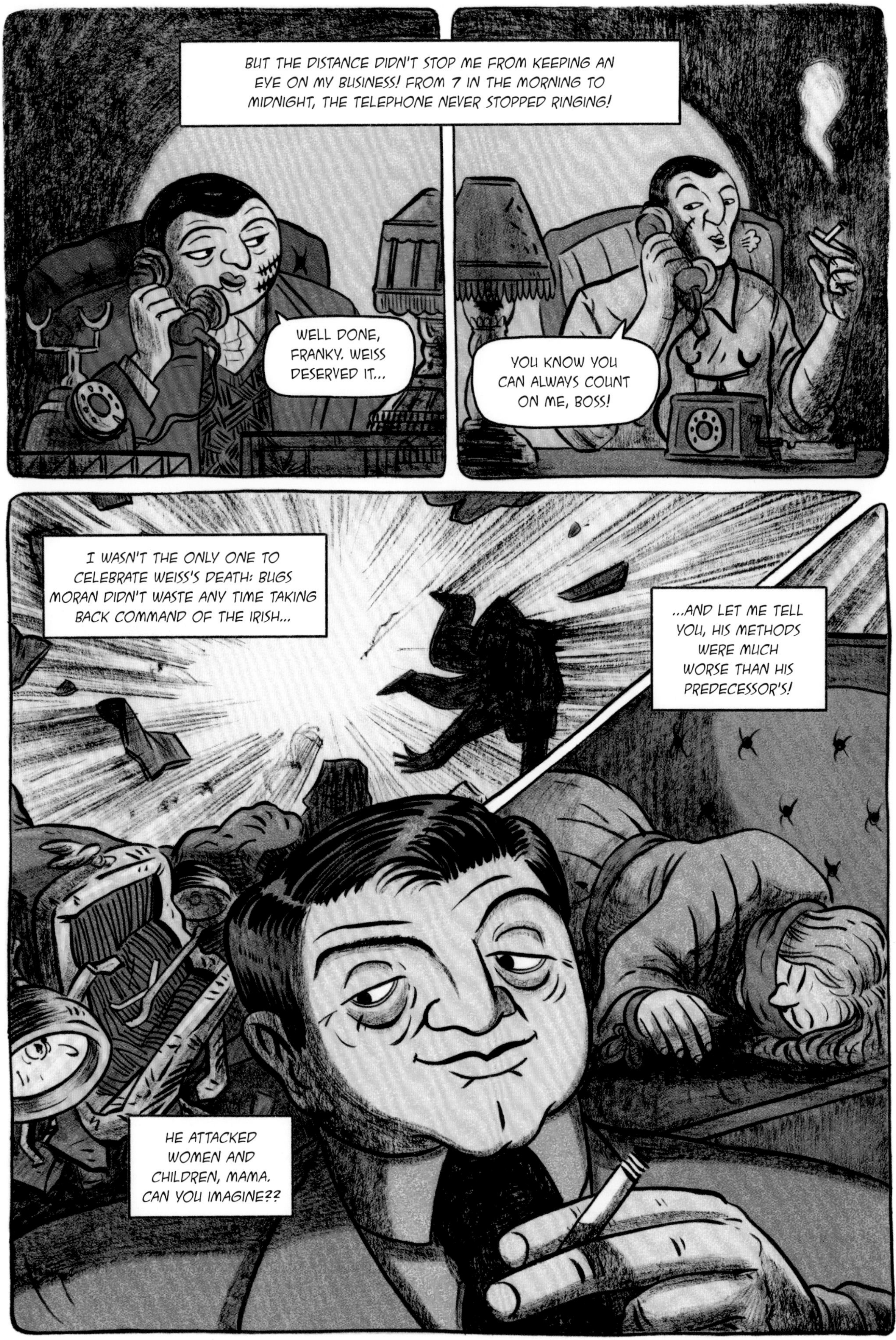
BUT THE DISTANCE DIDN'T STOP ME FROM KEEPING AN EYE ON MY BUSINESS! FROM 7 IN THE MORNING TO MIDNIGHT, THE TELEPHONE NEVER STOPPED RINGING!
WELL DONE, FRANKY. WEISS DESERVED IT...
YOU KNOW YOU CAN ALWAYS COUNT ON ME, BOSS!
I WASN'T THE ONLY ONE TO CELEBRATE WEISS'S DEATH: BUGS MORAN DIDN'T WASTE ANY TIME TAKING BACK COMMAND OF THE IRISH...
...AND LET ME TELL YOU, HIS METHODS WERE MUCH WORSE THAN HIS PREDECESSOR'S!
HE ATTACKED WOMEN AND CHILDREN, MAMA. CAN YOU IMAGINE??

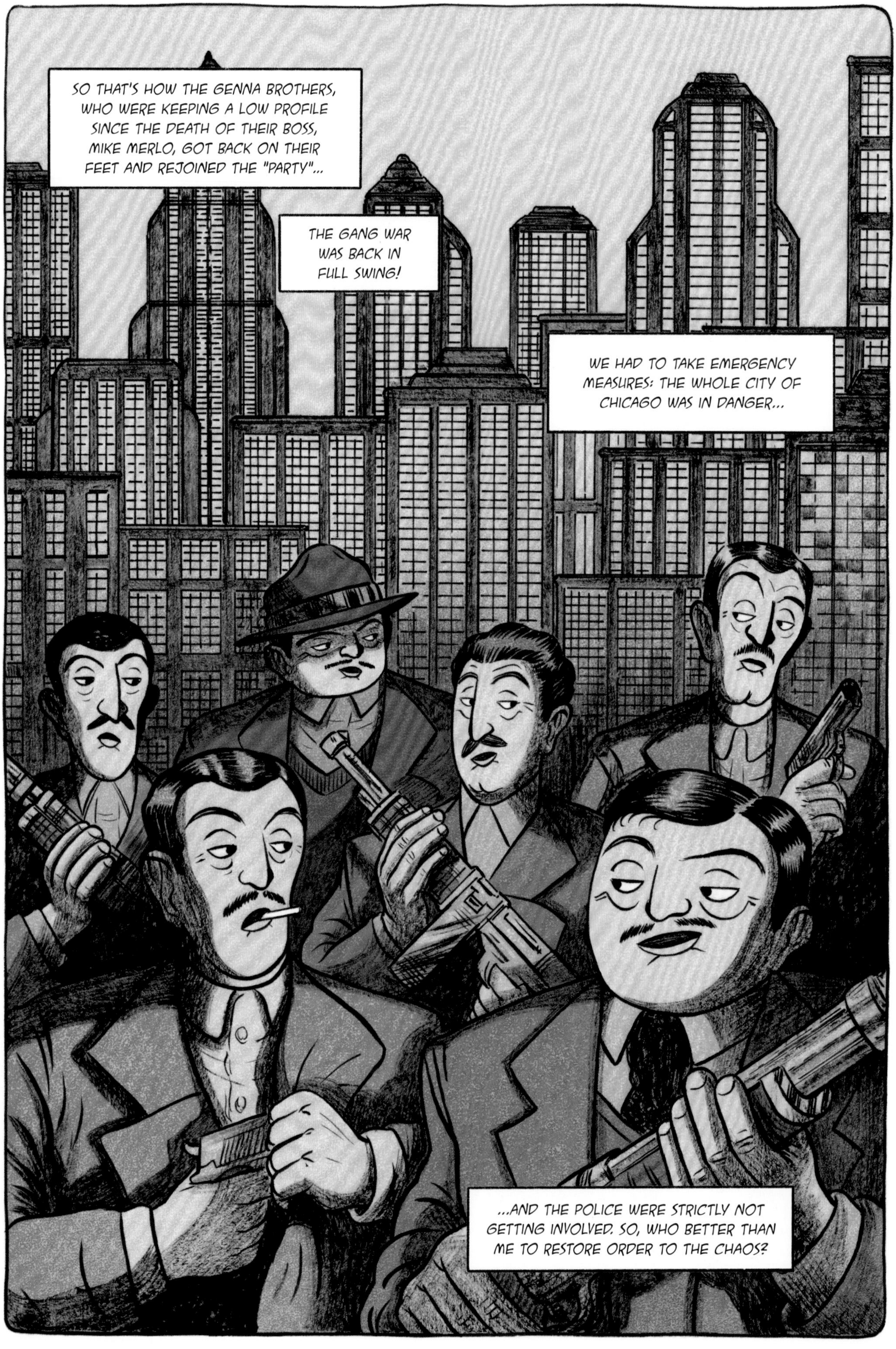
SO THAT'S HOW THE GENNA BROTHERS, WHO WERE KEEPING A LOW PROFILE SINCE THE DEATH OF THEIR BOSS, MIKE MERLO, GOT BACK ON THEIR FEET AND REJOINED THE "PARTY"...
THE GANG WAR WAS BACK IN FULL SWING!
WE HAD TO TAKE EMERGENCY MEASURES: THE WHOLE CITY OF CHICAGO WAS IN DANGER...
...AND THE POLICE WERE STRICTLY NOT GETTING INVOLVED. SO, WHO BETTER THAN ME TO RESTORE ORDER TO THE CHAOS?

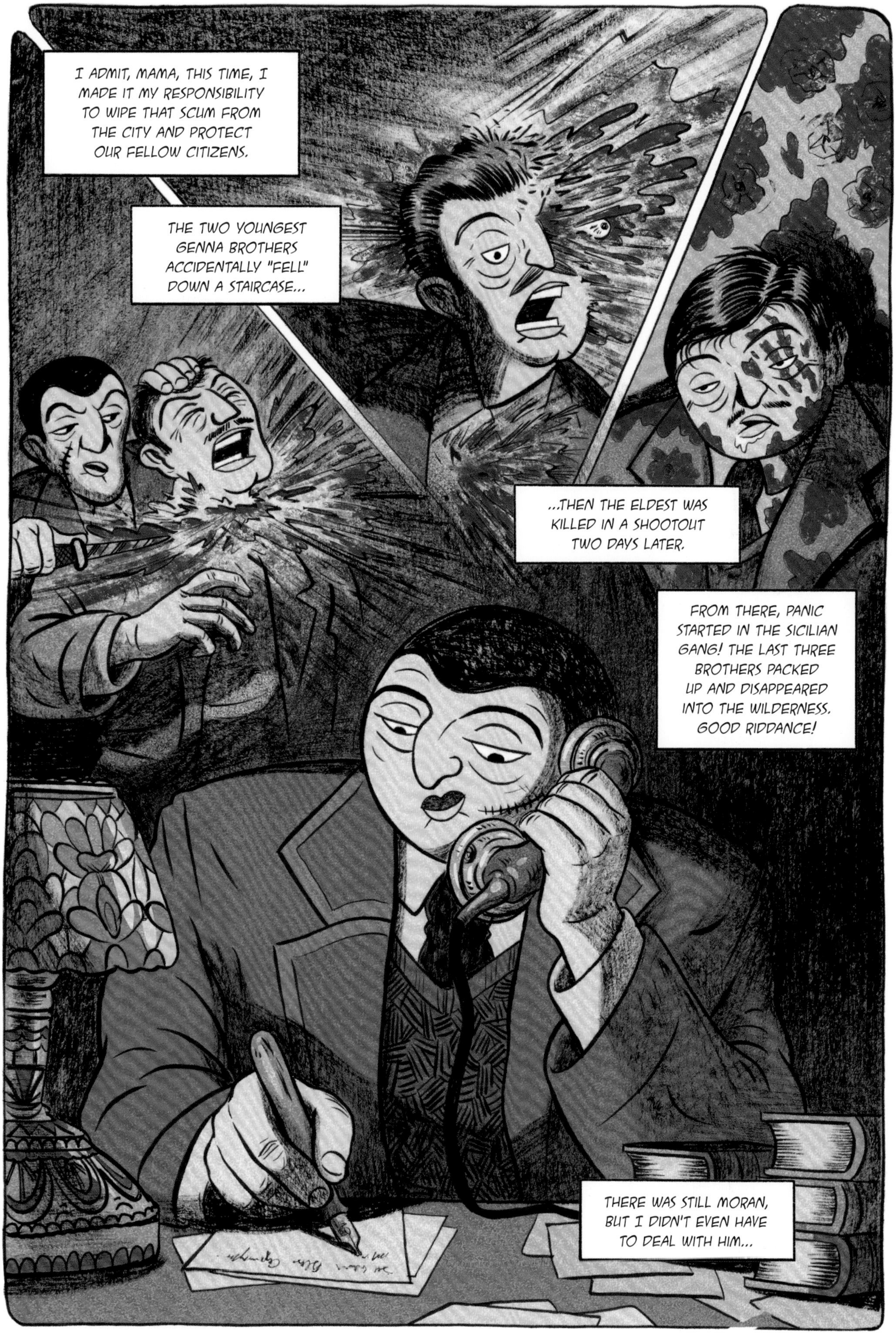
I ADMIT, MAMA, THIS TIME, I MADE IT MY RESPONSIBILITY TO WIPE THAT SCUM FROM THE CITY AND PROTECT OUR FELLOW CITIZENS.
THE TWO YOUNGEST GENNA BROTHERS ACCIDENTALLY "FELL" DOWN A STAIRCASE...
...THEN THE ELDEST WAS KILLED IN A SHOOTOUT TWO DAYS LATER.
FROM THERE, PANIC STARTED IN THE SICILIAN GANG! THE LAST THREE BROTHERS PACKED UP AND DISAPPEARED INTO THE WILDERNESS. GOOD RIDDANCE!
THERE WAS STILL MORAN, BUT I DIDN'T EVEN HAVE TO DEAL WITH HIM...

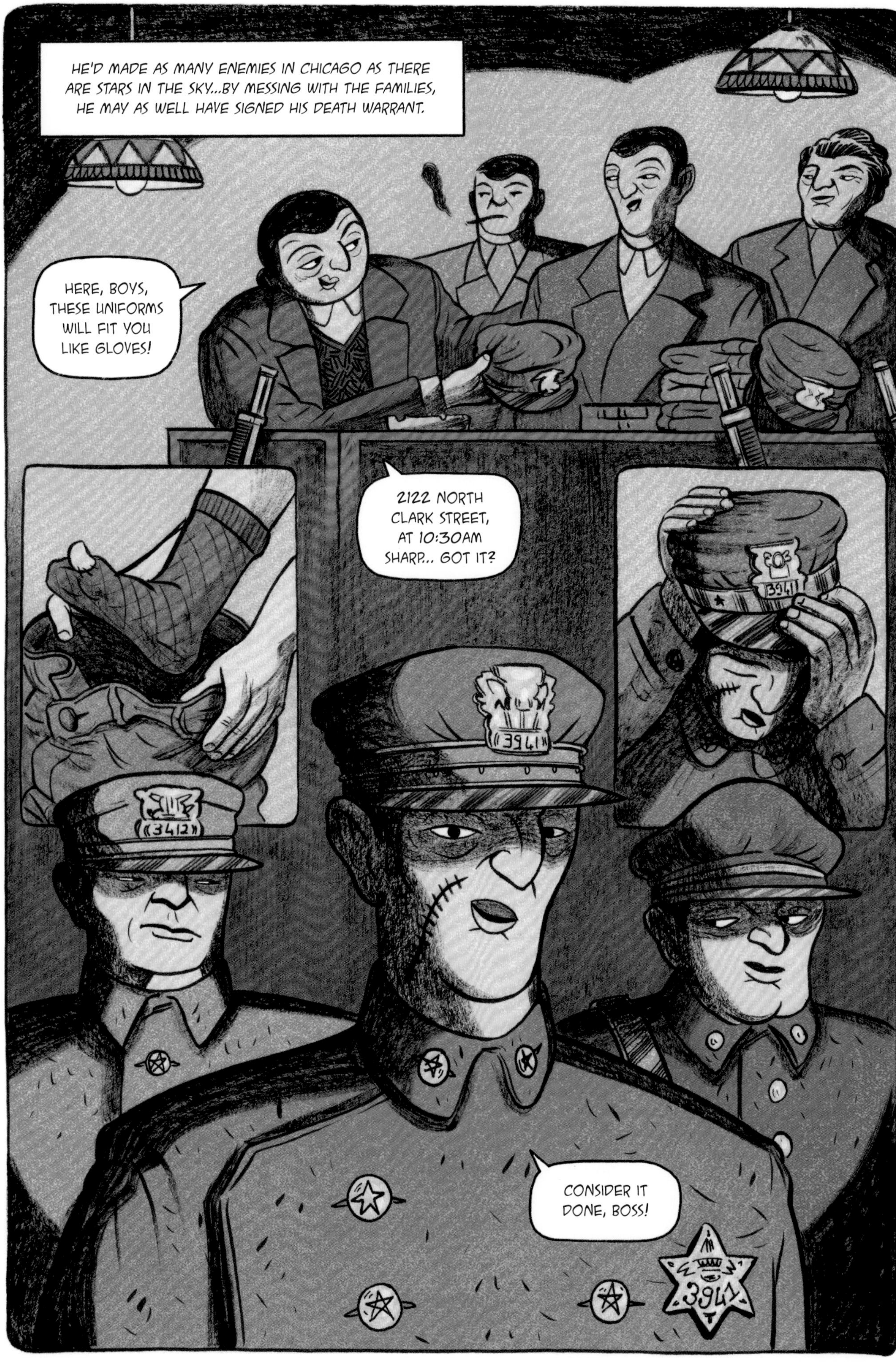
HE'D MADE AS MANY ENEMIES IN CHICAGO AS THERE ARE STARS IN THE SKY...BY MESSING WITH THE FAMILIES, HE MAY AS WELL HAVE SIGNED HIS DEATH WARRANT.
HERE, BOYS, THESE UNIFORMS WILL FIT YOU LIKE GLOVES!
2122 NORTH CLARK STREET, AT 10:30AM SHARP... GOT IT?
CONSIDER IT DONE, BOSS!

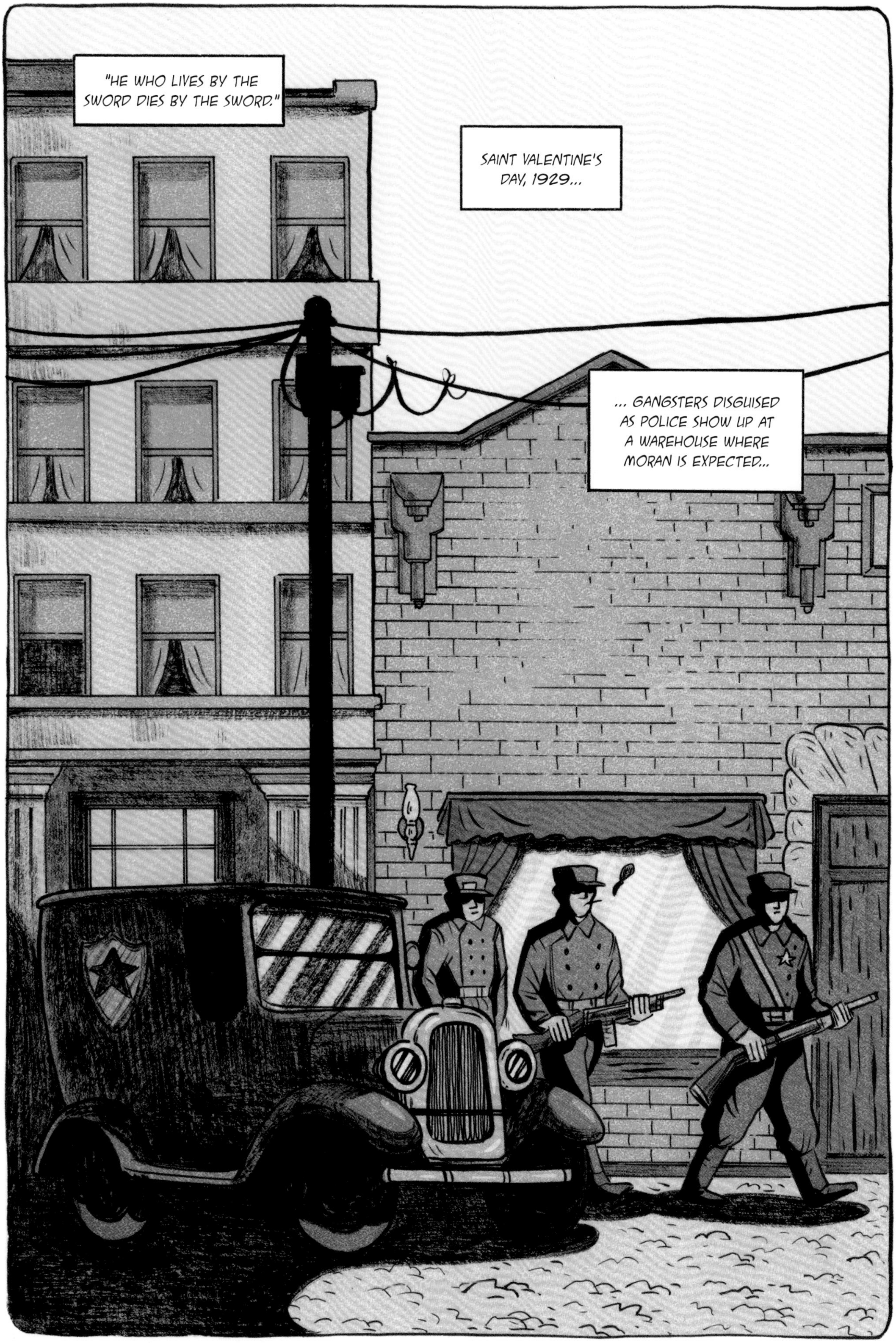
"HE WHO LIVES BY THE SWORD DIES BY THE SWORD."
SAINT VALENTINE'S DAY, 1929...
... GANGSTERS DISGUISED AS POLICE SHOW UP AT A WAREHOUSE WHERE MORAN IS EXPECTED...

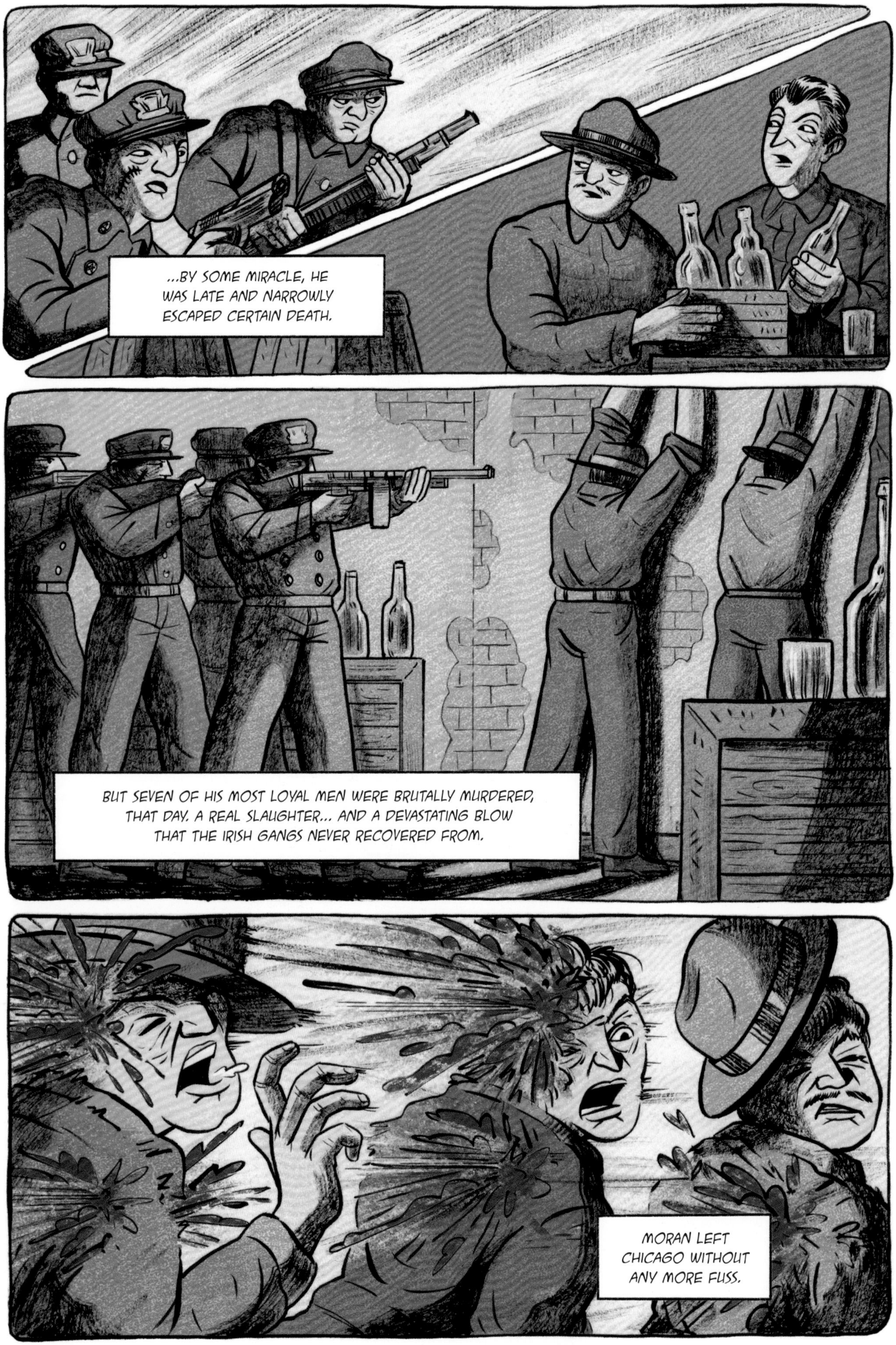
...BY SOME MIRACLE, HE WAS LATE AND NARROWLY ESCAPED CERTAIN DEATH.
BUT SEVEN OF HIS MOST LOYAL MEN WERE BRUTALLY MURDERED, THAT DAY. A REAL SLAUGHTER... AND A DEVASTATING BLOW THAT THE IRISH GANGS NEVER RECOVERED FROM.
MORAN LEFT CHICAGO WITHOUT ANY MORE FUSS.

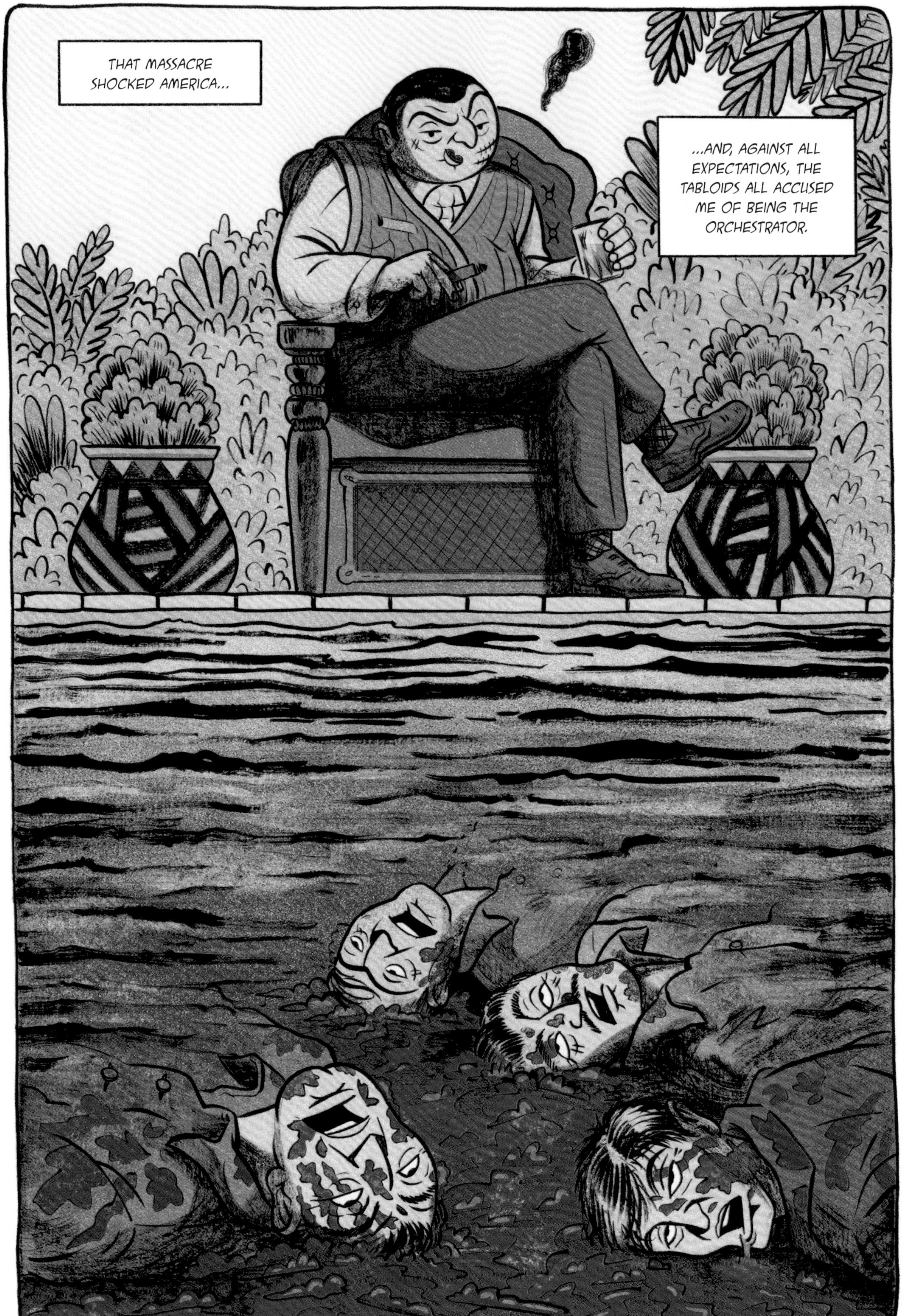
THAT MASSACRE SHOCKED AMERICA...
...AND, AGAINST ALL EXPECTATIONS, THE TABLOIDS ALL ACCUSED ME OF BEING THE ORCHESTRATOR.

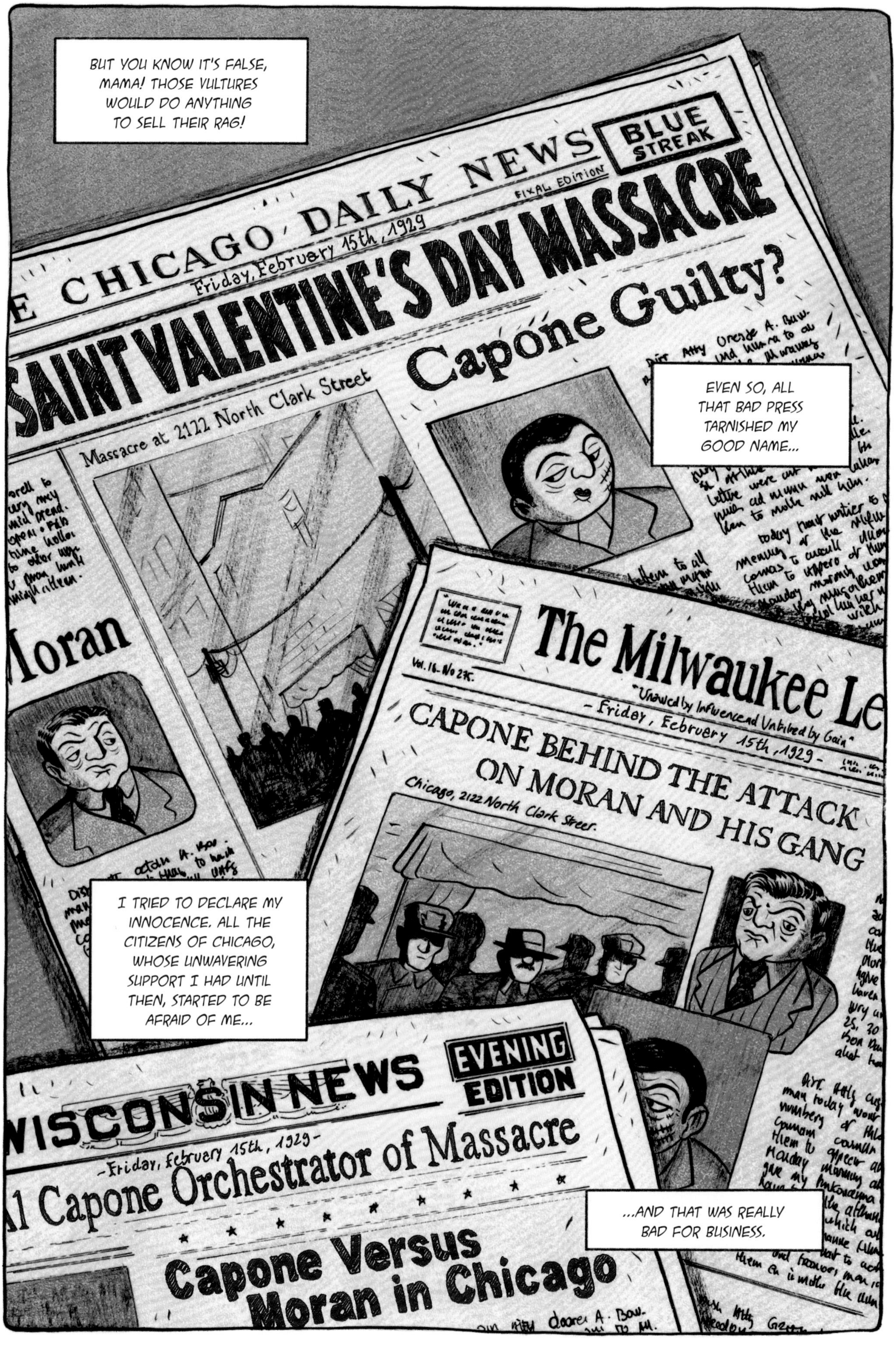
BUT YOU KNOW IT'S FALSE, MAMA! THOSE VULTURES WOULD DO ANYTHING TO SELL THEIR RAG!
THE CHICAGO DAILY NEWS
BLUE STREAK
FINAL EDITION
Friday, February 15th, 1929
SAINT VALENTINE'S DAY MASSACRE
Capone Guilty?
Massacre at 2122 North Clark Street
Moran
EVEN SO, ALL THAT BAD PRESS TARNISHED MY GOOD NAME...
The Milwaukee Le
Friday, February 15th, 1929
CAPONE BEHIND THE ATTACK ON MORAN AND HIS GANG
Chicago, 2122 North Clark Streer.
I TRIED TO DECLARE MY INNOCENCE. ALL THE CITIZENS OF CHICAGO, WHOSE UNWAVERING SUPPORT I HAD UNTIL THEN, STARTED TO BE AFRAID OF ME...
WISCONSIN NEWS
EVENING EDITION
Friday, february 15th, 1929
Al Capone Orchestrator of Massacre
Capone Versus Moran in Chicago
...AND THAT WAS REALLY BAD FOR BUSINESS.

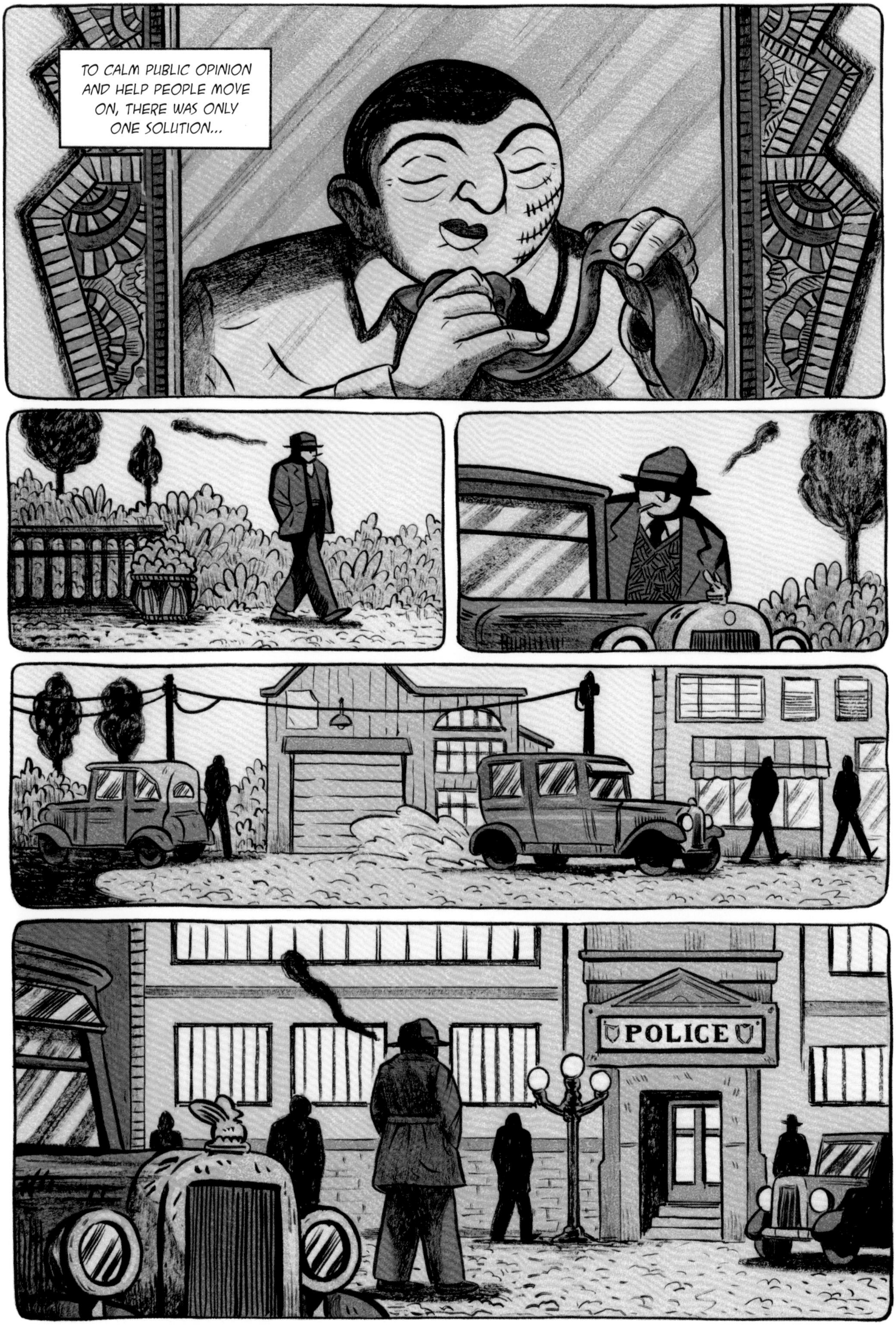
TO CALM PUBLIC OPINION AND HELP PEOPLE MOVE ON, THERE WAS ONLY ONE SOLUTION...
POLICE

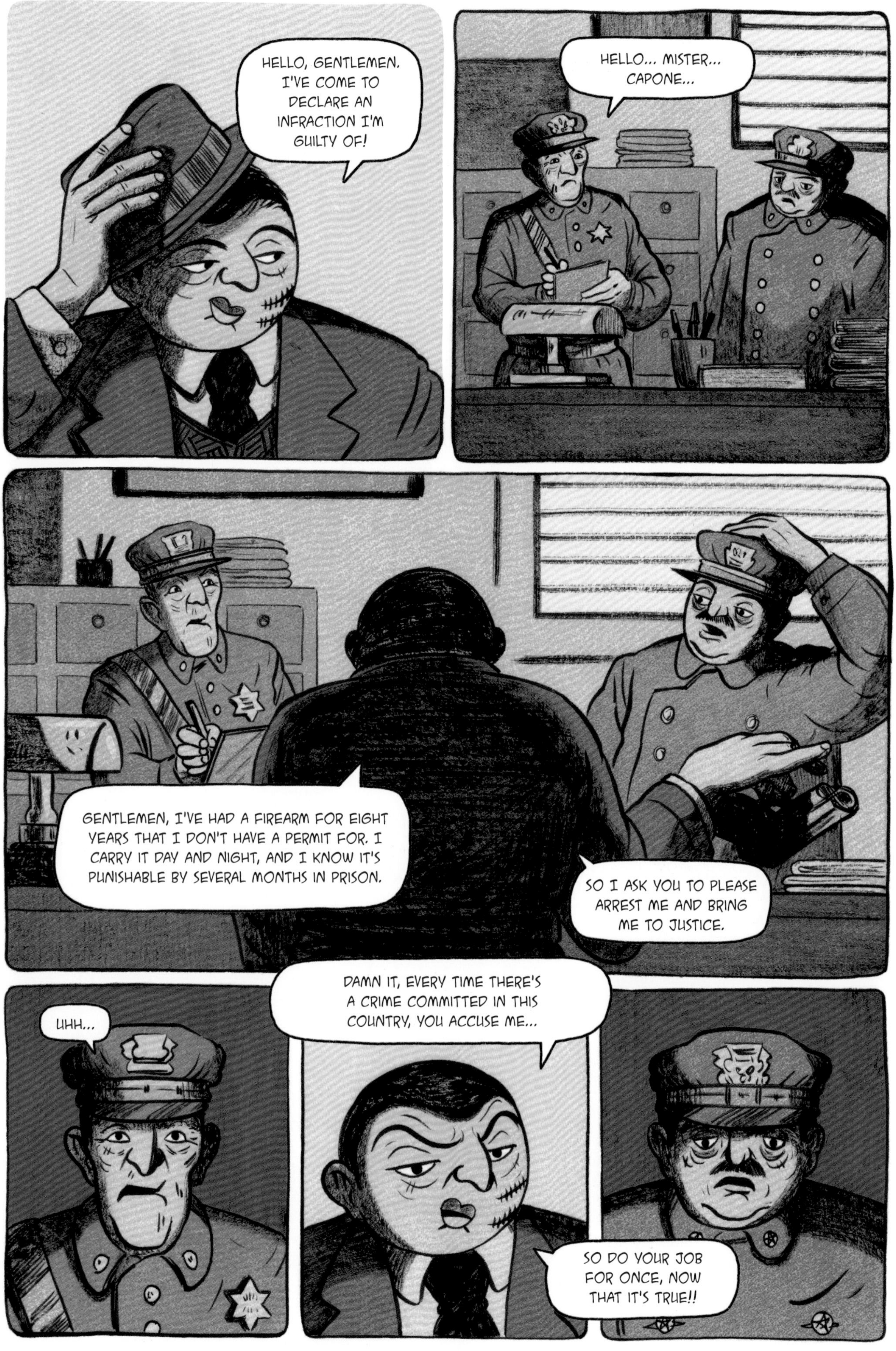
HELLO, GENTLEMEN. I'VE COME TO DECLARE AN INFRACTION I'M GUILTY OF!
HELLO... MISTER... CAPONE...
GENTLEMEN, I'VE HAD A FIREARM FOR EIGHT YEARS THAT I DON'T HAVE A PERMIT FOR. I CARRY IT DAY AND NIGHT, AND I KNOW IT'S PUNISHABLE BY SEVERAL MONTHS IN PRISON.
SO I ASK YOU TO PLEASE ARREST ME AND BRING ME TO JUSTICE.
UHH...
DAMN IT, EVERY TIME THERE'S A CRIME COMMITTED IN THIS COUNTRY, YOU ACCUSE ME...
SO DO YOUR JOB FOR ONCE, NOW THAT IT'S TRUE!!

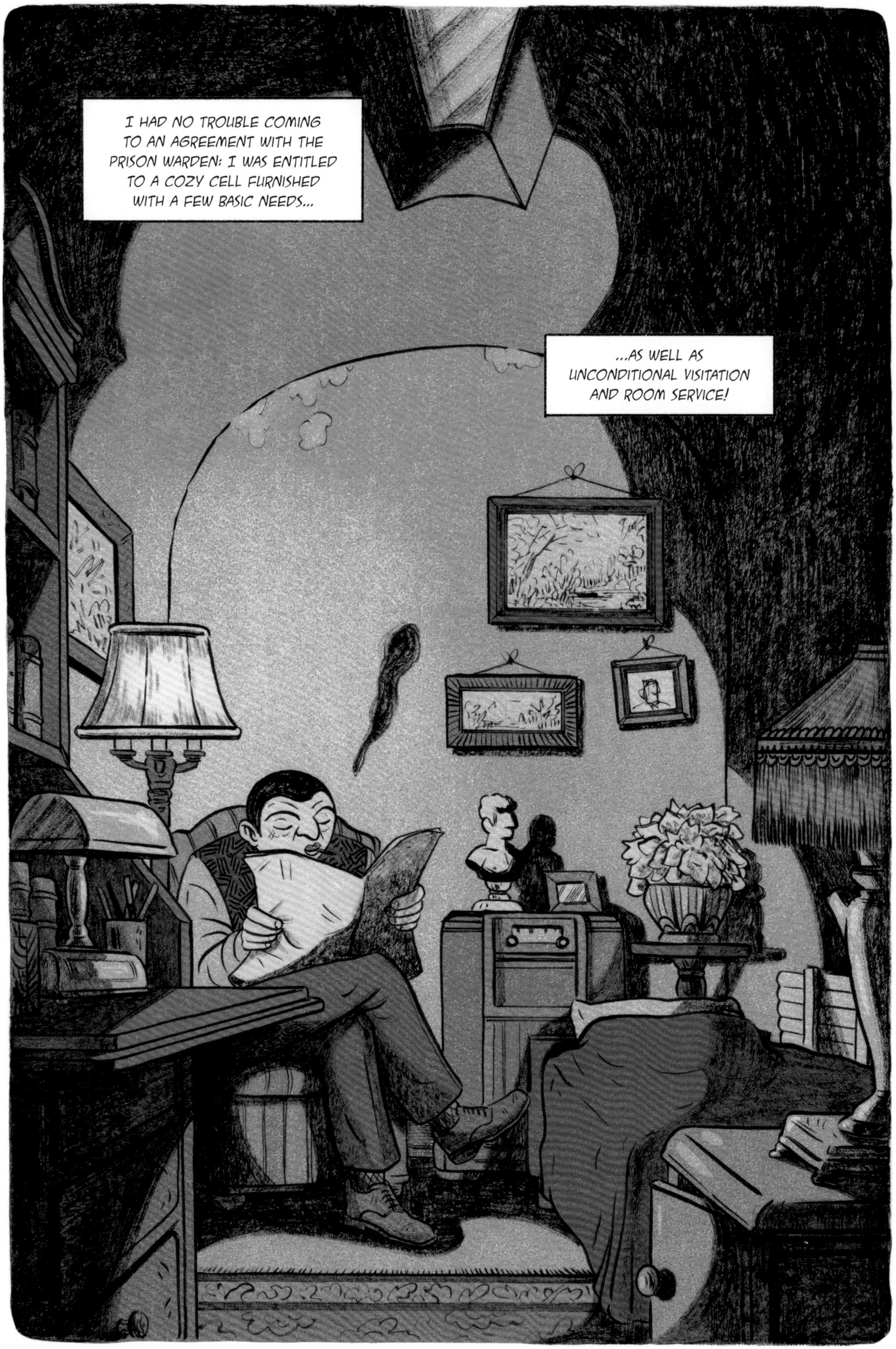
I HAD NO TROUBLE COMING TO AN AGREEMENT WITH THE PRISON WARDEN: I WAS ENTITLED TO A COZY CELL FURNISHED WITH A FEW BASIC NEEDS...
...AS WELL AS UNCONDITIONAL VISITATION AND ROOM SERVICE!

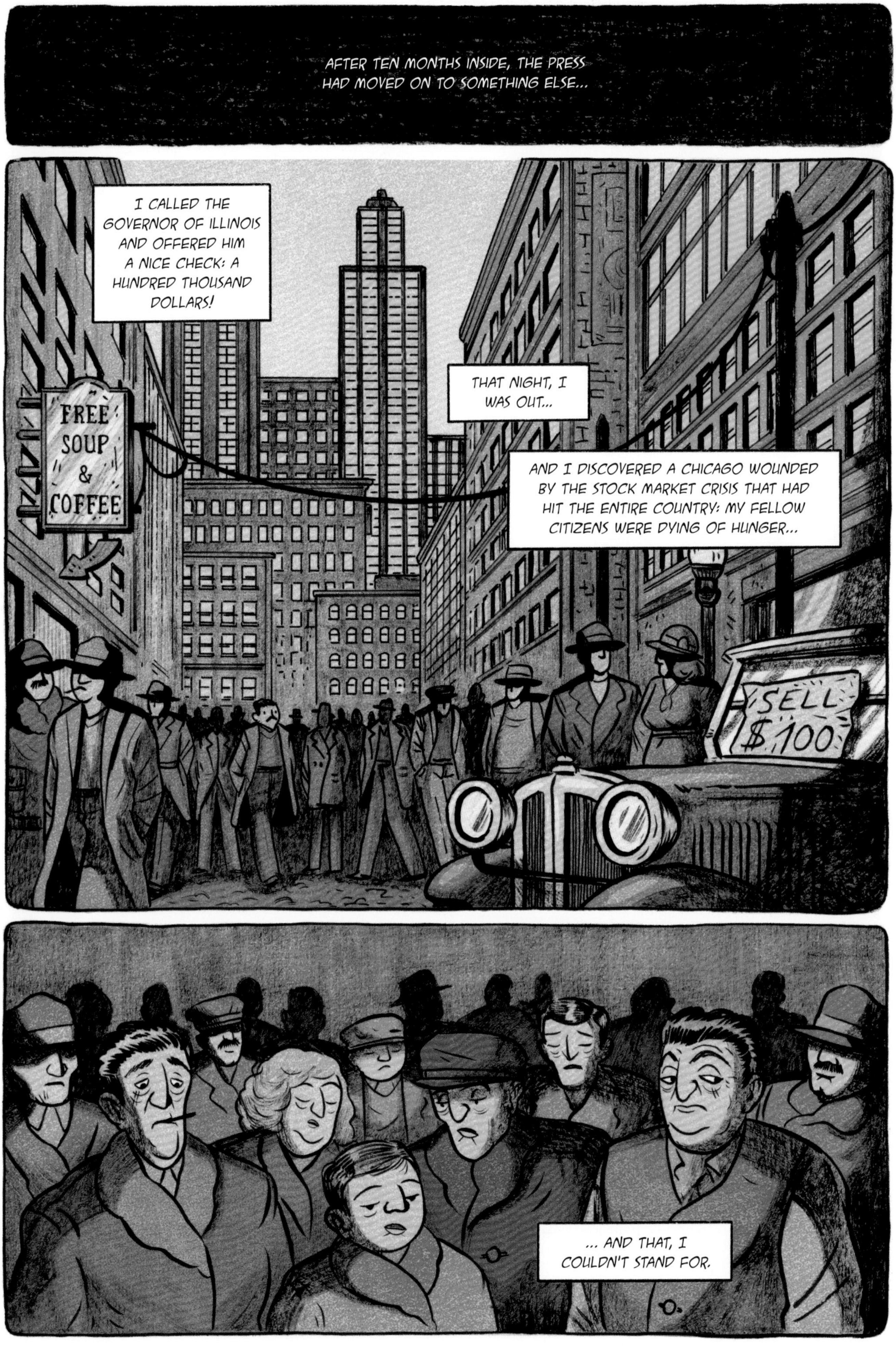
AFTER TEN MONTHS INSIDE, THE PRESS HAD MOVED ON TO SOMETHING ELSE...
I CALLED THE GOVERNOR OF ILLINOIS AND OFFERED HIM A NICE CHECK: A HUNDRED THOUSAND DOLLARS!
FREE SOUP & COFFEE
THAT NIGHT, I WAS OUT...
AND I DISCOVERED A CHICAGO WOUNDED BY THE STOCK MARKET CRISIS THAT HAD HIT THE ENTIRE COUNTRY: MY FELLOW CITIZENS WERE DYING OF HUNGER...
SELL $ 100
... AND THAT, I COULDN'T STAND FOR.

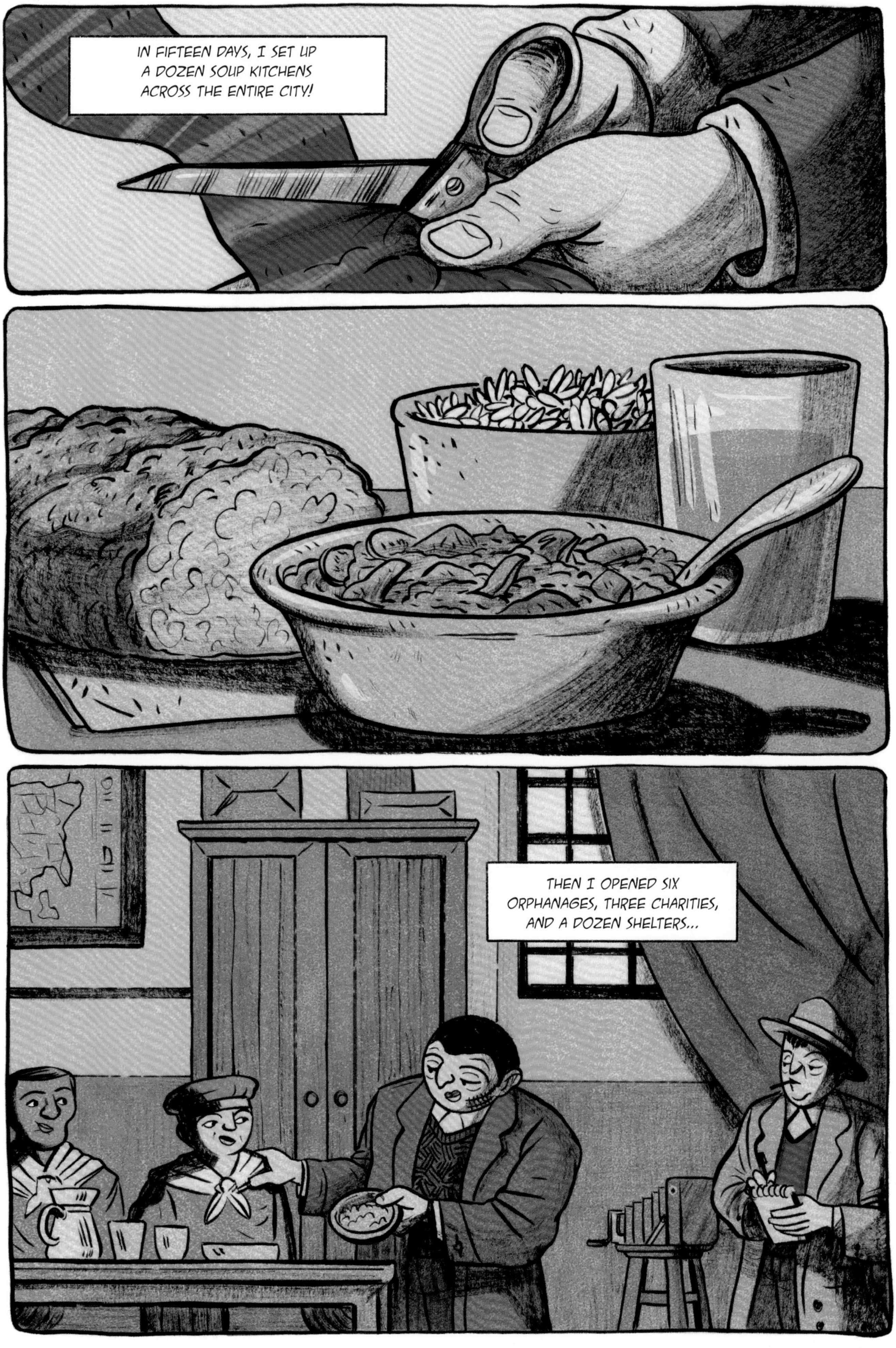
IN FIFTEEN DAYS, I SET UP A DOZEN SOUP KITCHENS ACROSS THE ENTIRE CITY!
THEN I OPENED SIX ORPHANAGES, THREE CHARITIES, AND A DOZEN SHELTERS...

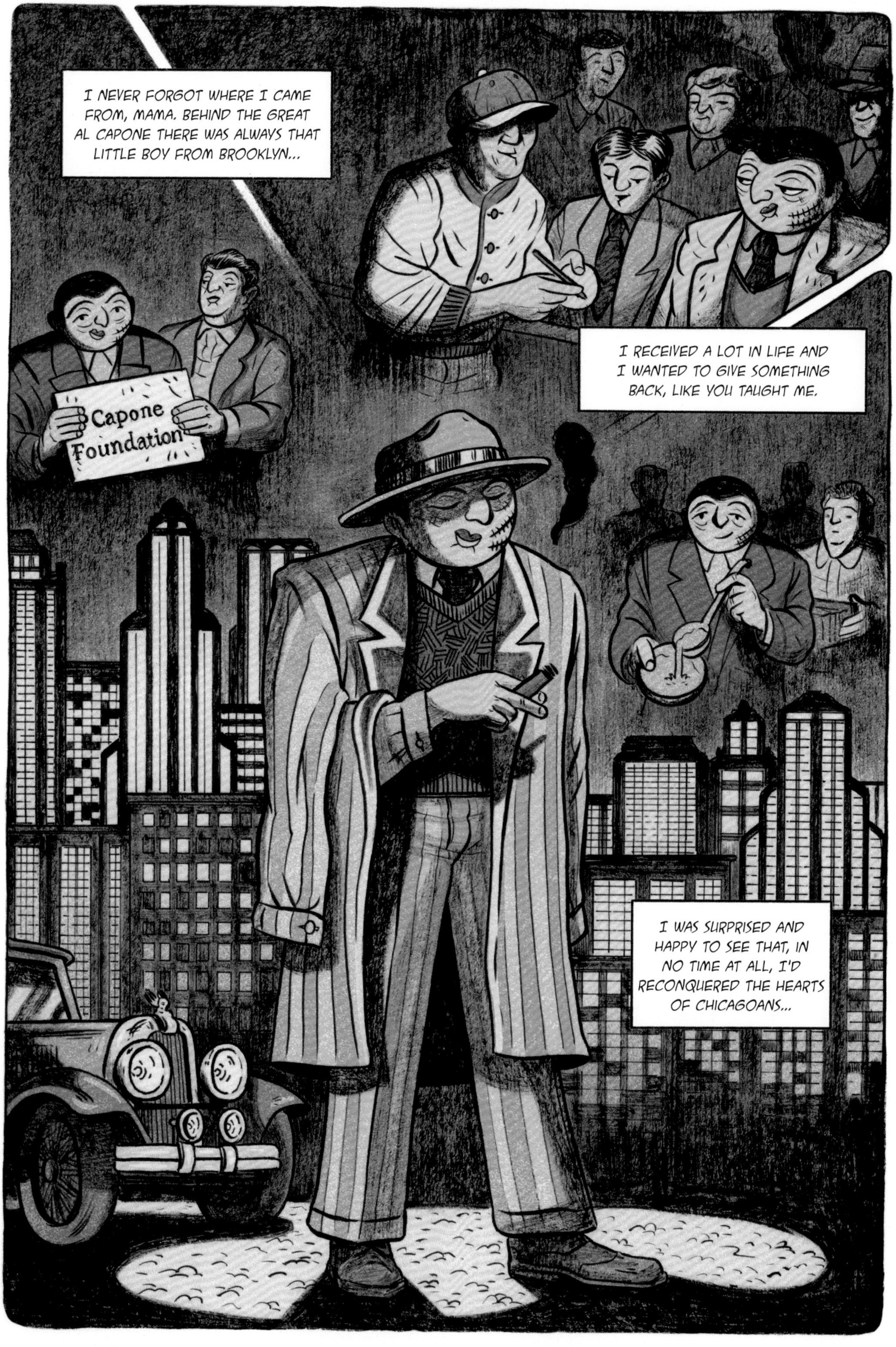
I NEVER FORGOT WHERE I CAME FROM, MAMA. BEHIND THE GREAT AL CAPONE THERE WAS ALWAYS THAT LITTLE BOY FROM BROOKLYN...
Capone Foundation
I RECEIVED A LOT IN LIFE AND I WANTED TO GIVE SOMETHING BACK, LIKE YOU TAUGHT ME.
I WAS SURPRISED AND HAPPY TO SEE THAT, IN NO TIME AT ALL, I'D RECONQUERED THE HEARTS OF CHICAGOANS...

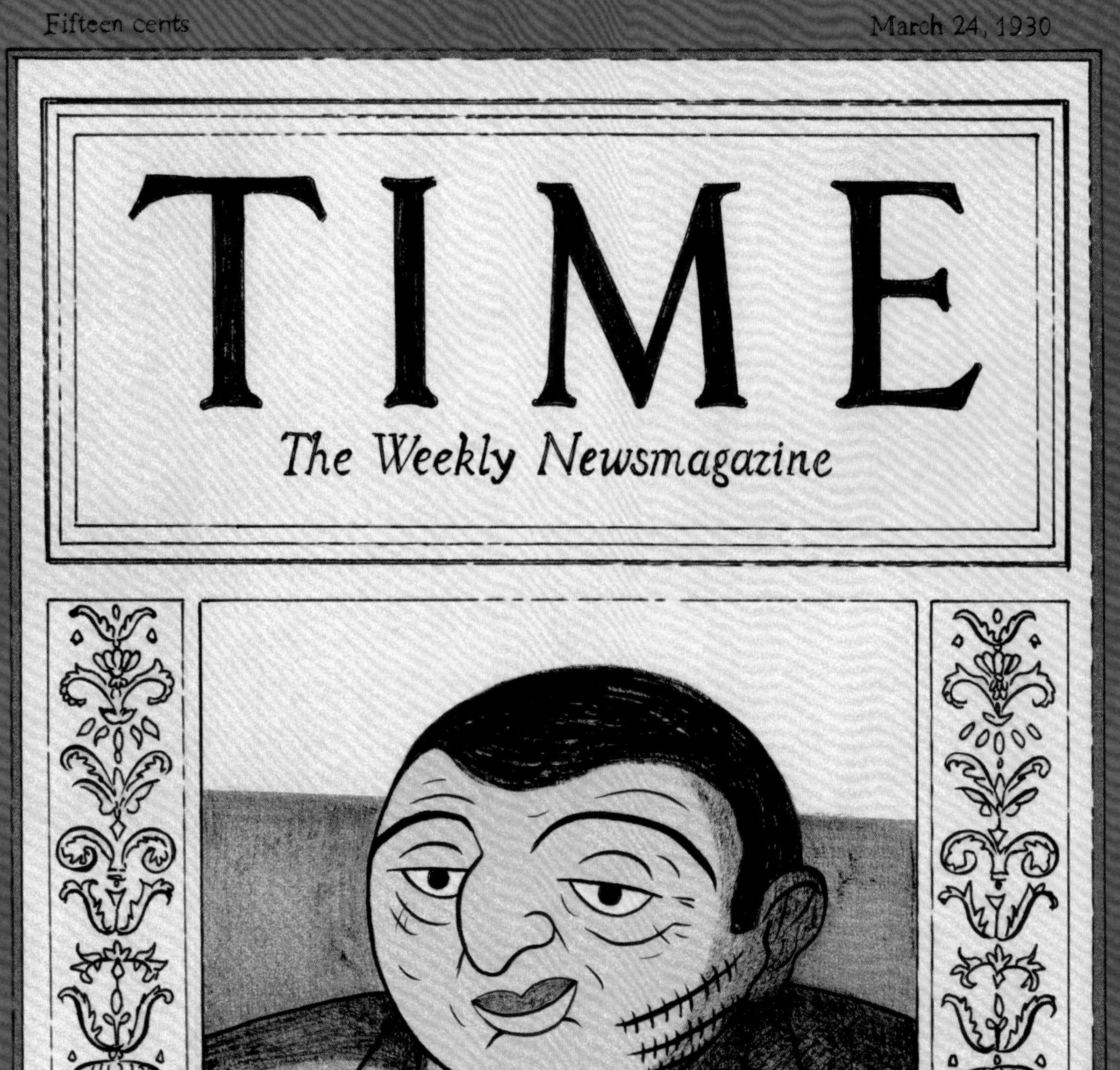

Fifteen cents
March 24, 1930
TIME
The Weekly Newsmagazine
MAMA, FINALLY, I'D BECOME THE UNCONTESTED KING OF CHICAGO!
Volume XV
ALPHONSE ("Scarface") CAPONE
A pink apron, a pan of spaghetti
Number 12

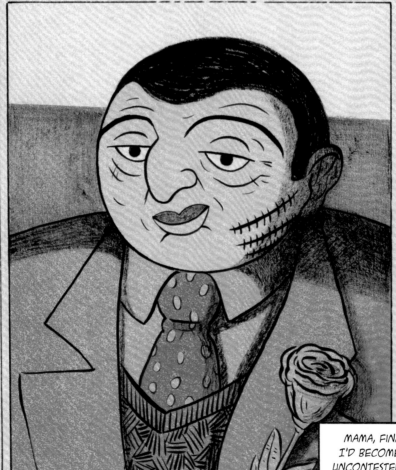

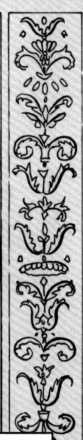

CHAPTER 5

Number 85-AZ

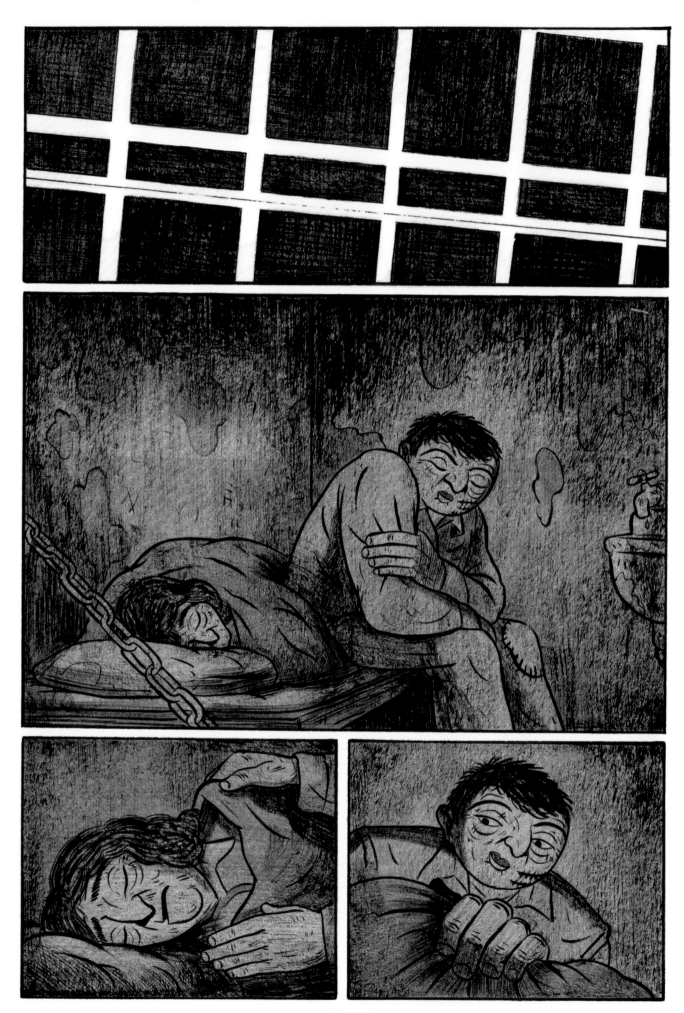

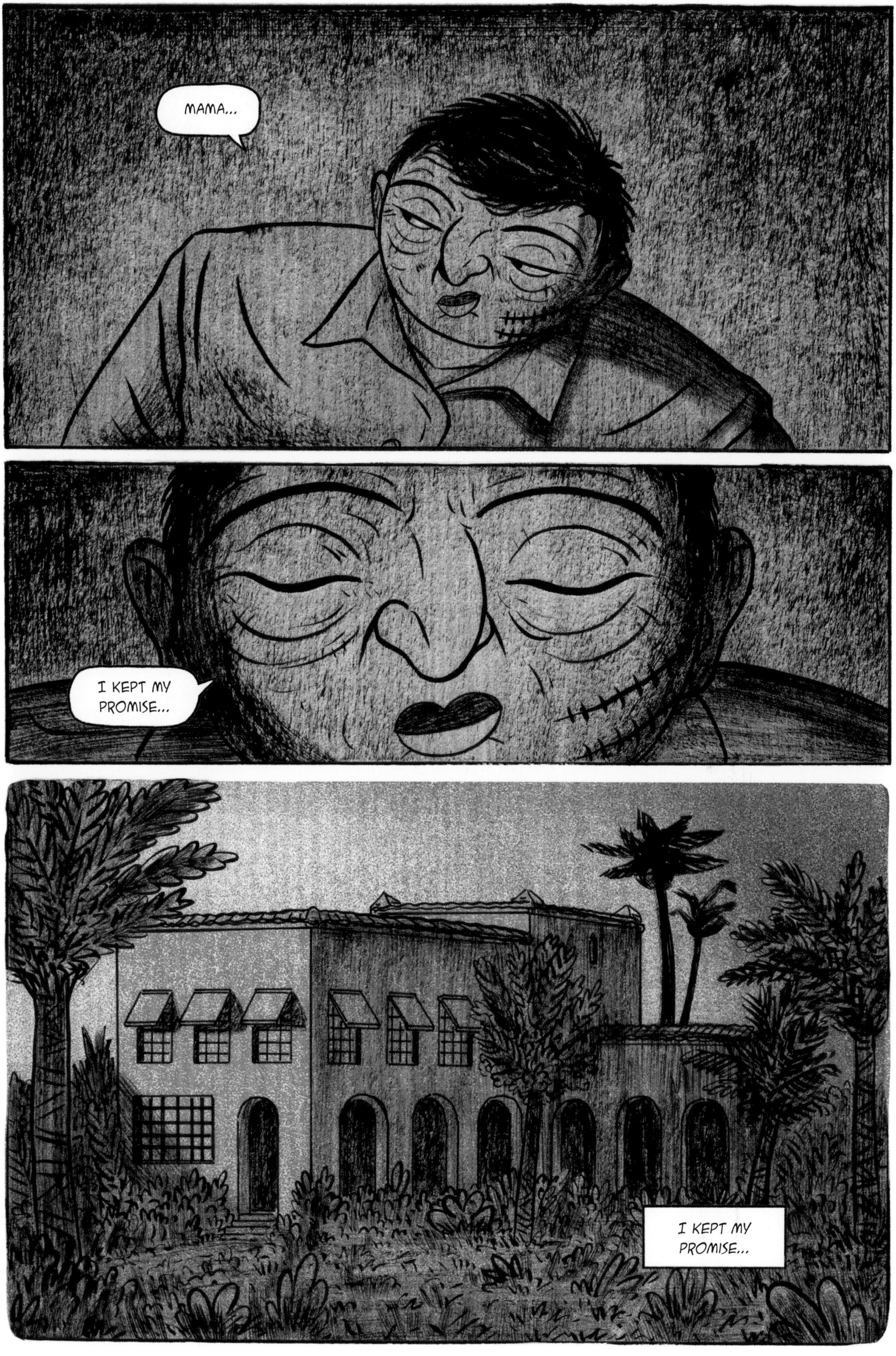
MAMA...
I KEPT MY PROMISE...
I KEPT MY PROMISE...

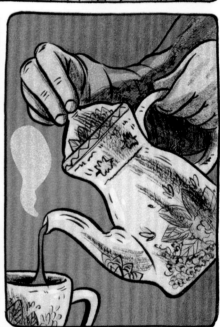

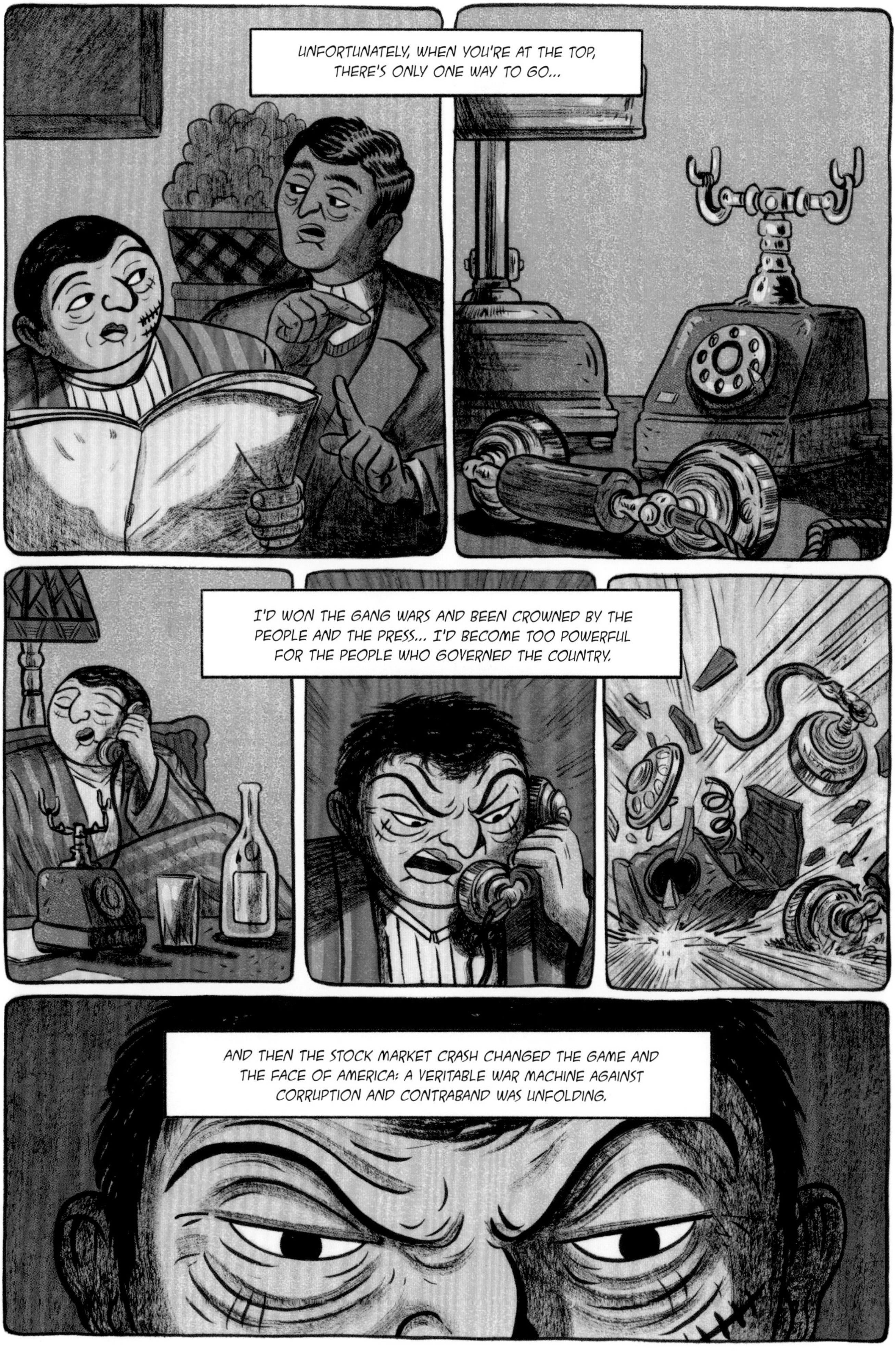
UNFORTUNATELY, WHEN YOU'RE AT THE TOP, THERE'S ONLY ONE WAY TO GO...
I'D WON THE GANG WARS AND BEEN CROWNED BY THE PEOPLE AND THE PRESS... I'D BECOME TOO POWERFUL FOR THE PEOPLE WHO GOVERNED THE COUNTRY.
AND THEN THE STOCK MARKET CRASH CHANGED THE GAME AND THE FACE OF AMERICA: A VERITABLE WAR MACHINE AGAINST CORRUPTION AND CONTRABAND WAS UNFOLDING.

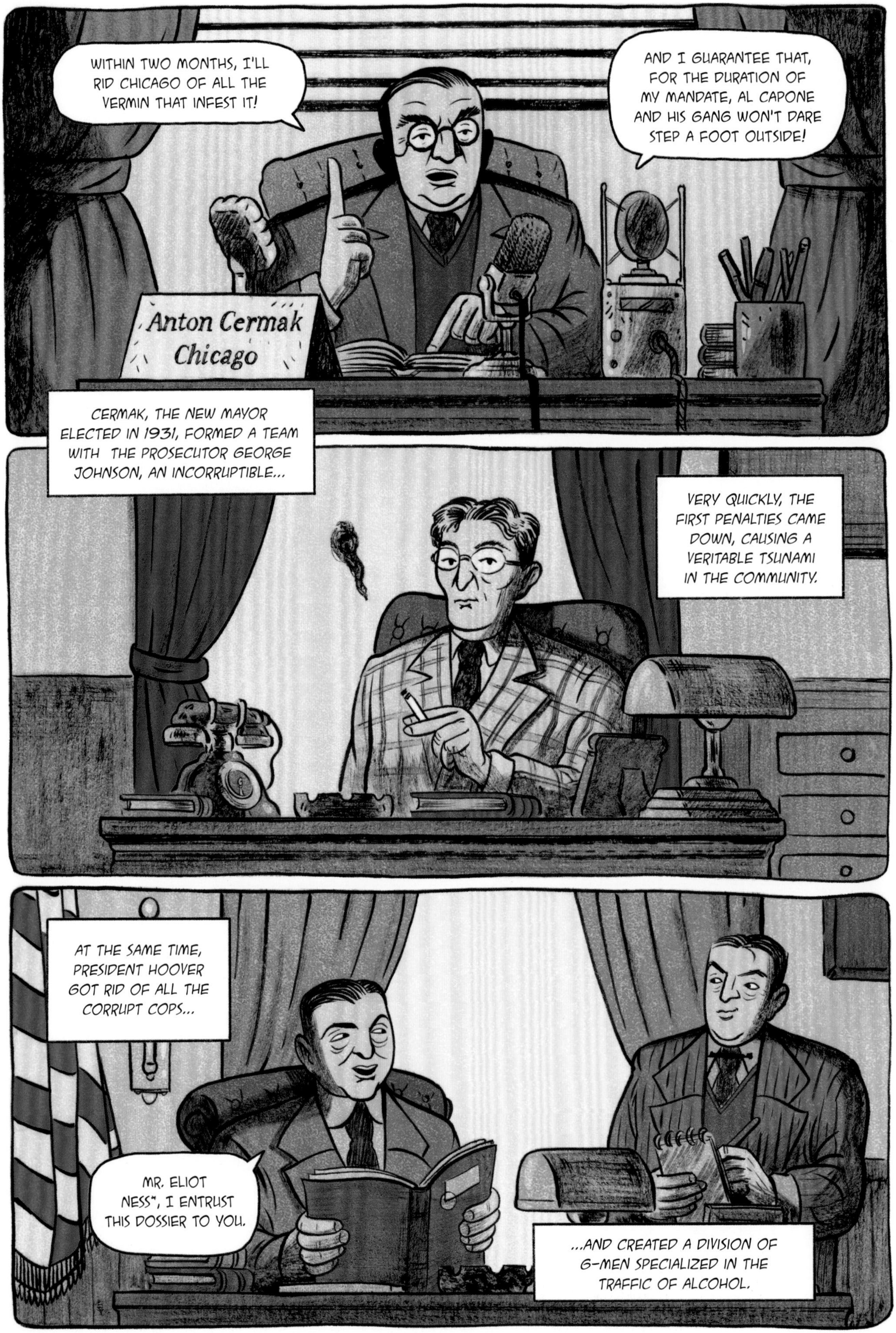
WITHIN TWO MONTHS, I'LL RID CHICAGO OF ALL THE VERMIN THAT INFEST IT!
AND I GUARANTEE THAT, FOR THE DURATION OF MY MANDATE, AL CAPONE AND HIS GANG WON'T DARE STEP A FOOT OUTSIDE!
Anton Cermak
Chicago
CERMAK, THE NEW MAYOR ELECTED IN 1931, FORMED A TEAM WITH THE PROSECUTOR GEORGE JOHNSON, AN INCORRUPTIBLE...
VERY QUICKLY, THE FIRST PENALTIES CAME DOWN, CAUSING A VERITABLE TSUNAMI IN THE COMMUNITY.
AT THE SAME TIME, PRESIDENT HOOVER GOT RID OF ALL THE CORRUPT COPS...
MR. ELIOT NESS*, I ENTRUST THIS DOSSIER TO YOU.
...AND CREATED A DIVISION OF G-MEN SPECIALIZED IN THE TRAFFIC OF ALCOHOL.

*FAMOUS US TREASURY AGENT WHO OPENLY FOUGHT AGAINST AL CAPONE.

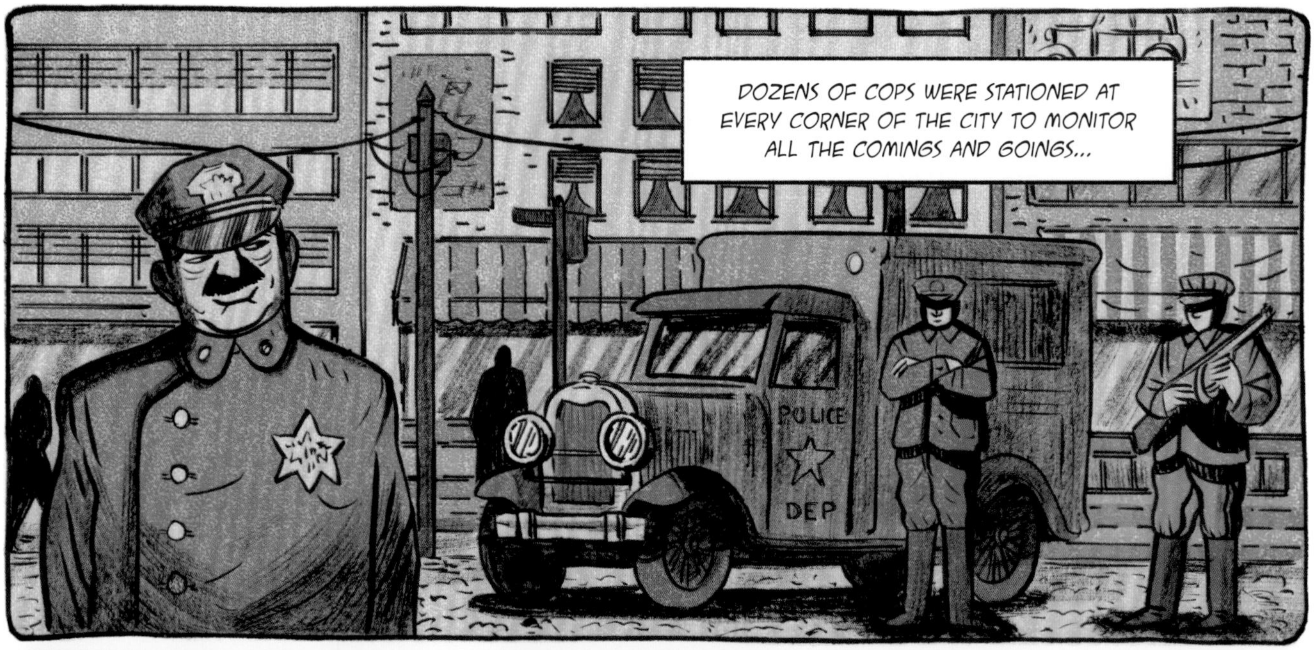
DOZENS OF COPS WERE STATIONED AT EVERY CORNER OF THE CITY TO MONITOR ALL THE COMINGS AND GOINGS...
POLICE
DEP

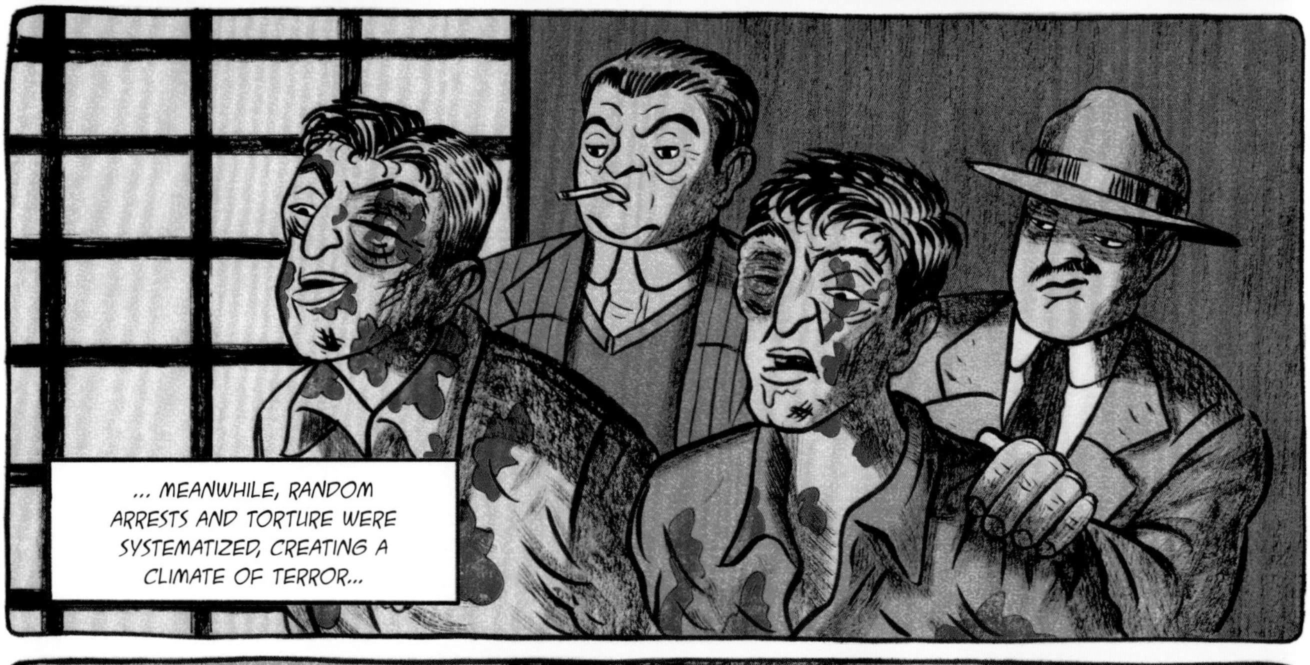
... MEANWHILE, RANDOM ARRESTS AND TORTURE WERE SYSTEMATIZED, CREATING A CLIMATE OF TERROR...

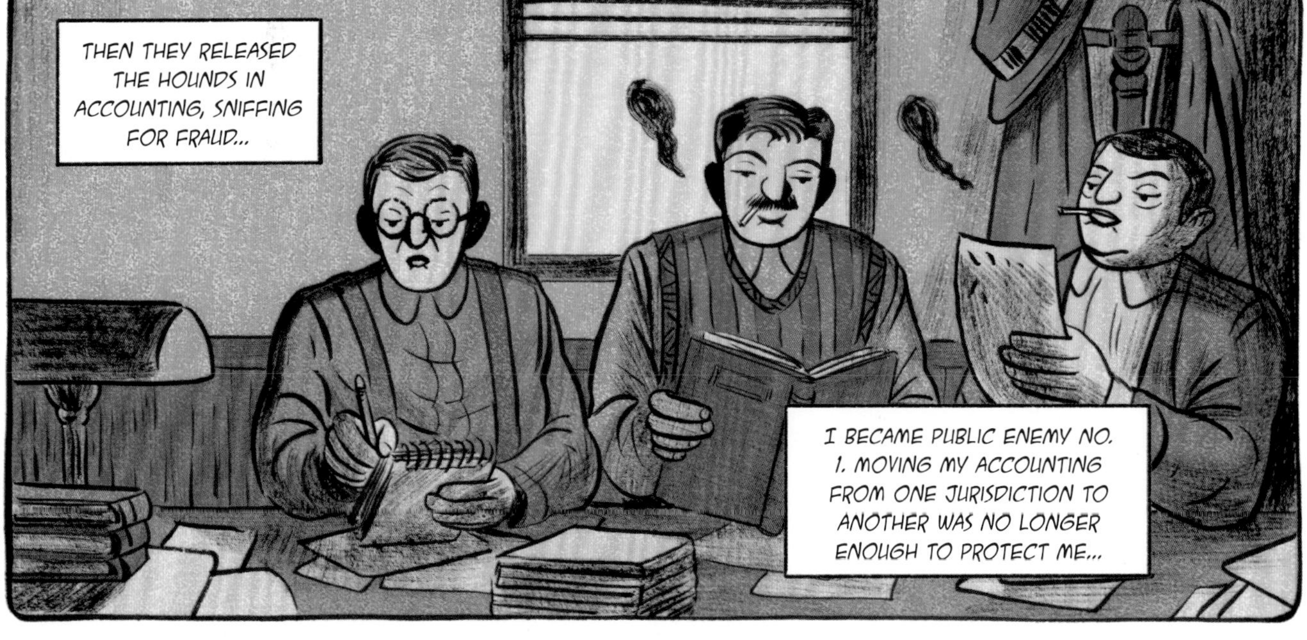
THEN THEY RELEASED THE HOUNDS IN ACCOUNTING, SNIFFING FOR FRAUD...
I BECAME PUBLIC ENEMY NO. 1. MOVING MY ACCOUNTING FROM ONE JURISDICTION TO ANOTHER WAS NO LONGER ENOUGH TO PROTECT ME...

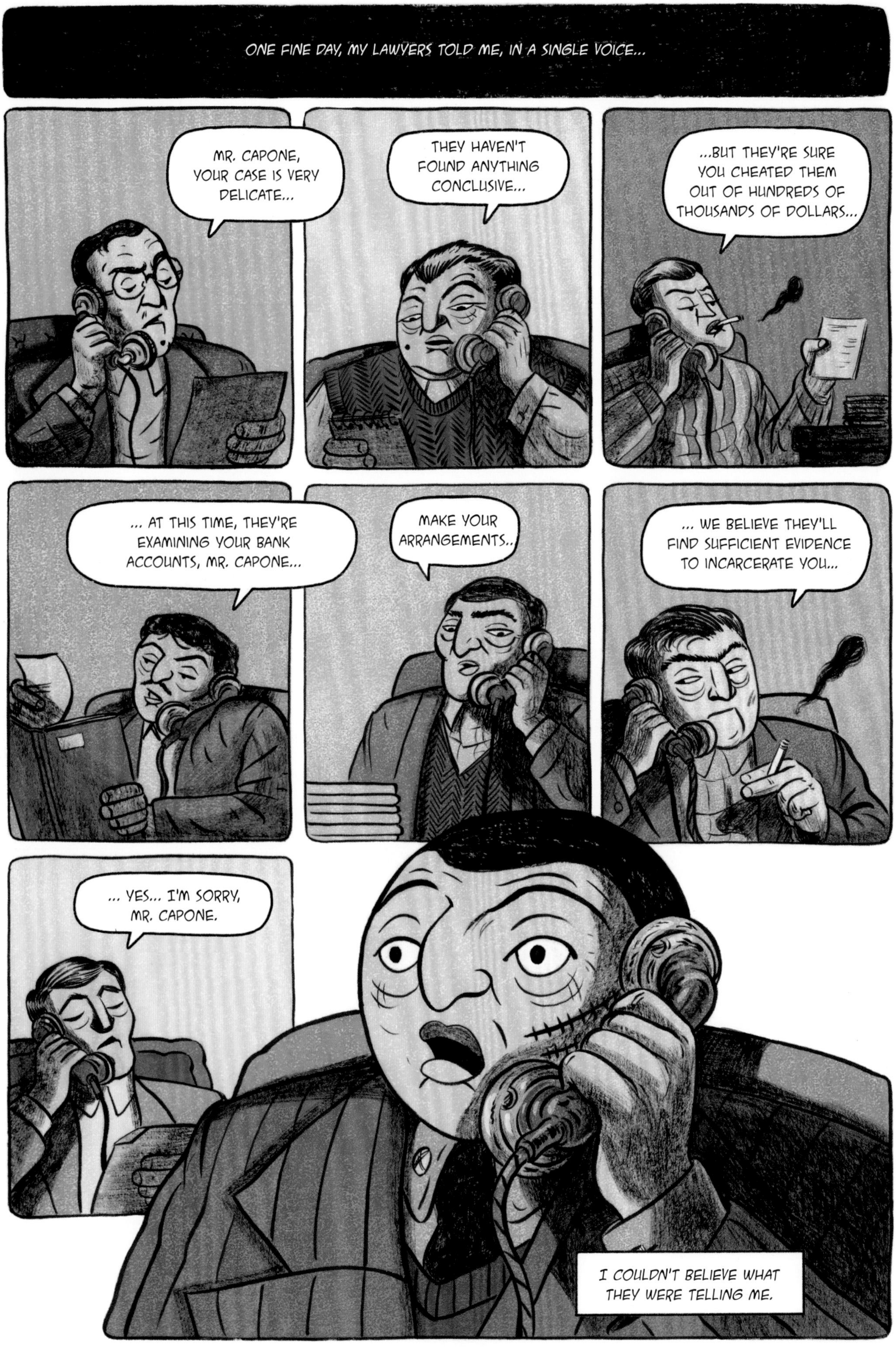

ONE FINE DAY, MY LAWYERS TOLD ME, IN A SINGLE VOICE...
MR. CAPONE, YOUR CASE IS VERY DELICATE...
THEY HAVEN'T FOUND ANYTHING CONCLUSIVE...
...BUT THEY'RE SURE YOU CHEATED THEM OUT OF HUNDREDS OF THOUSANDS OF DOLLARS...
... AT THIS TIME, THEY'RE EXAMINING YOUR BANK ACCOUNTS, MR. CAPONE...
MAKE YOUR ARRANGEMENTS...
... WE BELIEVE THEY'LL FIND SUFFICIENT EVIDENCE TO INCARCERATE YOU...
... YES... I'M SORRY, MR. CAPONE.
I COULDN'T BELIEVE WHAT THEY WERE TELLING ME.

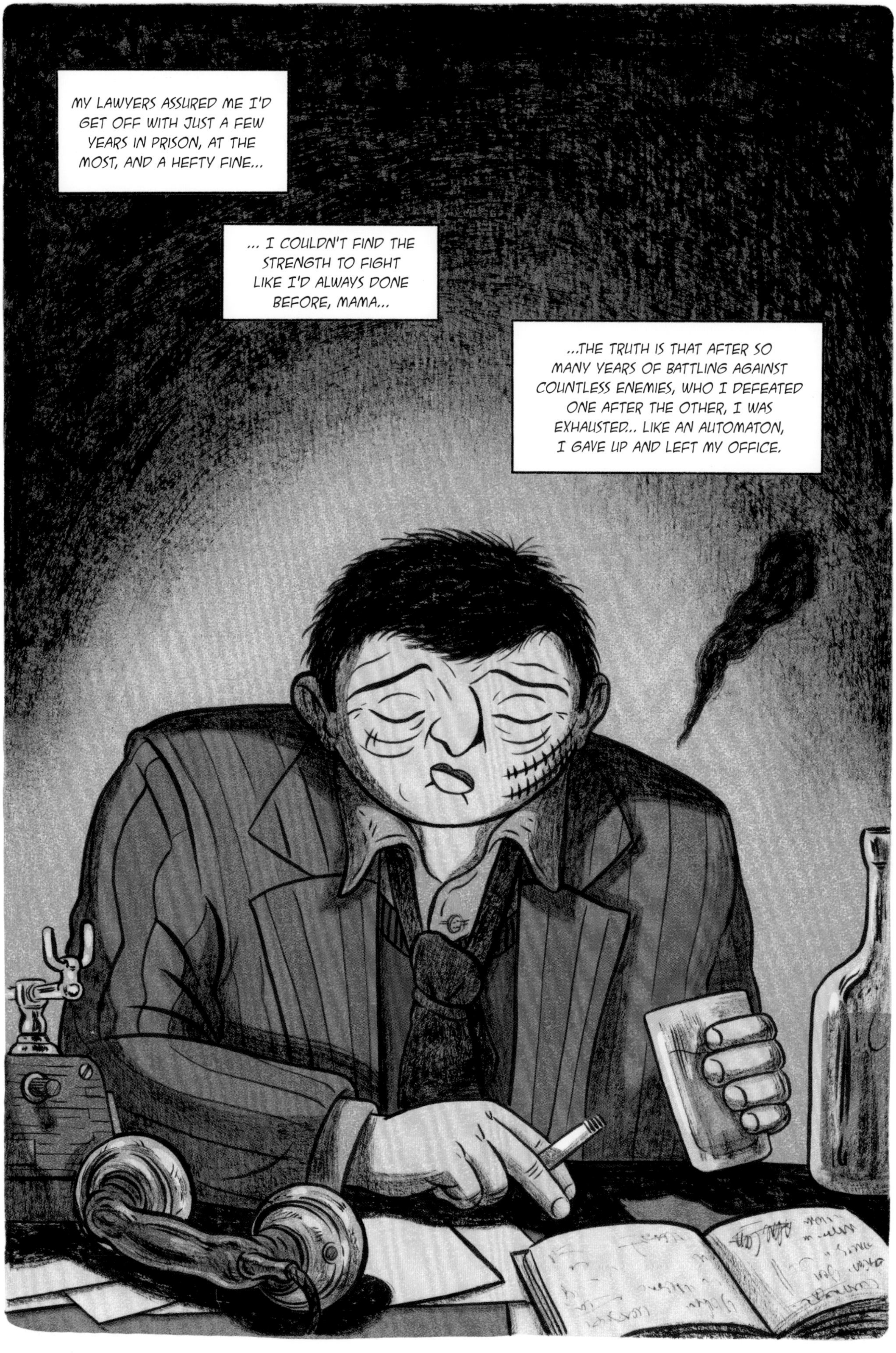
MY LAWYERS ASSURED ME I'D GET OFF WITH JUST A FEW YEARS IN PRISON, AT THE MOST, AND A HEFTY FINE...
... I COULDN'T FIND THE STRENGTH TO FIGHT LIKE I'D ALWAYS DONE BEFORE, MAMA...
...THE TRUTH IS THAT AFTER SO MANY YEARS OF BATTLING AGAINST COUNTLESS ENEMIES, WHO I DEFEATED ONE AFTER THE OTHER, I WAS EXHAUSTED... LIKE AN AUTOMATON, I GAVE UP AND LEFT MY OFFICE.

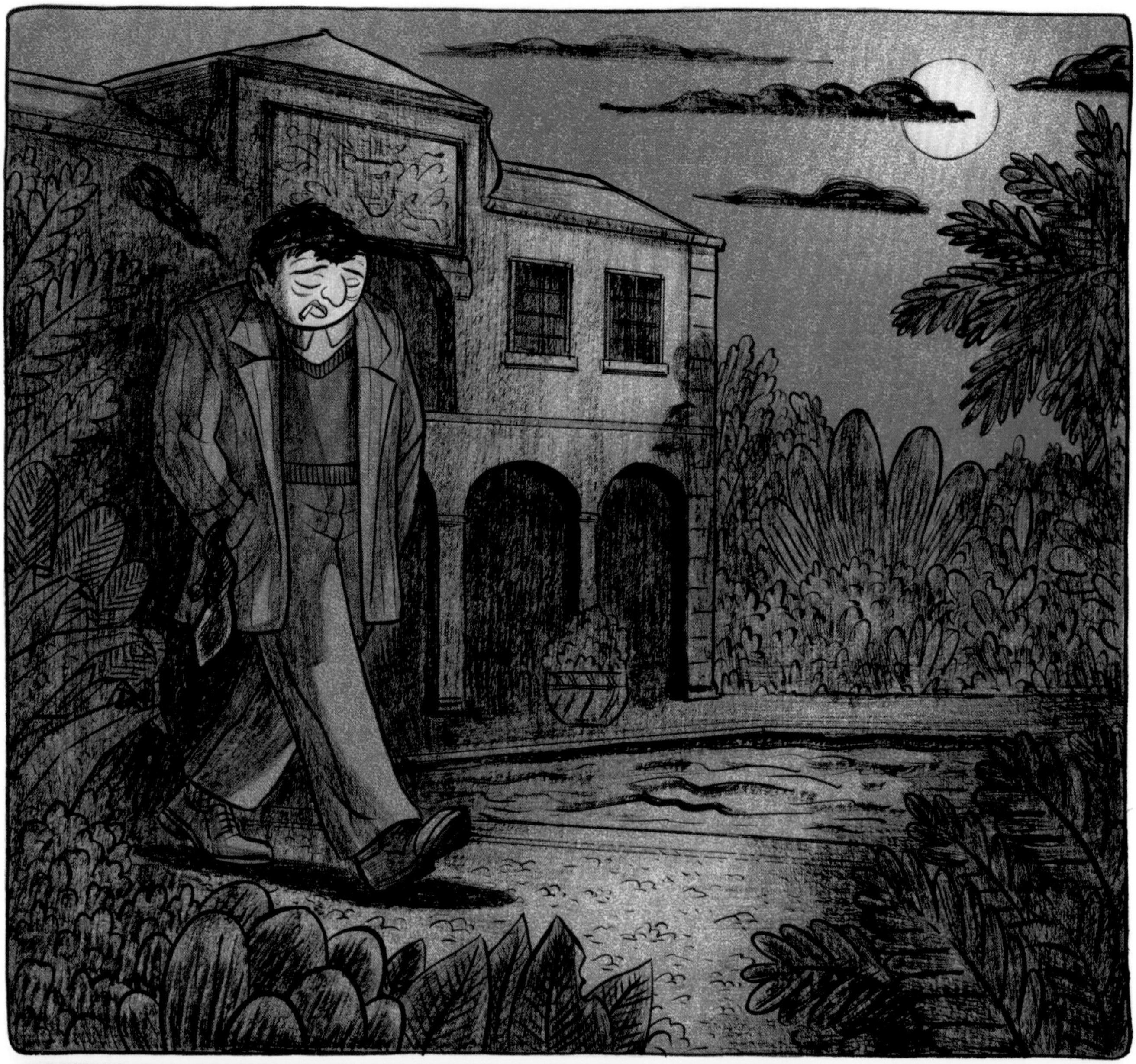

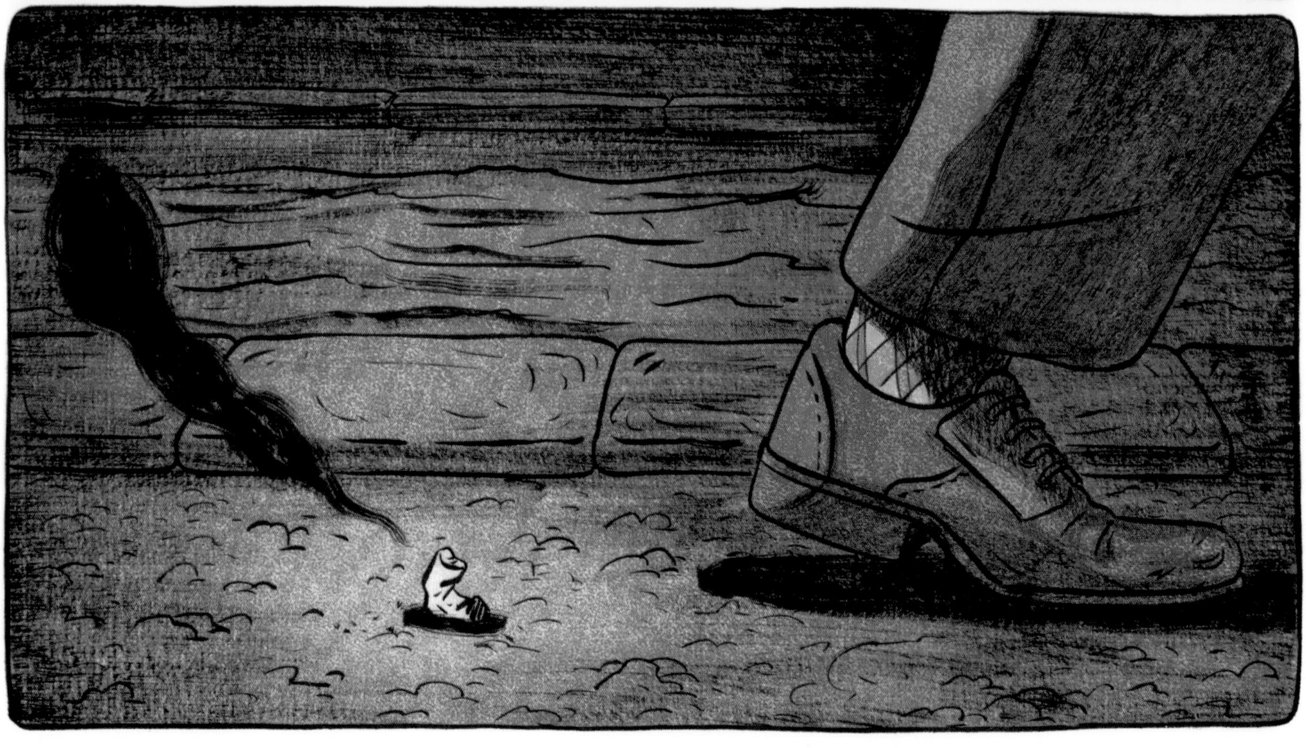

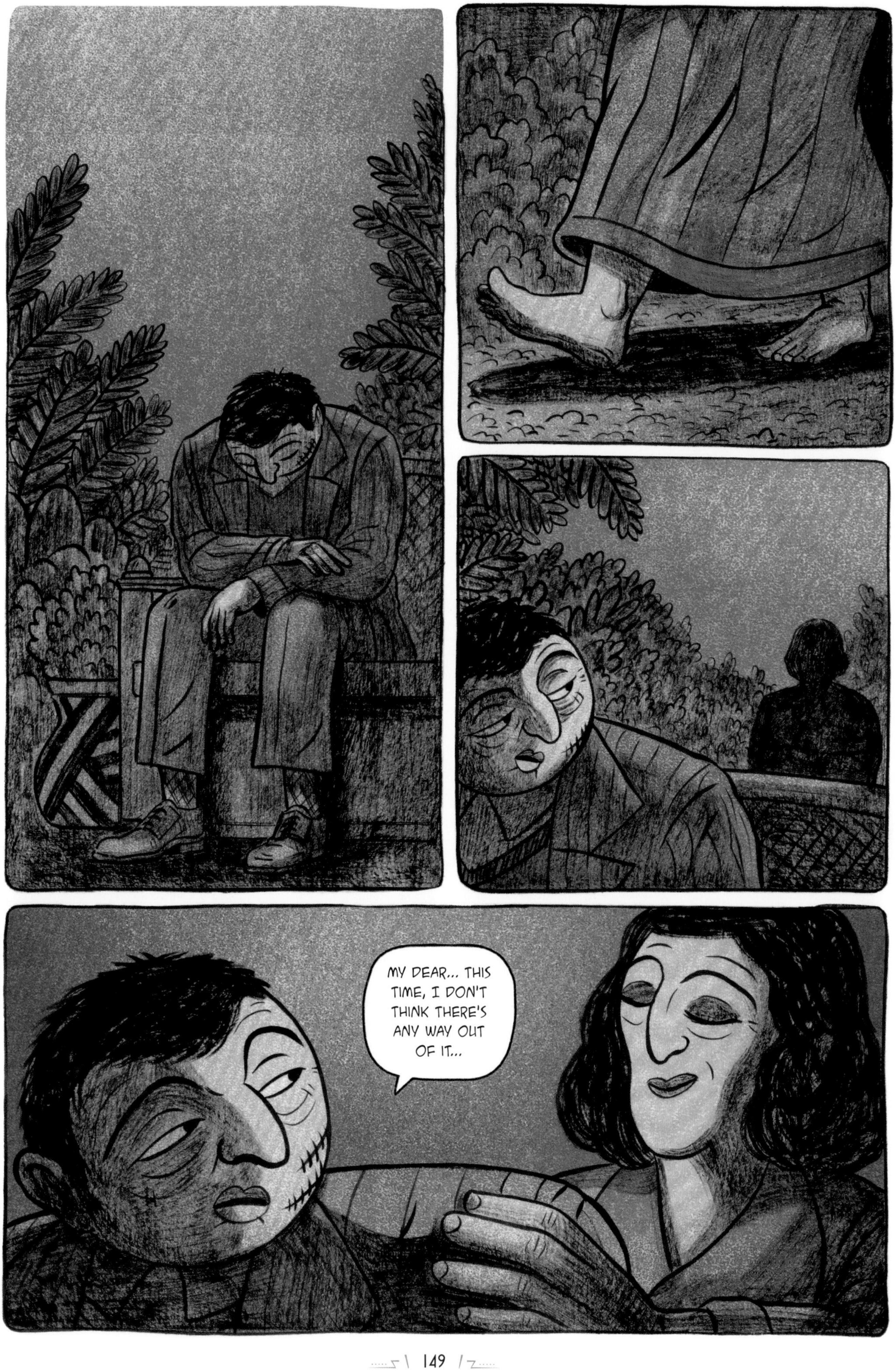
MY DEAR... THIS TIME, I DON'T THINK THERE'S ANY WAY OUT OF IT...

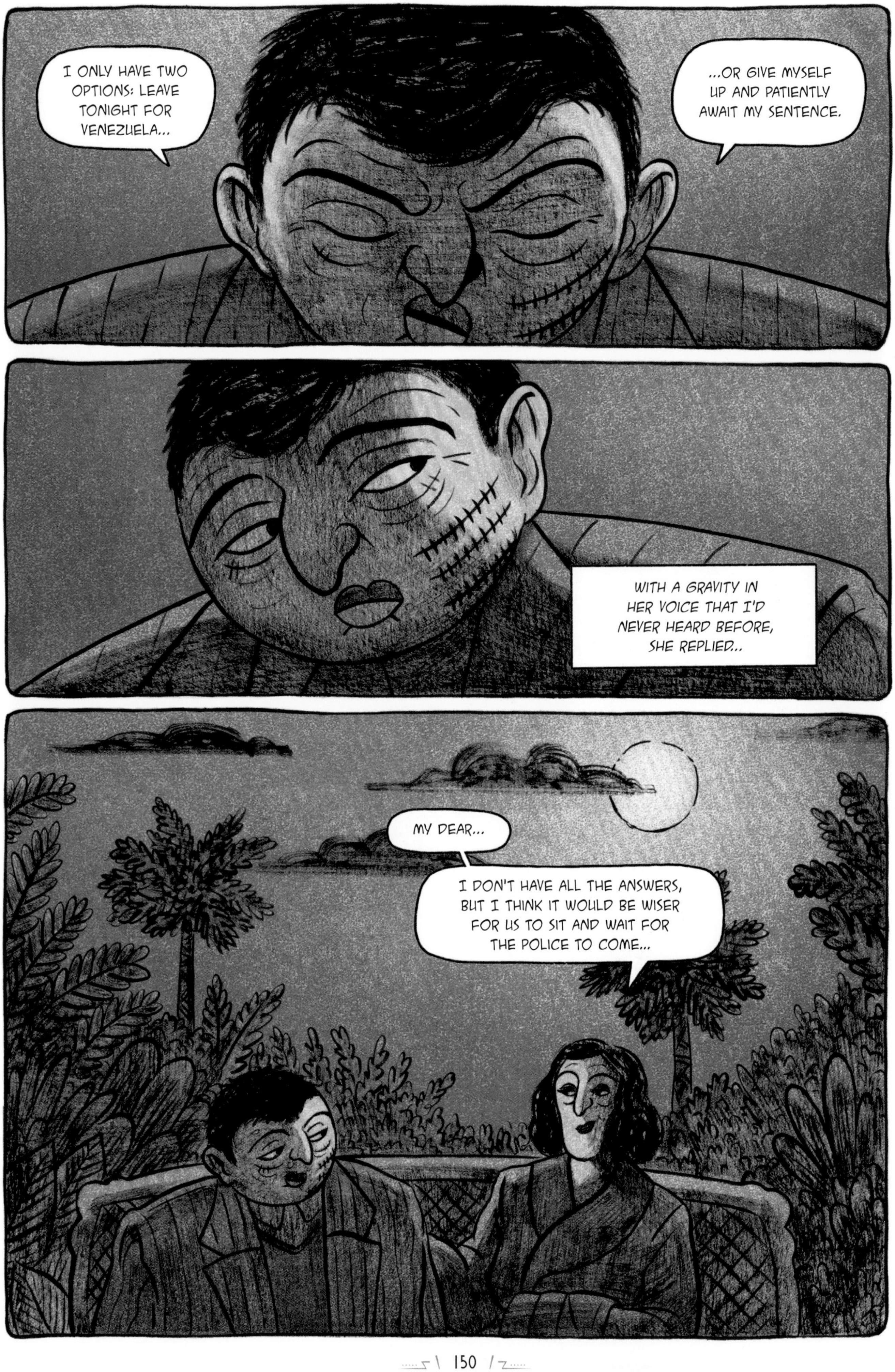
I ONLY HAVE TWO OPTIONS: LEAVE TONIGHT FOR VENEZUELA...
...OR GIVE MYSELF UP AND PATIENTLY AWAIT MY SENTENCE.
WITH A GRAVITY IN HER VOICE THAT I'D NEVER HEARD BEFORE, SHE REPLIED...
MY DEAR...
I DON'T HAVE ALL THE ANSWERS, BUT I THINK IT WOULD BE WISER FOR US TO SIT AND WAIT FOR THE POLICE TO COME...

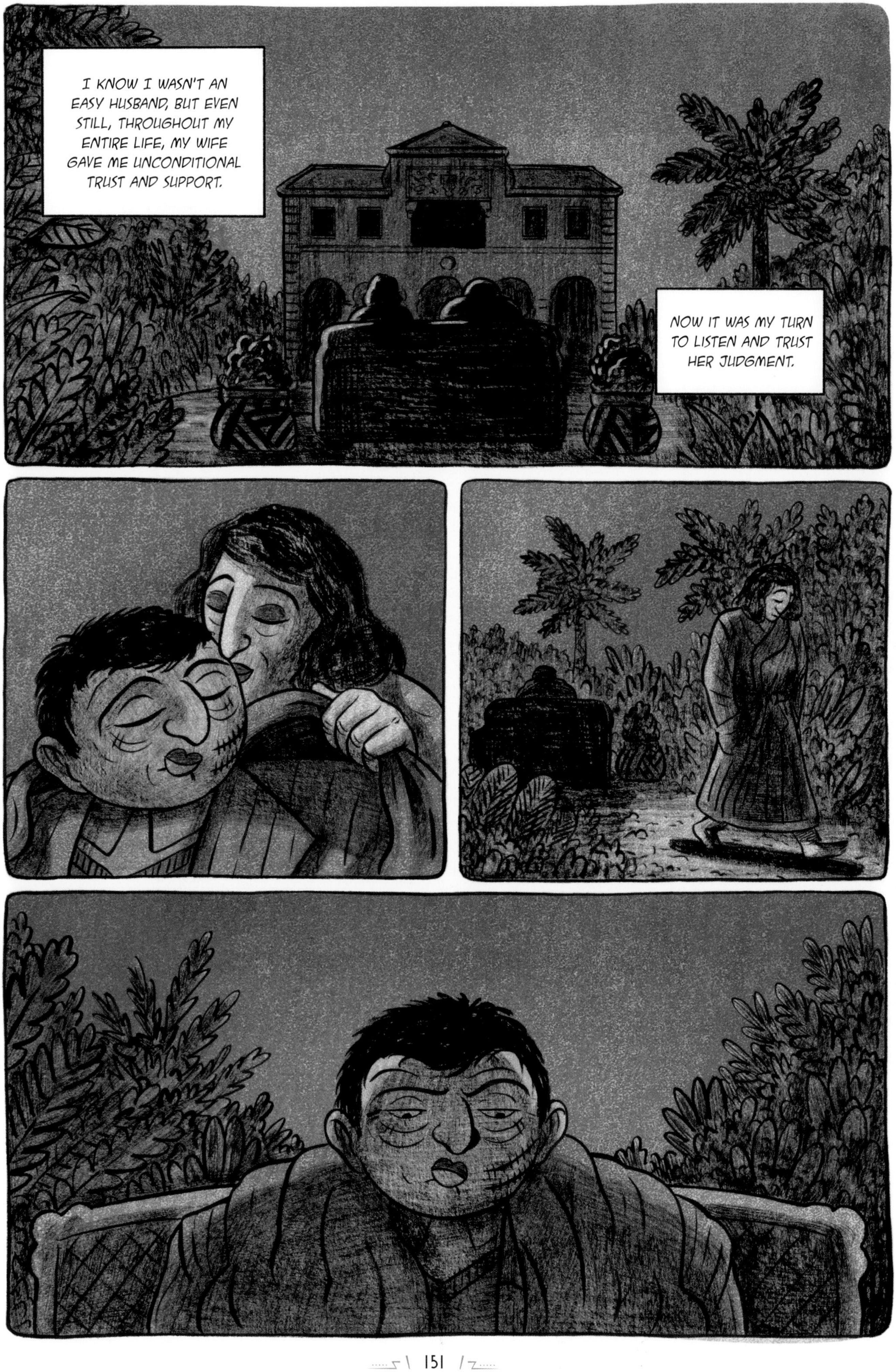
I KNOW I WASN'T AN EASY HUSBAND, BUT EVEN STILL, THROUGHOUT MY ENTIRE LIFE, MY WIFE GAVE ME UNCONDITIONAL TRUST AND SUPPORT.
NOW IT WAS MY TURN TO LISTEN AND TRUST HER JUDGMENT.

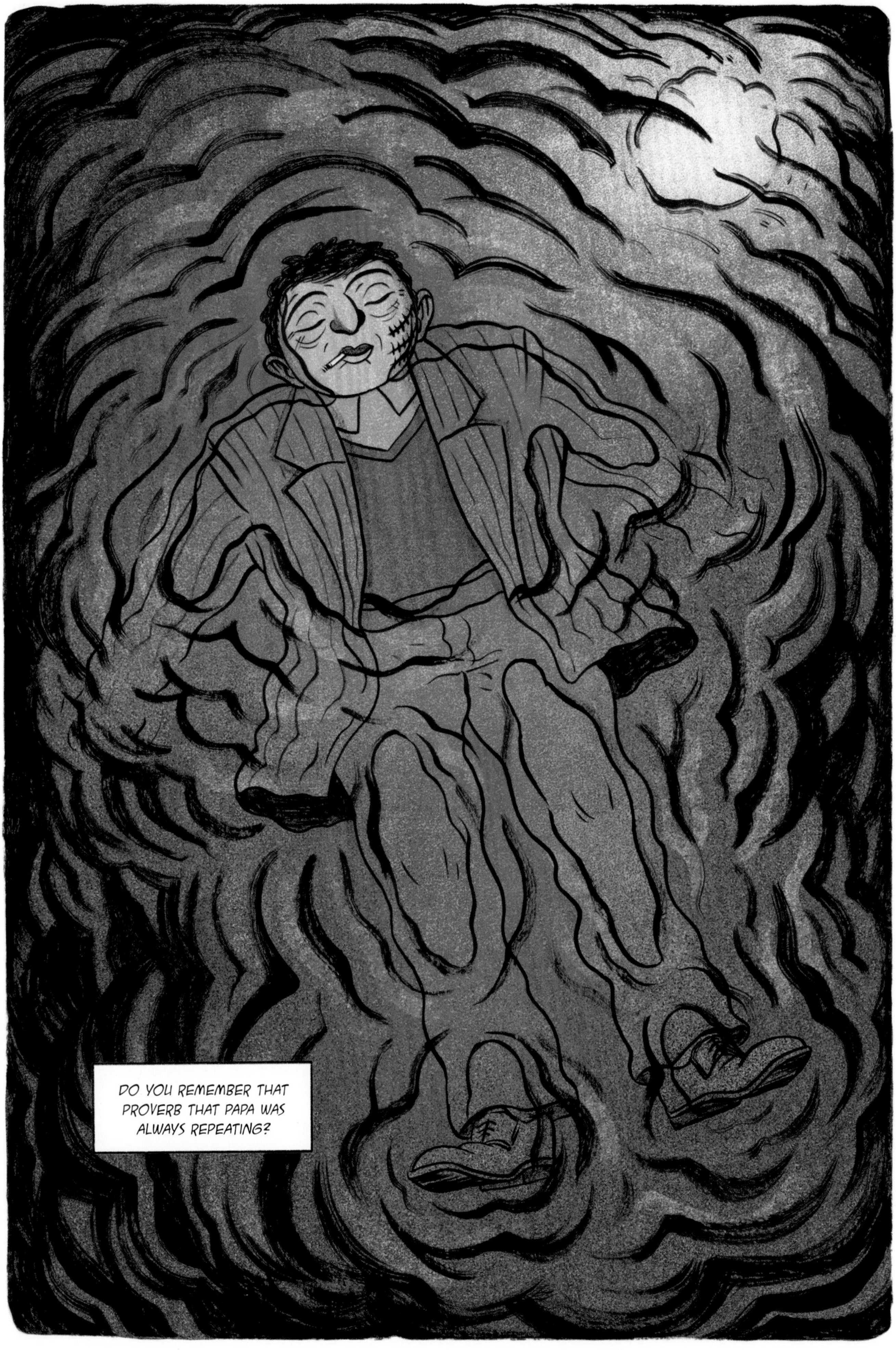
DO YOU REMEMBER THAT PROVERB THAT PAPA WAS ALWAYS REPEATING?

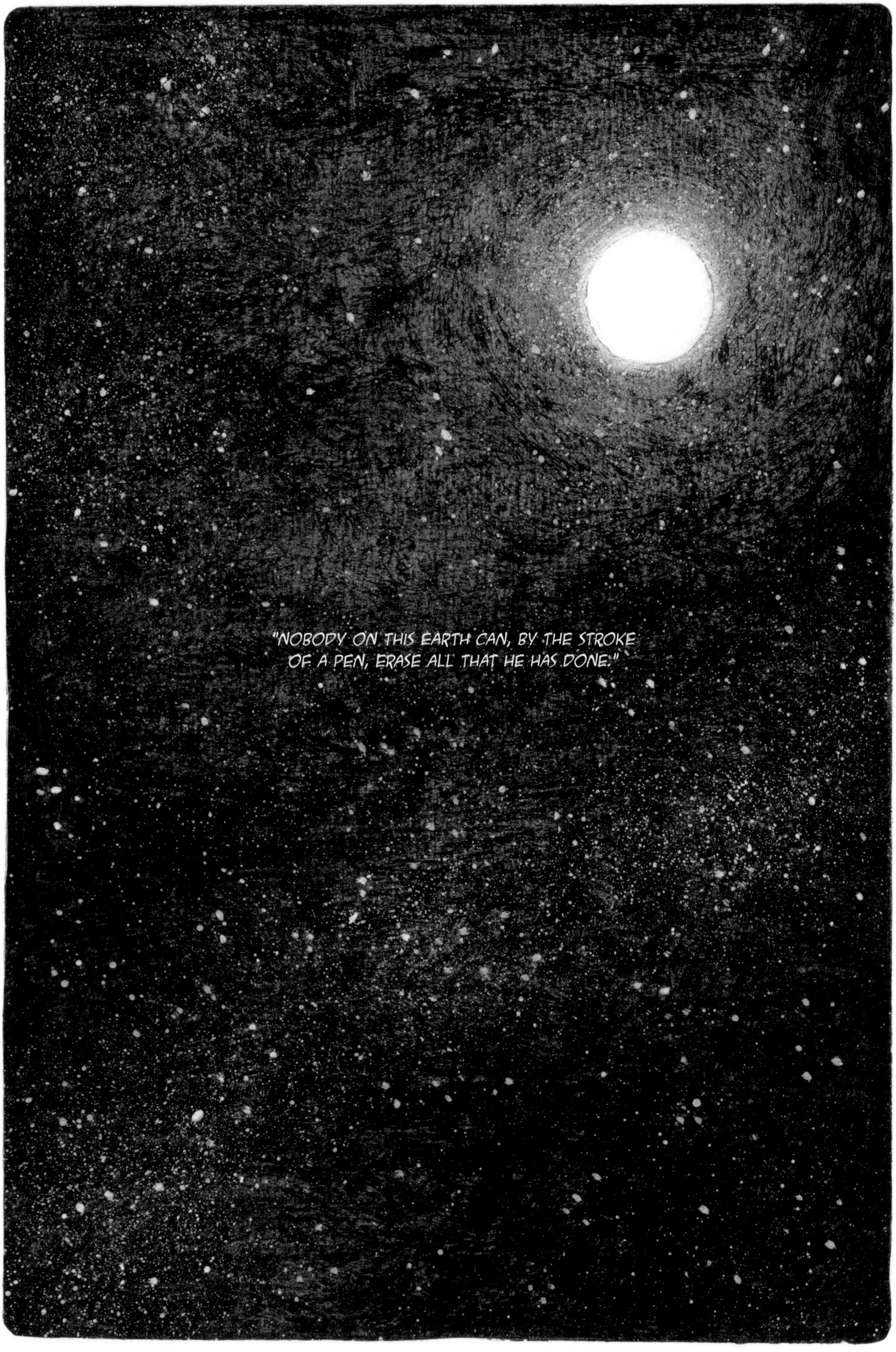
"NOBODY ON THIS EARTH CAN, BY THE STROKE OF A PEN, ERASE ALL THAT HE HAS DONE."

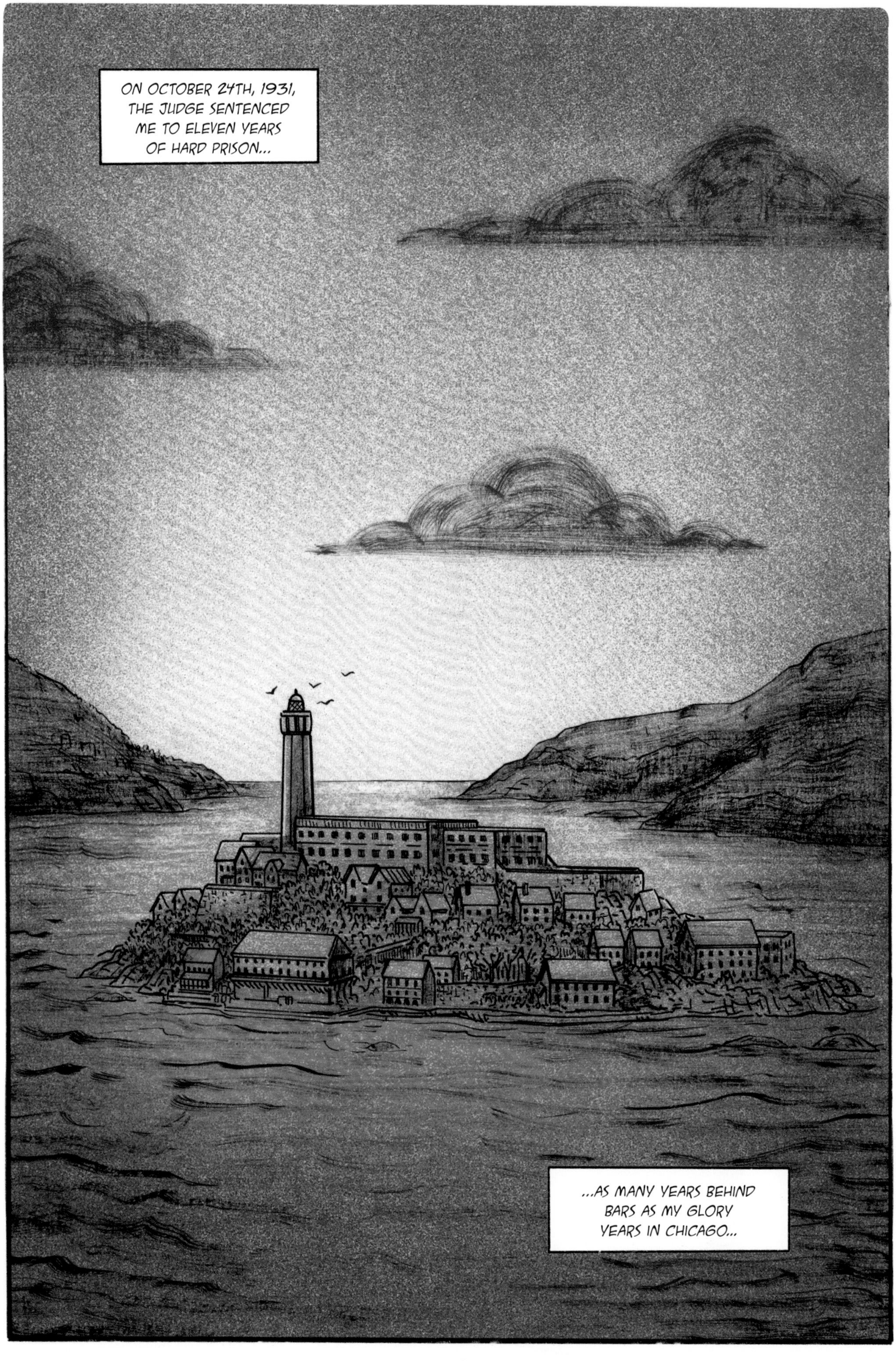
ON OCTOBER 24TH, 1931, THE JUDGE SENTENCED ME TO ELEVEN YEARS OF HARD PRISON...
...AS MANY YEARS BEHIND BARS AS MY GLORY YEARS IN CHICAGO...

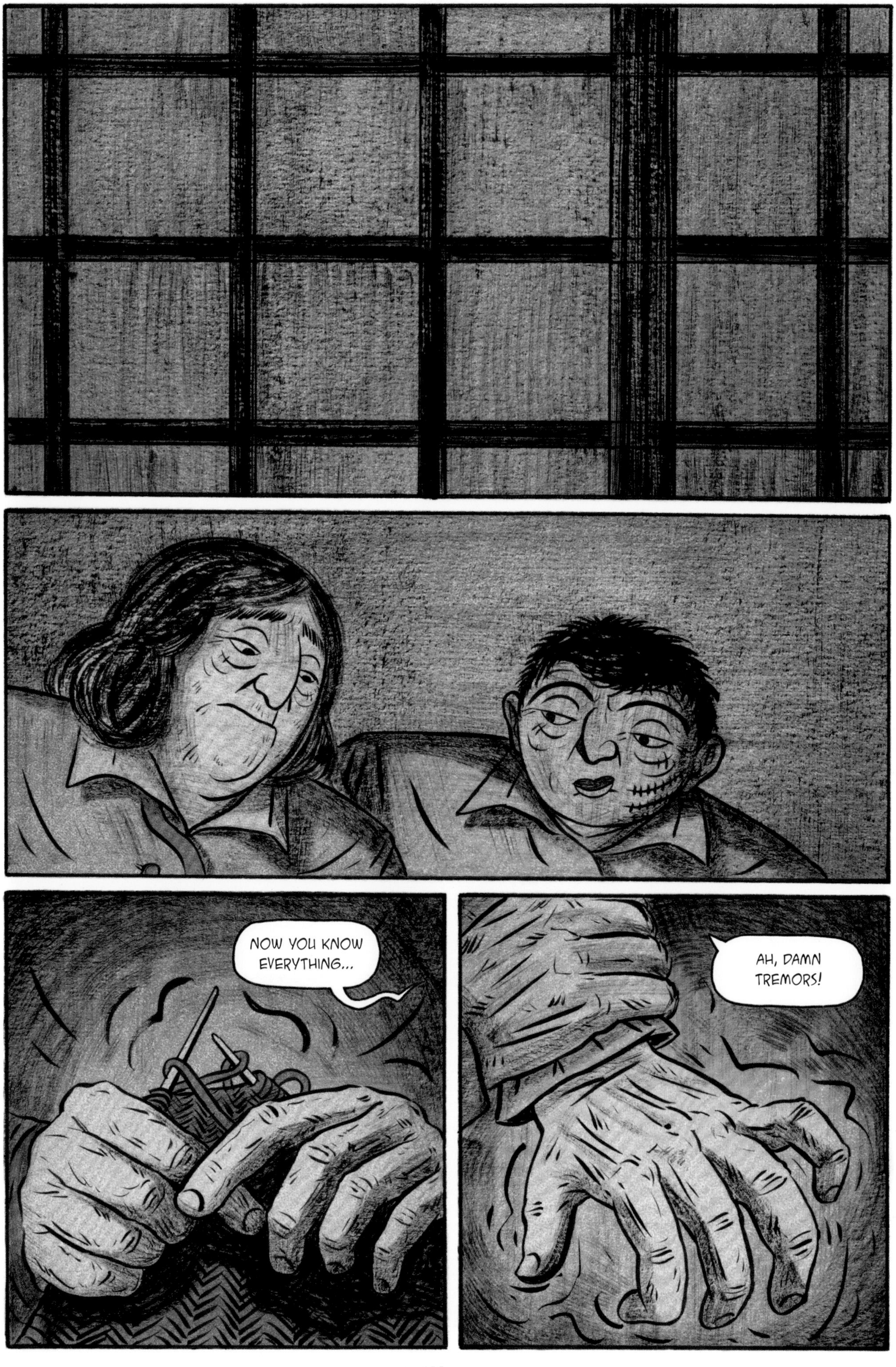
NOW YOU KNOW EVERYTHING...
AH, DAMN TREMORS!

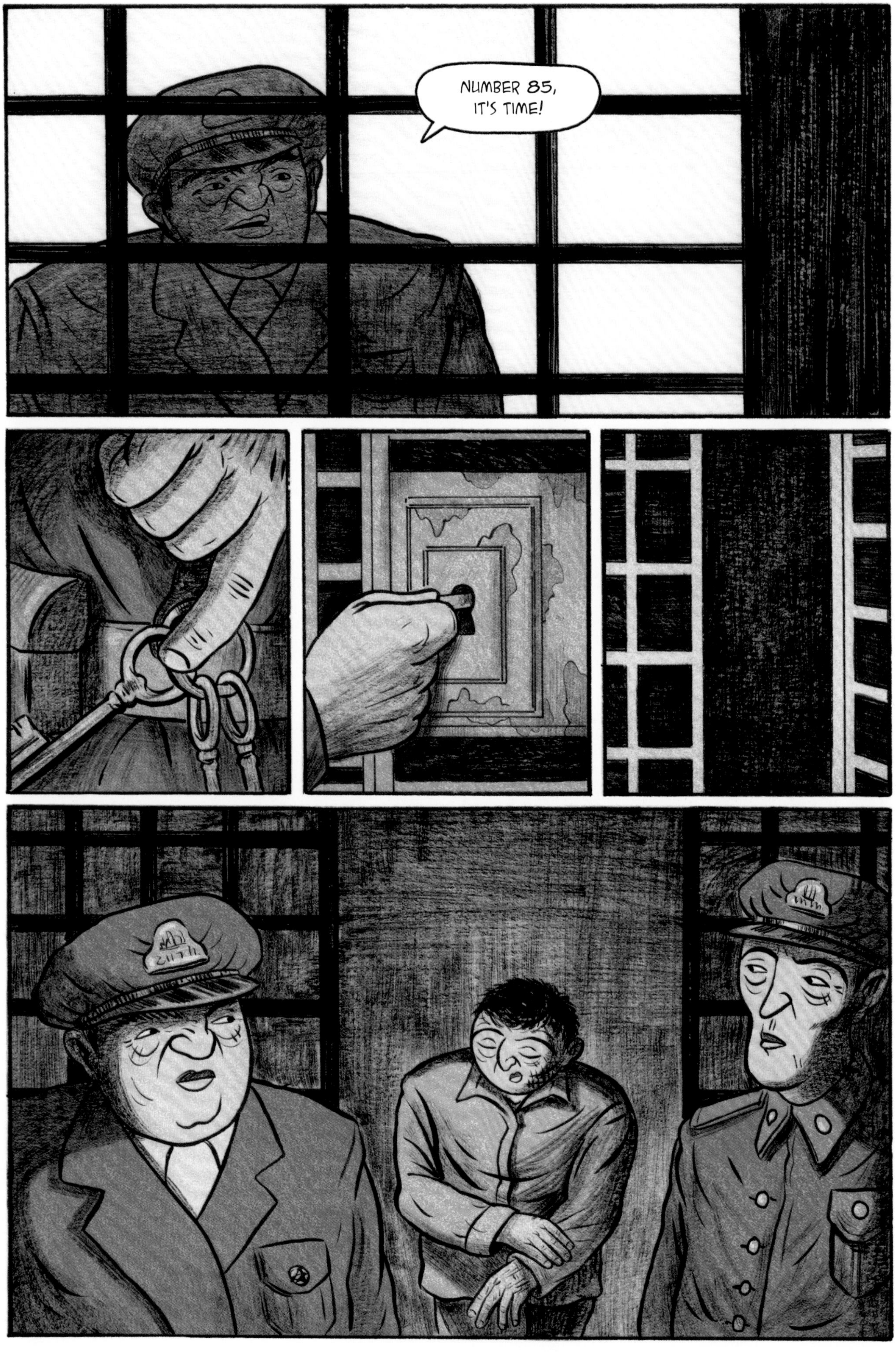
NUMBER 85,
IT'S TIME!

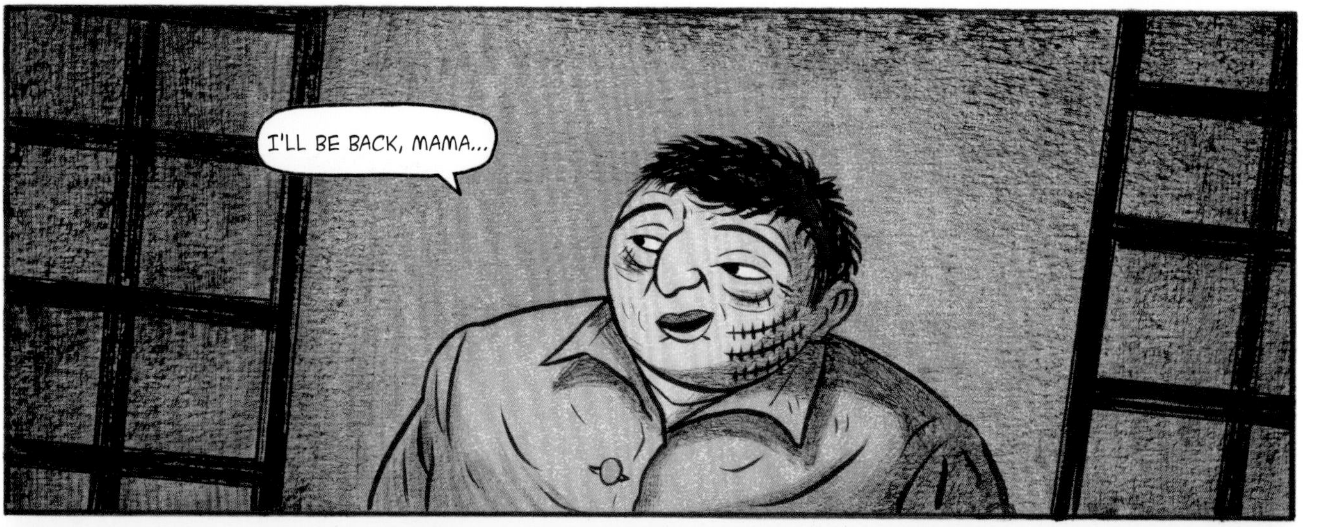
I'LL BE BACK, MAMA...

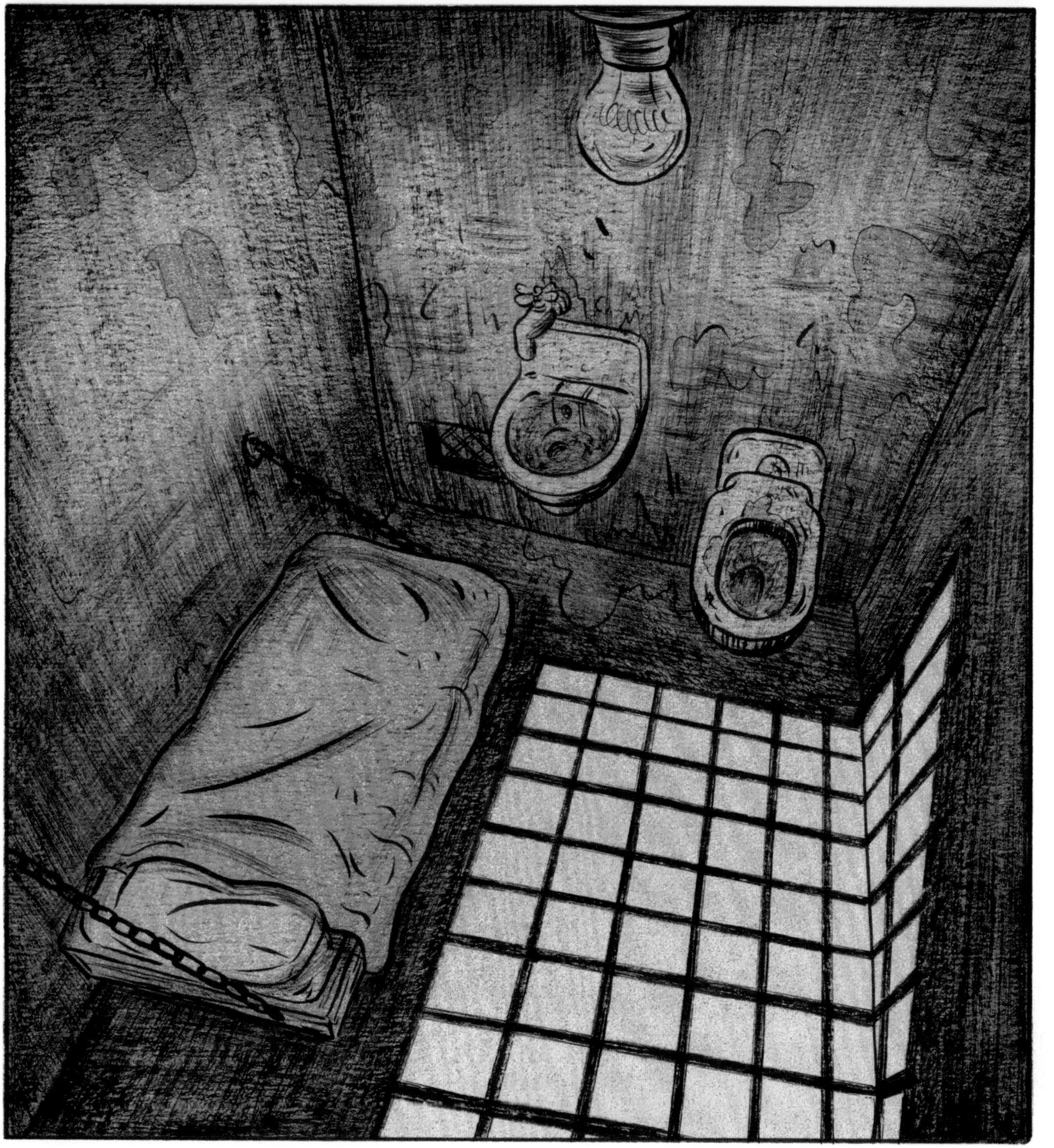

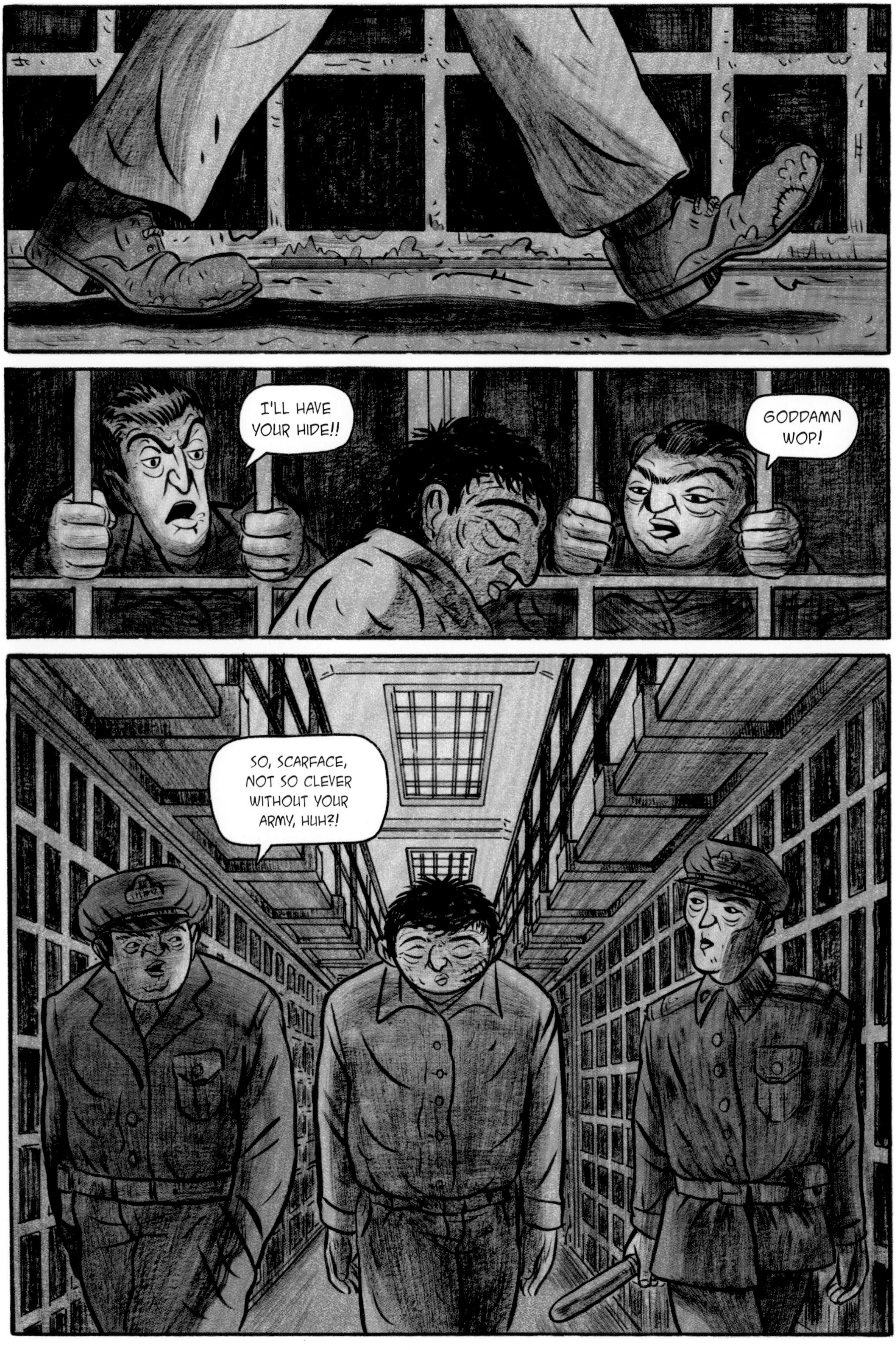
I'LL HAVE YOUR HIDE!!
GODDAMN WOP!
SO, SCARFACE, NOT SO CLEVER WITHOUT YOUR ARMY, HUH?!

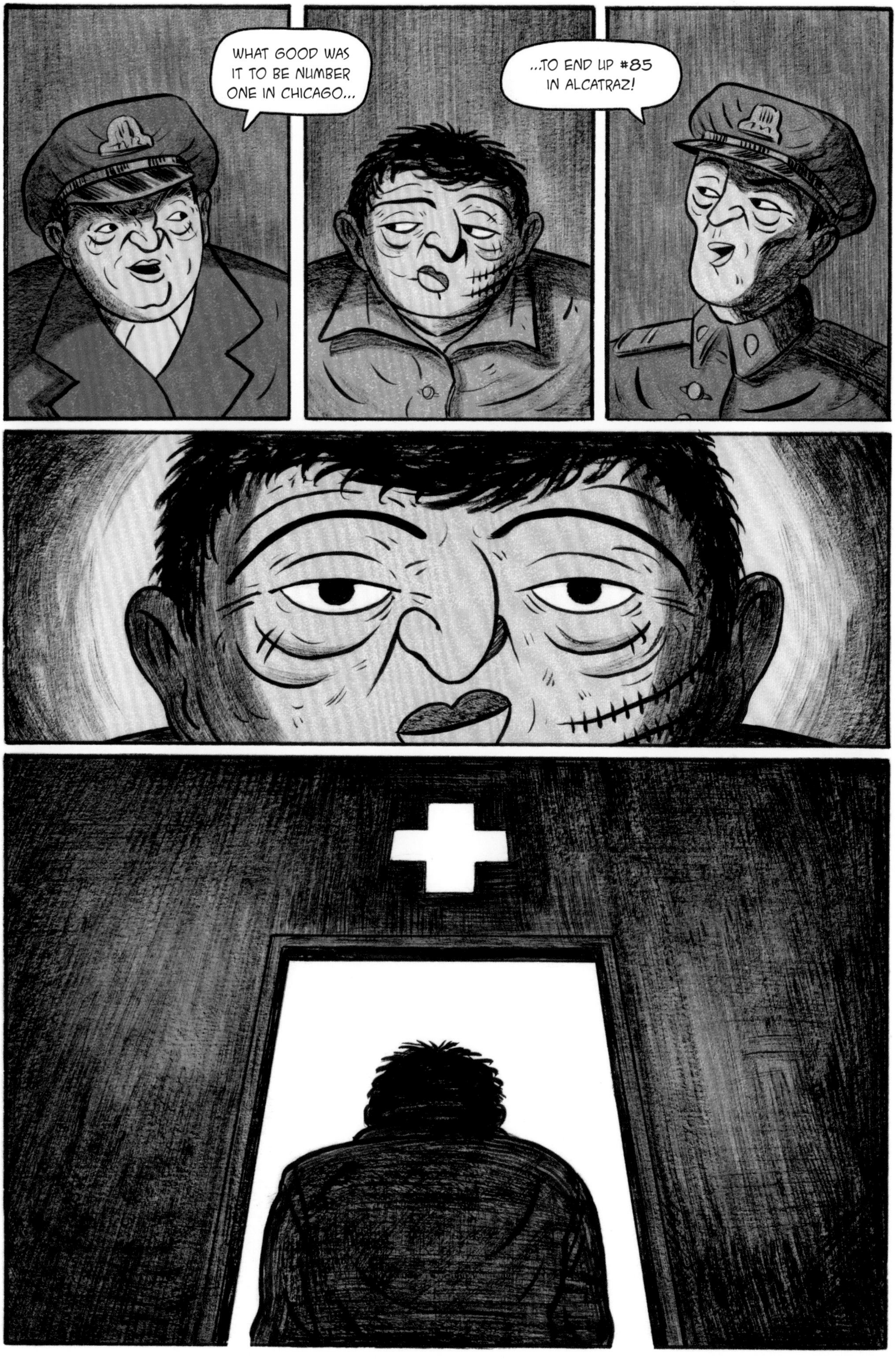
WHAT GOOD WAS IT TO BE NUMBER ONE IN CHICAGO...
...TO END UP #85 IN ALCATRAZ!

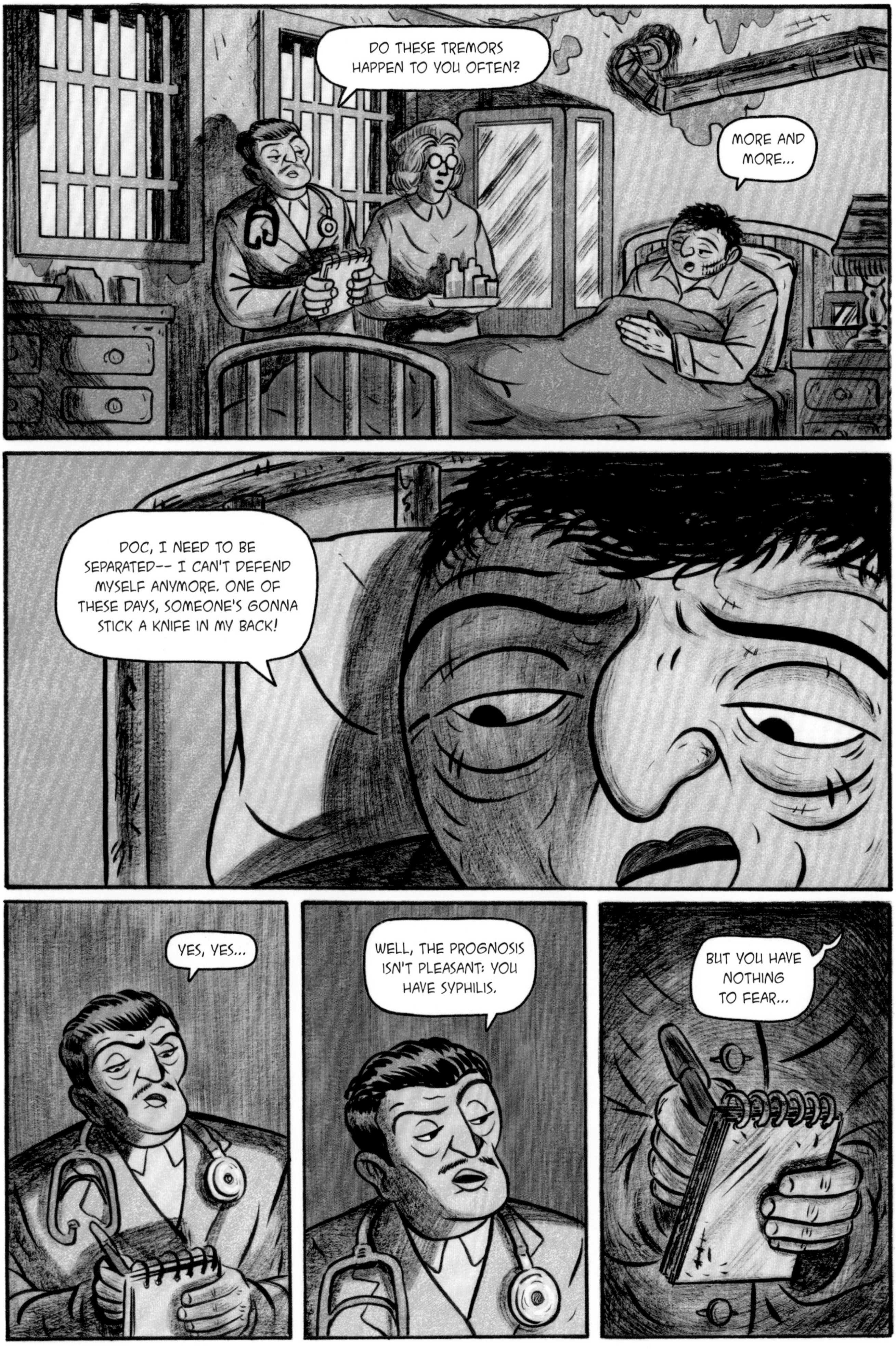
DO THESE TREMORS HAPPEN TO YOU OFTEN?
MORE AND MORE...
DOC, I NEED TO BE SEPARATED-- I CAN'T DEFEND MYSELF ANYMORE. ONE OF THESE DAYS, SOMEONE'S GONNA STICK A KNIFE IN MY BACK!
YES, YES...
WELL, THE PROGNOSIS ISN'T PLEASANT: YOU HAVE SYPHILIS.
BUT YOU HAVE NOTHING TO FEAR...

A COUPLE WEEKS OF REST, A LITTLE MEDICINE, AND EVERYTHING WILL BE BETTER.

YOU'LL STILL HAVE SOME TREMORS...

...BUT AS LONG AS YOU DON'T HAVE ANY HALLUCINATIONS, THE SICKNESS HASN'T SET IN YET.

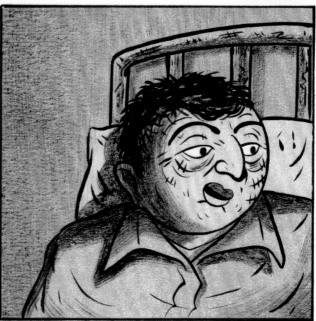

MY LITTLE ALFONSINO...

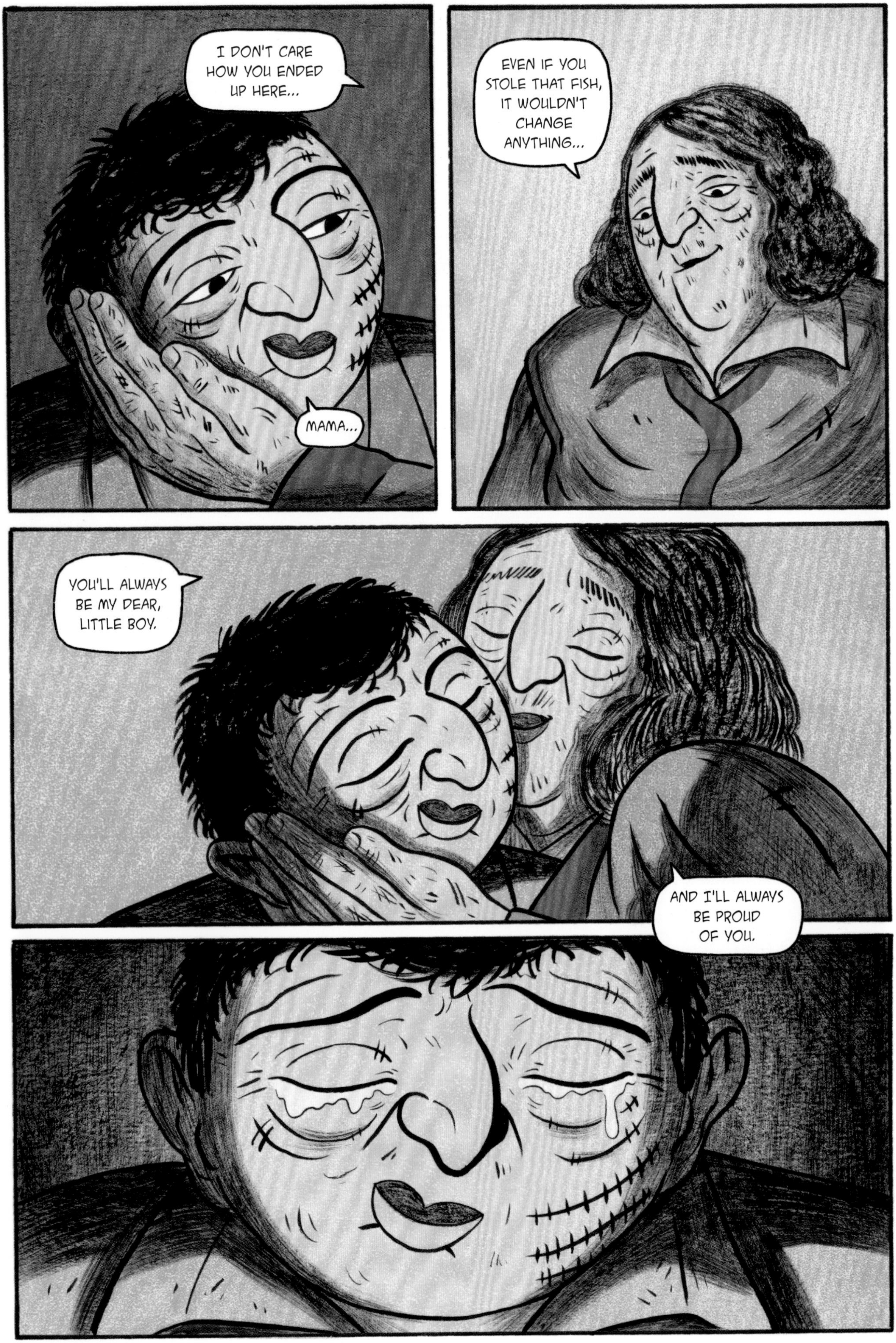
I DON'T CARE HOW YOU ENDED UP HERE...
MAMA...
EVEN IF YOU STOLE THAT FISH, IT WOULDN'T CHANGE ANYTHING...
YOU'LL ALWAYS BE MY DEAR, LITTLE BOY.
AND I'LL ALWAYS BE PROUD OF YOU.

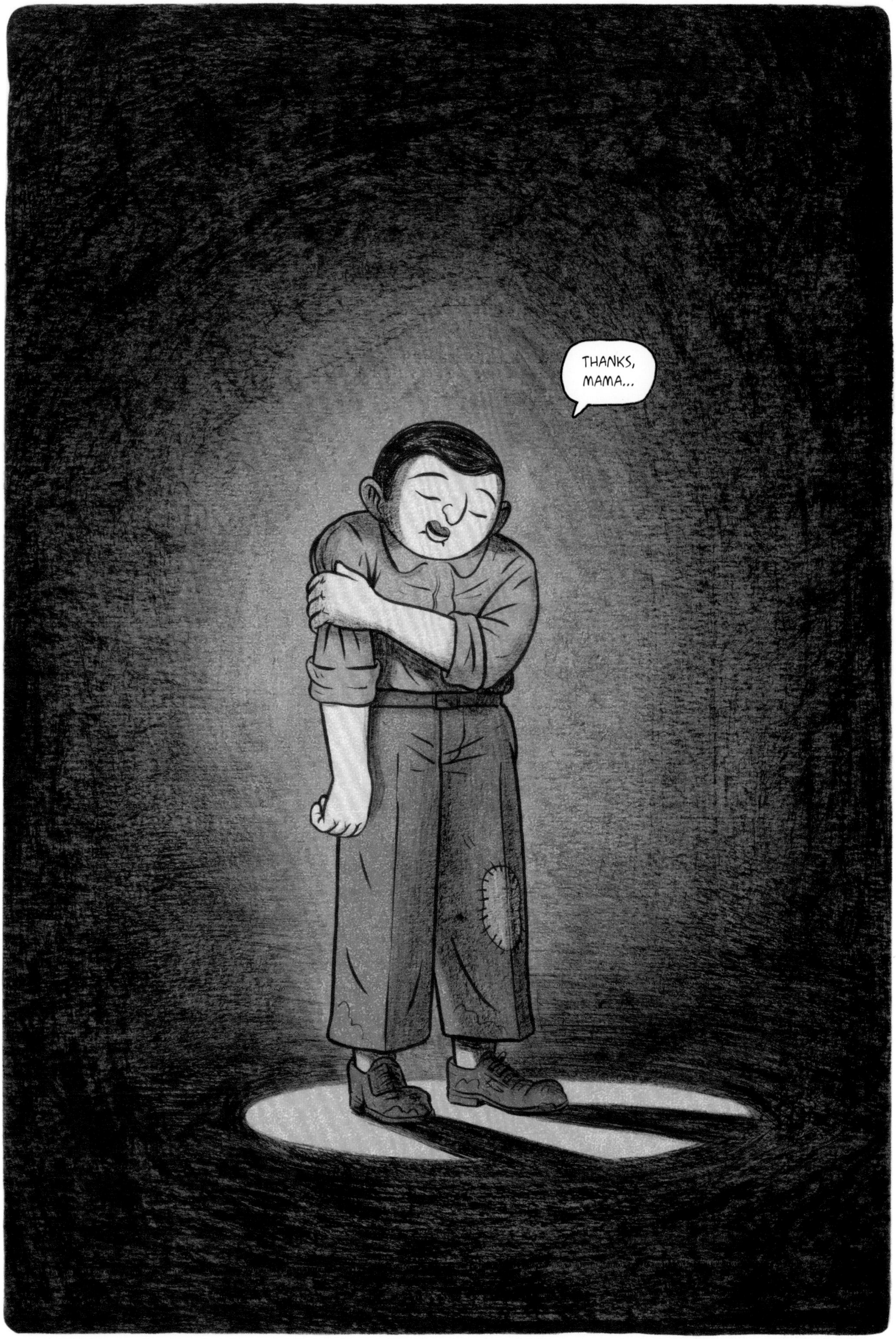
THANKS, MAMA...

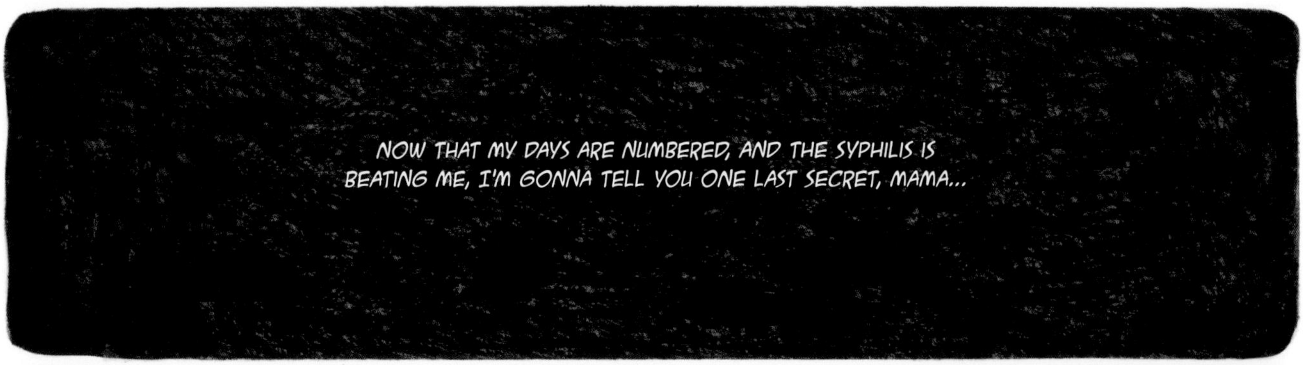
NOW THAT MY DAYS ARE NUMBERED, AND THE SYPHILIS IS BEATING ME, I'M GONNA TELL YOU ONE LAST SECRET, MAMA...

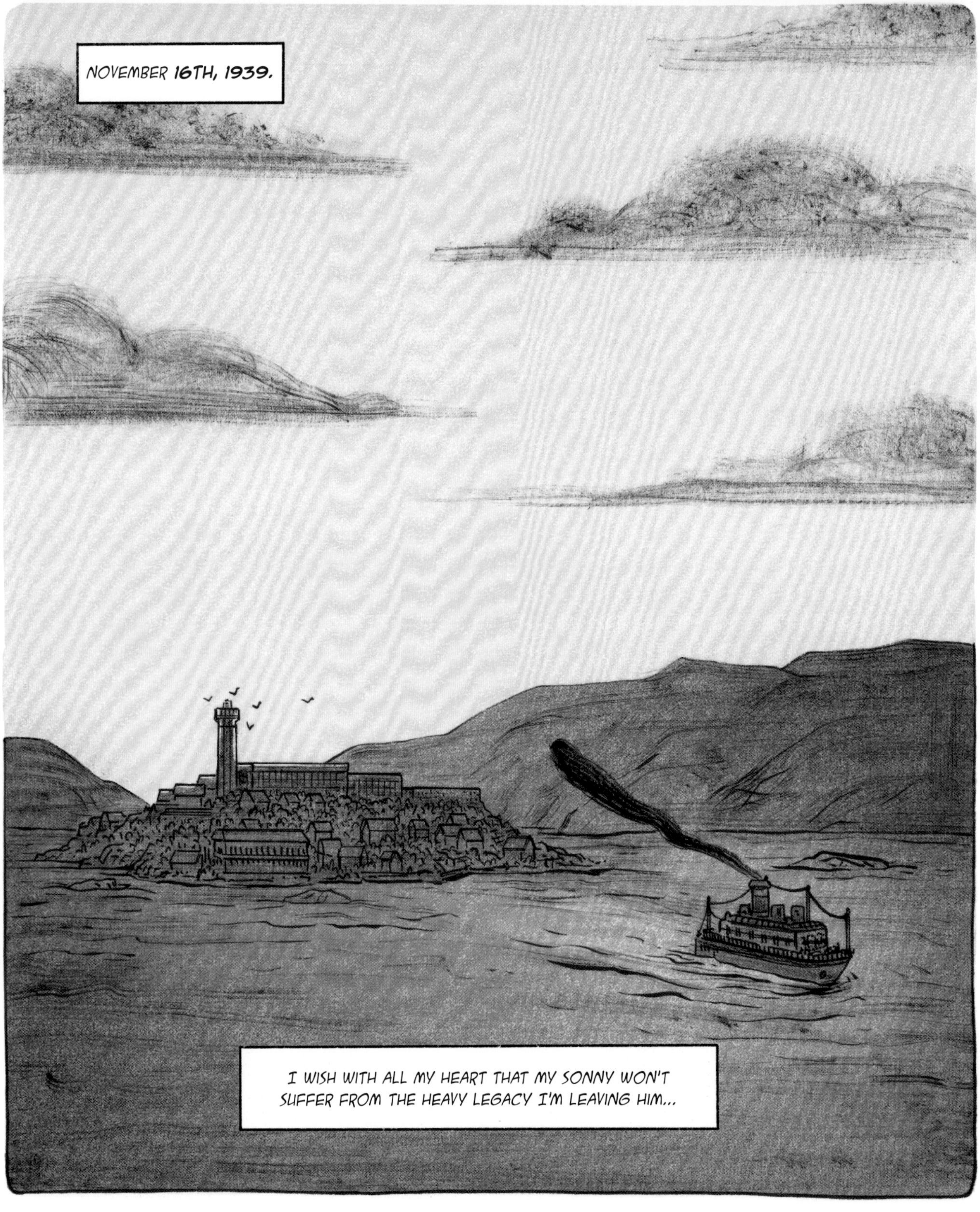
NOVEMBER 16TH, 1939.
I WISH WITH ALL MY HEART THAT MY SONNY WON'T SUFFER FROM THE HEAVY LEGACY I'M LEAVING HIM...

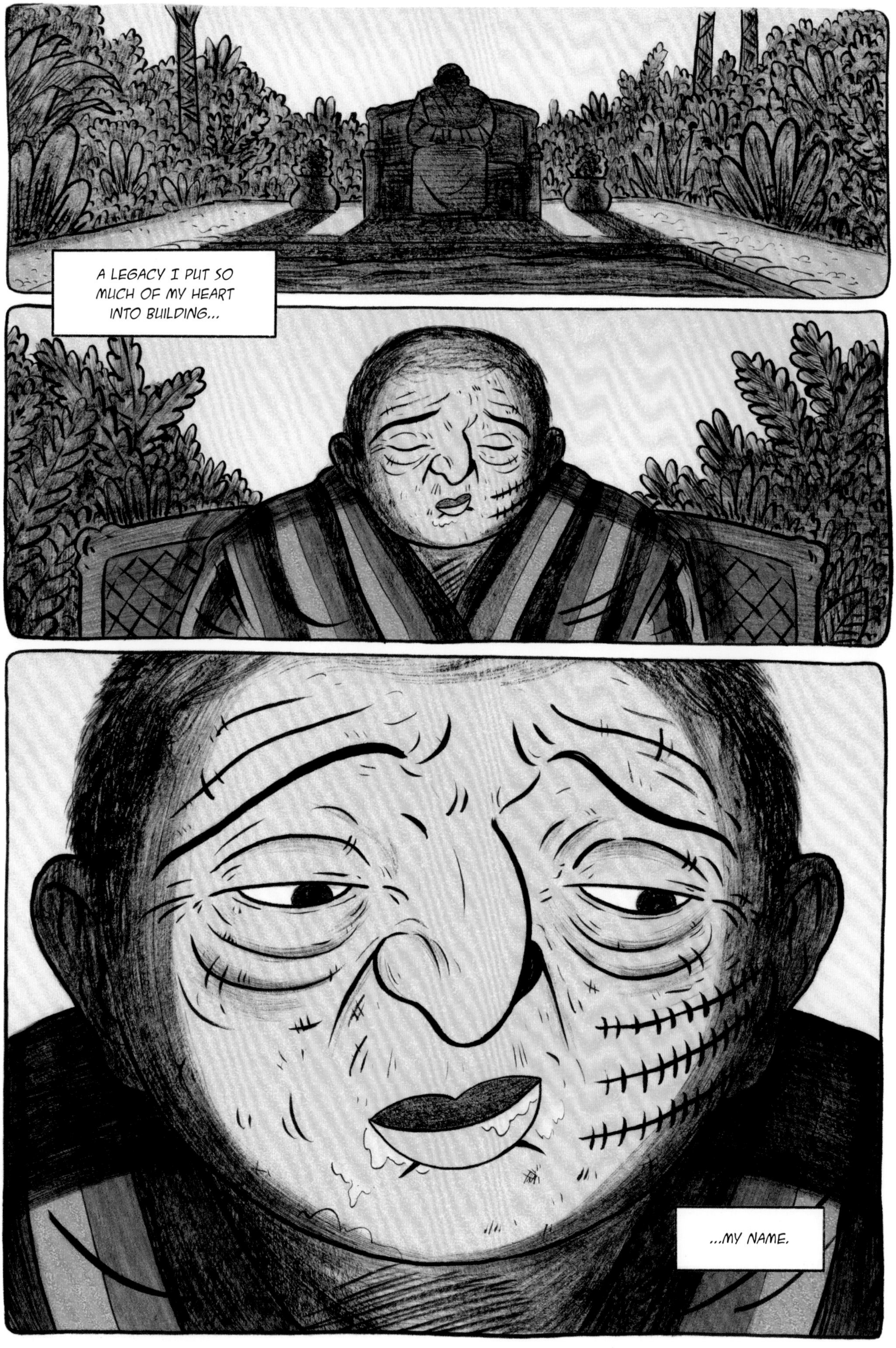
A LEGACY I PUT SO MUCH OF MY HEART INTO BUILDING...
...MY NAME.

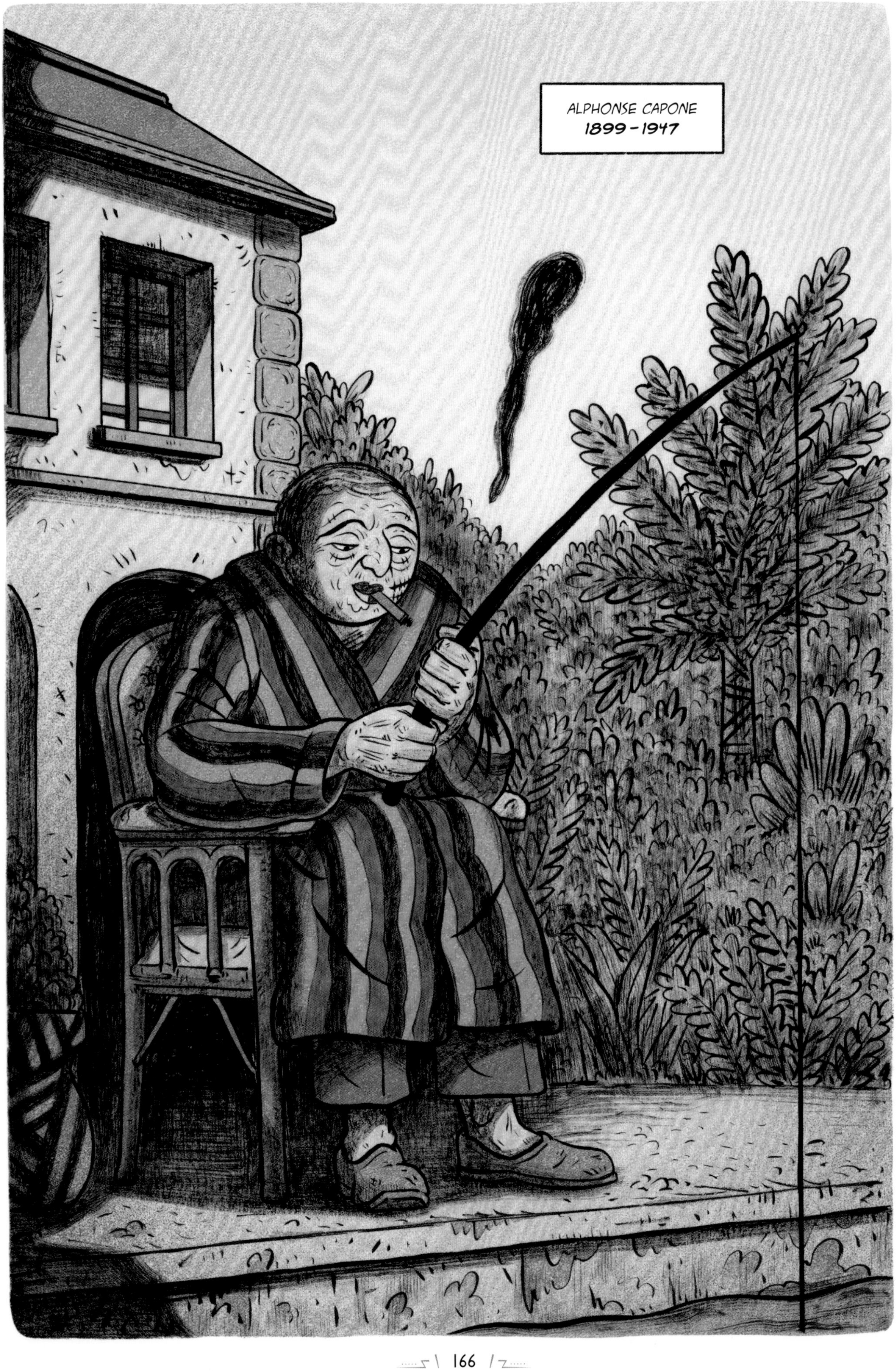
ALPHONSE CAPONE
1899-1947

THE END

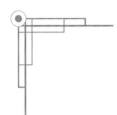

NOTE FROM THE EDITOR

SEVENTY-SIX YEARS AFTER THE DEATH OF AL CAPONE, THERE'S STILL MUCH DEBATE ABOUT HIS LIFE. DID HE REALLY HAVE SYPHILIS OR WAS IT MERCURY POISONING? HOW DID HE REALLY GET THE SCARS ON HIS FACE? IT DEPENDS WHO YOU ASK.

IN THIS BOOK, AUTHOR SWANN MERALLI MAKES AN EFFORT TO REPRESENT CAPONE'S LIFE AS ACCURATELY AS POSSIBLE WITH THE SOURCES AVAILABLE, WHILE FILLING IN THE GAPS IN A PLAUSIBLE WAY. THERE'S MUCH MORE INFORMATION OUT THERE ON HIS LATER YEARS, DUE TO THE OBVIOUSLY NEWSWORTHY NATURE OF HIS ACTIVITIES. SOME EVENTS ARE BASED ON CAPONE'S SUPPOSED AUTOBIOGRAPHY, ONLY AVAILABLE IN FRENCH, CONTAINING SOME QUESTIONABLE MATERIAL. SUCH AN AUTOBIOGRAPHY IS MOST LIKELY A FICTION, EVEN IF MOST OF THE DETAILS ARE ACCURATE, BUT IT MAKES FOR GOOD INSPIRATION.

HERE ARE SOME OF THE SOURCES THAT INSPIRED THE STORY. WE ENCOURAGE YOU TO DISCOVER THEM AND LEARN MORE ABOUT AL CAPONE'S LIFE.

BIBLIOGRAPHY

· MA VIE (AL CAPONE) — BY AL CAPONE

· AL CAPONE: HIS LIFE, LEGACY, AND LEGEND BY DEIRDRE BAIR.

· SON OF SCARFACE: A MEMOIR BY THE GRANDSON OF AL CAPONE.

· CAPONE (1975) — FILM.

· ENCYCLOPEDIA BRITTANICA — AL CAPONE

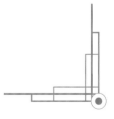

A big thank you to the entire Sarbacane team

and especially to Frédéric for trusting me

and allowing me to carry out this project

that's been so important to me.

A thank you to all my family, friends, Yann, Fabien and
all the others for their advice, support and kindness.

And an infinite thank you to my wife Sophie

and daughter Raphaëlle for being by my side,

for your help, encouragement, and valuable support.

Thank you for making all of this possible. I love you.

PF Radice

WWW.BLACKPANELPRESS.COM